The Princeton Review®

Cracking the

Praxis®

Tests

3rd Edition

The Staff of The Princeton Review

PrincetonReview.com

Penguin
Random
House

The Princeton Review
110 East 42nd St., 7th Floor
New York, NY 10017
Email: editorialsupport@review.com

Published in the United States by Penguin Random House LLC, New York, and in Canada by Random House of Canada, a division of Penguin Random House Ltd., Toronto.

ISBN: 978-1-5247-5820-2
eBook ISBN: 978-1-5247-5852-3
ISSN: 2163-6044

Editor: Colleen Day
Production Editors: Kathy Carter and Liz Rutzel
Production Artist: Deborah A. Weber
Content Contributors: Kevin Kelly, Heidi Torres, Christine Lindwall, Katie Chamberlain, and Jennifer Neale

Printed in the United States of America on partially recycled paper.

3rd Edition

Editorial

Rob Franek, Editor-in-Chief
Casey Cornelius, Chief Product Officer
Mary Beth Garrick, Executive Director of Production
Craig Patches, Production Design Manager
Selena Coppock, Managing Editor
Meave Shelton, Senior Editor
Colleen Day, Editor
Sarah Litt, Editor
Aaron Riccio, Editor
Orion McBean, Associate Editor

Penguin Random House Publishing Team

Tom Russell, VP, Publisher
Alison Stoltzfus, Publishing Director
Amanda Yee, Associate Managing Editor
Ellen Reed, Production Manager
Suzanne Lee, Designer

Acknowledgments

The Princeton Review would like to thank Kevin Kelly, Heidi Torres, Christine Lindwall, Katie Chamberlain, and Jennifer Neale, whose hard work and dedication made the third edition of this title possible. We are also, as always, greatly appreciative of the time and attention given to each page by Kathy Carter, Liz Rutzel, and Debbie Weber.

Contents

Get More (Free) Content

1 Go to **PrincetonReview.com/cracking.**

2 Enter the following ISBN for your book: 9781524758202

3 Answer a few simple questions to set up an exclusive Princeton Review account. (If you already have one, you can just log in.)

4 Click the "Student Tools" button, also found under "My Account" from the top toolbar. You're all set to access your bonus content!

Need to report a potential **content** issue?

Contact **EditorialSupport@review.com**.
Include:

- full title of the book
- ISBN number
- page number

Need to report a **technical** issue?

Contact **TPRStudentTech@review.com** and provide:

- your full name
- email address used to register the book
- full book title and ISBN
- computer OS (Mac/PC) and browser (Firefox, Safari, etc.)

The Princeton Review®

Once you've registered, you can...

- Access bonus study material, including a list of important math formulas and reference information, word roots to help you remember key vocabulary, as well as extra practice for the Math Subject Assessment and Principles of Learning and Teaching tests

- Read alternative solutions to math problems in the book for added insight into our math test-taking strategies

- Download a chapter on the Elementary Education Content Knowledge test, complete with practice questions and explanations

- Get our take on any recent or pending updates to the Praxis tests

- Check to see if there have been any corrections or updates to this edition

Look For These Icons Throughout The Book

 ONLINE ARTICLES

 PROVEN TECHNIQUES

 APPLIED STRATEGIES

 STUDY BREAK

 OTHER REFERENCES

Part I
Praxis
Orientation

Chapter 1
The Praxis Tests, The Princeton Review, and You

WHAT ARE THE PRAXIS TESTS?

The Praxis isn't a single exam but rather a series of computer-delivered exams designed and administered by the Educational Testing Service (ETS). The tests are used to measure various skills, knowledge, and general competence of candidates for teacher certification programs. Most states use at least one type of Praxis test, but specific test and score requirements vary by state. Therefore, it's crucial for you to know which tests are required in the state in which you plan to teach before registering for any exams or beginning your test preparation.

This book covers three sets of Praxis exams:

- **Praxis Core Academic Skills for Educators (aka Praxis Core)**—This is a series of three tests in Reading, Math, and Writing. Many colleges and universities use the Praxis Core tests as a comprehensive assessment of individuals entering teacher education programs. They are often taken early in one's college career. Each section can be taken separately or as a combined test.
- **Praxis Subject Assessments**—These exams focus on specific subject knowledge for grades K–12, as well as general and subject-specific teaching skills. There are numerous tests that fall into this category—you can take a Subject Assessment in anything from agriculture to psychology to technology to theater, but the most popular tests are the usual suspects: Math, English Language Arts, Science, and Social Studies.
- **Principles of Learning and Teaching (PLT) Tests**—This set of exams focuses on best pedagogical practices and classroom management techniques for each age range/grade level: Early Childhood, K–6, 5–9, and 7–12. Refer to your state's requirements to determine which test(s) you need to take.

You should also be aware of another group of Praxis exams: the Content Knowledge for Teaching (CKT) tests for Elementary Education, which include the regular CKT as well as a test called the Applied CKT. The CKT focuses on subject matter knowledge, while the Applied CKT tests specialized content knowledge used only in teaching. People who take these exams tend to be those seeking general elementary education licenses. For in-depth coverage of these exams, we recommend visiting the official test website: www.ets.org/praxis/about/ckt/. Your Student Tools contain a bonus chapter on Elementary Education, which, while geared toward the Content Knowledge test, also contains information relevant to the CKT.

STATE REQUIREMENTS AND SCORING

Figuring out the testing requirements for the state in which you plan to teach can be confusing. Your first resource is your college counselor, who can help you determine which tests you need to take and when. The ETS website also breaks down the testing requirements for each state, which you can read here: www.ets.org/praxis/states.

Scoring requirements also vary by state. For the most up-to-date scoring information, you should contact your teacher-training or education program or your state's licensing board.

There is also an abundance of information about scoring on the ETS website, including score-release dates, understanding your scores, the process for sending your scores to educational institutions, and how to cancel your score if necessary. See www.ets.org/praxis/scores/get/.

HOW TO REGISTER

While some Praxis tests are offered on an ongoing basis, others are administered only a handful of times each year. Be sure to check the test dates and locations ahead of time.

The easiest way to register for a Praxis test is online at www.ets.org/praxis/register. You can also register by mail by completing a Test Authorization Voucher Request form (which you can download from the website at the URL just given) and mailing it to ETS. If you register by phone, which is another option, you'll be charged an additional $35 fee. If you are planning to take a Praxis test outside of the United States, go to www.ets.org/praxis/register and follow the instructions there, as this may entail some additional restrictions and steps.

If you require special test-taking accommodations due to a disability or other needs, you must submit documentation with your accommodation request. You can read about the procedures in ETS's updated bulletin, which can be downloaded from their website: www.ets.org/praxis/register/disabilities/.

Understanding Your Praxis Score
You should understand how Praxis scoring works before you take a test. Check out ETS's "Understanding Your Praxis® Scores" bulletin, available on the official test website: www.ets.org/praxis/scores/get/. This document breaks down scoring ranges for each Praxis test type, along with key terms, frequently asked questions, and a summary of current statistics like number of test takers, median scores, and more.

The Praxis Is a Computer-Delivered Test
You should be aware that the Praxis tests are offered exclusively in computer-delivered formats (with the exception of Braille Proficiency test). The practice questions in this book imitate the types of question formats you will see on the computer-delivered tests.

WHAT IS THE PRINCETON REVIEW?

The Princeton Review is the leader in test prep. Our goal is to help students everywhere crack standardized tests for high school, graduate school, and beyond. Starting from humble beginnings in 1981, The Princeton Review is now one of the largest test preparation companies. We offer courses in more than 500 locations in 20 countries, as well as online; we also publish best-selling books, like the one you're holding.

This book will show you how to crack the Praxis test by teaching you to

- extract important information from tricky test questions
- take full advantage of the limited time allowed
- systematically answer questions, even if you don't fully understand them
- apply test-taking strategies to use the test to your advantage

HOW TO USE THIS BOOK

Cracking the Praxis is divided into several parts. In **Part I**, we cover some very general information about the tests (you just read them!) and go through a few of our key test-taking strategies, which you'll read about in Chapter 2. Some of the strategies employed in this book may be different from those you've used before. As a result, it may take time to integrate them into your test-taking approach. But believe us when we say that practice makes perfect! The strategies will become second nature in no time.

But Wait, There's More!
Prepping for an Elementary Education Praxis test? Check out your Student Tools to download a bonus chapter on the Elementary Education: Content Knowledge exam, complete with sample questions and a drill. Register your book now to access this chapter and more great content! Just follow the steps on the "Get More (Free) Content" page at the beginning of this book.

Part II covers the key Praxis exams: the Praxis Core Academic Skills for Educators Tests in Reading, Writing, and Math. There are three content review chapters (one for each subject) so that you can familiarize yourself with the material you'll be tested on and the types of questions you will see. **Part III** contains two practice tests for each subject (Reading, Writing, Math) for a total of six practice exams, along with detailed answers and explanations. We recommend using the first practice test in each subject area as a diagnostic tool to determine your strengths, as well as the areas in which you need to improve. Be sure to read the explanations to gain an understanding of why a certain answer is correct or incorrect. After you read the content review chapters, take the second practice test and compare your performance to that of the first test to see where you have improved and where you might need additional practice and review.

Part IV focuses on the most popular content areas for the Praxis Subject Assessments: Math, Science, English Language Arts, and Social Studies. These chapters contain content review and both guided and independent practice with the types of questions you will see on test day. The information in these chapters may not apply to the test(s) you are taking, but you may find a quick brush-up on other subject areas to be advantageous to your overall preparation.

Part V is all about the Principles of Learning and Teaching tests, or PLT tests for short. As the name implies, this set of exams measures your knowledge of teaching practices and other instructional concepts that teachers need to know for the classroom. Focused content review is provided for each grade band—K–6, 5–9, and 7–12—culminating in drills that mimic the question formats you will see on the real exam.

So, here are the main takeaways from this chapter:

- The Praxis tests are almost exclusively computer-delivered. Keep this in mind as you prepare for the test you are taking!
- Testing requirements vary by state. We recommend contacting your teacher certification program or consulting the official test website: www.ets.org/praxis/states.
- We want you to succeed, and we are here with you every step of the way.

Are you ready? Let's get cracking!

Go Online!
Your online Student Tools contain a bunch of great resources to boost your prep, including a bonus chapter on Elementary Education, quizzes for the PLT tests, and guided math practice.

Chapter 2
Test-Taking
Strategies for the
Praxis Tests

TIME MANAGEMENT IS YOUR FRIEND

Time management isn't just a big portion of any timed test—it's also a big portion of studying for any test. In both cases, you're trying to figure out the most efficient way to do something—to study or to solve—in a limited amount of time, and the answer to both is the same:

Plan ahead.

Timed Tests
We'll get into the test logistics in later chapters, including the time allotted for each test, the number of questions in total, and a breakdown of the different question formats.

As far as this book goes, start by figuring out what you need. If you're preparing for the Praxis Core, we suggest beginning with Practice Test 1 in the subject of your choice, timing yourself and sitting in conditions similar to those of the actual test.

When You Take a Practice Test

- **Time yourself strictly.** Use a timer, watch, or stopwatch that will ring and take note of where you were when you ran out of time. If you use a phone for this, make sure that you do not use any other functions, as you will not have access to your phone during the test.

- **Take the test (or at least each section) in one sitting.** The real exams range from 85–100 minutes long—the Reading and Math tests are 85 minutes each, and the Writing test is 100 minutes long, which means the combined test is 4 hours and 30 minutes. If you don't have that kind of time during your preparation, we recommend taking each individual test in a single sitting. While you might find it advantageous to pause for a few minutes to catch your breath and collect your thoughts between sections, be aware that time will keep counting down. Weigh the benefits of any mind-clearing break against that ticking clock, and work on building up your endurance for the real test.

- **Once your time is up, take note of how much of the test you completed.** Identify the question types or content areas that slowed you down the most. After that, go through and answer any remaining questions and then check to see which ones you answered incorrectly.

Once you know where you're stumbling—is it a speed issue? Content issue? Both?—you can start tackling the content sections of this book.

If you find yourself running out of time, work on applying The Princeton Review strategies to the questions in this book. (We'll get to those soon.) Like any standardized test, the Praxis tests are testing more than just your content knowledge; they are also testing your ability to manage your time effectively. For example, working through all the math for a question isn't always the most time-efficient way to get the right answer. (You'll learn more about this later.)

If there are questions you're misreading or that you fundamentally don't understand how to answer, pay close attention to the Crack It questions in the relevant content sections. Once you feel more comfortable with the content, take the second practice test on the same subject. Continue to study the sections you're struggling with. For more practice and preparation materials, you can check out the sample questions and study companions on the ETS website: www.ets.org/praxis/prepare/materials/.

GENERAL STRATEGIES

You likely will need to adjust your pacing depending on which test(s) you are taking. For example, on the Praxis Core Math Test, you have 85 minutes to answer 56 questions. If you approach the test believing that you need to put a lot of time and energy into every single question, you'll probably end up wasting valuable time working on a very difficult problem that you might get wrong anyway. Instead, we recommend the two-pass system.

THE TWO-PASS SYSTEM

Within any test, you will find three types of questions:

- those you can answer easily without spending very much time
- those that, if you had all the time in the world, you could solve
- those that you have absolutely no idea how to tackle

The two-pass system is this: on your first pass through the test questions, answer the first type of question—those you can answer easily without spending very much time. If you do not understand a particular question the first time you read it, skip it and go on to the next one. (The test-taking software should include a "Mark and Review" feature, which allows you to mark a question and then come back to it later.) Then, check the clock and determine how much time you have left.

After you've completed the first pass, begin your second pass, reviewing the questions you skipped, focusing on the second type of question—those you could solve if you had all the time in the world. Be careful not to spend too much time on any one question. For that third type listed above, we recommend making a reasonable guess, and moving on. You do not lose points for wrong answers on this test, so it never hurts to guess! In fact, it can only help you.

More Study Tools
When you prepare for an exam, you should utilize every possible resource available to you. The official test website offers a plethora of information and study help, including a computer-delivered testing demonstration, all of which you can find here: www.ets.org/praxis/prepare/materials/.

Calculator Policy
Some Praxis math tests provide access to an onscreen, four-function calculator. A few tests with more involved math may provide scientific or graphing calculators with additional functionality. For the most up-to-date policies and information about which tests allow which calculators, go to www.ets.org/praxis/test day/policies/calculators/.

Mark and Return
Know when to walk away from a question that leaves you completely stumped. Use the Mark button to facilitate this key skill. Skip early and often so that you always have questions to distract your brain when you get stuck. Come back to those questions later during your second pass through the test.

Note:
On test day, you will likely be given time before starting the test to acquaint yourself with various testing tools and buttons, like Review, Mark, Next, Back, and Help.

Use the Review Screen to Navigate

Similar to other computer-delivered tests like the GRE, the Praxis tests allow you to mark an answered or unanswered question and return to it later. In fact, you can skip any question you like and return to any question at any time you like. Navigating around a section is easy with the Review screen, which looks something like this:

Question Number	Marked	Status
1		Not Answered
2	✔	Not Answered
3		Not Answered
4		Not Answered
5		Not Answered
6		Not Answered
7		Answered
8		Answered
9	✔	Answered
10	✔	Answered
11		Answered
12		Not Answered

When you're ready to revisit a question, simply click on a question to return to it!

Process of Elimination

Here's a question you will not see on a Praxis test, but which will show you how powerful Process of Elimination (POE) can be.

What is the capital of Malawi?

○ New York

○ Paris

○ London

○ Lilongwe

○ Los Angeles

There are two ways to get this question right. The first is if you already have the specialized knowledge that the capital of Malawi is Lilongwe. If you don't, however, you can still get the question right—and that's by knowing what the capital of Malawi *isn't*. The computer that's scoring your test isn't going to know which method you used, and even if it did, it wouldn't care: a right answer is all that matters. Try to get into the habit of looking at a question and asking, "What are the wrong answers?" instead of "What is the right answer?"

By using POE this way, you can leave yourself with fewer answers to choose between. Statistically, this means that you'll pick right answers more often than not. That's the good thing about standardized tests like the Praxis—you don't have to come up with the answer from scratch. You just have to identify it.

Use Your Scratch Paper and Double-Check Your Answers

ETS doesn't give you many useful tools on this test, so you have to make good use of the ones they do give you—and one of those things is scratch paper. Mistakes happen in your head, but good technique happens on scratch paper. When you do work in your head, you are really doing two things at once. The first is figuring out the answer at hand, and the second is keeping track of where you've been. Mistakes happen when you try to do two things in your head at once. It's better to park your thinking on your scratch paper. Get it out of your head and onto the page. Good things happen when you do.

Scratch paper is crucial for math problems in particular. Not only is it important for performing calculations, but when used properly, it can actually help to direct your thinking as you work through multistep problems. For reading and writing questions, scratch paper is every bit as essential. It will help you to track your progress, to focus on only one answer choice at a time, and to work through a series of answer choices efficiently.

Get into the habit of double-checking all of your answers before you click on your answer choice—or answer choices. Make sure that you reread the directions and have done everything they asked you to—don't get the answer wrong just because you chose only one answer for a question that required you to choose two or more.

The only way to reliably avoid careless errors is to adopt habits that make them less likely to occur. Always check to see that you've transcribed information correctly to your scratch paper. Always read the question at least twice and note any key details that you might forget later. Always check your calculations. And always read the question one last time before selecting your answer.

No Penalty for Guessing
As you do not lose points for incorrect answers, it's always better to guess than it is to leave a question blank. At least by guessing, you stand a chance at getting lucky and guessing correctly.

By training yourself to avoid careless errors, you will increase your score.

STRATEGIES FOR MATH QUESTIONS

Math questions have to make sense within the context of the question, which means that there are a variety of strategies you can use on the multiple-choice questions to help find the answer from a different direction.

Guesstimating

Your answers on the test need to be exact. However, you don't need to be as precise when eliminating choices! Here's an example:

> A group of three men buys a one-dollar lottery ticket that wins $400. If the one dollar they paid for the ticket is subtracted and the remainder of the prize money is divided equally among the men, how much will each man receive?
>
> ○ $62.50
>
> ○ $75.00
>
> ○ $133.00
>
> ○ $200.00
>
> ○ $262.50

To solve this mathematically, you would take $400, subtract $1, and then divide the remainder by 3. But with a little bit of logic, you wouldn't have to do any of that.

The lottery ticket won $400. If there were four men, each one would have won about $100. However, there were only three winners, which means each one won more than $100, which instantly rules out (A), $62.50, and (B), $75.00. Next, consider (D): this is saying that each of the three men won half of the jackpot—but that's not possible. Therefore, (E), which is OVER half the jackpot, would also be incorrect. The only answer left is (C), which is correct.

Plugging In

On the Praxis Core Math Test, you may see questions in which numbers have been replaced with variables. For example:

> Mary Kate is two inches taller than Elaine, who is four inches shorter than Christine. If c represents Christine's height in inches, then in terms of c, what is an expression for Mary Kate's height?
>
> ○ $c + 4$
>
> ○ $c + 2$
>
> ○ c
>
> ○ $c - 2$
>
> ○ $c - 4$

When you see a chess-piece icon like the one above, it means we're showing you exactly how to use a specific strategy, like Guesstimating or Plugging In.

You might stumble on the representation of this problem if you aren't used to thinking of people's heights in terms of variables. To get around that, just pick a number to replace the variable. As a bonus, since you're the one picking numbers, you can choose ones that you find easiest to work with. They don't even have to be realistic: in this example, let's say that Christine is 10 inches tall, or to put it in terms of the math, $c = 10$.

We know that Elaine is 4 inches shorter than Christine, so $e = 6$. We also know that Mary Kate is 2 inches taller than Elaine, so $m = 8$. What you're looking for is the answer choice which, when you input $c = 10$, yields Mary Kate's height, 8. The only one that fits is $c - 2$.

Plugging In the Answers (PITA)

When the question provides you with an algebraic equation and the answer choices are numbers, you can use a more specific version of this strategy: Plugging In the Answers (PITA). The difference in this case is that instead of choosing your own numbers, you're testing the ones that have been so generously provided by the test writers. For example, here's a question you might see on the Praxis Core Math Test:

> Aaron's bookcase currently holds b books, but is capable of holding up to 80 books. If Aaron loans 3 books to his friend, Sonya, the bookcase is now three-quarters full. What is the value of b ?
>
> ○ 52
>
> ○ 54
>
> ○ 57
>
> ○ 60
>
> ○ 63

There's no need to make up your own numbers—in fact, it might be rather time-consuming to do so. We know that the answer is going to be 52, 54, 57, 60, or 63, so there's no need to test any other numbers. Note that when the answers are in ascending or descending order, you can save even more time by starting with the middle choice.

In this case, try starting with (C): if you have 57 books and take 3 away, you'll have 54 books, which is fewer than 60, three-quarters of the bookcase's capacity. Because you're going to need more books, you can also eliminate (A) and (B), and move up to the next choice. In this case, you can also eliminate (D), which is clearly incorrect because it's 60 before subtracting any books. That makes 63 the right answer.

Percentages and Fractions
Plugging In can help you on questions involving fractions and percentages, which can be tricky—choosing convenient numbers can make these questions easier to process. When dealing with percents, the easiest number to work with is generally 100.

The goal of these math strategies is to help you avoid algebraic mistakes, and to answer a question if you don't remember exactly how to solve it head-on. These can sometimes take a little more time, however, so take time throughout this book to really practice them. Find the methods that work best for you!

STRATEGIES FOR QUESTIONS IN OTHER CONTENT AREAS

Okay, so what about non-math questions, such as those on the Praxis Core Reading and Writing Tests, or perhaps a Subject Assessment in a content area like Social Studies? These questions require careful reading, as many are passage-based, particularly on the Core Reading Test. We'll provide more in-depth coverage later in this book on how to approach such questions, but for now, you should be aware of some common answer choices for these questions that fall into the following categories. These answer choices are usually wrong, so keep them in mind as you work on the questions.

Planning on grad school and need to take the GRE? Look no further than our all-in-one preparation guide, *Cracking the GRE.*

Extreme Answers

An extreme answer is too negative or too positive, or it uses absolute words like "all," "every," "never," or "always." If there are two answers that express a similar idea, there's a good chance that the one that's stated firmly is probably wrong, while the other, more moderate one, is probably correct.

Complicated Answers

Most passages on Praxis tests are not lengthy (though they might sometimes seem that way). As a result, there's little room to cover broad topics, make definitive claims, or have complicated conclusions. An answer should be to the point, and if it's not, it's likely trying to mask the fact that it wasn't actually mentioned in the passage. These choices might use words that *do* appear in the passage, so make sure there's more to that answer than just a key word.

Absent Answers

Above all else, if a question is passage-based, remember that answers need to be supported by the text. If you can't find evidence in the passage for something, then it is not correct.

TIPS FOR TEST DAY

Actually, let's start with the week or two leading up to test day. Here are some prep tips we recommend:

- **Establish a time routine.** If your test is scheduled for 9 A.M., but you usually don't wake up until 11 A.M., then you should change your habits about a week before the test. Force yourself to adopt a new routine so that your body has enough time to adjust to the new schedule.

- **Scope out the testing center.** If you can, find the location where you'll be taking the test several days before the actual test administration. You don't want to have to worry about finding the building, finding a parking space, and finding the exact testing room all on the day of the test.

- **Take it easy the night before.** Don't stay out late or spend the whole night cramming. The time for studying is over. A better approach is to relax with a movie or book, and then get a good night's sleep.

And here is some day-of advice:

- **Eat normally.** By this we mean what is normal for *you*. If you usually opt for a light breakfast and your test is scheduled for 9 A.M., today is not the day to have a hearty meal. If you never drink coffee, today is not the day to start. Still, it's important to eat beforehand, whether breakfast or lunch (depending on when your test is scheduled). Just don't eat anything weird, and take it easy with the liquids and caffeine.

- **Dress in layers.** In the event that your testing room is either too warm or too cold, layers will allow you to better adjust to whatever the thermostat says.

- **Familiarize yourself with ETS's testing policies.** Specifically, know your test's calculator policy, as not all exams allow them. Also remember that your personal belongings (including your cell phone) will be put away in a locker outside of the testing room. You can read about more policies and procedures here: www.ets.org/praxis/test_day/policies/.

- **Take photo identification to the test center.** Acceptable forms of identification include your driver's license, photo-bearing employee ID cards, and valid passports. If you registered by mail, you must also take the authorization voucher sent to you by ETS.

Stretch, drink some water, go to the bathroom, and do whatever you need to do in order to be prepared to sit for this test. You might also want to have a snack handy in case your particular exam has one or more scheduled breaks. Most importantly, remember that *you can do this*.

Give Your Mind a Rest
Avoid cramming as you prepare for your test. Don't attempt to read this book in one sitting, and don't study for hours on end. Giving your brain a break every now and then is crucial for keeping a clear head and absorbing the information.

Part II
Praxis Core
Academic Skills
for Educators

Chapter 3
Praxis Core
Reading

OVERVIEW OF THE PRAXIS CORE READING TEST

Welcome to the first chapter of your Praxis Core content review! We'll start by diving into Core Academic Skills: Reading (5712), an exam designed to measure your critical reading and thinking skills, as well as basic reading comprehension ability. The following table summarizes some key logistics of the Reading Test.

Format	Computer-delivered
Time	85 minutes
Number of Questions	56
Question Types	• Multiple choice • Select all that apply Questions will be based on statements, passages, and charts or graphs.
Guessing Penalty?	Nope! (So be sure not to leave any questions blank—when in doubt, make an educated guess.)

Most of the questions on the test are multiple choice—you will choose one answer from five possible answers. ETS calls these selected-response questions. However, you may see a few questions where you must "select all that apply"—that is, select one or more answers from a list of choices. These answers appear with checkboxes instead of the bubbles that you'll see on multiple-choice questions where you must select only one answer.

According to ETS, the Praxis Core Reading Test covers skills in three main categories:

1. Key Ideas and Details
2. Craft, Structure, and Language Skills
3. Integration of Knowledge and Ideas

The first two categories require you to understand what a passage says literally, as well as task you with critical and inferential comprehension. The third category requires you to compare information from paired passages, graphs, or tables as well as evaluate claims. Questions will be distributed more or less evenly among these categories, though you may see a few more in categories 1 and 3.

Praxis Core Reading: Breaking Down the Question Categories

Are you wondering what those three categories (Key Ideas and Details; Craft, Structure, and Language Skills; and Integration of Knowledge and Ideas) mean? Here's a summary:

- **Key Ideas and Details:** These questions require you to both understand the passage content itself (e.g., questions about the main idea or specific details within the passage) and make inferences about the content.
- **Craft, Structure, and Language Skills:** These questions focus more on word choice, organization, and various style techniques the author uses to convey his or her intended meaning. For example, you may be asked how a certain word reveals the author's tone or point of view.
- **Integration of Knowledge and Ideas:** Questions in this category usually require you to pull together (integrate) ideas and information from multiple sources and then interpret or apply that information. These questions may include a chart or graph that presents information visually.

The passages on the Reading Test will vary in length. The longest passages will probably be about 200 words, followed by four to seven questions. There will also be shorter passages (about 100 words in length), on which two to three questions will be based. You may also see a single statement followed by one question. The Reading Test will likely also include a dual passage set (each passage will be roughly 200 words) followed by four to seven questions, as well as anywhere from three to five questions about a chart or graph.

The passages are on a wide variety of often less-than-exciting topics, but don't let that bother you. The objective is to get in and out of a given question as quickly as possible.

HOW TO APPROACH READING QUESTIONS

When it comes to Reading questions, keep the following two ideas in mind:

It's an open-book test. No matter what, the information needed to answer any question will be right in front of you on the page. It doesn't matter whether you've never heard of the passage topic or whether it was the subject of your senior thesis—the information will be right in front of you. It's not like you have to memorize anything: you can always look back at the passage.

The right answer is the one that's better than the other four. The answer choices on the Praxis are designed to be confusing. We'll discuss strategies for the different types of questions that you're likely to see, but remember that here, as always, Process of Elimination (as discussed in Part I) is your best friend. Often, it will be easier to identify wrong answers than to pick the right one.

THE PASSAGES

There are two different styles of passages. Some passages are just collections of facts about a topic; these passages look like they might have come straight from a textbook. In the other style of passage, the author makes an argument, and tries to persuade you of his position. Both styles have distinct characteristics.

Textbook Passages

Textbook passages follow some basic structural rules. Each passage has a main idea and a topic sentence, and when the author moves from one topic to another, he or she will use transition words such as *although* or *in addition* to let you know how the topics are related.

Argument Passages

If the author tries to make an argument, she will have a conclusion, which will be backed up with evidence. You're not allowed to argue with the evidence (you have to assume it's factual), but you are allowed to argue with the conclusion that she reaches. In fact, if the author makes an argument, it's a safe bet that one or more questions about the passage will ask you about how the argument could be strengthened or weakened with new information.

Despite this variety, you should follow the same step-by-step process for all passages. We'll call this the Basic Approach.

The Basic Approach

Here are the four steps:

> 1. Read the questions first.
> 2. Ask yourself: What's the Big Idea?
> 3. Answer the question in your own words.
> 4. Use POE.

Let's break each one of these down:

1. Read the Questions First.

If you're like most people, you probably approach reading comprehension questions by reading the passage and trying to remember as much information as possible. By the time you read the first question, you've forgotten what the passage said about that particular topic, so you have to go back and read the passage again. But if you read the questions first, you'll know what the important parts of the passage are as you read them, and you'll be able to answer the questions far more efficiently.

For instance, if the question asks what the main point of the passage is, and that's the only question asked about the passage, how much time do you think you need to spend reading the nitty-gritty details? That's right, none. On the other hand, if there are two questions that ask about specific details, then you'll probably want to read more of the supporting information.

2. Ask Yourself: What's the Big Idea?

Your first objective as you read the passage should be to figure out, in broad terms, what the author is trying to say. What is the passage mostly about? We'll call this the Big Idea. If the questions haven't already tipped you off, you should decide as quickly as possible which type of passage you're reading. The format of the Big Idea will be slightly different depending on which type of passage it is.

Reading the questions before the passage also allows you to determine whether you're about to read a textbook passage or an argument passage. For example, if you see a question such as, "Which of the following, if true, would most support the author's contention?" then you can be sure that you're about to read an argument.

While reading a textbook passage, remember that you can rely on its organization. Let's try an example. Skim the following passage, reading only for the Big Idea. Use the structural clues in the passage to help find it.

Geologists classify rocks on the earth's surface into three categories: igneous, sedimentary, and metamorphic. The names
Line refer not to qualities of the rocks, such as
(5) texture or hardness, but rather to the way in which they were formed.

The first category, igneous, describes rocks that were formed by volcanic activity. Flowing red-hot lava burst forth from vents
(10) in the earth's surface and cooled quickly into solid rock.

By contrast, sedimentary rock is created over millennia by successive layers of silt from rivers and streams.

(15) Metamorphic rock is created by heat and pressure. The Himalayan mountain range is made up of metamorphic rock created by the collision of two continental plates. The heat and pressure caused by the collision
(20) recrystallized the original sedimentary rock and it became metamorphic rock.

So, what's the Big Idea? You should probably be thinking along these lines:

There are three kinds of rocks.

It really doesn't need to get any more complicated than that. You can look up the specific details later if you need them.

If you're faced with an argument, the Big Idea is what the author wants you to believe, and why he thinks you should believe it.

Try this one:

Some scientists and politicians have suggested that automobile engines will soon run on hydrogen fuel cells rather than gasoline.
Line They cite the rising cost of petroleum and
(5) a greater awareness of the threat of global warming as two reasons why this change is imminent. However, proponents of hydrogen fuel cell technology fail to consider the enormous cost of retooling auto factories to
(10) build these new engines, as well as the cost of upgrading gas stations to accommodate the new power source. Clearly, widespread use of hydrogen power for cars is years away.

What's the Big Idea?

> *We won't be converting to hydrogen fuel cells anytime soon because it'll cost too much.*

Since this is essentially an open-book test, all of the answers are either in the text or directly supported by the text. If you find the key piece of information, you should feel 100% confident that you can identify the correct answer choice.

3. Answer the Question in Your Own Words.

Many test takers neglect this step, and their scores suffer as a result. If you go into the answer choices saying to yourself, "I'll know the answer when I see it," you'll be more likely to get confused by the language of the wrong answer choices. If you go into the answer choices with a specific idea of what you're looking for, you'll be more likely to avoid the incorrect answers and choose the right one.

4. Use POE.

As we said earlier, a right answer is right only because it's better than all the others. We'll discuss typical patterns that ETS follows in creating wrong answers, and show you how to recognize them.

THE QUESTIONS

Before we apply the four steps to a specific example, let's talk a little more about the types of questions that you will be asked. As we mentioned earlier, ETS breaks the questions into three main categories: those that test literal comprehension, those that test critical and inferential comprehension, and those that test integration of knowledge and ideas.

Literal Comprehension

There are four types of literal comprehension questions that comprise about 45 percent of the questions you will see.

1. Main idea/purpose
2. Supporting idea
3. Vocabulary-in-context
4. Organization

Main Idea/Main Purpose

These are both closely related to the Big Idea, but there's an important distinction between the Main Idea and the Main Purpose. A Main Idea question asks, "What did the author say?" A Main Purpose question asks, "Why did the author write the passage?"

Supporting Idea

Supporting Idea questions ask about the evidence used to back up the Big Idea. These questions ask about specific pieces of information in the passage. These questions also ask not only *what* was said, but also *why* it was said.

Vocabulary-in-Context

These questions will ask you what a specific word or phrase means in the context of the passage. A sample question might look like this:

> As used in line 6 of the passage, the word "butaneous" most nearly means which of the following?

Organization

These questions ask about how the pieces of the passage fit together. A sample question might look like this:

> Which of the following best describes the organization of the third paragraph?

Critical and Inferential Comprehension

Critical and inferential comprehension questions comprise about 55 percent of the test and fall into the following three categories:

1. Evaluation
2. Inferential Reasoning
3. Generalization

Let's look at each of these.

Evaluation

These questions will ask you to do the following.

- Weaken or strengthen the author's position with an additional piece of evidence

  > Which of the following statements, if true, would most weaken the author's reasoning?

- Determine the role that evidence plays in the author's position

  > Which of the following supports the author's position?

- Distinguish between fact and opinion

  > Which of the following is a fact mentioned by the author?

While critical and inferential comprehension questions may require you to read between the lines a bit, they are as much supported by the words the author uses as are the literal comprehension questions.

Inferential Reasoning

These questions will ask you to do the following.

- Draw inferences and implications from the reading

  Which of the following exhibits what the author is implying from the text?

- Determine what unstated assumptions the author is making

  Which of the following is an assumption on which the author's argument depends?

- Find the Big Idea or what the author's general opinion is

  Which of the following best describes the author's feeling toward logging of old-growth forests?

Generalization

These questions will ask you to do the following.

- Predict and extend the things that are likely to happen based on the information in the passage

  If the trends mentioned in the passage continue, which of the following would be most likely to occur?

- Draw conclusions from the material

  Which of the following is the most likely conclusion to the passage?

- Apply the reasoning outlines in the passage in a similar scenario

  Which of the following best matches the chain of reasoning used by the author in the third paragraph?

Now let's look at longer examples of each question type.

Evaluation Questions

At a recent art museum exhibition, more
sculptures were shown than photographs or
oil paintings. The new curator of the museum
Line invited artists to submit works, and she alone
(5) selected the works to be displayed. The curator
of the museum is clearly biased in favor of
sculptors.

1 of 3

Which of the following statements, if true, would
weaken the author's argument?

- ○ At last year's exhibition, the old curator
  also selected more sculptures than
  photographs or oil paintings.

- ○ A recent survey concluded that most
  people prefer sculptures to oil paintings.

- ○ The new curator herself is a sculptor.

- ○ More sculptors than photographers or oil
  painters submitted works to be shown at
  the exhibition.

- ○ The oil paintings shown at the exhibition
  were of exceptionally high quality.

According to the flawed reasoning the author follows in the passage, in which of the following scenarios would the author be most likely to conclude that bias is present?

○ The coach of a little league team assigns his son to play pitcher even though another boy on the team has equally good skills at that position.

○ At a local grocery store, there is more shelf space devoted to Brand X than to Brand Y or Brand Z. The manager is solely responsible for allotting shelf space.

○ The manger of a local nostalgia movie house surveyed his frequent customers and decided to show more movies starring Cary Grant than either Katharine Hepburn or Henry Fonda, because his patrons had clearly expressed their preference for Cary Grant.

○ A moving company hires only people who can lift a 100-pound box over their heads. The new hires at the moving company this week were all men.

○ A man interviews for a job, but is told he lacks sufficient relevant experience. As he leaves the building, however, he notices that most of the employees at the firm are at least ten years younger than he is.

Which of the following is a fact mentioned by the author?

○ Museum visitors prefer to view sculptures rather than photographs.

○ Oil paintings are becoming rare works of art.

○ The new curator invited artists to submit works.

○ The new curator lacks experience and knowledge about oil paintings and photographs.

○ More photographs were shown at the art museum exhibition.

Here's How to Crack Them

As you learned from what you just read, evaluation questions ask you to read a passage and then evaluate that passage—pretty straightforward. The first question is an evidence question, the second is an application question, and the third is a fact-versus-opinion question. Each type can be worked using all or some of the steps in the four-step process that we just discussed.

You may find that for a given question, you can skip one step and jump right to another—that's fine. Work the questions in a way that works best for you. Let's work out these three.

Step 1: Read the Questions First.

> 1 of 3
>
> Which of the following statements, if true, would most weaken the author's argument?

> 2 of 3
>
> According to the flawed reasoning the author follows in the passage, in which of the following scenarios would the author be most likely to conclude that bias is present?

> 3 of 3
>
> Which of the following is a fact mentioned by the author?

Step 2: What's the Big Idea?

Based on the passage, the Big Idea is something like this:

> *The curator is biased because she picked more sculptures to display in the art exhibition.*

Step 3: Answer the Question in Your Own Words.

> 1 of 3
>
> Which of the following statements, if true, would most weaken the author's argument?

We're looking for something that suggests that just because she picked more sculptures doesn't necessarily mean she's biased. For instance, maybe most of the submitted oil paintings and photographs were just plain bad.

Step 4: Use POE.

> (A) At last year's exhibition, the old curator also selected more sculptors than photographs or oil paintings.

Does this show that the new curator isn't necessarily biased? No. What happened last year is not relevant to what happened this year.

Notice that we're just getting an idea of what we're looking for rather than an exact answer. Many different statements would weaken the author's argument.

Answer Choices on the Computer-Delivered Test

On the actual exam, you won't see answer choices (A) through (E). Instead, each answer choice will be preceded by a bubble, and you will click on the one that you are choosing as your answer. But for the purposes of walking through practice questions in this book, we'll be assigning the answer choices a letter (A) through (E), based on the order they're listed. In other words, the first choice listed is (A), the second is (B), and so on.

(B) A recent survey concluded that most people prefer sculptures to oil paintings.

Does this show that the new curator isn't necessarily biased? No. What most people believe is not relevant to what the curator believes.

(C) The new curator herself is a sculptor.

No. If anything, this would serve to strengthen the author's argument by showing that the curator is biased because she is a sculptor and is therefore in favor of sculptors.

(D) More sculptors than photographers or oil painters submitted works to be shown at the exhibition.

Does this show that the new curator isn't necessarily biased? Yes. If there were more sculptures submitted, then the fact that there are more sculptures in the exhibition wouldn't necessarily mean the curator was biased. Keep this one.

(E) The oil paintings shown at the exhibition were of exceptionally high quality.

No. This is irrelevant. The quality of the paintings has nothing to do with whether or not the curator is biased in favor of sculptors. The best answer is (D).

Now let's try another one. We already read all of the questions and decided on the big idea of the passage, so we can jump to Step 3.

Step 3: Answer In Your Own Words.

2 of 3

According to the flawed reasoning the author follows in the passage, in which of the following scenarios would the author be most likely to conclude that bias is present?

This is an example of an evaluation question. The question asks you to find the scenario in which the author would find bias, assuming he applied the flawed reasoning in the passage. To give yourself an idea of what you are looking for, try to state the flawed reasoning in general terms before you look at the answer choices. For instance, in this case you might say:

The fact that someone picked more of one thing than another thing means that the person is biased.

Your own opinion is irrelevant—you're just looking to summarize the author's reasoning. Now we look for an answer choice that follows the same (flawed) logic.

Step 4: Use POE.

    (A) The coach of a little league team
             assigns his son to play pitcher even
             though another boy on the team has
             equally good skills at that position.

Does this talk about someone picking more of something? No. Cross it out.

    (B) At a local grocery store, there is more
             shelf space devoted to Brand X than
             to Brand Y or Brand Z. The manager
             is solely responsible for allotting shelf
             space.

Does this talk about someone picking more of something? Kind of. Let's keep it for the moment and see what the other choices are.

    (C) The manger of a local nostalgia
             movie house surveyed his frequent
             customers and decided to show more
             movies starring Cary Grant than
             either Katharine Hepburn or Henry
             Fonda, because his patrons had clearly
             expressed their preference for Cary
             Grant.

This talks about someone picking more of something, but there's a reason explicitly stated that shows the manager isn't biased. Cross it out.

    (D) A moving company hires only people
             who can lift a 100-pound box over
             their heads. The new hires at the
             moving company this week were all
             men.

This, too, talks about someone picking more of something (in this case, all men and no women), but here also there's a reason that suggests there's no bias involved. Cross it out.

    (E) A man interviews for a job, but is told
             he lacks sufficient relevant experience.
             As he leaves the building, however, he
             notices that most of the employees at
             the firm are at least ten years younger
             than he is.

Does this talk about someone picking more of something? The person doing the hiring isn't explicitly mentioned, and the hiring of the younger people happened earlier than the older man's interview, so this doesn't seem like the best match. But let's look at (B) again:

> (B) At a local grocery store, there is more shelf space devoted to Brand X than to Brand Y or Brand Z. The manager is solely responsible for allotting shelf space.

Here, as in the original passage, we have one identifiable person in charge of making the decision. We also are asked to compare one item to two others. According to the reasoning in the passage, the author should conclude that the manager is in favor of brand *X*. Overall, this seems like the best choice. Pick (B).

Let's try the last one, and we'll jump to Step 3 again.

Step 3: Answer In Your Own Words.

> 3 of 3
> Which of the following is a fact mentioned by the author?

This is an example of a fact versus opinion question that asks that you to decipher the difference between them given the passage.

Step 4: Use POE.

> (A) Museum visitors prefer to view sculptures rather than photographs.

While the passage compares sculptures over photographs by showing more sculptures in the exhibition, this is not evidences in the passage. Cross it out.

> (B) Oil paintings are becoming rare works of art.

From the passage, we are unable to determine that this is a fact. Get rid of it.

> (C) The new curator invited artists to submit works.

Yes. We know that the new curator invited artists to submit works. Let's keep it.

> (D) The new curator lacks experience and knowledge about oil paintings and photographs.

The passage does not mention her experience. Throw it out.

> (E) More photographs were shown at the art museum exhibition.

No. In fact, more sculptures were shown. The best answer is (C).

Inferential Reasoning Questions

The next question type that we will discuss is the inferential reasoning question. This is a question for which you will, again, be asked to read a passage and answer some questions about the passage. However, you will be expected to make a few more leaps of logic with inferential reasoning questions. You'll need to make inferences, that is, derive conclusions from the information presented in the passage. Let's try a few examples.

Some scientists and politicians have suggested that automobile engines will soon run on hydrogen fuel cells rather than gasoline. They cite the rising cost of petroleum and a greater awareness of the threat of global warming as two reasons why this chance is imminent. However, proponents of hydrogen fuel cell technology fail to consider the enormous cost of retooling auto factories to build these new engines, as well as the cost of upgrading gas stations to accommodate the new power source. Clearly, widespread use of hydrogen power for cars is years away.

1 of 3

Which of the following did the passage mention as a reason that some people believe that hydrogen will soon replace gasoline as the main form of fuel cars?

○ The cost of fossil fuel-based energy sources is rising.

○ The burning of gasoline contributes to global warming.

○ The cost of retooling auto factories is negligible compared to the costs associated with global warming.

○ Hydrogen is a cleaner-burning fuel than gasoline.

○ Hydrogen will be cheaper than gasoline in the near future.

Which of the following is an assumption on which the author's argument depends?

○ Fuel-based energy sources are rising each year.

○ Hydrogen will be cheaper than gasoline in the near future.

○ Global warming is diminishing and does not need to be addressed by scientists and politicians.

○ It will be only a few years until hydrogen-powered cars are vastly used.

○ Gasoline is becoming less expensive when compared with hydrogen gas.

3 of 3

Which of the following best describes the author's feeling toward hydrogen powered cars?

○ Hydrogen-powered cars will be vastly used in only a few years.

○ Retooling factories is cost effective and will benefit the creation of hydrogen-powered engines.

○ Even though the change to hydrogen powered cars is likely, it will not happen for many years.

○ The burning of gasoline contributes to global warming.

○ Hydrogen will be cheaper than gasoline in the near future.

Here's How to Crack Them
Step 1: Read the Questions First.

1 of 3

Which of the following did the passage mention as a reason that some people believe that hydrogen will soon replace gasoline as the main form of fuel cars?

2 of 3

Which of the following is an assumption on which the author's argument depends?

Which of the following best describes the author's feeling toward hydrogen powered cars?

The first question asks you to draw inferences and implications from the reading. The second asks what assumptions the author is making to lead him to his argument. The last question asks you to determine the author's feelings.

Step 2: What's the Big Idea?

Based on the passage, the Big Idea can be one of two things:

> *The rising cost of petroleum is leading scientists and politicians to consider hydrogen powered engines, or hydrogen powered engines are years away and may require much cost.*

Step 3: Answer the Question in Your Own Words.

1 of 3

Which of the following did the passage mention as a reason that some people believe that hydrogen will soon replace gasoline as the main form of fuel cars?

We're looking for a reason hydrogen will replace gasoline. Notice that we're just getting an idea of what we're looking for rather than an exact answer. There are many reasons we can think of.

Step 4: Use POE.

(A) The cost of fossil fuel-based energy sources is rising.

Was this a reason listed in the text? Yes. Let's keep it and review the other answers.

(B) The burning of gasoline contributes to global warming.

Did the passage state that burning of gasoline contributes to global warming? No. It states that there is a greater awareness of the threat of global warming.

(C) The cost of retooling auto factories is negligible compared to the costs associated with global warming.

Did the passage compare the costs of retooling auto factories to global warming? No.

(D) Hydrogen is a cleaner-burning fuel than gasoline.

No. The passage does not state this. Cross it out.

(E) Hydrogen will be cheaper than gasoline
in the near future.

No. The passage does not discuss the differences in cost between gasoline and hydrogen. The best answer is (A).

Let's tackle the next one. Remember that we have already completed Steps 1 and 2, so we'll jump straight to Step 3 here.

Step 3: Answer the Question in Your Own Words.

2 of 3

Which of the following is an assumption on which
the author's argument depends?

This is an example of an assumption question. The question asks you to find the assumption being made by the author on which he bases his arguments. To give yourself an idea of what you are looking for, try to state the flawed reasoning in general terms before you look at the answer choices. For instance, in this case you might say:

The author assumes that hydrogen will be more expensive and will take more time to convert automobiles to than people realize because of the cost of retooling auto factories.

Step 4: Use POE.

(A) Fuel-based energy sources are rising
each year.

Does this support the author's argument that the automobile industry will take longer to convert cars over to hydrogen powered engines? Yes. Keep it.

(B) Hydrogen will be cheaper than gasoline
in the near future.

The author does not state that hydrogen will be cheaper than gasoline, but it does state that gasoline prices are rising. It actually states that it can be years away instead of the near future. This would not support the author's argument.

(C) Global warming is diminishing and
does not need to be addressed by
scientists and politicians.

Is this an assumption you determine after reading the passage? No.

(D) It will be only a few years until
hydrogen-powered cars are vastly used.

No. In fact, the passage states the opposite. This would refute the author's stance.

(E) Gasoline is becoming less expensive
      when compared with hydrogen gas.

Does the passage state gasoline will be less expensive than hydrogen? No. It implies that it is more expensive. Cross it out. The best answer is (A).

Now let's try the last one.

Step 3: Answer the Question in Your Own Words.

3 of 3

Which of the following best describes the author's feeling toward hydrogen powered cars?

What are the author's thoughts about hydrogen powered cars? Notice that we're just getting an idea of what we're looking for rather than an exact answer. There are many feelings that may come across in the author's writing.

Step 4: Use POE.

(A) Hydrogen-powered cars will be vastly
      used in only a few years.

No. The author specifically states that it can take many years to convert cars to hydrogen.

(B) Retooling factories is cost effective and
      will benefit the creation of hydrogen-
      powered engines.

No. The author states that politicians and scientists are not thinking about the large costs associated with retooling auto factories.

(C) Even though the change to hydrogen
      powered cars is likely, it will not
      happen for many years.

Yes. This is how the author feels. Let's keep it.

(D) The burning of gasoline contributes to
      global warming.

The author does not discuss the relationship between burning gasoline and global warming.

(E) Hydrogen will be cheaper than gasoline
      in the near future.

No. We cannot determine that the author feels this way after reading the passage. The best answer is (C).

Generalization

Now, let's take a look at one last passage that deals with generalization questions.

Consumers spent far more money on recordings of popular music than on classical music last year, and a similarly disproportionate amount was spent on live popular music concert tickets than on classical concert tickets. Because popular music lovers outnumber classical music aficionados by a wide margin, these disparities should come as no great shock, and in a free society, people have the right to spend money on whatever legal product they choose. But because only classical music has the ability to elevate a listener's soul, the people who bought popular music recordings and concert tickets simply wasted their money.

1 of 2

If the trends mentioned in the passage continue, which of the following would be most likely to occur?

○ Classical music recording and live concerts will continue to decline.

○ Popular music will begin to build soul.

○ Classical music listeners will waste money on recordings and concert tickets.

○ The government will begin to restrict spending on certain music related products.

○ More classical concert tickets will be sold.

2 of 2

Which of the following statements follows the author's chain of reasoning?

○ Popular music should be banned.

○ Elevation of one's soul should be one's top priority.

○ Popular music has no value whatsoever.

○ People should spend more money on classical music recordings than on popular recordings.

○ More people would listen to classical music if it were taught in the schools.

Here's How to Crack Them

You've worked through the steps enough times that this last batch of generalization questions should be a breeze. Remember the steps that you've learned and let's tackle these last few questions.

Step 1: Read the Questions First.

> 1 of 2
>
> If the trends mentioned in the passage continue, which of the following would be most likely to occur?

Step 2: What's the Big Idea?

Popular music lovers are spending more money on their beloved music, but they are missing out on soul-elevating classical music.

Step 3: Answer the Question in Your Own Words.

That passage was certainly opinionated. What is the gist of this first question? *If popular music continues to grow in popularity, what will happen next?*

Step 4: Use POE.

Now, compare your take on the question with the answer choices:

> (A) Classical music recording and live concerts will continue to decline.

This seems likely and agrees with our answer. Keep it.

> (B) Popular music will begin to build soul.

We can't determine from the passage that popular music will begin to build soul. Cross it out.

> (C) Classical music listeners will waste money on recordings and concert tickets.

This is an opinion that doesn't follow the trends of the passage.

> (D) The government will begin to restrict spending on certain music related products.

The government is not mentioned in the paragraph.

> (E) More classical concert tickets will be sold.

This refutes the argument in the passage. Cross it out. The best answer is (A).

Now let's try the last question. We already read the question, so let's jump to Step 3.

Step 3: Answer the Question in Your Own Words.

Which of the following statements follows the author's chain of reasoning?

This is an application question. ETS asks you to take what you know about the author and pick the statement with which he or she would be most likely to agree. It's impossible to predict what the right answer will be, but you should remind yourself of what you know so far.

The author prefers classical music to popular music and thinks that people are foolish to spend money on popular music.

Step 4: Use POE.

Let's look at the choices and use Process of Elimination.

    (A) Popular music should be banned.

This seems awfully extreme. It's hard to defend an extreme answer choice on an extend/predict question. Right answers are usually more middle-of-the road. Cross it out.

    (B) Elevation of one's soul should be one's top priority.

There's no evidence to suggest it should be one's top priority. Cross it out.

    (C) Popular music has no value whatsoever.

No value whatsoever? Again, that seems extreme. Get rid of it.

    (D) People should spend more money on classical music recordings than on popular recordings.

That's better. Of course the author would agree with what he believes—that spending money on popular music is wasteful and that classical music is uplifting. It's not too much of a stretch to believe that he thinks that everyone should spend more money on classical music than on popular music.

    (E) More people would listen to classical music if it were taught in the schools.

We have no idea whether the author would agree with his or not. Cross it out. The best answer is (D).

Integration of Knowledge and Ideas

One final question type is the integration of knowledge and ideas. This may be presented as two passages offering different perspectives on a single issue or as a graph or table. Take a look at the question below.

Joel's basketball team in Philadelphia (denoted by PHL) had a busy two weeks. Below are the results of their games from the past two weeks, along with a summary of Joel's points, rebounds, and assists (passes to a scoring player) in each game.

	Sunday	Monday	Tuesday	Wednesday	Thursday	Friday	Saturday
Week 1	PHL 112 NYC 110 **Joel's stats** 15 points 8 assists 7 rebounds			PHL 90 BOS 99 **Joel's stats** 20 points 11 assists 9 rebounds	PHL 102 CLE 94 **Joel's stats** 16 points 9 assists 8 rebounds		PHL 118 BKN 120 **Joel's stats** 10 points 6 assists 6 rebounds
	Sunday	Monday	Tuesday	Wednesday	Thursday	Friday	Saturday
Week 2		PHL 88 PHX 95 **Joel's stats** 12 points 10 assists 9 rebounds	PHL 109 MIA 100 **Joel's stats** 24 points 8 assists 5 rebounds		PHL 106 OKC 103 **Joel's stats** 11 points 14 assists 4 rebounds	PHL 94 DET 80 **Joel's stats** 17 points 13 assists 9 rebounds	

Based on the last two weeks of games, which of the following conclusions are valid?

Select **all** that apply.

☐ Joel had at least seven rebounds in each game that his team won.

☐ Joel did not score fewer than 10 points per game during the two weeks.

☐ Joel's points always exceeded his assists.

Here's How to Crack It

Make sure that you understand what the table and the introduction say. In this case, we learn that the table shows us two weeks of Joel's basketball results. The information on top of each entry is the scores of the two teams, while the information on the bottom provides three stats on Joel's performance.

The question itself asks us to identify the true statements. To find out which statements are supported, we need to integrate information. For instance, the first statement claims that "Joel had at least seven rebounds in each game that his team won." To evaluate this claim, look only at the games his team won. You can find these on Sunday and Thursday of week one and on Tuesday, Thursday, and Friday of Week 2. By looking at those games, we can see that Joel had at least 7 rebounds in only three of those games. On Tuesday and Thursday of Week 2, he only had 5 and 4 rebounds, respectively. Eliminate (A).

The second statement is easy to verify since a simple glance would show us that he scored in the double digits in all eight games, meaning that he never scored fewer than 10 points per game. Click (B), the second checkbox.

Finally, you once again need to compare information for the third statement. Compare his points and assists. If the points are always greater than the assists, we can click this box. However, if we find at least one exception, we need to eliminate it. Thursday of Week 2 is the only example of Joel's points not exceeding his assists. Since we have at least one contradicting example, we must eliminate (C). The only correct answer is (B).

KEY TAKEAWAYS

You've probably noticed that the two key ideas we discussed at the very beginning are fundamental to being able to answer each question, regardless of the question type.

- It's an open-book test.
- The right answer is the one that's better than the other four.

Keep both ideas firmly in mind, and remember to follow the four-step Basic Approach as you work through the following drill. Then check your answers using the explanations at the end of the chapter.

READING DRILL

Each statement or passage is followed by a question or questions based on its content. After reading a statement or passage, choose the best answer to each question from among the five choices given. Answer all questions following a statement or passage on the basis of what is stated or implied in that statement or passage; you are not expected to have any previous knowledge of the topics treated in the statements or passages. Answers and explanations can be found at the end of the chapter.

1 of 8

In 1994, approximately two percent of humans who were admitted to hospital emergency rooms after suffering a scorpion bite in Texas died from the attack. Ten years later, this figure has jumped to four percent. Clearly, the venom of the scorpion has become much more toxic to humans.

Which of the following statements, if true, most seriously weakens the above conclusion?

○ The scorpion population in Texas has remained steady since 1994.

○ There have been few innovations in the treatment of scorpion bites since 1994.

○ Most people who suffer scorpion bites are inexperienced hikers who are unaware of the best methods to avoid contact with a scorpion.

○ Since 1994, people have learned that most scorpion bites can be treated in the home as long as they are detected early.

○ People who survive one scorpion bite tend to have a better than average chance of surviving a second bite.

Questions 2–4 are based on the following passage.

Mounting evidence suggests that any musical stimulus, from Beethoven to Outkast, can have therapeutic effects. Whether you've had heart
Line surgery or a bad day at the office, soothing
(5) sounds may help to lessen stress and promote well-being. Music therapy isn't mainstream health care, but recent studies suggest it can have a wide range of benefits. Most studies have been done with patients recovering from illnesses such as a
(10) stroke or cancer.

No one really knows how music helps the body. It is known that listening to music can directly influence pulse, the electrical activity of muscles, and lower blood pressure. Neuroscientists
(15) suspect that music can actually help build and strengthen connections among nerve cells. This is probably why listening to Mozart before an IQ test boosts test scores an average of nine points.

2 of 8

Which of the following is NOT mentioned as a benefit of listening to music?

○ Relieved stress

○ Increased neural activity

○ Lowered blood pressure

○ Increased coordination

○ Improved pulse

3 of 8

Which of the following best summarizes the content of the passage?

○ Music therapy has become so widely accepted that many healthcare organizations are adding music therapy coverage to their insurance policies.

○ The passage presents a detailed analysis on how music helps the body.

○ Neuroscientists are tracking the neurological effects of music on the body.

○ Evidence suggests that music therapy helps the body, even if we aren't sure exactly how.

○ Students can perform better on standardized tests if they listen to more classical music.

4 of 8

The author's use of the word "mainstream" in the first paragraph means

○ conventional

○ radical

○ musical

○ medicinal

○ experimental

Terry, a high-school senior from State A, expressed an interest in attending Lewis State College, which was located in State B. Terry's parents discovered that Lewis State College offered residents of State B a substantial discount from its normal tuition cost. Therefore, the parents decided to move to State B.

Which of the following, if true, is the most important reason why the parents might reconsider their decision?

○ Scholarships are given only to applicants who establish financial need.

◉ To qualify for the lower tuition, applicants must prove they have lived in State B for a minimum of three years.

○ Several colleges in State A offer tuition discounts.

○ State B does not have the same property values as State A.

○ Regular tuition at Lewis State College is lower than that of most state colleges.

A survey of 1,200 residents of a certain state revealed that 34 percent found hunting to be morally wrong and 59 percent had never hunted before. From this information, the surveyors concluded that _____.

Which of the following best completes the passage above?

○ some respondents expressed their moral convictions more strongly than others

○ the people who expressed an objection to hunting had never hunted before

○ moral objection is not the only reason why people do not hunt

○ the people who had hunted before but stopped because of a moral objection outnumbered those who had never hunted but didn't find it morally wrong

○ some people hunt even though they are morally opposed to it

Questions 7 and 8 are based on the following passage.

Forced to hunt for new prey, killer whales are upsetting the sea otter population off the Alaskan coast, disrupting the food chain and
Line setting off an ecological cascade. The whales have
(5) created damage with such alarming efficiency that a vast ecosystem now seems to be at risk of collapse.

The problem began when fish stocks started to decline in the Bering Sea, probably as a result
(10) of commercial fishing, or changes in the ocean currents and temperatures. Because of this lack of food, seals and sea lions are thinning out, losing some of their insulating blubber. Killer whales, therefore, aren't getting the same diet from seals
(15) and sea lions as they once did, forcing them to feed on sea otters. The otter populations have collapsed, allowing their prey, sea urchins, to multiply out of control. Sea urchins have now begun to devour the kelp forests on the ocean
(20) floor at an alarming rate. The kelp forests are crucial to a number of habitats.

Otter populations have declined off the Alaskan coast primarily because

○ sea urchins are multiplying at record rates

○ the kelp forests are being destroyed

◉ whales have been forced to search for additional food

○ commercial fishing nets trap otters

○ global warming and current changes are making the otters sick

Which of the following best outlines the structure of the passage?

○ A statement is made, and then supported through an example.

◉ A theory is stated, and the steps leading up to that theory are then explained.

○ A question is raised, and then answered.

○ An experiment is stated, followed by its conclusion.

○ An argument is stated, and then refuted.

READING DRILL ANSWERS AND EXPLANATIONS

1. **D** In order to weaken the conclusion, you need to show that the increase in the death rate to 4% from 2% is due to reasons beyond the toxicity of scorpion venom. Why is a higher percentage of emergency room admits dying if the venom is not more dangerous? Choice (A) is not relevant. Choice (B) indicates that the rates should stay the same, but it does not weaken the argument. Choices (C) and (E) are also irrelevant. Choice (D) indicates that many people are treating their bites at home. This indicates that only severe cases end up in the emergency room, and these severe cases have a higher death rate. Choice (D) helps to weaken the conclusion, so it is the correct answer.

2. **D** On a "NOT" question, eliminate any answer choice that is true. Choice (A), which is about stress relief, can be found in line 5, so eliminate (A). Choice (B) can be eliminated because it is stated in lines 15–16 that *music can actually help build and strengthen connections among nerve cells.* Lowered blood pressure can be found in line 14, so eliminate (C). Finally, eliminate (E) because improved pulse is found in line 13. This leaves (D) as the correct answer.

3. **D** The first paragraph states that music therapy helps a number of people with varying conditions. The second paragraph attempts to give some information on how music may help the body. This best aligns with (D), which states that there is evidence to show how music therapy helps the body. You can eliminate (A) because the text explicitly states in line 6 that music therapy is not mainstream health care. Choice (B) is incorrect because the text does not explain *how* music therapy helps the body, only that evidence suggests that it does help the body. Choices (C) and (E) are also incorrect because they each deal only with a supporting detail from the passage, not the main idea.

4. **A** Without looking at the answer choices, replace the word in question with an alternate word that functions equally well. You could replace *mainstream* with the phrase "widely accepted," and the sentence would retain the original meaning. Therefore, the author uses the word *mainstream* to point out how music therapy is beyond the normal practices in medicine. Choice (A), *conventional*, is correct. You can eliminate (B) and (E) because *radical* and *experimental* both mean the opposite of "widely accepted." Choices (C) and (D) are deceptive answer choices, as both words are topics covered in the text. However, that does not mean that those words have anything to do with *mainstream*. Eliminate (C) and (D).

5. **B** Terry's parents chose to move with the belief that it would help get Terry a lower tuition. In order for that to happen, Terry's parents must be residents of State B. Choice (B) indicates that residency alone is not sufficient, which would weaken the decision to move.

6. **C** The number of people who have never hunted exceeds the number of people who find hunting to be morally wrong. Therefore, some people who do not hunt do not find hunting to be morally wrong. If this is the case, there must be other reasons why people choose not to hunt. No other statement can be logically drawn from the information presented in the brief passage. Choice (C) is the answer.

7. **C**   The third sentence in the second paragraph addresses sea otters. The whale needs additional food because the sea lions are not as readily available for the whale's diet. Therefore, (C) is correct. The rapid growth of the sea urchin population is mentioned as an effect of the sea otter decline, not a cause of it, so eliminate (A). Choice (B) can be eliminated as well because the kelp forest destruction is an effect of the growth of the sea urchin population. Be careful with (D); commercial fishing is mentioned in the passage, but the text does not say that commercial fishers are trapping otters. Eliminate (D). Choice (E) is incorrect for a similar reason: global warming is referenced *(changes in the ocean currents and temperatures)*, but there is no evidence that it is making otters sick.

8. **B**   The passage starts with the claim that the otter population is in great danger. The theory is supported by explaining how whales are feeding. This kind of structure best aligns with (B). Choice (A) is incorrect because the claim is not supported by only a single example. There is no question raised in the first part of the passage, so you can eliminate (C). There also is no experiment introduced, which makes (D) incorrect. Finally, (E) is incorrect because there is no contradictory information given.

Chapter 4
Praxis Core Writing

Write Smart!
This chapter is all about the writing skills and rules you need to know for the Praxis Core Writing Test. But if you want to expand your writing knowledge, check out *Writing Smart,* our concise guide to all types of writing, such as timed essays, research papers, and more.

OVERVIEW OF THE PRAXIS CORE WRITING TEST

The Praxis Core Academic Skills for Educators: Writing (5722) is a computer-delivered test that is 100 minutes long and consists of both multiple-choice ("selected response") and essay questions. There may be some questions that will not count toward your score. Points earned on the essay and multiple-choice sections are reported separately on your score report. The following table summarizes some key logistics of the Praxis Core Writing Test.

Format	Computer-delivered
Time	100 minutes • Selected response (multiple choice): 40 minutes • Essays: 60 minutes
Number of Questions	42 • 40 selected-response questions • 2 essays
Question Types	• Usage ("Error ID") • Sentence Correction • Revision in Context • Research Skills
Guessing Penalty?	Nope! (So be sure not to leave any questions blank—when in doubt, make an educated guess.)

As indicated in the table, the test has two parts: 40 selected-response (multiple-choice) questions and two essays. The multiple-choice questions, which you'll have 40 minutes to complete, are broken down into the following categories:

> • 19 Usage ("Error ID") questions
> • 11 Sentence Correction questions
> • 6 Revision-in-Context questions
> • 4 Research Skills questions

The two essays are as follows:

> • Essay #1 (30 minutes): Argumentative essay
> • Essay #2 (30 minutes): Source-based essay

This chapter discusses each of these question types in detail. Let's start with the multiple-choice section.

Multiple-Choice Questions on the Writing Test

Usage Questions

The first type of multiple-choice question asks you to identify an error in a sentence. Here's an example of a usage question:

> Statistically, <u>one</u> is more likely to die in an
>   A
> automobile accident than in a <u>plane crash</u>, yet
>   B
> paradoxically people feel safer in their <u>car</u> <u>than</u> in
>   C   D
> airplanes. <u>No error</u>
>   E

All you have to do with these questions is determine which one of the underlined portions of the sentence, if any, contains a grammar or usage error. You don't have to correct the error or explain why it's wrong; you just have to find it. If there's no error, the correct answer is (E).

If you spot an error immediately, that's great. If not, the easiest way to approach these questions is to apply your knowledge of grammar to each of the underlined portions of the sentence. For instance, in the example above you would do this:

(A)   *One* is a singular pronoun. Does that match with the verb *is*? Yes. So that's not an error.

(B)   Is *plane crash* an acceptable use of words? Yes. So that's not an error.

(C)   *Car* is a singular noun. Does that match with the other nouns and pronouns in that clause? No. "People" and "their" are both plural. So *car* is incorrect. Choice (C) is the right answer. You don't even need to look at (D) and (E).

Please note that on the actual exam, the answer choices will not be labeled (A) through (E), as shown here. Rather, each choice will be underlined as shown, and you will click on the answer you're selecting. For our purposes here, we will be using letters (A) through (E) for easier reference.

Sentence Correction Questions

The second type of multiple-choice question asks you to correct errors in a sentence. Here's an example of a sentence correction question:

> To get through an emergency, <u>it demands remaining calm</u> and collected.
>
> ○ it demands remaining calm
>
> ○ it demands calmness
>
> ○ one is demanded to remain calm
>
> ◉ one should remain calm
>
> ○ demands one to remain calm

A sentence correction question gives you a sentence, underlines a portion (or all) of it, and asks you to pick the answer choice that best rewrites the underlined portion. If the underlined portion is correct as written, the answer is (A).

Reminder

In this book, we will use letters—(A), (B), (C), etc.—to more easily refer to the answer choices. On the actual test, the answer choices will not be labeled; you will simply click on the bubble of the choice you are selecting.

If you spot an error immediately on a sentence correction question, that's great. Eliminate (A) and all choices that repeat the same error. Then compare the remaining answer choices and eliminate those that contain other errors.

If you don't spot an error immediately, you can use the answer choices to help you. For instance, notice in the example that two answers begin with the word *it*, and two begin with the word *one*. Which is correct? Well, according to the portion of the sentence that's not underlined (which is the part you can't change) someone has to get through an emergency. Therefore, the answer should start with the word *one*. Now we're down to (C) and (D). Which is better? Is someone demanding that you remain calm? No. The best answer is (D).

Revision-in-Context Questions

Revision-in-context questions ask you to make improvements to a flawed passage that has a variety of errors and problems. These questions test your ability to develop and organize your thoughts and to express them clearly and effectively in accordance with the conventions of good English. Here's an example of a revision-in context question that pertains to a passage about college athletes:

> **(1)** At many American colleges star athletes are viewed as critical assets to the reputation and financial well-being of the university. **(2)** While often envied and even idolized by their peers, these young athletes in fact face many unique and difficult challenges. **(3)** The demands on their time are often so great that these students face the dilemma of having to choose between playing sports and completing their schoolwork. **(4)** This is an upsetting dilemma.

Which is the best way to revise and combine the underlined portion of sentences 3 and 4 (reproduced below)?

The demands on their time are often so great <u>these students face the dilemma of having to choose between playing sports and completing their schoolwork. This is an upsetting dilemma.</u>

○ these students face the dilemma of having to choose between playing sports and completing their schoolwork; an upsetting dilemma.

○ these students face the dilemma of having to choose between playing sports and completing their schoolwork, this is an upsetting dilemma.

○ these students face the dilemma of having to choose between playing sports and completing their schoolwork; which is an upsetting dilemma.

○ these students face the upsetting dilemma of having to choose between playing sports and completing their schoolwork.

○ these students face the dilemma of having to choose between playing sports and completing their schoolwork, which is an upsetting dilemma.

Revision-in-context questions might ask you to choose the best way to deal with a particular sentence (e.g., delete it, change it, or move it elsewhere in the passage), or to simply choose the best revision. You might be given a choice of five additional sentences and asked which one would best conclude the passage, or be provided with one additional sentence and asked to decide where in the passage that sentence would fit. You might also be asked (as in the example above) to revise and combine two sentences. When dealing with these questions, you should remember that you are being tested on more than your knowledge of grammar, punctuation, and spelling. Succinctness and clarity of expression are greatly valued, as is your ability to arrange your ideas in logical order. The shortest answer choice that does not introduce additional errors is often your best bet here.

In the sample question above, both (A) and (C) introduce the error of incorrect use of the semicolon (which is properly used to separate two independent clauses and should not be used with sentence fragments). Choice (B) introduces the error of incorrect use of the comma (which, unlike the semicolon, should not be used to separate two independent clauses). While (E) is grammatically correct, it is still a bit wordy and repetitive. The second sentence under consideration here offers nothing new except for the idea that the dilemma at issue is upsetting. Choice (D) succinctly expresses this idea without introducing additional errors and is therefore the best choice.

On the Writing Test, less is definitely more! When faced with two or more grammatically correct answer choices, choose the shortest one.

Usage, Sentence Correction, and Revision-in-Context: What's Tested?

These question formats test the same rules of English, which we'll go over in great detail. You have one minute per question on the multiple-choice section, so you'll need to be very familiar with the question types and the grammar rules.

The grammar content tested on the Praxis Core Writing Test is actually quite limited. There are literally thousands of English grammar rules that ETS could test, but they stick to a very small subset. Here are the big categories:

Grammatical Relationships	• Subject/verb agreement • Pronoun agreement and proper use • Verb tense agreement and form
Structural Relationships	• Comparison • Coordination • Correlation • Negation • Parallelism • Subordination
Word Choice and Mechanics	• Diction • Capitalization • Punctuation

We'll start with an overview of the fundamentals, but don't worry if you start feeling overwhelmed by definitions. Because the questions ask you only to identify errors or correct sentences, ETS can't test you on the definitions of these ideas. You'll be tested only on usage.

GRAMMATICAL RELATIONSHIPS PART I

In case you're wondering, the category ETS doesn't test is *articles—the, a, an.*

Parts of Speech

The Praxis Core Writing Test covers the following eight parts of speech:

- noun
- adverb
- interjection
- verb
- preposition
- conjunction
- adjective
- pronoun

Nouns and Proper Nouns

> A **noun** is a person, place, thing, or idea.

The doctor walked into the store.

The nouns are *doctor* (a person) and *store* (a place).

Beauty is in the eye of the beholder.

The nouns are *beauty* (an idea), *eye* (a thing), and *beholder* (a person).

Proper nouns are nouns that name a specific person, place, thing, or idea. They should be capitalized.

George Washington was raised on a farm in Virginia.

The nouns are *George Washington* (a specific person, and therefore a capitalized proper noun), *farm* (an unspecified place and therefore not capitalized), and *Virginia* (a specific place, and therefore a capitalized proper noun).

Verbs

> A **verb** is an action word that tells you what's happening.

The policeman apprehended the criminal.
I have eaten worms.
You are a doctor.

The verbs are *apprehended*, *have eaten*, and *are*.

Any form of the verb *to be*, such as *am, are, were, was, will be*, and so on, is called a **state of being verb**.

Stop! It's Grammar Time
Looking to brush up on some grammar? Check out *Grammar Smart*, our guide to need-to-know grammar rules for the classroom, workplace, and beyond.

Verb Tense

The **tense** of a verb tells you when the action occurred. The most common tenses are past, present, and future, but there are variations that you should be familiar with. Let's look at the ones that get tested:

Present	Shannon walks to the store every day. Shannon is walking to the store right now.
Past	Shannon walked to the store yesterday.
Future	Shannon will walk to the store tomorrow.

There are two others that show up a lot:

Present perfect	Shannon has walked to the store every day since she got her cast removed.
Past perfect	Shannon had walked to the store every day until she broke her leg.

You use the present perfect tense to show that an action 1) started in the past and continues into the present (e.g., *I have known Sue for years*), or 2) occurred at an unspecified point in the past (e.g., *I have visited London*). You use the past perfect tense to show that a continued action happened before some specified point in the past (e.g., *My uncle had played tennis every day until he took up golf*).

Brian <u>had shown</u> no signs of <u>dissatisfaction</u> with his
         A   B
<u>job</u> before he <u>quit</u>. <u>No error</u>
C   D   E

Here's How to Crack It

The correct answer is (E). *He quit* is in the past, and before that time, *he had shown* no signs of dissatisfaction. The sentence correctly uses the past perfect tense, and there are no errors with the words *dissatisfaction* or *job*.

Adjectives

> **Adjectives** are used to describe (or modify) nouns.

The cat was lazy.
The lazy cat slept on the windowsill.

The adjective in both sentences is *lazy*.

Adverbs

> **Adverbs** are words that modify verbs, adjectives, and other adverbs.

I quickly climbed to the top.

In this case, the adverb *quickly* modifies the verb *climbed*.

The dog was very stupid.

In this case, the adverb *very* modifies the adjective *stupid*.

He painted the house very neatly.

There are two adverbs here: *neatly* modifies the verb *painted*, and *very* modifies the adverb *neatly*.

Try this one:

I was real excited to see my girlfriend.

- ○ I was real excited to see my girlfriend.
- ○ I was real excitedly to see my girlfriend.
- ◉ I was really excited to see my girlfriend.
- ○ I was really excitedly to see my girlfriend.
- ○ I was real, real excited to see my girlfriend.

Here's How to Crack It

In this case, the word *real* is modifying *excited*. *Excited* is an adjective, so the word that modifies it should be an adverb. *Real* is an adjective, so (A) is incorrect, as well as (B) and (E). *Really* is an adverb, correctly modifying *excited* in (C). In (D), there is no adjective at all. Choice (C) is the best answer.

Prepositions

> **Prepositions** are words that show how objects are related with respect to time or space.

I ran to the store.

The preposition is *to*.

By now, you should be able to identify nouns.

The preposition is *by*.

Other common prepositions are *of*, *at*, *in*, and *on*.

Subjects and Objects

> The **subject** of the sentence tells you who or what is performing the action.

I ate the sandwich.

The verb is *ate*, so the subject is the person or thing that is doing the eating. In this case, the subject is *I*.

There are two ways that a noun can be an **object**: it can receive the action that the subject performs (*sandwich*, in the above example), or it can be the noun following a preposition.

John sped past the policeman.

Past is the preposition, so *policeman* is the object of the preposition.

If we're using the full name of each noun, the distinction between subject and object isn't very important. However, the difference between the two becomes very important (especially to ETS) when we use pronouns. Let's return to parts of speech.

Pronouns

> **Pronouns** are short words that take the place of nouns.
>
> *I, you, he, she, it, me, they, them, us, him,*
> and *her* are all pronouns.

Pronouns are convenient because they're typically shorter than the nouns they replace. For instance, you could say:

> *James bought a dictionary as a birthday present for Elizabeth, and when Elizabeth came over that night, James gave the dictionary to Elizabeth.*

But you could say it much more succinctly like this:

> *James bought a dictionary as a birthday present for Elizabeth, and when she came over that night, he gave it to her.*

Not all pronouns are created equal. What if we wanted to use pronouns to shorten this sentence?

> *Paul went to the store.*

What's wrong with this pronoun?

> *Him went to the store.*

That should read:

> *He went to the store.*

The trick is that some pronouns replace subjects, and some pronouns replace objects. Here's the list:

Subject	Object
I	me
you	you
he	him
she	her
we	us
they	them
it	it

Let's see how this works out:

I have a twin brother. Mom loves us, and we love pie, so on our birthday she baked us a banana cream pie. He and I ate most of it that night. The next day, she split the leftovers evenly between him and me.

So, when the twins are the objects of Mom's love, the correct pronoun is *us*, but when they do the loving (of pie, in this case), the correct pronoun is the subject pronoun *we*. Similarly, when they are the subjects eating the pie, the correct pronouns are *he* and *I*, but when the twins are the objects of the preposition *between*, the correct pronouns are *him* and *me*.

One last oddity: state of being verbs (*am, are, was*, etc.) always use subject pronouns. So no matter how strange this may sound, *It is I* is correct, and *It's me* is incorrect. Similarly, if Betty answers the phone and the caller asks to speak with her, she should reply, "This is she," not "This is her." Look at the following example.

────────────────○────────────────

Between <u>you</u> and <u>I</u>, this test isn't <u>really</u> that <u>bad</u>.
       A   B   C   D
<u>No error</u>
   E

Here's How to Crack It

The answer is (B). *I* is a subject pronoun, and the sentence requires an object pronoun there, because of the preposition *between*.

────────────────○────────────────

Possessive Pronouns

We're not done with pronouns yet. You also use pronouns to show possession more concisely. Possessive pronouns can be used in two ways: as an adjective and as a word following a "to be" verb. Look at the following sentence:

Ahmed drove Ahmed's car.

Ahmed's is an adjective modifying *car*. You could use a possessive pronoun to shorten it this way:

Ahmed drove his car.

His replaces *Ahmed's*, but still modifies *car*, and is therefore an adjective. Here's another example:

That pillow is my pillow.

My modifies *pillow*, and again the possessive pronoun functions as an adjective. But you'd probably write it this way:

That pillow is mine.

Aha! Here we have one word that indicates possession replacing another. The possessive adjective *my* and the noun that it modifies, *pillow,* are replaced by the possessive pronoun *mine.* Remember that it's not important to know what these things are called, as long as you understand how they're used.

So here's the chart with the possessive pronouns added in:

Subject	Object	Possessive Adjective	Possessive Pronoun
I	me	my	mine
you	you	your	yours
he	him	his	his
she	her	her	hers
we	us	our	ours
they	them	their	theirs
it	it	its	its (not used much)

OK, so think about these sentences:

I ate a sandwich.
The sandwich was eaten by <u>me</u>.
That's <u>my</u> sandwich.
That sandwich is <u>mine</u>.

Try reading these aloud, and then again with each row of the pronouns from the chart. If anything sounds weird to you, think about the rules and persuade yourself that what you're reading is grammatically correct, even if it sounds bad. Most English speakers are notoriously lazy about speaking with correct grammar, so it can be misleading to trust your ear on the exam.

Don't fall into the trap of simply eliminating answers that sound wrong. "It is I" may sound like something out of a Shakespearean play, but it is 100% correct.

If you're not sure whether to use "who" or "whom," simply substitute "he" or "him." To who/whom should I address the letter? I address it to **him**. *Him* is the object pronoun, so the object pronoun *whom* must be correct.

Who and *whom* are two other pronouns that are tested a lot. You'll never confuse them again if you remember that *who* is used as a subject and *whom* is used as an object. The possessive form (both types) is *whose*. So let's add one last row to our list:

Subject	Object	Possessive Adjective	Possessive Pronoun
I	me	my	mine
you	you	your	yours
he	him	his	his
she	her	her	hers
we	us	our	ours
they	them	their	theirs
it	it	its	its (not used much)
who	whom	whose	whose (also not used much)

<u>Who</u> ate the sandwich?
The sandwich was eaten by <u>whom</u>?
<u>Whose</u> sandwich is that?
That sandwich is <u>whose</u>?

Notice also that none of the possessive pronouns is spelled with an apostrophe. This confuses many people, because we do use apostrophes with regular possessive nouns, like this:

The car is Monique's.

But it would be incorrect to write:

The car is her's.

Instead, you should write:

The car is hers.

Perhaps the most common error in this regard is the misspelling of the possessive pronoun *its*. This is correct:

The dog licked its paws.

This is incorrect:

The dog licked it's paws.

The word *it's* is a contraction of the words *it is*, and is therefore not a possessive pronoun at all, but a subject and verb together. It would be nonsensical to say:

The dog licked it is paws.

Just remember that possessive pronouns never use apostrophes.

Interjections

Interjections are words that show excitement or emotion.

They're usually set apart from a sentence by an exclamation point:

Wow! I aced the writing test!

But you can also use a comma if the feeling isn't as strong:

Hey, that's pretty good.

Conjunctions

There are three types of **conjunctions**: coordinate, subordinate, and correlative.

Coordinate conjunctions are the words *and, but, for, or, nor*, and *yet*.

They link equivalent parts of speech or complete thoughts together. This statement uses the conjunction *and* to link two nouns:

Malika bought a jar and a spoon.

This one links two verbs using the conjunction *or*:

I don't know whether to laugh or to cry.

This one links two complete sentences with the conjunction *but*:

I love you, but I don't want to marry you.

Notice that in each of these examples the items linked by the conjunctions could have come in either order without altering the meaning of the sentence.

Malika bought a spoon and a jar.

means the same thing as

Malika bought a jar and a spoon.

> By contrast, a **subordinate conjunction** suggests that one part of the sentence is more important than the other.

Because and *although* are two examples of subordinate conjunctions.

Although he hadn't showered in three days, he didn't smell that bad.
Adam was fired because his job was eliminated.

Notice that in these sentences you can't necessarily switch the order without substantially changing the meaning:

Adam's job was eliminated because he was fired.

> **Correlative conjunctions** always come in pairs. Some examples are *either...or,*
> *neither...or,* and *not only...but also.*

Either that wallpaper goes, or I do.
Neither bats nor rats scare me.

Now that we've got the parts of speech defined, let's look at how they relate to each other, and apply that knowledge to actual questions.

GRAMMATICAL RELATIONSHIPS PART II

All parts of speech in a sentence need to agree with one another. For instance, it wouldn't make sense to say

Harriet Tubman will be remembered for his heroic actions.

because *Harriet Tubman* is a woman, and *his* is a male pronoun. That's considered a pronoun gender disagreement, and that's an error. Let's look at all the parts of speech that must agree in a sentence.

Subject-Verb Agreement

Singular subjects should match with singular verbs, and plural subjects should match with plural verbs. This is called "agreeing in number." Try this one:

---○---

The sonnet, a poetic form used by Shakespeare and other writers, <u>has a strict rhyme scheme</u>.

- ○ has a strict rhyme scheme
- ○ has a rhyme scheme that is considered strict
- ○ have a strict rhyme scheme
- ○ have strictly a rhyme scheme
- ○ have a scheme that rhymes strictly

Here's How to Crack It

If you see the verb of the sentence underlined, make sure that it agrees in number with the subject of the sentence. How will ETS try to trick you? By separating the subject and the verb with a bunch of extra words. To help you locate the subject, cross out prepositional phrases and words that are separated by commas (called subordinate clauses). In this case we'd be left with:

The sonnet has a strict rhyme scheme.

What's the subject? *The sonnet.* Is *the sonnet* singular or plural? Well, it says *the son-net*, so it must be singular. What's the verb? *has.* Is *has* singular or plural? Singular. So the subject and verb match as written. If you look at the answer choices, you'll notice that (A) and (B) start with *has*, while (C), (D), and (E) start with *have*. We've decided that *has* is correct, so we can eliminate (C), (D), and (E).

Now, if we compare (A) and (B), we see that (B) adds an unnecessary new idea (*considered strict?* By whom?) and is longer than (A). Both of these characteristics tend to make answer choices incorrect, so the best answer is (A).

---○---

If there's more than one subject of a sentence, things can change. If the multiple subjects are connected by *and*, then the subject is taken to be plural:

Carolyn and Betty walk to school.

If the subjects are connected by *or* or *nor*, the verb should match with the subject closest to it. Both of these sentences are correct:

Neither Akil nor the girls are wrong.
The girls or Akil is wrong.

Pronoun Agreement and Proper Use

Pronouns have to agree with the nouns they replace in both number and gender, and each pronoun must refer unambiguously to exactly one noun in the sentence.

When Ben's girlfriend told him that <u>she</u> didn't like
A

<u>his</u> dog Tabitha, <u>he</u> decided to get rid of <u>her</u>.
B   C   D
<u>No error</u>
E

Here's How to Crack It

Let's take a look at each of the underlined pronouns. Choice (A), *she,* is correctly used. At this point in the sentence there has only been one female introduced, Ben's girlfriend. Similarly, (B) and (C) refer to Ben, because he is the only male in the sentence that those pronouns could refer to. Choice (D), however, could refer to either Tabitha or Ben's girlfriend. The ambiguous pronoun is an error, and the correct answer is (D).

Verb Tense Agreement and Form

The tense of a sentence should be consistent with respect to the action of the sentence.

Since 1920, <u>when</u> the 19th Amendment to the U.S.
A
Constitution <u>was ratified</u>, women <u>will have the right</u>
B C
to vote <u>to elect</u> the President. <u>No error</u>
D E

Here's How to Crack It

The sentence begins with the words *Since 1920,* which suggests that an action started in the past and continues to the present time. But later in the sentence, the future tense is used *(will have the right)*. These tenses are inconsistent, so the correct answer is (C).

Try this one:

———————————○———————————

> Although Jorge ate tuna regularly, he stopped after he learned that it might be unhealthy in large amounts due to high levels of mercury.

- ○ Although Jorge ate tuna regularly
- ○ Although Jorge ate tuna regularly once
- ○ Although Jorge was eating tuna regularly
- ○ Although Jorge had eaten tuna regularly
- ○ Although Jorge was at one time eating tuna regularly

Here's How to Crack It

In this case, we have an action that happened (Jorge's eating) further in the past than another action (his learning that it might be unhealthy). When this situation occurs, ETS believes that you need the past perfect tense to show that time relationship. The correct answer is (D).

———————————○———————————

STRUCTURAL RELATIONSHIPS

Now that we have a handle on the parts of speech and some basic grammar rules, let's see how we can string words together to form the sorts of long, convoluted sentences that you're likely to see on the exam.

Subjects and Predicates

For a sentence to stand alone and make sense, it needs a subject and an action for that subject to perform. That action is called the **predicate**, and in its simplest form it can consist of nothing but a verb. This is a complete sentence:

> *Kim works.*

Kim is the subject, and *works* is the predicate. A more complex sentence looks like this:

> *Kim works regularly at the grocery store on the corner of Main Street and Elm Avenue every Monday and Wednesday afternoon.*

Notice that there's still only one subject and one predicate, but in this case the predicate is much longer. The complete predicate is *works regularly at the grocery store...Wednesday afternoon*.

Phrases and Clauses

At the grocery store, *on the corner of Main Street and Elm Avenue*, and *every Monday and Wednesday afternoon* are all examples of **phrases**. A phrase is a group of words that functions as a unit but does not contain a subject and a predicate. Therefore, it can't stand alone as a sentence. Look at the following example:

> *Standing on the sidewalk, Joan was hit by an out-of-control skateboarder.*

The phrase *standing on the sidewalk* has an action, but we don't know who was standing until later in the sentence, after the comma.

A **clause**, then, is anything that has both a subject and an action. However, just because something is a clause doesn't necessarily mean it can stand alone as a sentence.

> *Although Xian loved her brother.*

That doesn't make sense by itself, even though the clause has both a subject (Xian) and an action (loved). This is an example of a **dependent clause**, because it needs another clause to make it a whole sentence:

> *Although Xian loved her brother, she didn't want to take him to the movies.*

She didn't want to take him to the movies is a clause that could stand alone as a complete sentence. It's called an **independent clause**.

You may have noticed that the word *although* was the only thing that kept the dependent clause from being an independent clause. *Although,* as we mentioned earlier, is an example of a subordinating conjunction. One rule of sentence construction is that in a complete sentence you can't have a dependent clause without an independent clause. Look at this one:

> *Although Fred was taller than Jim, but Jim was a better basketball player.*

What's the problem here? There are two dependent clauses, one using the conjunction *although*, and the other using the conjunction *but*. We could rewrite this two ways:

> *Although Fred was taller than Jim, Jim was a better basketball player.*
> *Fred was taller than Jim, but Jim was a better basketball player.*

In both cases, we changed one of the dependent clauses into an independent clause by removing the conjunction. You can even have multiple dependent clauses, as long as there's an independent clause in the sentence somewhere.

> *Although Fred was taller than Jim, Fred couldn't shoot a free throw to save his life, so Jim was a better basketball player.*

So far, in every example we've seen, clauses and phrases have been separated by commas. There's one important exception: if you have two closely related independent clauses, you can put them together in the same sentence, but they should be separated by a semicolon. Here is an example:

> *Jim is an asset to the team; he has a great free throw.*

Each of these could stand alone as a complete sentence.

Misplaced Modifiers

Modifiers are words that more fully explain other words. The examples we've seen so far have been adjectives and adverbs. ETS likes to test the idea that modifiers can change the meaning of a sentence in different ways depending on their location in the sentence. Let's start with a short sentence.

> *Paula eats fish.*

The subject is *Paula,* the verb is *eats,* and the noun that receives the action is *fish.* Now let's add the modifier *only* in different places. *Only* can function as an adjective or an adverb.

> *Only Paula eats fish.*

Here, we mean that Paula and no one else eats fish.

> *Paula only eats fish.*

This is what we'd probably say in everyday conversation if we meant that Paula didn't eat anything other than fish. A conversation might go like this:

> *I heard that Paula's on some weird new diet.*
> *Yes, Paula only eats fish.*

Again, though, most of us are very bad about the correctness of our spoken English. This sentence means that Paula eats fish, but she doesn't do anything else to them—she doesn't throw them at people, dance with them, or paint them. The conversation should go like this:

> *I heard that Paula's on some weird new diet.*
> *Yes, Paula eats only fish.*

Now, *only* modifies *fish,* which more fully explains what Paula eats. The general rule is this: a modifier needs to go right next to the thing that it modifies. If the modifier is a single word, it usually goes right before the thing that it modifies. How will ETS test this? Like so:

Standing on the sidewalk, <u>a tomato hit Joan in the face</u>.

○ a tomato hit Joan in the face

○ a tomato facially hit Joan

○ Joan, in the face, was hit by a tomato

○ Joan was in the face hit by a tomato

○ Joan was hit in the face by a tomato

Here's How to Crack It

The first thing you should notice is that *Standing on the sidewalk* is a phrase—there's an action but no subject. Given that a modifier should go right next to the thing it modifies, we look for the first noun right after the comma. In this case, we find *a tomato.* Does it make sense that a tomato was standing on the sidewalk? No. In fact, we can tell from context that the first noun after the comma should be *Joan,* and we can therefore cross out (A) and (B).

Compare (C), (D), and (E), and you'll notice that the only difference among them is the placement of the modifying prepositional phrase *in the face.* Ask yourself what that phrase is supposed to describe more fully. You should conclude that it describes where she was hit. Unless they're at the beginning of a sentence, prepositional phrases usually go right after the thing that they're describing.

Cross out (C) because *in the face* seems to modify *Joan.* Cross out (D) because *in the face* seems to modify where she was. Choice (E) is the best answer because *in the face* correctly describes where she was hit.

Comparison

The Writing Test also tests comparisons. Look at the following sentence.

Adults eat more vegetables than children.

This sentence is supposed to compare the amount of vegetables that adults eat to the amount of vegetables children eat. The way it's written, however, this sentence compares the number of vegetables that adults eat to the number of children that adults eat.

You could correct it this way:

Adults eat more vegetables than children eat.

But you're more likely to see it this way:

Adults eat more vegetables than children do.

Try the following example.

The works of John Grisham <u>sell better than Stephen King</u>.

- ○ sell better than Stephen King
- ○ sell better than Stephen King does
- ○ sell better than does Stephen King
- ○ sell better than the works of Stephen King
- ○ sell better than those of Stephen King

Here's How to Crack It

If you're saying to yourself, "I didn't realize Mr. King was for sale," then you've spotted the error. We're supposed to compare the authors' works, but we're comparing John Grisham's works to Stephen King, the man. Cross out (A). Because (B) and (C) repeat the same error, you can cross them out as well.

Now compare the remaining answer choices. Both compare the works of the authors, but in (E), the pronoun *those* replaces the works. Both sentences are grammatically correct. When faced with two grammatically correct answer choices, pick the shorter of the two. Choice (E) is the correct answer.

Negation

Negation is making sentences negative by adding the word *not* to the first auxiliary verb. Look at the following table.

Tense	Negative Element	Examples
Present Simple	do + not = don't does + not = doesn't	I do not run. She doesn't run.
Past Simple	did + not = didn't was + not = wasn't	I didn't run. I wasn't running.
Present Progressive	is + not = isn't are + not = aren't	She isn't running. They aren't running.

Parallelism

One way ETS can make sentences more complex is to introduce lists or comparisons. ETS considers it important that items in lists or items being compared be in the same form as one another. That idea is called **parallelism,** and it's a frequently tested concept on the Praxis Core Writing Test.

Lists

Two or more elements make up a list. When there are only two elements, you create a list by joining them together with the word *and:*

I went to the store and bought bread and butter.

If there are more than two elements, you still need an *and* at the end, but you'll also need to separate the earlier elements with commas:

I went to the store and bought milk, cereal, bread, and butter.

Notice there is a comma after *bread* but before *and*. This comma, called a serial comma, is not required, but ETS prefers it to be there. ETS won't test you on that one, though. They'll test you on parallelism. Let's try another one:

Bo's life goals were <u>a successful career and to be a good father</u>.

○ a successful career and to be a good father

○ a successful career and good fatherhood

○ a successful and good career and fatherhood

○ to have a successful career and a good father

○ to have a successful career and to be a good father

Here's How to Crack It

The two items in the list have something to do with a successful career and being a good father. Choice (A) is incorrect because the two items in the list are *a successful career,* which is a noun, and *to be a good father,* which is a verb. *Good fatherhood* isn't quite the same thing as being a good father, so get rid of (B) and (C). In (D), the items are parallel (*a successful career* and *a good father* are both nouns), but Bo doesn't want to *have* a good father; he wants to *be* a good father. Choice (E) fixes all the problems. *Have a successful career* and *be a good father* are parallel and accurately describe his goals.

Parallel constructions tend to sound much better than nonparallel ones, so you can rely on your ear a bit more for these questions.

The questions on the Praxis Core Writing Test become more challenging with really long sentences that try to cause you to get lost in the thicket of words. Here is an example:

Last weekend, George washed his car, made his bicycle safer by installing reflectors on the front and back and replacing the brake pads, and mowed the lawn.

○ Last weekend, George washed his car, made his bicycle safer by installing reflectors on the front and back of the frame and replacing the brake pads, and mowed the lawn.

○ Last weekend, George, washing his car, made his bicycle safer by installing reflectors on the front and back, and replacing the brake pads, and mowed the lawn.

○ Last weekend, George washed his car and made his bicycle safer by installing reflectors on the front and back and replacing the brake pads and mowed the lawn.

○ Last weekend, George, washing his car, making his bicycle safer by installing reflectors in the front and back, and replacing the brake pads, mowed the lawn.

○ Last weekend, George washed his car, making his bicycle safer by installing reflectors on the front and back, replacing the brake pads, and mowing the lawn.

Here's How to Crack It
Break this down into smaller lists.

- What are the things that George did? He washed his car, made his bicycle safer, and mowed the lawn. Are those three ideas parallel? Yes.
- What about the reflectors? Well, they're part of making his bicycle safer. How did he do that? By installing reflectors and replacing the brake pads. Are those ideas parallel? Yes.
- Where did he install the reflectors? On the front and back. Are those ideas parallel? Yes. There's no problem with the sentence as it stands. The best answer is (A).

Subordination

A subordinate conjunction suggests that one part of the sentence is more important than the other.

Because and *although* are two examples of subordinate conjunctions.

> *Although he hadn't showered in three days, he didn't smell that bad.*
> *Adam was fired because his job was eliminated.*

Notice that in these sentences you can't necessarily switch the order without substantially changing the meaning:

> *Adam's job was eliminated because he was fired.*

WORD CHOICE AND MECHANICS

Finally, ETS has some very specific ideas about what constitutes good writing style. We'll start with word choice, or diction.

Word Choice

Word choice, or **diction,** means using a specific word in a specific context. ETS will try to fool you with words that sound similar.

> *Don't go outside in your bear feet!*

Here the word *bear* ("to endure") was mistaken for the word *bare* ("unclothed or uncovered"), resulting in a diction error. Such errors are common, especially when words have multiple meanings (e.g., a "bear" is also a large carnivorous mammal).

> *I can't bear the thought of the bear chewing on my bare leg!*

ETS frequently uses more complicated words to test diction, so be on your toes if you see a relatively complicated-looking word that just doesn't seem right somehow.

Punctuation

We've seen commas show up a lot so far, so let's pause here for a moment and talk about punctuation.

The Praxis Core Writing exam tests comma usage the most, but it also tests usage of colons, semicolons, and apostrophes.

Commas

Here are the four places you use a comma. We've already talked about three of them. Use a comma to do the following:

To join independent clauses together with a conjunction	*He didn't like walking to school, but he didn't own a bicycle.*
To separate an introductory phrase or dependent clause from the independent clause	*Although he hated walking to school, he had no choice.*
To make lists	*Eat, drink, and be merry.*

Here's the new one:

| To separate a clause or phrase within the sentence that adds information that is not crucial to the meaning of the sentence | *My grandfather, a World War II veteran, was born in 1902.* |

Notice that you could omit everything between the commas and still preserve the original meaning of the sentence.

Colons and Semicolons

Colons can be used to begin lists or to show that something is anticipated.

> *I want only three things out of life: fame, wealth, and happiness.*
> *This is what I think: you smell.*

Semicolons, as we mentioned earlier, are used to join two closely related independent clauses. You don't need a conjunction when you use a semicolon.

> *I knew she was dead; she wasn't moving.*

Apostrophes

Apostrophe misuse is rampant, so you can't trust what you see in everyday life.

Use Apostrophes	
To replace letters in contractions	*You are not going to that.* becomes *You **aren't** going to do that.*
To make the possessive form of singular nouns	*The **teacher's** grade book was stolen.*
To make the possessive form of plural nouns that don't end in *s*	*The **men's** clothes were old-fashioned.*
To make the possessive form of plural nouns that do end in *s* (Note that the apostrophe goes after the *s* in this case.)	*The **students'** grades were abysmal.*

Don't Use Apostrophes	
In personal pronouns	*The book is your's.* should be *The book is **yours**.*
To make nouns plural	*Two dog's fought over a bone.* should be *Two **dogs** fought over a bone.*
To make a singular noun that ends in *s* plural	*We want to keep up with the Jones's.* should be *We want to keep up with the **Joneses**.*

These next four sentences are all correct:

> *Mr. Jones owned a dog.*
> *Mr. Jones's dog ran away.*
> *The Joneses bought a new dog.*
> *The Joneses' new dog ran away, too.*

Mechanics

Idiomatic Expressions

Idiomatic expressions are collections of words that are used together by linguistic convention. In other words, people say something a certain way because everyone says it that way. To ETS, idiomatic expressions are all about prepositions. Look at this one:

> *She is regarded to be one of the top professionals in her field.*

What's wrong with that? The words *regarded to be* may sound wrong to you. Try this instead:

> *She is regarded as one of the top professionals in her field.*

The correct idiom is *regarded as.* Why? Just because. This is one place on the Writing Test where you can trust your ear a lot of the time, because many idioms are familiar to English speakers. There are some, however, that you're just going to have to memorize. The following is a list of some commonly tested idioms, organized by preposition.

About	
Worry...about	Don't *worry about* me; I'll be fine.
Dispute...about	We had a *dispute about* the amount of money she spent.
Debate...about	The senate *debated about* the bill for three days.
As	
Define...as	A square is *defined as* a polygon with four equal sides and four equal angles.
Regard...as	Tom is *regarded as* New York's finest badminton player.
Not so...as	She is *not so* much beautiful *as* classy.
So...as to be	The movie was *so* bad *as to be* unwatchable.
Think of...as	*Think of* it *as* a vacation rather than a prison sentence.
See...as	Many people *see* the death penalty *as* barbaric.
The same...as	She gave *the same* number of cookies to me *as* to you.
As...as	The boy is *as* dumb *as* a post.

At	
Target...at	The movie was *targeted at* pre-adolescent girls.
For	
Responsible...for	You are *responsible for* your baby.
From	
Prohibit...from	James was *prohibited from* playing baseball in the glass gazebo.
Different...from	After spending more time with her, I discovered that she was not all that *different from* me.
That	
So...that	He was *so* naive *that* he thought politicians told the truth.
Hypothesis...that	The *hypothesis that* dinosaurs were killed off by a meteor crash is increasingly plausible.
To	
Forbid...to	I *forbid* you *to* marry that boy!
Ability...to	He has the *ability to* start fires using his mind.
Attribute...to	The painting, previously *attributed to* Rembrandt, was shown to be a forgery.
Require...to	You are *required to* take the Praxis.
Responsibility...to	You have a *responsibility to* do your job well.
Permit...to	You are *permitted to* leave the hospital grounds only with an escort.
Superior...to	Your math skills are *superior to* mine.
Try...to	*Try to* stay awake during the Praxis.
With	
Credit...with	Marie Curie is *credited with* discovering many radio-active elements.
Associate...with	*Associating with* criminals is unwise.

No Preposition	
Consider...	Many people *consider* the Taj Mahal the most beautiful building in the world.
More Than One Preposition	
Distinguish...from	She can't *distinguish* her elbow *from* a hole in the ground.
Distinguish between...and	Many color-blind people can't *distinguish between* red *and* green.
Native *(noun)***...of**	Arnold Schwarzenegger is a *native of* Austria.
Native *(adjective)***...to**	The Nene goose is *native to* Hawaii.
Comparisons and Links	
Not only...but also	He is *not only* strong, *but also* fast.
Not...but	The soup was *not* perfect *but* was still edible.
Either...or	*Either* Serena *or* Tara will win the award.
Neither...nor	*Neither* Gabe *nor* Aaron will be chosen for the team.
More...than; less...than	I like ice cream *more than* cabbage, but *less than* beets.
As *(to compare actions)*	She ate *as* many cookies *as* I did.
Like *(to compare nouns)*	Her computer is just *like* mine.
Such as *(to list examples)*	Karen likes bright colors *such as* hot pink and yellow.
More...the -er	The *more* spinach I eat, *the stronger* I get.
From...to	He led the race *from* start *to* finish.
Just as...so too	*Just as* I did well on the Praxis, *so too* will you.

Clarity

For the purposes of this exam, writing is considered clear if it is (1) not wordy and (2) not redundant.

Wordiness

In a sentence correction question, if you're faced with two grammatically correct answer choices, pick the shorter one. Try the following example:

The fingernails of male orangutans tend to be shorter than females.

- ○ than females
- ○ than female orangutans
- ○ than female orangutans are
- ○ than those of female orangutans
- ○ than the fingernails of female orangutans

Here's How to Crack It

The error in the sentence as written is a comparison error. The author intends to compare the length of the orangutans' fingernails, but the sentence compares the length of the males' fingernails to the length of the females' whole bodies. Choices (B) and (C) repeat the same error in different forms, so cross both of those out, too.

Now compare (D) and (E). Both make the comparison accurately, but (D) replaces *the fingernails* with the pronoun *those*. Because shorter grammatically correct answers are preferred, (D) is the best answer.

Redundancy

As far as the test is concerned, repeating an idea in a sentence is stylistically incorrect. Let's look at a question that addresses errors of redundancy:

If you <u>want</u> to lose weight, <u>you</u> should exercise at
     A   B
least three times <u>per</u> week <u>or more</u>. <u>No error</u>
            C   D   E

Here's How to Crack It
Because the sentence already says *at least,* it's unnecessary to add *or more.* Choice (D) is the best answer.

Research Skills Questions

Unlike the rest of the multiple-choice section and the essays, research skills questions test neither writing ability nor knowledge of grammar, usage, or mechanics. They test your understanding of effective research strategy. Limited to only a few items on the test, these questions often measure your ability to recognize the various elements of citations, assess the credibility of sources, distinguish relevant from irrelevant information, and understand effective research procedure. Here's an example of a research skills question:

Which of the following sources would likely be the most useful in writing a research paper about the history of ballet?

- ○ A memoir published by a famous American ballerina in 1997

- ○ A video demonstrating basic ballet poses for beginners

- ○ A book detailing the history of a prominent ballet company in New York City since its establishment in 1975

- ○ A journal article discussing how ballet has developed as an art form from the fifteenth through the twenty-first centuries

- ○ Transcripts of interviews with several well-reputed European ballet instructors

Here's How to Crack It
A video about basic ballet poses would provide little or no information about the history of ballet, so (B) can be easily eliminated. The memoir of a famous ballerina would deal mostly with her own personal experience, which would be of limited use for this purpose (especially since the 1997 publication date identifies her as an individual of our modern era); (A) can be eliminated. Interviews with ballet instructors would be similarly confined to the individuals' own personal experiences and would be of limited use as well, so (E) can be eliminated. A book about the history of a prominent ballet company might provide some useful

information, but this would be limited to the past forty years or so and deal mostly with one NYC ballet company; eliminate (C). A journal article discussing the development of ballet over the past 600 years would be perfect for present purposes, so (D) is the best answer.

Research Skills: What's Tested?

Primary vs. Secondary Sources

The research skills section usually contains a question that requires you to distinguish primary from secondary sources. Just remember that primary sources are contemporaneous sources that provide firsthand information about a person, thing, or event. Examples of **primary sources** include legal and historical documents, photographs, interviews, memoirs, emails, speeches, diaries, artifacts, literature, experimental results, works of art, audio and video recordings, letters, and books and articles *written at the time the events occurred*. In contrast, **secondary sources** interpret, summarize, discuss, analyze, or comment upon original source material and are usually *not* contemporaneous. Examples of secondary sources include documentaries, treatises, textbooks, biographies, literary criticism, and newspaper articles *written about events from an earlier time*.

Citation

The main systems of citation for present purposes are APA (American Psychological Association) style, which is used mostly in the social sciences, and MLA (Modern Language Association) style, which is used mostly for liberal arts and humanities. Both systems are updated frequently. The good news is that the Writing Test will not require you to create proper citations in either format, distinguish one system from the other, or identify citation errors. You will, however, be required to identify what type of source is being cited. Consider the following examples:

Jefferson, K.A. (1998). Birth order and familial discord. *The American Journal of Psychodynamic Family Therapy, (7)*31, 37–49.

Kellerman, Carol. "Shakespeare's Comedies: A Feminist Perspective." *The American Journal of Women in Literature*, vol. 18., no. 4, Nov. 2007, pp. 78–86.

The first journal article citation is in APA style and the second in is MLA. While there are minor stylistic differences between the two, the basic elements are the same: the author is listed first, then the title of the article, followed by the name of the journal, the volume/issue number, and the page reference. For either of these two citations, it is clear that a journal article in print is the source material being referenced. Keep in mind that book citations list the publisher, while journal articles in print list the volume, issue, and page numbers of the article. Online works can be distinguished from print material by the presence of a URL (webpage address) or a DOI (Digital Object Identifier), which is a string of numbers, letters, and symbols that identifies that particular work on the Internet.

Source Relevance

This really comes down to a little thoughtful analysis and a bit of common sense. A question might ask you to choose which source would be the most (or least) relevant for a particular purpose, or whether a particular source would serve to narrow or broaden the scope of a given research topic. For example, if you were writing a report about pet dogs, a book about poodles would have a much more narrow scope. In contrast, a book about household pets would have a broader scope; it would likely contain some useful material about dogs, but also some irrelevant material about other kinds of domestic animals. A book about cats would likely be completely irrelevant.

THE ARGUMENTATIVE ESSAY

You'll spend the first 30 minutes of the essay section writing an argumentative, or persuasive, essay. Because you have only 30 minutes, no one (including the essay grader) expects this essay to be a masterpiece of literature. Instead, it's supposed to demonstrate your ability to organize your thoughts and express them clearly through writing.

Scoring

The essay is scored by two independent graders, both of whom give the essay a score ranging from 1 (lowest) to 6 (highest). If the two scores differ by more than one point, a third scorer is brought in.

It is possible to get a 0, but only if you don't respond to the topic. For instance, a perfectly written diatribe on the evils of standardized testing would get you a score of zero.

It is important to realize that graders will spend about 50–60 seconds grading your essay. That's it. You'll get a high score if you give them what they want. This is what you should do:

- Respond to the prompt
- Organize
- Fill 'er up
- Proofread

Let's look at each of these.

Respond to the Prompt

The directions will look something like this:

> Read the opinion stated below. Discuss the extent to which you agree or disagree with this point of view. Support your position with specific reasons and examples from your own experience, observations, or reading.

Then you are given a statement to write about. It will be a statement of opinion, not fact. Some topics are related to education; some aren't. The statements are purposefully written so that you could easily support either side. Let's try this one:

> "Because professional athletes have such a strong influence on children, they have a responsibility to act as positive role models."

First, pick a side. It doesn't matter which side you choose, but choose one and defend it. If you're not sure which way to go, spend no more than 30 seconds brainstorming reasons for and against the opinion. (You will be given scratch paper to plan your essay.) Then pick the side for which you came up with more support. For the purpose of this example, let's argue against the opinion.

Once you've chosen the side you want to take, come up with two or three reasons that you'll use to support your position. For example:

- *People known for certain abilities or qualities shouldn't be expected to demonstrate unrelated abilities.*
- *Parents should be primary role models for their children.*
- *Children will learn more about the world if they understand that no one's perfect.*

Organize

If you had only 50 seconds to read and grade an essay, wouldn't you want it to be well organized? So will your graders. Take about 3–5 minutes and plan your essay before you start writing. Here's the format you should use:

Paragraph 1	Introduce the topic and let the reader know what side you've chosen. If appropriate, give a short preview of the reasons and examples you'll be using. You may restate the prompt directly, or paraphrase it as part of the introduction.
Paragraph 2	Take the first reason and develop it.
Paragraph 3	Take the second reason and develop it.
Paragraph 4	Take the third reason and develop it.
Paragraph 5	Conclude the essay by recapping the major points.

Don't worry if you'd be ashamed to have your favorite English teacher read what you end up creating. This essay isn't supposed to be award winning; it's just supposed to be well organized and clear.

Fill 'Er Up

Keep in mind that *what* you write is much more important than *how much* you write. However, if your essay is too short and underdeveloped, you will not receive a high score. Discussing three reasons, each with a sentence or two of support, and including an introduction and a conclusion should be more than adequate.

As you're writing, keep the following in mind:

> - Use good transition words. Words like *although* and *however* show the reader how your next idea relates to the previous idea. Graders like that, because it makes their jobs easier.
> - Don't attempt to spell a six-syllable word that you think you know the meaning of. Keep your writing simple and direct.

The following is a sample essay based on the prompt about athletes and role models:

The author of the opinion believes that athletes have a responsibility to be positive role models simply because such celebrities face extensive media coverage and therefore influence children. This belief is unfounded. Athletes are just as human as everyone else, and it is unreasonable to hold them to a standard that the rest of society wouldn't be able to meet simply because they are more visible.

Would you expect your auto mechanic to be fluent in French? Would you expect your piano teacher to be able to kick a 35-yard field goal? Of course you wouldn't, even though fluency in French and the ability to kick a 35-yard field goal are both admirable traits. So why would you expect a professional athlete to be a paragon of virtue in his or her everyday life? Granted, I might expect such a high standard of behavior from a priest or a rabbi, because their professions are directly related to morality, but there's no reason to expect such a standard from an athlete.

If the author is concerned about positive role modeling, perhaps he should focus his attention on parental involvement. Parents have a far greater effect on the moral development of their children than any athlete celebrated in the media. Professional athletic leagues filled with positive role models couldn't possibly negate the effects of an abusive home life on a child's development. Conversely, children raised by strong, involved, moral parents are unlikely to be swayed by images of star athletes acting in immoral ways.

In fact, with the right guidance, the visible presence of athletes engaging in questionable activities can be a useful moral lesson. Consider the Kobe Bryant case. Regardless of his guilt or innocence, parents could use his situation to show children that money doesn't buy happiness, that no one is above the law, and that it's important to treat women with respect. In fact, if Mr. Bryant were a perfect moral citizen, parents would be deprived of this lesson because the media certainly wouldn't devote similar time and attention to stories showing him volunteering in a soup kitchen or donating to charity.

So, although the author clearly has the best interests of society in mind, his opinion that athletes have a responsibility to be positive role models is groundless. Let athletes be athletes, let parents be parents, and let us all strive to teach our children well.

Proofread

Leave two or three minutes at the end to proofread your essay. No one's expecting a polished final draft, but you don't want to leave the false impression that you don't understand the conventions of written English. If you can quickly correct a few careless errors, you should.

That's it. Ideally, this should be a formulaic exercise, but you should definitely practice this a few times. Keep in mind that 30 minutes isn't a very long time. Practice writing essays using the following prompts:

> "Prospective teachers in any field should be required to study a foreign language."
>
> "Advertisements that promote the use of alcohol or tobacco should be banned."
>
> "Job satisfaction is more important than high wages."

You're almost done with this chapter! After you complete the Writing Drill, consider taking a break before moving on to the Praxis Core Math content review. Your mind deserves a rest!

THE SOURCE-BASED ESSAY

You'll spend the second 30 minutes of the essay section writing a source-based essay. The difference between this essay and the argumentative essay is that here you'll be required to incorporate information from two passages that will be provided for you. The passages may not address the same exact issues, but they will be written essentially on the same topic. For example, the first passage might discuss the rising popularity of the "selfie" craze and its cultural significance. The second passage might focus more on the dangers of taking selfies and the psychological reasons why teenagers engage in this practice. You will be asked to incorporate ideas from BOTH passages into an essay that discusses the most important concerns about the issue as stated in the prompt (e.g., "the selfie phenomenon and its impact").

Unlike the argumentative essay, you are not required to "pick a side" of the argument and defend your position; you should simply discuss the main issues that pertain to the topic as you see them. As with the argumentative essay, it is acceptable (and encouraged) to use examples from your own experience, reading, and observations. However, an essay based *only* on personal experience and outside information (in other words, one that doesn't rely heavily on the two sources that are provided) will be judged inadequate.

When writing the source-based essay, you must appropriately cite the passages whenever you quote or paraphrase them, not just discuss their ideas. Don't worry —you won't be required to construct formal citations, you can simply identify the passages by the author's last name, the title of the piece, or any other "clear identifier" (e.g., "Source 1" or "Source 2"). It is also extremely important to cite BOTH sources; essays that address only one passage do not typically receive scores above a 3. Moreover, it is much better to skillfully interweave the two sources throughout the essay, as opposed to, for example, discussing the ideas presented in Source 1 in the second paragraph and then discussing the ideas presented in Source 2 in the third. It is important to LINK the ideas expressed in the two passages, not just consider them separately.

A high-scoring essay is one that develops and expands upon the ideas presented in the two passages, as opposed to simply restating them. You will be expected to provide relevant and appropriate examples in support of your position. It is not enough to list and discuss the main issues about the topic—you must also explain WHY these issues are important. Failing to do so is often the difference between a score of 5 or 6 and a mid-range score. The sources provided should serve as the foundation upon which you will build a well-developed essay.

As with the argumentative essay, you will be judged on your writing and organizational skills and your knowledge of grammar, usage, and mechanics. Good writing technique involves displaying variety in sentence structure (e.g., avoid using a series of short declarative sentences). Your essay need not be perfect and one or two grammatical or spelling errors will not negatively affect your score. However, an accumulation of errors will certainly be held against you. As with the argumentative essay, it is critical to proofread your work and choose words with which you are familiar.

Now it's time to test your knowledge in the following drill. Answers and explanations can be found at the end of the chapter.

Remember to make a positive first impression on the reader by starting your essay with a clearly stated and thoughtful introductory sentence. Also keep in mind that your conclusion will shape the reader's final impression of you (right before that person determines your score)!

WRITING DRILL

Answers and explanations can be found at the end of the chapter.

Neither <u>my</u> pet rattlesnake <u>nor</u> my sister's teddy
      A   B

bear <u>is</u> able <u>to talk</u>. <u>No error</u>
   C   D   E

2 of 9

<u>Next year</u>, the Florida legislature is changing
    A

<u>their procedures</u> used <u>to evaluate</u> teacher quality
      B   C

<u>and</u> tenure eligibility. <u>No error</u>
 D   E

3 of 9

Like many other blockbuster hits of the last five

years, <u>the movie</u> <u>had been</u> full of special <u>effects</u>,
      A   B   C

<u>but shy of</u> character development. <u>No error</u>
   D   E

4 of 9

After the thief <u>left</u> the bank with thousands of
          A

dollars, <u>he</u> quickly realized <u>he was</u> surrounded by
     B   C

the police <u>on all sides</u>. <u>No error</u>
        D   E

5 of 9

Having searched for his glasses for hours, <u>they were</u>
<u>not found by Paul until morning</u>.

- ⃝ they were not found by Paul until morning
- ⃝ they were not found from Paul until morning
- ⃝ they had not been found until morning
- ⃝ Paul did not find them until morning
- ⃝ Paul was not found until morning

6 of 9

Andrea only bought the toaster <u>because she wanted</u>
<u>the free gift that came with it.</u>

- ⃝ because she wanted the free gift that came with it.
- ⃝ because she was wanting the free gift that came with it.
- ⃝ because she wanted the gift that came with it.
- ⃝ because the gift that came with it was something that she had been wanting.
- ⃝ because she had wanted the free gift that came with it.

7 of 9

Arthur, who loves all animals, <u>has always pet</u>
<u>strange dogs until one bit him last year.</u>

- ⃝ has always pet strange dogs until one bit him last year.
- ⃝ had always pet strange dogs until one of the dogs bit him last year.
- ⃝ has always pet strange dogs, one having bitten him last year,
- ⃝ had always pet strange dogs that bit him last year.
- ⃝ had always pet strange dogs until one bit him last year.

After the successful IPO, <u>Steve decided to retire over searching for another job</u>.

- ○ Steve decided to retire over searching for another job
- ○ Steve had decided to retire over searching for another job
- ○ Steve decided to retire rather than searching for another job
- ○ Steve decided to retire rather than to search for another job
- ○ Steve decided retirement rather than searching for another job

Sally, a high school senior, is working on a research project about soldiers' personal experiences in World War II. Use of the official transcript of a 1944 BBC interview with a British army private in which he reflects upon having fought in several World War II battles would

- ○ broaden the scope of the project
- ○ be more reliable than a video recording of the same interview
- ○ likely contain no relevant information
- ○ be a primary source
- ○ probably be unreliable because of how long ago the interview took place

WRITING DRILL ANSWERS AND EXPLANATIONS

1. **E** This sentence contains no error. The correlative conjunction *neither...nor* is used correctly, and the singular verb aligns with the singular pronoun. The infinitive is structured correctly.

2. **B** This sentence contains an error in subject/pronoun agreement. The subject of the sentence is *legislature*, which is a singular noun. The pronoun *their* is plural and therefore incorrect.

3. **B** There is no reason to use the past perfect tense, *had been*, here. The simple past tense, in this case *was*, is sufficient (the movie *was* full of special effects). *Had been* should be used only to describe an event that takes place before another past event.

4. **D** *Surrounded on all sides* is redundant. If one is surrounded one is, by definition, enclosed on all sides. You will find questions where redundancy is the only error.

5. **D** The phrase *having searched for his glasses for hours* is a misplaced modifier. It modifies *Paul,* who must therefore be the subject of the sentence. You can eliminate (A), (B), and (C), in which the glasses are the subject (they are receiving the action). Choice (E) does not convey the proper meaning—Paul was not lost; his glasses were!

6. **C** *Free gift* is redundant; gifts are, by definition, free. You can eliminate (A), (B), and (E), which all repeat this error. Choice (D) corrects the redundancy but is wordy and awkward. Therefore, (C) is correct.

7. **E** This sentence describes an action continuing in the past (petting strange dogs) that was interrupted by another action (the dog biting Arthur last year). Accordingly, the past perfect tense (*had always pet*) is required. You can eliminate (A) and (C) because they both repeat the error of using the present perfect tense (*has pet*) instead. Choice (D) changes the meaning of the sentence, stating that Arthur used to pet strange dogs *that bit him.* Choice (B) is grammatically correct but repetitive and wordy, unnecessarily repeating the word *dogs.*

8. **D** This question tests parallel construction. The infinitives *to retire* and *to search* are consistent, which makes (D) correct. All other answer choices do not keep the sentence structure consistent.

9. **D** The source described here—the transcript of an interview with a soldier who is discussing his personal World War II experiences—would be highly relevant, so (C) can be eliminated. The source would not broaden the topic of the research project because it would be precisely on point; eliminate (A). There is no reason to believe that a written transcript of an interview would be more reliable than a video recording (the opposite is probably true), so (B) is wrong as well. However, there is also no reason to believe that the official BBC transcript is unreliable because the interview took place in the 1940s; eliminate (E). The best answer is (D) because the transcript, which provides a contemporaneous firsthand account by the soldier, is a primary source.

Chapter 5
Praxis Core Math

OVERVIEW OF THE PRAXIS CORE MATH TEST

The third and final part of the Praxis Core Academic Skills for Educators Test is Math (5732). Before we get into the content of the exam, you should be familiar with the basics of the test format. Let's outline those right now:

Format	Computer-delivered
Time	85 minutes
Number of Questions	56
Question Types	• Multiple choice • Select all that apply • Numeric entry (in which you type your answer into a box on the screen)
Calculator Allowed?	Yes; an onscreen, five-function calculator is available.
Guessing Penalty?	Nope! (So be sure not to leave any questions blank—when in doubt, make an educated guess.)

Most of the questions on the test are multiple choice, or selected response—you will choose one answer from five possible answers. However, there are a few questions that will use a different format. For some questions, you will select one or more answers from a list of choices (these answers appear with checkboxes instead of bubbles). Some other questions will ask you to type a numeric answer into a box. ETS calls these *numeric entry questions*.

According to ETS, the Praxis Core Math Test covers skills in four categories:

> • Number and Quantity
> • Algebra and Functions
> • Geometry
> • Statistics and Probability

On the actual test, about 60% of the questions will be on topics in the first two categories—Number and Quantity (~30%) and Algebra and Functions (~30%). The other two categories, Geometry and Statistics and Probability, each comprise about 20% of the questions.

The test content is at a high school level, with an emphasis on reasoning skills rather than straightforward calculations. This means that some questions will contain tricky phrasing, combine multiple concepts in a single question, and require you to analyze information. Not to worry! In this book, you have the opportunity to thoroughly familiarize yourself with the test content and question types, as well as the strategies you can use to conquer them.

Before we get into the test content areas, let's go over calculator use on this exam. On this computer-delivered test, you will be provided with an onscreen calculator that will look something like this:

Remember that not every Praxis exam allows calculator use. Check www.ets.org/praxis/ test_day/policies/ calculators for up-to-date calculator policies.

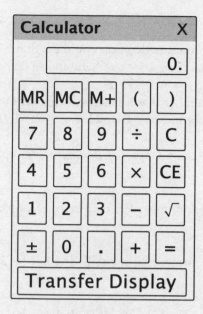

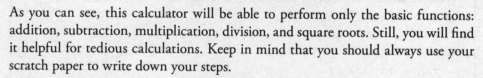

As you can see, this calculator will be able to perform only the basic functions: addition, subtraction, multiplication, division, and square roots. Still, you will find it helpful for tedious calculations. Keep in mind that you should always use your scratch paper to write down your steps.

That about covers the basics of this test. Let's get into the math you'll see!

NUMBER AND QUANTITY

The best place to start is with a vocabulary list. Here are some key math terms you should know:

Real number—Any number that exists on the number line, including integers, fractions, decimals, negative numbers, and so on.

Integer—A whole number that is positive, negative, or zero. Fractions and mixed numbers are not integers. Examples: –3, –2, –1, 0, 1, 2, 3…

Positive number—A number greater than zero. Examples: 1, 2, 3, 1/2, 2/3, 0.75

Negative number—A number less than zero. Examples: –3, –2, –1, –3/4, –1/8, –0.3

Even number—An integer that is evenly divisible by 2. Examples: 2, 4, 6, –4, –6

Odd number—An integer that is NOT divisible by 2. Examples: 3, 5, 7, –3, 5

Zero—
- 0 is an integer.
- 0 is neither positive nor negative.
- 0 is even.
- Anything times 0 is 0.
- You cannot divide by 0.

Factor—An integer that divides evenly into another integer. For example, the factors of 15 are 1, 3, 5, and 15. Factors can be negative as well (e.g., –3 × –5 = 15).

- The **greatest common factor** of two or more numbers is the greatest factor that the numbers have in common. For example, the greatest common factor of 12 and 18 is 6. The factors of 12 are {1, 2, 3, 4, 6, 12}, and the factors of 18 are {1, 2, 3, 6, 9, 18}. They have the factors {1, 2, 3, 6} in common, and 6 is the greatest common factor.

(Continued)

Multiple—The result of multiplying an integer by another integer. For example, the multiples of 3 include 3, 6, 9, 12, and so on. Multiples can be negative as well.

- The **least common multiple** of two or more numbers is the lowest positive multiple that the numbers have in common. For example, the least common multiple of 6 and 15 is 30. The multiples of 6 are {6, 12, 18, 24, 30, …}, and the multiples of 15 are {15, 30, 45, …}. They have many multiples in common, such as {30, 60, 90}, but the least common multiple is 30.

Prime number—A number that is divisible only by itself and 1, such as 2, 3, 5, 7, and 11. The smallest prime number is 2. The number 1 is not a prime number.

Consecutive numbers—Integers that are in order from smallest to largest, with no gaps. For example, {7, 8, 9, 10}. You can also have consecutive numbers in a certain pattern, such as consecutive even numbers {2, 4, 6, 8, …} or consecutive multiples of 5 {5, 10, 15, …}.

Rational number—A number that can be expressed as a fraction of two integers. For example, 2/3 is a rational number, and so is 317/524. All integers are rational numbers as well, since they can be expressed as fractions. For example, 4 can be expressed as 4/1 or 12/3.

- Decimal numbers might or might not be rational. If a rational number is expressed as a decimal, it must have an end, or it must have a repeating pattern. For example, 1/4 expressed as a decimal is 0.25, so it has an end. 1/3 expressed as a decimal is 0.333…, and repeats forever. Both 1/3 and 1/4 are rational numbers.

Irrational number—A number that *cannot* be expressed as a fraction of two integers. For example, $\sqrt{2}$ is not rational. Its decimal value does not have an end or a repeating pattern. (Its value is 1.41421356…and continues with an infinite amount of non-repeating numbers). Most irrational numbers we encounter are the result of roots. That is, if you take the root of an integer, and the result is *not* an integer, then it is irrational. You'll learn more about roots later in this chapter.

Another irrational number is π (pronounced "pi"), which is a constant used in geometry. (Its value is 3.14159265… and continues with an infinite amount of non-repeating numbers). You'll learn more about pi in the Geometry section.

Now that we've covered some vocabulary, we're ready to discuss the major test topics in more depth. Let's begin with decimals.

Decimals

One way to represent numbers that are not integers is to use **decimals.** We use them all the time to represent monetary amounts that aren't whole dollars. For instance, if the price of an item is $3.92, we know that means three whole dollars, and $\frac{92}{100}$ of another dollar.

Numbers expressed as decimals are especially easy to multiply and divide by powers of 10. To multiply by 10, move the decimal point over one place to the right. To divide by 10, move the decimal point over one place to the left. For instance, $413.25 \times 10 = 4{,}132.5$ and $413.25 \div 10 = 41.325$.

For larger powers of 10, such as 100, 1,000, and so on, move the decimal over as many times as there are zeroes. Try this:

$$23.41735 \times 1{,}000 =$$

There are three zeroes, so we should move the decimal to the right three places:

$$23.41735 \times 1{,}000 = 23{,}417.35$$

This works for dividing by powers of 10, too:

$$41{,}325.1 \div 10{,}000 =$$

There are four zeroes, so move the decimal over four places to the left.

$$41{,}325.1 \div 10{,}000 = 4.13251$$

Scientific Notation

Scientific notation is a special way of writing numbers. In real life, it's usually used to represent very large or very small numbers, but you'll see it used for regular-sized numbers on the Praxis Core Math Test. Here's an example of a hard-to-read number:

$$452{,}300{,}000$$

In scientific notation, the number looks like this:

$$4.523 \times 10^8$$

In scientific notation, the first number being multiplied must be an integer greater than or equal to 1 and strictly less than 10. (In other words, the decimal point must come right after the first non-zero digit of the number.) The second part of the number tells you how many decimal places to move the number over.

Remember that the exponent tells you how many times to multiply a number by itself. So, $10^2 = 10 \times 10 = 100$, $10^3 = 10 \times 10 \times 10 = 1,000$, and so forth. Do you see the pattern? When 10 is the base, the exponent tells you how many zeroes there are. So 4.523×10^8 simply means, "start with 4.523 and move the decimal point over to the right 8 times."

If the decimal point has to move over more spaces than there are decimal places, you have to add zeroes to the end of the number for each extra decimal place required.

Take a look at this example:

Which of the following is equivalent to 923,000 ?

○ 923×100

○ $(9.23 \times 10^4) \times 100$

○ $923,000,000 \div 10$

○ $92.3 \times 1,000$

○ 9.23×10^5

Write down the answer choices on your scratch paper in order to work through the problem.

(A) $923 \times 100 = 92,300$. Cross out (A).
(B) $(9.23 \times 10^4) \times 100 = 92,300 \times 100 = 9,230,000$. Cross out (B).
(C) $923,000,000 \div 10 = 92,300,000$. Cross out (C).
(D) $92.3 \times 1,000 = 92,300$. Cross out (D).
(E) $9.23 \times 10^5 = 923,000$. Choice (E) is the correct answer.

Fractions

First thing's first. Here are a few terms to get you started in this section:

A **fraction** is a part of a whole. An example of a fraction is $\frac{2}{3}$. In the fraction $\frac{2}{3}$, 2 is the *numerator*, and it represents the part; 3 is the *denominator*, and it represents the whole. $\frac{2}{3}$ means "2 out of 3"—you have 2 *parts*, and it would take 3 of those parts to make a *whole*. A fraction can be bigger on the top ($\frac{4}{3}$), or bigger on the bottom ($\frac{3}{4}$), or equal in the numerator and denominator ($\frac{3}{3} = 1$).

The **reciprocal** of a fraction is its inverse; it's what you get when you switch the numerator and denominator. For example, the reciprocal of $\frac{3}{5}$ is $\frac{5}{3}$. You can also take the reciprocal of an integer by putting a 1 on top. For example, the reciprocal of 4 is $\frac{1}{4}$.

A **ratio** is a *part to part* comparison of two or more numbers. For example, 2:3 means "2 for every 3." This is different from a fraction, because the bottom number represents another *part*, not the whole. For instance, if the *ratio* of boys to girls in a classroom is 2:3, that means that there are 2 girls for every 3 boys. That also means that there are 2 girls for every 5 *students*, so the *fraction* of girls in the class is $\frac{2}{5}$ (not $\frac{2}{3}$).

Adding and Subtracting Fractions

To add or subtract fractions, use the **Bowtie method.** Let's say we wanted to add these two fractions:

$$\frac{2}{3} + \frac{1}{5} = —$$

The first thing we do is multiply the two denominators together, and write the result on the bottom of the new fraction:

$$\frac{2}{3} + \frac{1}{5} = \frac{}{15}$$

Now, start the bowtie. Multiply the denominator of the second fraction by the numerator of the first fraction and write the number on the top of the new fraction:

$$\frac{2}{3} + \frac{1}{5} = \frac{10}{15}$$

Since we're adding the fractions, write a plus sign next to the 10:

$$\frac{2}{3} + \frac{1}{5} = \frac{10+}{15}$$

Now, complete the bowtie by multiplying the denominator of the first fraction by the numerator of the second fraction:

$$\frac{2}{3} + \frac{1}{5} = \frac{10 + 3}{15}$$

Finally, add the numerators.

$$\frac{2}{3} + \frac{1}{5} = \frac{10 + 3}{15} = \frac{13}{15}$$

Subtracting works the same way, except there's a minus sign instead of a plus sign. Try this one:

$$\frac{3}{4} - \frac{1}{7} =$$

Multiply the denominators:

$$\frac{3}{4} - \frac{1}{7} = \frac{}{28}$$

Multiply the denominator of the second by the numerator of the first. Draw that line of the bowtie.

$$\frac{3}{4} \quad \frac{1}{7} = \frac{21}{28}$$

Copy the minus sign:

$$\frac{3}{4} - \frac{1}{7} = \frac{21 -}{28}$$

Complete the bowtie:

$$\frac{3}{4} - \frac{1}{7} = \frac{21 - 4}{28}$$

Subtract the two numbers:

$$\frac{3}{4} - \frac{1}{7} = \frac{21 - 4}{28} = \frac{17}{28}$$

Mixed Numbers

A **mixed number** (also known as a **mixed fraction**) is a number with an integer part and a fractional part (for example, $2\frac{1}{3}$, $5\frac{3}{8}$, etc.). In other words, a mixed number is the sum of an integer and a fraction. The mixed number $2\frac{1}{3}$ is the same as $2 + \frac{1}{3}$.

In simplest form, a fraction's numerator should be smaller than its denominator. If the numerator is larger, the fraction is an **improper fraction**, and should normally be rewritten as a mixed number.

For example, $\frac{8}{5}$ is an improper fraction. It can instead be written as $1\frac{3}{5}$, because $\frac{8}{5} = \frac{5}{5} + \frac{3}{5} = 1 + \frac{3}{5}$.

For some arithmetic involving mixed numbers, you may need to convert the mixed number to an improper fraction first. The simplest way to do that is to convert the integer part to a fraction, and add the two parts of the mixed number together. Let's try an example:

What is the reciprocal of $3\frac{2}{7}$?

Here's How to Crack It

First, convert 3 to a fraction with the denominator 7. You want the same denominator as the fraction in your mixed number.

$$\frac{3}{1} = \frac{21}{7}$$

Then, add the two parts of the mixed number.

$$\frac{21}{7} + \frac{2}{7} = \frac{23}{7}$$

Now, you can flip the fraction. The reciprocal of $\frac{23}{7}$ is $\frac{7}{23}$.

Multiplying and Dividing Fractions

Multiplying fractions is easy: Multiply the numerators together and the denominators together. Try this problem:

$$\frac{3}{5} \times \frac{4}{7}$$

Multiply the numerators:

$$\frac{3}{5} \times \frac{4}{7} = \frac{12}{}$$

Multiply the denominators:

$$\frac{3}{5} \times \frac{4}{7} = \frac{12}{35}$$

To divide fractions, invert (flip over) the *second* fraction and then multiply:

$$\frac{3}{5} \div \frac{1}{3}$$

$$\frac{3}{5} \times \frac{3}{1}$$

$$\frac{3}{5} \times \frac{3}{1} = \frac{9}{5}$$

But a fraction bar means "divided by" too, so sometimes you'll see division problems written like this:

$$\frac{\frac{7}{9}}{\frac{1}{4}}$$

In cases such as this, you can rewrite the fraction to look like this:

$$\frac{7}{9} \div \frac{1}{4}$$

Then invert and multiply:

$$\frac{7}{9} \times \frac{4}{1}$$

$$\frac{7}{9} \times \frac{4}{1} = \frac{28}{9}$$

Comparing Fractions

Sometimes you'll need to be able to tell whether a fraction is bigger or smaller than another. You can use the bowtie for this, too. For example, which is bigger, $\frac{5}{7}$ or $\frac{7}{11}$? First, write the fractions side by side:

$$\frac{5}{7} \quad \frac{7}{11}$$

Use the bowtie, always working upward and crosswise. Write each product at the top of its corresponding arrow:

$$55 \quad 49$$
$$\frac{5}{7} \times \frac{7}{11}$$

The larger number will appear above the larger fraction. Because 55 is bigger than 49, $\frac{5}{7}$ is bigger than $\frac{7}{11}$.

Simplifying Fractions

Sometimes when you're manipulating fractions, you can end up with large, unwieldy numbers on the top and bottom. Because the fractions on the Praxis Core Math Test are often in the simplest form, you should know how to simplify the fraction. In other words, find an equivalent fraction with smaller numbers. To do this, look for factors that are present in both the numerator and denominator, and divide them away. Take a look at this fraction:

$$\frac{21}{49}$$

This fraction can be simplified because both the numerator and denominator are divisible by 7. We could rewrite the fraction like this:

$$\frac{7 \times 3}{7 \times 7} = \frac{7}{7} \times \frac{3}{7}$$

We can cancel out a 7 from the top and bottom because there's nothing going on here besides multiplication. That leaves us with:

$$\frac{3}{7}$$

Important note: Canceling works only with fractions that have nothing but multiplication in the numerator and denominator. For example, we couldn't get away with canceling if the fraction looked like this:

$$\frac{7 + 3}{7 + 7}$$

With larger numbers, you may have to simplify several times to get down to simplest form. Try simplifying this:

$$\frac{15}{75}$$

Because both numbers end in a 5, we know that 5 must be a factor of both:

$$\frac{15}{75} = \frac{5 \times 3}{5 \times 15} = \frac{3}{15}$$

But 3 is a factor of 15, so we can simplify again:

$$\frac{3}{15} = \frac{3 \times 1}{3 \times 5} = \frac{1}{5}$$

So, $\frac{15}{75} = \frac{1}{5}$.

Try simplifying the following fractions:

$$\frac{25}{100} \qquad \frac{60}{360} \qquad \frac{48}{144}$$

Depending on which factors you started with, your work may look different, but you should arrive at the same solutions:

$$\frac{25}{100} = \frac{25 \times 1}{25 \times 4} = \frac{1}{4}$$

$$\frac{60}{360} = \frac{10 \times 6}{10 \times 36} = \frac{6}{36} = \frac{6 \times 1}{6 \times 6} = \frac{1}{6}$$

$$\frac{48}{144} = \frac{12 \times 4}{12 \times 12} = \frac{4}{12} = \frac{4 \times 1}{4 \times 3} = \frac{1}{3}$$

Percents

Percentages always compare other numbers to 100 (*percent* literally means "out of 100") because 100 is a nice round number and many of us have developed an intuitive understanding of how other numbers relate to it. For instance, we all know that 50 percent is the same as the fraction $\frac{1}{2}$. We also understand that although a sale sign advertising "10% off" is a good thing, it's probably not worth making a special trip to the store.

Converting Between Decimals and Percents

Because *percent* means "out of 100," you can write percentages as fractions by putting 100 in the denominator and simplifying, or as decimals by moving the decimal two places to the left. For example, $25\% = \frac{25}{100} = \frac{1}{4}$, and $25\% = 0.25$. Try the following examples.

What is 23% expressed as a decimal?

Here's How to Crack It
Divide 23 by 100.

$$\frac{23}{100} = 0.23$$

Note: you can read 0.23 as "23 hundredths," which is the same as $\frac{23}{100}$.

If the percent has a decimal in it, you still follow the same steps: move the decimal two places to the left.

─────────────○─────────────

What is 124.7% expressed as a decimal?

Here's How to Crack It
Divide 124.7 by 100:

$$\frac{124.7}{100} = 1.247$$

─────────────○─────────────

Converting Percents to Fractions

To convert a percent to a fraction, simply write a fraction with the percent number as the numerator, and 100 as the denominator. Then, reduce completely.

─────────────○─────────────

What is 85% expressed as a fraction?

Here's How to Crack It
Write as a fraction with 100 on the bottom:

$$\frac{85}{100}$$

Reduce completely:

$$\frac{85}{100} = \frac{17}{20}$$

─────────────○─────────────

If a percent has decimals in it, keep multiplying the top and the bottom by 10, until the percent number becomes an integer. Try the next example.

What is 85.2 expressed as a fraction?

Here's How to Crack It

Write as a fraction with 100 on the bottom:

$$\frac{85.2}{100}$$

Multiply the top and the bottom by 10:

$$\frac{85.2 \times 10}{100 \times 10} = \frac{825}{1,000}$$

Reduce completely.

$$\frac{852}{1,000} = \frac{426}{500} = \frac{213}{250}$$

Tip: Since the denominator is a power of 10, we know that the fraction could reduce by only 2, 5, and/or 10. That makes it a little easier to check for factors!

Converting Fractions to Percents

To convert a fraction to a percent, first divide the numerator by the denominator. Then, multiply by 100.

What is $\frac{3}{8}$ expressed as a percent?

Here's How to Crack It

Divide the numerator by the denominator. You can use the on-screen calculator on the test, or use long division.

$$3 \div 8 = 0.375$$

This is the decimal value of the fraction $\frac{3}{8}$. To convert it to a percent, we need to multiply by 100. That is, move the decimal point two places to the right. Don't forget to include the percent symbol!

$$0.375 = 37.5\%$$

You'll learn more about tricky percent questions in the Algebra and Functions section.

You should be familiar with these common percentages and their fraction/decimal equivalents:

Percent	Fraction	Decimal
10	$\frac{1}{10}$	0.1
25	$\frac{1}{4}$	0.25
33.3	$\frac{1}{3}$	0.333
50	$\frac{1}{2}$	0.5
66.6	$\frac{2}{3}$	0.666
75	$\frac{3}{4}$	0.75
100	1	1
200	2	2

Percent Change

When a question asks for the "percent change," "percent increase," or "percent decrease," use this formula:

$$\frac{\text{difference}}{\text{original}} = \text{percent change}$$

In this formula, "difference" means subtract. The "original" number is the number before it was "changed."

Try the following example.

Last year, the cost of a subway ride changed from $1.50 to $2.00. By what percent did the cost of a subway ride increase?

If the question asks for "percent increase," then you know the "original" number is the *smaller* number. If it asks for "percent decrease," then you know the "original" number is the *larger* number.

If the question asks for "percent change," then you might need to think carefully. For example, in the phrase "change from 3 to 5," we know that 3 is the *original*, because we start with 3 and change to 5.

A question might also mention time, such as "on Monday, there were 3 boxes, and on Friday, there were 5 boxes." This tells you that 3 is the *original*, because Monday comes before Friday.

Here's How to Crack It

Use the formula $\frac{\text{difference}}{\text{original}}$ = percent change.

To find the *difference*, subtract the smaller number from the larger number:

$$\$2.00 - \$1.50 = \$0.50$$

The *original* number is $1.50, since that's the price before the change. So,

$$\frac{\text{difference}}{\text{original}} = \frac{0.50}{1.50} = 0.333..., \text{ or } \frac{1}{3}$$

Let's try one more.

During a sale, the price of a $40 video game is decreased to $32. What is the percent change of the discount?

Here's How to Crack It

Use the formula $\frac{\text{difference}}{\text{original}}$ = percent change. The difference is $40 - $32 = $8. The original number is 40, since the price is higher before the change. Calculate $\frac{8}{40}$.

$$8 \div 40 = 0.2, \text{ or } 20\%$$

Powers and Roots

You may see test questions involving powers and roots. Here are some terms you should know.

A **power** is the result of multiplying a number by itself one or more times. For example, 5^3 means $5 \times 5 \times 5 = 125$. In 5^3, 5 is called the **base,** and the 3 is called the **exponent** (it can also be called the *index*). The exponent tells you the number of times to multiply the base by itself. (In 5^3, you write 5 *three* times, and multiply them together). You can read 5^3 as *five to the third power.*

Square is another word for the *second power* of a number. For example, the *square* of 7 is 49, because $7^2 = 49$.

A **root** is an inverse of a power. For example, $\sqrt[3]{8} = 2$, because $2 \times 2 \times 2 = 8$. The expression "What is $\sqrt[3]{8}$?" means "What number, when taken to the *third power*, equals 8?" (in other words, $number^3 = 8$). In $\sqrt[3]{8}$, the 3 is called the *index*, and the 8 is called the **radicand.** The $\sqrt{\ }$ symbol is called a **radical symbol,** and an expression with a radical is called a **radical expression.**

Square root is another word for the *second root* of a number. For example, $\sqrt[2]{25} = 5$. Note that square roots are often written without an index, as in $\sqrt{25} = 5$. If you see a root written without an index, it means that the index is 2.

It will be helpful to you to memorize the 2nd and 3rd powers of numbers 1 through 20. This will make some problems easier, and it will also help you estimate. For example, what is the square root of 150? Well, if you know that $12^2 = 144$ and $13^2 = 169$, then you know that $\sqrt{150}$ must be between 12 and 13. (In fact, its value is approximately 12.247.) You can use the table below for reference.

Number	2nd power	3rd power
1	1	1
2	4	8
3	9	27
4	16	64
5	25	125
6	36	216
7	49	343
8	64	512
9	81	729
10	100	1,000
11	121	1,331
12	144	1,728
13	169	2,197
14	196	2,744
15	225	3,375
16	256	4,096
17	289	4,913
18	324	5,832
19	361	6,859
20	400	8,000

Logic

You can expect some questions about logic. That is, the question will provide one or more logical statements, and ask you about the truth or untruth of other statements. Logic statements generally fall into one of two categories: *if/then* statements and *all/some* statements.

If/Then Statements

Here's an example of an **if/then statement**: If we are in Los Angeles, then we are in California.

An if/then statement gives a *condition* (the *if* portion of the statement) and a *conclusion* (the *then* portion of the statement). When given an if/then statement, there is only one other statement that *must* be true. It is called the **contrapositive**.

> The contrapositive of **If A, then B** is **If not B, then not A.**

The contrapositive of

> *If we are in Los Angeles, then we are in California.*

is

> *If we are not in California, then we are not in Los Angeles.*

Notice that since the first statement is true, the contrapositive statement must also be true. However, if this were a multiple-choice question, you might see options like these:

> *If we are in California, then we are in Los Angeles.*
> *If we are not in Los Angeles, then we are not in California.*

Neither of those two statements is true—of course, we can be in another city in California. For these types of questions, the correct answer will always be the contrapositive!

All/Some Statements

When a logical statement uses the word *all,* it's really just an if/then statement. For example, *all cows are mammals* can be rewritten as *if an animal is a cow, then it is a mammal.* For *all* statements, use the contrapositive rule as shown above. It's true that *if an animal is not a mammal, then it is not a cow.* It is not true that *all mammals are cows,* or that *some cows are not mammals.*

When a statement uses the word *some,* it means "at least one." It might be one, or a few, or a lot—don't assume. For example, if it is true that *some students drove to school today,* then it follows that *not all students walked to school today.* You shouldn't assume that *more students walked to school,* or *some students rode a horse to school.*

ALGEBRA AND FUNCTIONS

The Praxis Core Math Test will also cover topics related to algebra and functions. Algebra questions will mainly focus on concepts of variables and equations. You will use algebra to simplify expressions, solve for unknown values in equations, and derive equations to solve problems.

Order of Operations

The **order of operations** is the order in which we perform calculations in math. When you have multiple steps in a problem, using the correct order of operations ensures that you will get the correct answer. The correct order of operations is **P**arentheses, **E**xponents, **M**ultiplication, **D**ivision, **A**ddition, **S**ubtraction—or PEMDAS for short.

Parentheses (also known as brackets) are always dealt with first. For example:

$$72 \div (2 \times 9) =$$

$$72 \div 18 = 4$$

Exponents have the highest priority *after* parentheses. For example:

$$72 \div 3^2 =$$

$$72 \div 9 = 8$$

Multiplication and **Division** have higher priority than addition and subtraction.

$$18 \times 2 - 5 =$$

$$36 - 5 = 31$$

Also, remember to solve multiplication and division together, from **left to right**. For example:

$$18 \div 2 \times 3 =$$

$$9 \times 3 = 27$$

Addition and **Subtraction** have the lowest priority. Remember to solve addition and subtraction together, from **left to right**. For example:

$$15 - 5 + 3 =$$

$$10 + 3 = 13$$

The Distributive Property

The **Distributive Property** states that there are two ways to multiply a sum by a number. You can either (1) take the sum first and then multiply, or (2) multiply each addend by the number separately, and then add the products together.

> **Distributive Property:** $a(b + c) = ab + bc$

Try this next problem.

What is the value of $20 \times (4 + 3)$?

Here's How to Crack It

You can do the steps inside the parentheses first:

$$20 \times (4 + 3) =$$
$$20 \times 7 = 140$$

Or, you can use the Distributive Property:

$$20 \times (4 + 3) =$$
$$20 \times 4 + 20 \times 3 =$$
$$80 + 60 = 140$$

The results are the same, and both are valid processes.

Algebraic Expressions and Equations

You should also know how to solve simple algebraic equations. An **equation** is a mathematical sentence that contains an equals sign. For example, $5 - 2 = 3$ is an equation. An **algebraic equation** is an equation that contains one or more variables. The following examples are algebraic equations:

$$5 + x = 9 \qquad (x + 2)^3 = 27 \qquad 2x + 9 = \frac{x}{4} \qquad y = 3x - 5$$

You should be able to create and recognize algebraic representations of mathematical relationships. Try this example:

Which of the following expressions best represents "the difference of a certain number and the square of another number"?

○ $\dfrac{x}{y^2}$

○ $x - y^2$

○ $(x - y)^2$

○ $x + y^2$

○ $x^2 - y^2$

Here's How to Crack It

The word *difference* means subtraction, so we can eliminate (A) and (D). The phrase tells us that only one of the variables is squared, so the best answer is (B).

Solving Equations

To solve equations, you must follow one golden rule:

> Whatever operation you do to one side of the equation, you must also do to the other side.

For example, to solve the equation $x + 11 = 24$, subtract 11 from both sides.

$$x + 11 = 24$$
$$x + 11 - 11 = 24 - 11$$
$$x = 13$$

Now work through this example:

Solve for x:

$3x + 4 = -2x + 7$

Here's How to Crack It

First, you need to make sure that all the x's are on the same side of the equals sign. Whatever operation you perform on one side, you must perform on the other. Start by adding $2x$ to both sides:

$$
\begin{array}{r}
3x + 4 = -2x + 7 \\
+2x \qquad\quad +2x \\
\hline
5x + 4 = \qquad\ 7
\end{array}
$$

Next, make sure all of the numbers are on the other side. In this case, you must subtract 4 from both sides of the equation.

$$
\begin{array}{r}
5x + 4 = 7 \\
-4\ \ -4 \\
\hline
5x \quad\ = 3
\end{array}
$$

Finally, divide both sides by 5 to get x by itself.

$$\frac{5x}{5} = \frac{3}{5}$$

$$x = \frac{3}{5}$$

Note: Cross-multiplication is ONLY for equations. Do not cross-multiply when you are performing arithmetic with fractions (e.g., $\frac{3}{x} \times \frac{6}{10}$ is not the same as $3 \times 10 \times 6 \times x$).

Cross-Multiplying

Use cross-multiplying when there is a fraction on both sides of an equation.

$$\frac{3}{x} = \frac{6}{10}$$

Since there is a fraction on both sides of the equals sign, cross-multiply. This is similar to the Bowtie method previously described. Multiply the bottom right number by the top left number, and write the result on the left side of the equals sign:

$$\frac{3}{x} \diagdown \frac{6}{10}$$

$$30 =$$

Then, multiply the bottom left number by the top right number and write the result on the right side of the equals sign:

$$\frac{3}{x} \diagup\!\!\!\!\diagdown \frac{6}{10}$$

$$6x = 30$$

Now, solve as usual by dividing both sides by 6:

$$\frac{6}{6}x = \frac{30}{6}$$

So, $x = 5$.

Ratios and Proportions

Many questions on the Praxis Core Math Test will ask you to compare relationships between numbers. One way to do this is to use a **ratio.** For example, in the town of Surf City, immortalized in the Jan and Dean recording, there are "two girls for every boy." This is a ratio, which can also be expressed in the following ways:

with the word "to":	2 to 1
or with a colon:	2:1
or even as a fraction:	$\frac{2}{1}$

All of these are equivalent. The 2-to-1 ratio is not meant to imply that there are only two girls in the entire town. Instead, it means that regardless of the number of people in the town, there will always be twice as many girls as boys.

Why Cross-Multiplying Works

Cross-multiplying is a shortcut for performing several steps. It is used specifically for an equation of two fractions. To solve this example equation, we could have done the following:

$$\frac{3}{x} = \frac{6}{10}$$

$3 = x \times \dfrac{6}{10}$ (multiply both sides by x)

$3 \times 10 = x \times 6$ (multiply both sides by 10)

$30 = 6x$

You can solve ratio problems by setting up a *proportion*, which is just two ratios (usually written as fractions) side by side with an equals sign in between. For instance, let's say you were asked this question:

In Surf City there are two girls for every boy. If there are 30 boys in Surf City, how many girls are there?

○ 2

○ 15

○ 30

○ 32

○ 60

Here's How to Crack It

Set up the proportion like this:

$$\frac{2}{1} = \frac{x}{30}$$

On one side of the equals sign, write the ratio you're given. Put the number of girls on top, and the number of boys on the bottom (but you could have written it the other way, too). On the other side, create another ratio, making sure you keep the girls and boys in the same order. Since you don't know the number of girls (that's what you're being asked to find), write an x on the top. The problem states that there are 30 boys, so fill that in on the bottom. Now, cross-multiply:

$$30 \times 2 = x \times 1$$

$$60 = x$$

So, there are 60 girls.

What if the question had looked like the following?

---○---

In the town of Surf City, there are two girls for every boy. If there are 120 people in the town (and there are no adults), how many boys are there?

- ○ 1
- ○ 20
- ○ 40
- ○ 60
- ○ 80

Here's How to Crack It

This question asks something a little different. Instead of simply focusing on the number of girls and boys, we're asked about the relationship between the total number of girls and boys in the town and the number of boys. To solve a question like this, you need to think about the original ratio and its implications for the total number of people.

The original ratio is a part-to-part relationship. In other words, we're comparing two parts to each other: the number of girls relative to the number of boys. If you're asked about a part-to-whole relationship, first add the parts together.

Girls	Boys	Whole
2 +	1 =	3

Now we have a way of expressing the relationship of the parts to the whole, because it's now clear that out of every three people in Surf City, two will be girls and one will be a boy. Armed with this knowledge, we can set up another proportion to answer the question. As we analyzed earlier, the problem asks us to compare the number of boys to the total population. So we can write:

$$\frac{1}{3} = \frac{x}{120}$$

Cross-multiplying and solving, we find that:

$$120 \times 1 = 3 \times x$$
$$120 = 3x$$
$$40 = x$$

---○---

Sometimes questions will ask you about proportions without mentioning ratios at all. Try this one:

On a certain map, two towns that are 100 miles away from each other are represented by dots that are $\frac{7}{8}$ inches apart. How far apart would two dots be if they represented towns that were 200 miles away from each other?

○ $\frac{3.5}{8}$ inches

○ $\frac{7}{8}$ inches

○ $\frac{10.5}{8}$ inches

○ $\frac{14}{8}$ inches

○ $\frac{20}{8}$ inches

Here's How to Crack It

Set up the proportion just as we did for the ratio problems, making sure you keep the things you're comparing in the same relative order:

$$\frac{\frac{7}{8}}{100} = \frac{x}{200}$$

$$200 \times \frac{7}{8} = 100 \times x$$

Before multiplying the left-hand side of the equation, save yourself some trouble and divide both sides by 100 first, giving you:

$$\frac{200}{100} \times \frac{7}{8} = x$$

Reducing $\dfrac{200}{100}$ gives us 2, so now we have:

$$2 \times \frac{7}{8} = x$$

$$\frac{14}{8} = x$$

Percents as Proportions

You can solve percent problems with proportions, too. For example, to convert the fraction $\dfrac{29}{88}$ to a percent, you could write it as a proportion:

$$\frac{24}{88} = \frac{x}{100}$$

To solve for x, use cross-multiplication.

$$24 \times 100 = x \times 88$$

$$2{,}400 = x \times 88$$

$$\frac{2{,}400}{88} = x$$

$$27.272727\ldots = x$$

Using this concept, we can solve some trickier percent questions with unknown values. Use the following proportion rule for word problems:

$$\frac{\text{part}}{\text{whole}} = \frac{\text{percent}}{100}$$

Let's try a few examples.

———————————○———————————

What is 3% of 45 ?

Here's How to Crack It

Fill in the given values into the proportion above. The "percent" is 3, and the "whole" is 45. The "part" is the unknown value we are solving for.

$$\frac{x}{45} = \frac{3}{100}$$

Cross-multiply:

$$x \times 100 = 3 \times 45$$

$$x \times 100 = 135$$

Now divide both sides by 100:

$$x = \frac{135}{100}$$

$$x = 1.35$$

To check the result, try substituting the number into the original question:

1.35 is 3% of 45

$1.35 = 0.03 \times 45$ True!

———————————○———————————

Here's another example.

———————————○———————————

12 is 6% of what number?

Here's How to Crack It

Read carefully. The question says *6% of what number*, so that means the "whole" is the unknown value. The "part" is 12.

$$\frac{12}{x} = \frac{6}{100}$$

Cross-multiply:

$$12 \times 100 = x \times 6$$
$$1{,}200 = x \times 6$$

Divide both sides by 6:

$$x = \frac{1{,}200}{6}$$
$$x = 200$$

To check, try substituting the number into the original question.

12 is 6% of 200

$12 = 0.06 \times 200$ True!

Okay, just one more.

4 is what percent of 72 ?

Here's How to Crack It

The question says *what percent*, so we are solving for the *percent* part of the equation. The "part" is 4, and the "whole" is 72.

$$\frac{4}{72} = \frac{x}{100}$$

Cross-multiply:

$$4 \times 100 = 72 \times x$$
$$400 = 72 \times x$$

Divide both sides by 72:

$$x = \frac{400}{72}$$
$$x = 5.555\ldots$$

Check the result:

4 is 5.555% of 72

$4 = 0.0555 \times 72$

True! This value is approximate, since we rounded the repeating decimal.

Strategies for Algebra Questions (and Beyond)

Before going any further in our content review, let's take a moment to review a few strategies that will help you in the types of algebra questions we just discussed, as well as some more complex problems we'll take a look at later in this chapter. We discussed these strategies in Part I, but they're worth repeating here as a reminder.

Plugging In

For many multiple-choice questions involving algebra, you can use a strategy we call Plugging In. Basically, you'll "plug in" numbers for the variables or unknowns, and treat the question like an arithmetic question. This strategy can help you avoid mistakes, and can also make challenging and multistep algebra problems easier to understand and solve. If you practice the Plugging In approach on as many problems as possible, you will find it very helpful on test day! There are two different types of Plugging In: Plugging In the Answers and plugging in your own number.

Plugging In the Answers (PITA) means testing the numerical answer choices that are provided in multiple-choice and select-all-that-apply questions. You can recognize the following clues to tell you to use Plugging In the Answers: the question has numerical answer choices, there might not be actual variables in the question (but there are one or more unknown values), and you'll probably feel like you should set up an equation to solve it. Let's walk through the approach with an example.

A caterer serves 124 meals at a school function. If the meal choices were vegetarian for $3.00 or steak for $4.50, and the total cost of all the meals was $423, how many meals were vegetarian meals?

- ○ 60
- ○ 70
- ○ 80
- ○ 90
- ○ 100

Here's How to Crack It

First, **recognize the opportunity** to PITA: there are numerical answer choices, the question has unknown values, and you might have felt the need to make an equation. Don't write an equation; plug in!

Identify the unknown that you're being asked to solve: in this case, it's the number of vegetarian meals (see: *how many meals were vegetarian meals?*) This is the value that we are plugging in from the answer choices.

When you plug in the answers, start with (C), the third answer choice. We start with the answer in the middle, because if it is wrong, we can easily eliminate two more answer choices! Here, (C) is 80. Plug that in for the *number of vegetarian meals*, and work through the problem arithmetically:

A caterer serves 124 meals...

If 80 were vegetarian, that means 44 were steak meals (124 − 80 = 44).

...vegetarian for $3.00 and steak for $4.50

Calculate the cost. 80 × $3.00 = $240.00, and 44 × $4.50 = $198.00. $240 + $198 = $438.

What other information do we have?

the total cost of all the meals was $423

For 80 vegetarian meals and 44 steak meals, we calculated the cost to be $438. This cost is too high. Eliminate (C). We want a *lower* total cost, so do we want fewer vegetarian meals? Actually, the vegetarian meals were cheaper, so we'll get a lower cost if we have *more* vegetarian meals and fewer steak meals. So we should eliminate (A) and (B), and try (D) next.

Plug in once more (this time, 90). If 90 were vegetarian meals, that means 34 were steak meals (124 − 90 = 34). Now calculate the cost: 90 × $3.00 = $270.00, and 34 × $4.50 = $153.00. $240 + $153 = $423.

What other information do we have? For 90 vegetarian meals and 34 steak meals, we calculated the cost to be $423. This cost is just right, so the correct answer is (D).

─────────────○─────────────

The other option is to **plug in your own number,** which means choosing an easy number and plugging it in for the variable in the problem. You can recognize the opportunity to plug in your own number when the answer choices have variables, and often the question will use the phrase "in terms of." Let's work through the process with a practice question.

Remember to write down all of the arithmetic steps on your scratch paper!

Don't worry if you're ever unsure about which number to test after (C). Just try either (B) or (D) next. See if the result brings you closer to—or farther from—the result you need.

Allen gives Cristian *c* dollars. He gives Brittany 20 fewer dollars than he gives to Cristian. He gives Destiny 30 more dollars than he gives Brittany. How much money, in dollars, did Allen give away to Brittany, Cristian, and Destiny, in terms of *c* ?

○ $3c - 10$

○ $3c$

○ $3c + 10$

○ $3c + 20$

○ $c - 20$

Here's How to Crack It

First, **recognize the opportunity** to plug in. The answer choices have variables, and the question contains the phrase "in terms of." Don't solve algebraically—Plug In!

Let's **choose a number** for *c*. The number should be a straightforward and simple one, but it should also make sense in the problem. Let's try 50.

Work through the problem arithmetically: *Allen gives Cristian 50 dollars. He gives Brittany 20 fewer dollars then he gives to Cristian.* Brittany gets $30 ($50 – $20 = $30). *He gives Destiny 30 more dollars than he gives Brittany.* Destiny gets $60 ($30 + $30 = $60). *How much money, in dollars, did Allen give away?* $50 + $30 + $60 = $140. This result ($140) is our **target value**. That is, the correct answer should equal $140, when *c* is equal to $50.

When you plug in your own number, you must check all of the answer choices.

(A) $3(50) - 10$ $150 - 10 = 140$ Looks good! *Check all of the answers.*

(B) $3(50)$ $3(50) = 150$ Not equal to 140. Eliminate.

(C) $3(50) + 10$ $150 + 10 = 160$ Not equal to 140. Eliminate.

(D) $3(50) + 20$ $150 + 20 = 170$ Not equal to 140. Eliminate.

(E) $50 - 20$ $50 - 20 = 30$ Not equal to 140. Eliminate.

Here, we eliminated (B), (C), (D), and (E), because they did not match our target value. The only answer left is (A), so this is the correct answer.

Reminder About Answer Choices

On the actual test, the answer choices will not be labeled with letters. We're using them here in order to more easily refer to the answer choices.

What if more than one answer choice matches your target value? That's a possibility, because the answer choices will vary depending on the number you pick. If it happens, try another number and plug in again from the first step. You don't need to check the answers that you already eliminated—only the answers that remain.

Linear Equations and Inequalities

Now that you have some basic strategies in your back pocket, let's move on to some higher-level topics in algebra: namely, linear equations and inequalities.

A **linear equation** is an equation that forms a straight line when it is graphed. The equation itself represents all of the points that exist on the line. The equation will be true for every point that exists on the line. For example, if the equation is $y = x + 3$, then points on the line include (0, 3), (1, 4), (2, 5), and so on. The line also includes fractional, irrational, and negative numbers, such as (0.5, 3.5) in this example.

In a linear equation, the **slope** is the measure of the gradient, or slant, of the line. To calculate slope, use the following formula, comparing any two points $\{(x_1, y_1)$ and $(x_2, y_2)\}$ from the line:

$$\frac{y_1 - y_2}{x_1 - x_2}$$

You can also remember this formula as $\frac{rise}{run}$ or $\frac{change\ in\ y}{change\ in\ x}$. Let's try an example.

———————————◯———————————

What is the slope of a line containing the points (6, 12) and (3, 7) ?

Here's How to Crack It

In the formula, the two coordinate pairs are (x_1, y_1) and (x_2, y_2), respectively. Plug in the numbers as follows:

$$\frac{12 - 7}{6 - 3} = \frac{5}{3}$$

The slope of the line is $\frac{5}{3}$.

———————————◯———————————

You should also remember the following rules regarding slope:

The slope of a horizontal line is **0**. (There is no change in y, so the numerator is 0.)

The slope of a vertical line is **undefined**. (There is no change in x, so the denominator is 0.)

Lines that are **parallel** to each other have the *same* slope.

Lines that are **perpendicular** to each other have *opposite reciprocal* slopes (e.g., example, $\frac{3}{4}$ and $-\frac{4}{3}$).

Slope-Intercept Form

An equation is said to be in **slope-intercept form** if it is in the form $y = mx + b$. For example, $y = 5x + 2$ is written in slope-intercept form. It's called slope-intercept form because it is easy to identify the slope and the y-intercept of the line. Slope is the gradient (slant) of the line. The **y-intercept** is the point at which the line crosses the vertical axis. In other words, it's the value of y when $x = 0$.

In slope-intercept form, **m** represents the slope, and **b** represents the y-intercept. The variables x and y represent any given coordinate pair on the line. Normally in a linear equation, you'll see x and y as variables, and numerical values for m and b. For example, in the equation $y = 5x + 2$, the slope is 5, and the y-intercept is 2.

Try this practice question.

Which of the following coordinates represents a point on the line $y = (\frac{2}{3})x + 4$?
Select **all** that apply.

☐ (0, 6)

☐ (1.5, 5)

☐ (3, 9)

☐ (4.5, 5)

☐ (6, 8)

Here's How to Crack It

Since coordinate points are given, Plug In! You'll be looking to see if the equation is true with the given coordinate pairs.

(A) $y = (\frac{2}{3})x + 4$

$6 = (\frac{2}{3}) \times 0 + 4$

$6 = 0 + 4$

$6 = 4$ False. Eliminate (0, 6).

(B) $y = (\frac{2}{3})x + 4$

$5 = (\frac{2}{3}) \times 1.5 + 4$

$5 = 1 + 4$

$5 = 5$?   True. Select (1.5, 5).

(C) $y = (\frac{2}{3})x + 4$

$9 = (\frac{2}{3}) \times 3 + 4$

$9 = 2 + 4$

$9 = 6$ False. Eliminate (3, 9).

(D) $y = (\frac{2}{3})x + 4$

$5 = (\frac{2}{3}) \times 4.5 + 4$

$5 = 3 + 4$

$5 = 7$?   False. Eliminate (4.5, 5).

(E) $y = (\frac{2}{3})x + 4$

$8 = (\frac{2}{3}) \times 6 + 4$

$8 = 4 + 4$

$8 = 8$ True. Select (6, 8).

The two correct answers are (1.5, 5) and (6, 8).

Point-Slope Form

The **point-slope form** of a line is $y - y_1 = m(x - x_1)$. This form is convenient to use when you know the slope of the line as well as one of its coordinates. In point-slope form, the m represents the slope, and x_1 and y_1 represent a known coordinate pair from the line (x_1, y_1). The x and y are normally seen as variables, which represent any coordinate pair from the line. For example, the equation $y - 5 = 2(x - 3)$ is written in point-slope form. The slope is 2, and a known coordinate from the line is $(3, 5)$.

To change an equation from point-slope form to slope-intercept form, get the y by itself, and simplify. Try the following example.

Which of the following is equivalent to the equation $y - 6 = 2(x + 4)$?

Here's How to Crack It

Suppose the answer choices are equations in slope-intercept form. Therefore, we need to change the equation to slope-intercept form.

First, you can get the y by itself.

$$y - 6 = 2(x + 4)$$

Add 6 to both sides of the equation.

$$y = 2(x + 4) + 6$$

Then, simplify completely, using the Distributive Property.

$$y = (2 \times x + 2 \times 4) + 6$$

$$y = 2x + 8 + 6$$

$$y = 2x + 14$$

The slope-intercept form of the equation is $y = 2x + 14$.

Inequalities

An **inequality** is a number sentence that uses an inequality symbol ($<$, $>$, $\leq$, or $\geq$) instead of the equals sign. Inequalities are solved the same way that equations are solved, with one important difference. If you multiply or divide an inequality by a *negative* number, you must reverse the inequality symbol.

Inequality Symbols

$<$	less than
$>$	greater than
$\leq$	less than or equal to
$\geq$	greater than or equal to

Let's try a question.

Solve the inequality for x:

$-2x + 10 > 24$

Here's How to Crack It

Proceed as though solving an equation, but remember the rule above.

$-2x + 10 > 24$

$\qquad -2x > 14 \qquad$ Subtract 10 from both sides.

$\qquad\quad x < -7 \qquad$ Divide both sides by -2. Reverse the inequality symbol.

If it helps you to remember the rule, you can solve the last step in two parts:

$-2x > 14$

$\quad -x > 7 \qquad\qquad$ Divide both sides by 2.

$\quad\ x < -7 \qquad\qquad$ Divide both sides by -1. Reverse the inequality symbol.

The **solution** to an inequality is said to be a *range* of values. For example, the solution $x < -7$ means "x is any value less than -7." In practical terms, you could use an inequality to solve a scenario involving limits, such as "Maria can spend no more than \$30 on a birthday gift." If Maria's spending is represented by m, then you would say that $m \leq \$30$.

Linear Inequalities

Inequalities can be **linear** as well, meaning that the inequality has two variables (e.g., x and y) and can be graphed as a straight line in the coordinate plane. To identify the graph of a linear inequality, put the inequality in slope-intercept form first (i.e., $y < mx + b$). Find the y-intercept and the slope, as you would with a linear equation. Finally, the appearance of the line and shading of the graph depend on the inequality symbol being used.

Why Dashed?

The dashed line (for $<$ and $>$ inequalities) indicates that the points on the line are *not solutions* to the inequality. Rather, the solutions are either below ($<$) or above ($>$) the line.

$<$	Dashed line; shading below the line
$>$	Dashed line; shading above the line
$\leq$	Solid line; shading below the line
$\geq$	Solid line; shading above the line

The figures below (continued on the next page) show the graphs for $y = x$ and the corresponding inequalities for that line.

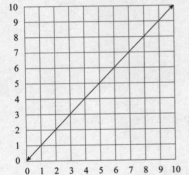

$y = x$

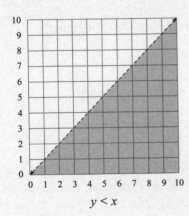

$y < x$

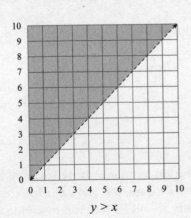

$y > x$

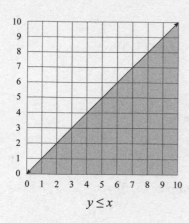

$y \leq x$

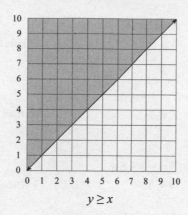

$y \geq x$

Systems of Linear Equations

A **system of equations** is a set of two or more equations that are solved *together*. The **solution** to a system is the set of values that are true for ALL of the equations in the system. In a system of linear equations, the solution is the point at which the lines intersect.

If you are asked to identify the solution to a system of equations, and the question is multiple choice, try Plugging In!

$$y = -x + 8$$
$$y = 2x - 1$$

What is the solution to the system of equations shown above?

○ (2, 3)

○ (3, 5)

○ (4, 7)

○ (5, 3)

○ (6, 11)

Here's How to Crack It

The solution must be true for BOTH equations. Try Plugging In the Answers to the first equation.

$$y = -x + 8$$

(A)   (2, 3)

   $3 = -2 + 8$

   $3 = 6$ False. Eliminate (2, 3).

Here's PITA in action!

In a coordinate pair, the two values are always in the order (x, y). So in the case of $(3, 5)$, $x = 3$ and $y = 5$.

(B)   (3, 5)
        $5 = -3 + 8$
        $5 = 5$ True. Don't eliminate (3, 5) yet.

(C)   (4, 7)
        $7 = -4 + 8$
        $7 = 4$ False. Eliminate (4, 7).

(D)   (5, 3)
        $3 = -5 + 8$
        $3 = 3$ True. Don't eliminate (5, 3) yet.

(E)   (6, 11)
        $11 = -6 + 8$
        $11 = 2$ False. Eliminate (6, 11).

We are left with two choices: (3, 5) and (5, 3). Plug these answer choices into the second equation.

$$y = 2x - 1$$

(3, 5)
$5 = 2(3) - 1$
$5 = 6 - 1$
$5 = 5 ?$ True. (3, 5) is true for **both** equations, so it is the solution.

You can verify that the other remaining choice is *not* the solution:

$3 = 2(5) - 1$
$3 = 10 - 1$
$3 = 9$ False. Eliminate (5, 3).

The figure below shows the graphs of both equations. Notice that the solution (3, 5) is where the two lines intersect.

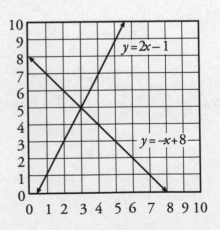

If plugging in is not an option, you can use **substitution** to solve a system of linear equations. Look at this example:

$$y = (\frac{3}{2})x + 3 \qquad\qquad y = x + 5$$

First, make sure each equation has y by itself on one side. Next, since we have two expressions that equal y, we can set the two expressions equal to each other. That is, we are substituting an expression for y.

$$(\frac{3}{2})x + 3 = x + 5$$

Solve for x:

$3x + 6 = 2x + 10$	You can multiply both sides by 2, which "clears" the fraction.
$3x = 2x + 4$	Subtract 6 from both sides of the equation.
$x = 4$	Subtract $2x$ from both sides of the equation.

The x-value of the solution is 4. Now that we know this, we can plug it in to solve for y. You don't have to plug in to both equations; one equation is sufficient to find y. Here, we will show the work for both:

$y = x + 5$	$y = (\frac{3}{2})x + 3$
$y = 4 + 5$	$y = (\frac{3}{2})(4) + 3$
$y = 9$	$y = \frac{12}{2} + 3$
	$y = 6 + 3$
	$y = 9$

The solution to this system is (4, 9). The figure below shows the graphs of both equations. Notice that the solution (4, 9) is where the two lines intersect.

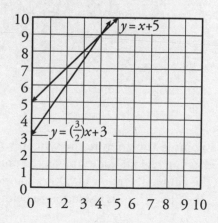

You should know these rules for the number of solutions in a system:

- If two distinct lines are **not parallel**, then they intersect exactly **once**, and their equations have **one solution**. To intersect, the lines must have **different slopes**.

  The equations $y = 3x + 8$ and $y = 2x - 5$ have *one solution*.

- If two lines are **parallel**, then they do **not intersect**, and their equations have **no solution**. To be parallel, the lines must have the **same slope**, but **different y-intercepts**.

  The equations $y = 3x + 5$ and $y = 3x - 9$ have *no solution*.

- If two lines have the **same slope** and the **same y-intercept**, then they are actually the **same line**. The two equations are **equivalent**, and they have an **infinite number of solutions**.

  The equations $y = 4x + 3$ and $2y = 8x + 6$ are the *same line*. (Note: What happens when you divide the second equation by 2?)

Systems of Inequalities

A **system of inequalities** is a set of two or more inequalities that are solved together. Systems of inequalities often have an *infinite number* of solutions. In a graph, the **solution** is where the shaded regions overlap.

The figure below shows the graphs of two inequalities. The solution is where the two shaded regions overlap.

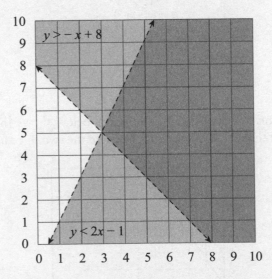

To determine whether a point is a solution to the system, you can check to see if the point lies in the overlapping region. For example, the point (8, 5) is a solution to the system shown in the figure. The point (4, 2) is a solution to only *one* of the inequalities ($y < 2x - 1$). The point (1, 4) is a solution to neither.

Recall that every line has an infinite number of points. The phrase "infinite number of solutions" does not mean that *every point in the coordinate plane* is a solution. Rather, it refers to the infinite number of points *on the line*.

You can also plug in to both inequalities. Let's try plugging in (8, 5):

$y > -x + 8$
$5 > -8 + 8$
$5 > 0$ True.

$y < 2x - 1$
$5 < 2(8) - 1$
$5 < 16 - 1$
$5 < 15$ True.

Since the point (8, 5) makes both inequalities true, it is a solution to both inequalities.

Functions

A **function** is a mathematical relationship that takes an **input** (the value that "goes into" the function) and produces an **output** (the value that "comes out of" the function). An example of function notation is the following:

$$f(x) = x + 9$$

The f in $f(x)$ is the **name** of the function. A function can also have different names, like g or h. The name of a function does not represent a variable, or multiplication. Think of $f(x)$ as "We have a function and we're going to call it f. Here's what f does to x."

The (x) in parentheses represents the *input*—it's a variable for any number that can go into the function. (Note that the variable doesn't have to be x). The expression after the parentheses represents the *output*—it's what the function "does" to the input. In the example above, the function f takes the input x, and simply adds 9 to it. The output is $x + 9$.

There is a rule for functions:

Each input must have exactly one output.

A function cannot produce two or more outputs for the same input. If a relationship does not follow this rule, then it is not a function. Instead you can use the broader term **relation**. Examples of relations might simply be plots of data. For instance, there is no *function* relationship between a person's height and their weight—people with the same height can have many different weights.

The Vertical Line Test

Functions and relations can be graphed in the coordinate plane. The input is on the *x*-axis, and the output is on the *y*-axis. The **vertical line test** is a way to identify graphs of *functions*. It means that if a straight vertical line can pass through more than one point of the graph, then the graph is not a function. (Horizontal lines, however, can cross more than once.)

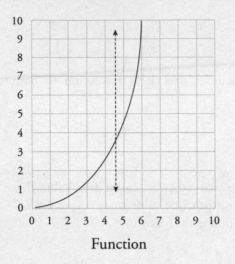
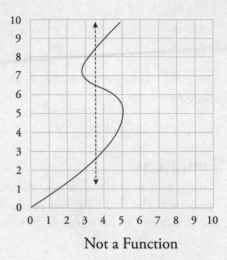

Function   Not a Function

The graph on the left is a function; there is only one output for any one input. The graph on the right is not a function; some inputs have more than one output.

GEOMETRY

Another math topic you will likely encounter on the Praxis Core Math Test is geometry. This is a large category, so let's cover the key geometry concepts separately.

Lines and Angles

Let's review some terms.

Lines

A straight line extends forever in both directions. A **line** is named by any two points on it, in either order. For instance, the line below could be named *AB*, *BC*, *AC*, *BA*, *CB*, or *CA*. The arrows tell you the line extends past what is drawn.

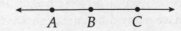

Line Segments

A **line segment** is a finite section of a line with endpoints at either end. Line segments are named by their endpoints. In the line above, *AB* is an example of a line segment.

Parallel Lines

Parallel lines are lines that never intersect. The symbol ∥ means parallel.

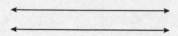

Perpendicular Lines

Perpendicular lines meet at a 90-degree angle. The symbol ⊥ means perpendicular. The lines below are perpendicular. In the figure below, the ⌐ symbol means that the lines meet at a 90-degree angle, which also means that the lines are perpendicular.

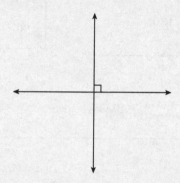

Rays

A **ray** has one endpoint, but extends infinitely in the other direction. A ray is named by its endpoint and any other point on it. The ray below could be named *PQ* or *PR*.

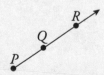

Angles

When two lines, line segments, or rays intersect, **angles** are formed. The point of intersection is called a **vertex.** Angles are named with the vertex point in the middle.

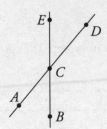

A straight line, which can also be called a **straight angle,** measures 180 degrees. A 90-degree angle is called a **right angle.**

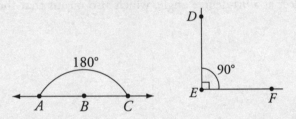

Try applying what you've reviewed so far:

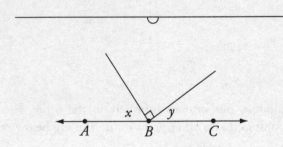

What is the value of x in terms of y ?

○ $90 + y$

○ $90 - y$

○ $180 - y$

○ $180 + y$

○ $360 - y$

Here's How to Crack It

A straight line has 180 degrees, so $x + y$ + the right angle = 180. Because a right angle has 90 degrees, we know that $x + y + 90 = 180$, or $x + y = 90$. We want the value of x in terms of y, so subtract y from both sides. That leaves $x = 90 - y$, and the best answer is (B).

Polygons

A **polygon** is a closed plane figure made up of at least three straight lines. Both triangles and rectangles are examples of polygons.

Triangles

A **triangle** is a three-sided closed figure. The sum of the interior angles of a triangle is 180 degrees. **Equilateral triangles** have equal side lengths, and each angle measure is 60 degrees. **Isosceles triangles** have two equal sides, and the angles opposite those sides are equal in measure. **Right triangles** contain one right angle. The side opposite the right angle (always the longest side of a right triangle) is called the **hypotenuse**. The other sides of a right triangle are called *legs*.

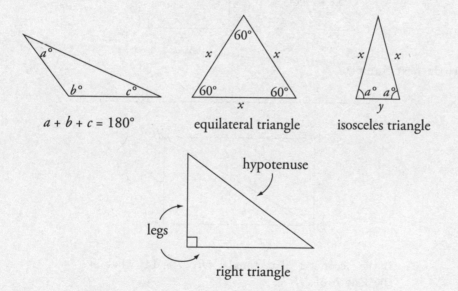

$a + b + c = 180°$ equilateral triangle   isosceles triangle

right triangle

The Pythagorean Theorem

There's one important formula to know about right triangles: the **Pythagorean Theorem,** which states that the sum of the squares of the legs equals the square of the hypotenuse.

$$a^2 + b^2 = c^2$$

In the right triangle below, $3^2 + 4^2 = 5^2$. In the triangle next to it, $5^2 + 12^2 = 13^2$.

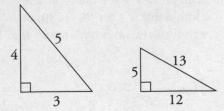

Rectangles

A **rectangle** is a four-sided closed figure with four right angles. The opposite sides are parallel and equal in length to each other. If all four sides of a rectangle are of equal length, the rectangle becomes a square.

Perimeter

The **perimeter** of a figure is the sum of the lengths of all sides of that figure. The perimeter of the triangle below is 12 (3 + 4 + 5). The perimeter of the rectangle next to it is 20 (7 + 3 + 7 + 3).

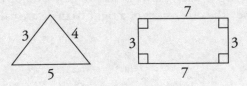

Try the next example.

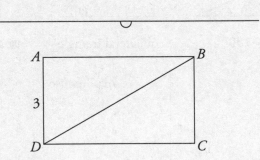

If the perimeter of rectangle *ABCD* is 14, what is the length of *BD* ?

- ○ 3
- ○ 4
- ○ 5
- ○ 8
- ○ 14

Here's How to Crack It

The perimeter is the sum of all four sides, so $AB + BC + CD + AD = 14$. Remember that the opposite sides of a rectangle are equal in length. If $AD = 3$, then BC also equals 3. So we have $AB + 3 + CD + 3 = 14$, or $AB + CD = 8$. We know that AB and CD are equal too, so they must both equal 4. Now, use the Pythagorean Theorem, which says that $3^2 + 4^2 = BD^2$. So $9 + 16 = BD^2$, or $BD^2 = 25$, so $BD = 5$. The best answer is (C).

Area and Volume

Area is the measurement of the amount of flat space enclosed by a figure. Area is always expressed in square units (e.g., square inches, square feet). The formula for the area of a rectangle is $A = lw$, where l is the length of the rectangle and w is the width. The area for the rectangle below is $7 \times 3 = 21$. The area of the square next to it is $5 \times 5 = 25$ (which is also why that amount is called "five squared" or 5^2).

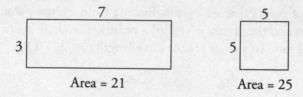

Area = 21   Area = 25

The formula for the area of a triangle is $A = \dfrac{1}{2}bh$, where b is the base of the triangle and h is the height of the triangle. The height of the triangle is always measured by dropping a perpendicular line from the high point of the triangle to the line containing the base. The area of the triangle below is $\dfrac{1}{2} \times 6 \times 5 = 15$.

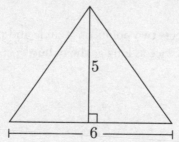

Volume is the measurement of the three-dimensional space closed by a figure. Volume is expressed in cubic units (e.g., cubic feet, cubic meters). The formula for the volume of a box is $V = lwh$, where l is the length, w is the width, and h is the height. The volume of the box below is $3 \times 4 \times 5 = 60$.

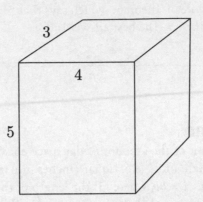

Circles

A **circle** is a set of points that are a given distance from a given point. The point is called the **center,** and the distance is called a **radius**. The circle below has center O and radius 4. All radii in a circle are the same length, so $OP = OQ$.

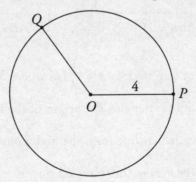

A line segment that connects two points on a circle and passes through the center is called a **diameter.** It is twice as long as the radius.

Finding the Area and Circumference of Circles

The formula for the area of a circle is $A = \pi r^2$, where r is the length of the radius. The area of the circle below is $\pi \times 3^2$, or 9π.

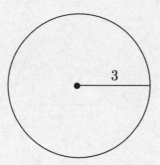

Try this example, which combines your knowledge of both triangles and circles.

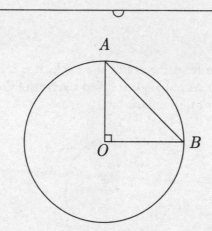

If the area of the circle is 16π, what is the area of triangle AOB ?

- ○ 4
- ○ 8
- ○ 4π
- ○ 16
- ○ 8π

Here's How to Crack It

If the area of the circle is 16π, the radius must be 4. Because the radius of the circle is the length of the line from the center to any point on the circle, both AO and BO must equal 4. AOB is a right triangle, so AO is the height if BO is the base. The area of the triangle is therefore $\frac{1}{2} \times 4 \times 4 = 8$. The best answer is (B).

The **circumference** of a circle is the distance you would travel if you were to walk around its edge. You can think of circumference as the perimeter of a circle. The formula for the circumference of a circle is $C = 2\pi r$, where r is the length of the radius. The circle below (the same one from page 142) with radius = 4 has a circumference of $(2)(\pi)(4) = 8\pi$.

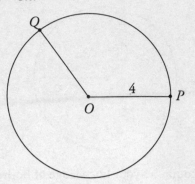

Arcs

When an angle is drawn from the center of a circle, it is called a **central angle**. The region bound by the central angle is called a **sector** of the circle. A portion of a circle's circumference is called an **arc**.

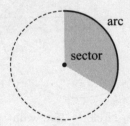

To solve problems involving arcs or sectors, use a proportion.

$$\frac{\text{part}}{\text{whole}} = \frac{\text{central angle}}{360°} = \frac{\text{arc length}}{\substack{\text{total circumference} \\ (2\pi r)}} = \frac{\text{sector area}}{\substack{\text{total area} \\ (\pi r^2)}}$$

You can solve for ALL of these parts if you have just two pieces of information: something that tells you the size of the full circle, and something that tells you the size of the "slice."

Here's an example.

A survey showed that 40% of people voted for Candidate Y in an election. If a circle graph is made to represent the results, what is the degree measure of the sector representing the people who voted for Candidate Y?

Here's How to Crack It

Note: a "circle graph" is otherwise known as a "pie chart." This question is essentially asking, "What is the degree measure of 40% of a circle?" We can use a proportion. The $\frac{\text{part}}{\text{whole}}$ relationship is 40%, or $\frac{40}{100}$. We need to solve for the central angle, so use the relationship $\frac{\text{central angle}}{360°}$. Let's use the variable x to represent the central angle.

$$\frac{\text{part}}{\text{whole}} = \frac{\text{central angle}}{360°}$$

$$\frac{40}{100} = \frac{x}{360}$$

Cross-multiply and then divide both sides by 100 to get

$$100x = 14,400$$

$$x = 144$$

The measure of the central angle is 144°.

Try another one.

If a pizza has a radius of 8 inches, and is sliced into 10 congruent pieces, what is the area (in square inches) of each piece?

Here's How to Crack It

We know the radius, which means that we can also find both the area and the circumference of the pizza. We need to find the area of one piece, so we'll start with the relationship $\dfrac{\text{sector area}}{\text{total area}}$. We also know that the $\dfrac{\text{part}}{\text{whole}}$ relationship is $\dfrac{1}{10}$ (the problem says that the pizza is sliced into 10 congruent pieces). Let's use the variable x to represent the sector area.

$$\frac{\text{sector area}}{\text{total area}} = \frac{1}{10}$$

$$\frac{x}{\pi r^2} = \frac{1}{10}$$

$$\frac{x}{\pi \times 8^2} = \frac{1}{10} \qquad \text{Substitute 8 for } r.$$

$$\frac{x}{\pi \times 64} = \frac{1}{10}$$

$$\frac{x}{\pi} = \frac{64}{10} \qquad \text{Multiply both sides by 64.}$$

$$x = \frac{\pi \times 64}{10} \qquad \text{Multiply both sides by } \pi.$$

$$x = \pi \times 6.4 \qquad \text{Simplify.}$$

The area of the sector is 6.4π square inches, or approximately 20.11 square inches.

Tangent Lines

A line is **tangent** to a circle if it touches the circle at exactly one point. The radius that intersects the point of tangency is **perpendicular** to the tangent line. If a question mentions a tangent line, it will be important to remember this definition.

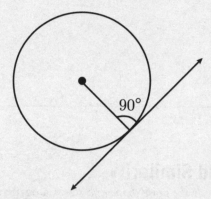

Try the following question.

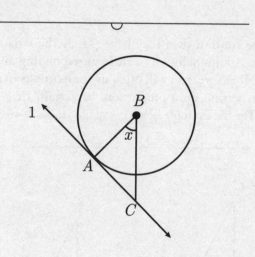

Line 1 is tangent to circle B at point A. If segment AB is congruent to segment AC, what is the measure of angle x, in degrees?

Here's How to Crack It

Since line 1 is tangent to the circle, we know that it is perpendicular to the radius AB. Therefore, the measure of BAC is 90°.

Additionally, since segments AB and AC are congruent we know that triangle ABC is isosceles. Since it is isosceles, then the angles ABC and ACB are congruent. You can use $180 - 90 = 2x$ to find x.

$$180° - 90° = 2x$$
$$90 = 2x$$
$$x = 45$$

The measure of angle x is 45°.

Congruence and Similarity

Congruent means *exactly the same shape and size*. Congruent angles have the same measure, and congruent segments have the same length. If two polygons are congruent, that means that each pair of corresponding angles and side lengths is congruent.

If two figures are **similar**, then they have exactly the same shape, but they may be different sizes. Additionally, all of their corresponding angles and side lengths are *proportional*. Therefore, you will often use proportions to solve questions about similarity. When setting up a proportion, be certain that you are using corresponding sides. Try the example below.

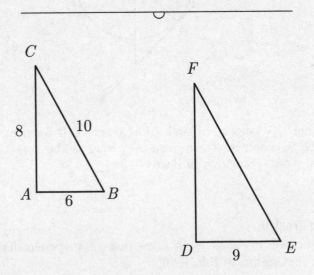

In the figure above, if triangle ABC is similar to triangle DEF, what is the length of segment DF?

Here's How to Crack It

Since the triangles are similar, we can use a proportion. The corresponding side lengths that we can use are DF (unknown) with AC (8), and DE (9) with AB (6). Let's use the variable x to represent side length DF.

$$\frac{x}{8} = \frac{9}{6}$$

$$6x = 9 \times 8$$

$$x = \frac{9 \times 8}{6}$$

$$x = \frac{72}{6}$$

$$x = 12$$

You should also know the following rules about angles, as these are often used as a means of testing for congruence and similarity.

Properties of Angles

The two main angle terms you should know are:

> **Supplementary angles**—Two angles whose measures have a sum of 180°
>
> **Complementary angles**—Two angles whose measures have a sum of 90°

Here are some other key angle properties.

Vertical Angles

Whenever two lines intersect, they form two pairs of congruent angles. The angles opposite each other (known as **vertical angles**) are congruent. In the figure on the next page, angles A and C are vertical angles, and angles B and D are vertical angles.

The adjacent angles are *supplementary*. Angles *A* and *B* are supplementary, *B* and *C* are supplementary, and so on.

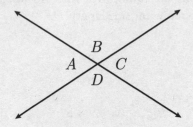

Transversals

A **transversal** is a line that intersects two other lines. Whenever a transversal intersects two *parallel* lines, there are several pairs of congruent angles, as discussed below.

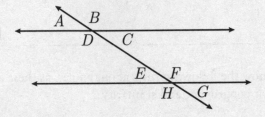

Corresponding angles in the above figure are congruent. These are angles that are in the "same spot" relative to each parallel line. In the figure above, the following angle pairs are corresponding:

    A and *E*   *B* and *F*   *C* and *G*   *D* and *H*

Alternate interior angles in the figure are also congruent. These are angles that are on opposite corners in the interior of the parallel lines. In the figure above, the following angle pairs are alternate interior angles:

    C and *E*   *D* and *F*

Additionally, adjacent angles in the figure are *supplementary*. Angles *A* and *B* are supplementary, angles *B* and *C* are supplementary, and so on. Overall, this means that the following angles are congruent:

    A, *C*, *E*, and *G* are congruent.

    B, *D*, *F*, and *H* are congruent.

When you are presented with two parallel lines crossed by a transversal, look at the two different angle measures represented. If one is obviously bigger than the other, that makes the whole thing easier! All of the "big" angles are congruent to each other, and all of the "small" angles are congruent to each other.

STATISTICS AND PROBABILITY

The last major category we'll cover in this section is statistics and probability. The relevant topics that might pop up on the test include mean, median, mode, and range; probability (independent and dependent events); graphs like pie charts and histograms; and samples. Let's get to it!

Mean, Median, Mode, and Range

On the test you will likely see questions about sets of numbers. A set can look like this, {1, 3, 7, 9}, or it can be described in context (e.g., a list of test scores). There are four values you need to be able to find with respect to sets.

Mean (or Arithmetic Mean)

The **mean** is also known as the **average.** To find the mean, add all of the elements of a set together and divide by the number of elements in the set. To find the mean of the set {1, 7, 3, 9}, first find the total: $1 + 3 + 7 + 9 = 20$. Then, divide by the number of elements in the set: $\frac{20}{4} = 5$. The average of the set {1, 7, 3, 9} is 5.

Median

The **median** is the middle number in the set when the elements of the set are placed in order from smallest to largest. If the set contains an odd number of elements, the median is the number that is in the middle. For example, to find the median of the set $\left\{5, \ -1, \ 0, \ -4, \ -\frac{1}{2}\right\}$, you'd first arrange the elements in order: $\left\{-4, \ -1, \ -\frac{1}{2}, \ 0, \ 5\right\}$. Then, pick the middle one: $-\frac{1}{2}$. If there is an even number of elements, the rules change slightly. In that case, the median is the average of the middle two numbers after the set is ordered. So, to find the median of the set {1, 7, 3, 9}, you'd order the set: {1, 3, 7, 9}, and then take the average of the middle two numbers. $\frac{3+7}{2} = 5$. So the median of the set {1, 7, 3, 9} is 5.

Here is an interesting rule regarding mean and median:

If a set of numbers is *consecutive*, then the mean and median are equal.

Consecutive numbers are in order from smallest to largest with no missing numbers. For example, {1, 2, 3, 4, 5} is a set of consecutive numbers. Consecutive numbers can also be in a pattern, such as {5, 10, 15, 20, 25}.

For example, in the set {10, 20, 30, 40, 50}, we can find that the median is 30. And according to the rule above, we also know that the *mean* is 30, since the set is consecutive numbers. This can save time on some questions involving mean and median!

This rule is also very helpful when calculating the *sum* of a consecutive list. Since we can find the mean easily, we can also find the sum, using the relationship $mean = \frac{total}{count}$. Let's see how we can quickly calculate the sum of a consecutive set. Look at the following example.

What is the sum of the set of integers from 1 to 25 ?

Here's How to Crack It

We could calculate the sum by hand, by adding all 25 numbers, but that would take a lot of time. Let's find the median first.

{1, 2, 3, 4, 5, 6, 7, 8, 9, 10, 11, 12, 13, 14, 15, 16, 17, 18, 19, 20, 21, 22, 23, 24, 25}

The median of the set is 13. Since the set is consecutive numbers, the mean is also 13.

Use the relationship $mean = \frac{total}{count}$ to find the sum:

$$mean \times count = total$$

$$13 \times 25 = 325$$

The sum of the set is 325.

Mode

The **mode** is the element member that occurs *most* frequently in a list. For instance, the mode of the list {−1, −1, 3, 5, 7, −4, 5, −1} is −1, because −1 appears the *most* (three times in the list).

Range

To find the **range** of a set, take the largest element member in the set and subtract the smallest member. That result is the range. For example, the range of the set {1, 7, 3, 9} is 8, because 9 − 1 = 8.

Try this one:

───────────────○───────────────

What is sum of the average, range, and median of the set {3, 5, 7} ?

- ○ 15
- ○ 14
- ○ 7
- ○ 5
- ○ 3

Here's How to Crack It

The average of the set is $\dfrac{3+5+7}{3} = \dfrac{15}{3} = 5$.

The range of the set is 7 − 3 = 4, and the median of the set is 5. 5 + 4 + 5 = 14, which is (B).

───────────────○───────────────

Probability

You can expect to see a few questions involving probability on the test. The **probability** of an event occurring is expressed as a fraction or a percentage, always between 0 (meaning that there's no chance of the event occurring) and 1 (meaning that the event will definitely occur). To calculate a probability, fill in the following fraction:

$$\frac{\text{The number of ways the event can occur}}{\text{The total number of possible outcomes}}$$

For instance, let's say you want to calculate the probability of drawing a queen at random from a full deck of cards. Because there are four queens in the deck, there are four ways the event (drawing a queen) could occur. Because there are 52 cards in the deck, there are 52 possible outcomes. Therefore, the probability of drawing a queen is $\frac{4}{52}$, or $\frac{1}{13}$.

There's one other important idea about probability: the probability of an event *not* happening is equal to 1 minus the probability of the event happening. For instance, if there's a 30% chance of rain, there's a 1 − 30% or 70% chance of it *not* raining.

> *The probability that an event WILL NOT occur =*
> *1 − the probability that the event WILL occur*

Try this question:

What is the probability that on a single roll of a fair die the result will NOT be a multiple of three?

- ○ $\frac{1}{6}$
- ○ $\frac{1}{3}$
- ○ $\frac{1}{2}$
- ○ $\frac{2}{3}$
- ○ $\frac{5}{6}$

Here's How to Crack It

There are six outcomes possible, the numbers 1 through 6. Of those, the numbers 3 and 6 are the only multiples of 3, so there are two ways of getting a multiple of 3. However, the questions asks to find the probability that the result will NOT be a multiple of 3, so write:

$$1 - \frac{2}{6} = \frac{4}{6} = \frac{2}{3}$$

The answer is (D).

Independent Events

If events are **independent** of one another, it means that the outcome of the first event does *not* affect the outcome of the second. Examples of independent events include most random chance events, such as flipping a coin. To calculate the probability of two independent events happening together, multiply their two probabilities:

$$Probability(A \text{ and } B) = Probability(A) \times Probability(B)$$

Try an example.

At the Riverwood Trader, there is a 15% probability that food items are on sale. There is also a 22% probability that clothing items are on sale. What is the probability that food items *and* clothing items are on sale at the same time?

Here's How to Crack It

Since the events are independent, multiply the two probabilities together:

$$15\% \times 22\%$$

$$0.15 \times 0.22 = 0.033$$

The probability of both sales happening together is 0.033, or 3.3%.

Dependent Events

Events are **dependent** if the outcome of one event affects the outcome of the other. A common example of dependent events is removing objects from a set *without replacement*. Since objects have been removed, this affects the probability when you remove another object.

To calculate the probability of two dependent events happening together, multiply their two probabilities, taking into account the outcome of the first event:

*Probability(A and B) = Probability(A) × Probability(B **after** A)*

Here's a question for you to try.

A candy jar contains 24 strawberry candies, 16 peppermint candies, and 15 butterscotch candies. If two candies are chosen at random, what is the probability that both candies are butterscotch?

Here's How to Crack It

These events are *dependent*. If you remove a candy from the jar, then the number of candies has changed, so the probability changes for the second candy. Here's how to calculate the two probabilities:

The probability that the first candy is butterscotch is $\dfrac{15}{total\ candies}$. Calculate the total candies: 24 + 16 + 15 = 55. Therefore, the probability that the first candy is butterscotch is $\dfrac{15}{55}$, or $\dfrac{3}{11}$. After removing the first candy, there are now 54 total candies remaining, 14 of which are butterscotch. Therefore, the probability that the second candy is butterscotch is $\dfrac{14}{54}$, or $\dfrac{7}{27}$.

Multiply the two probabilities:

$$\left(\frac{3}{11}\right) \times \left(\frac{7}{27}\right) =$$

$$\frac{21}{297} = \frac{7}{99}$$

The probability that both candies are butterscotch is $\dfrac{7}{99}$.

Charts and Graphs

You're likely to see many questions on the Praxis Core Math Test that ask you to interpret data on charts and graphs. We'll review the most common graphs you'll see and show you some sample questions so you can see how you'll be expected to apply your knowledge.

Bar Graphs

One common type of graph is a bar graph, in which data is arranged next to each other for ease of comparison. Look at the following bar graph and answer the questions that follow.

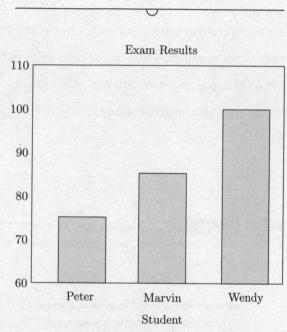

Exam Results

Wendy's score is approximately how many points greater than Marvin's score?

- ○ 5
- ○ 10
- ○ 15
- ○ 20
- ○ 25

Here's How to Crack It

This problem is very straightforward, but it's easy to make a careless mistake either by misreading the student's name or by misreading the score scale on the left. Just read the information on the graph and perform the necessary calculation. In this case, Wendy scored 100 and Marvin scored about 85, because the column corresponding to Marvin's score is about halfway between 80 and 90. 100 − 85 = 15, which is the correct answer.

Try another.

> Wendy's score is approximately what percent greater than Peter's?
>
> ○ 10%
>
> ○ 25%
>
> ○ 33%
>
> ○ 50%
>
> ○ 75%

Here's How to Crack It

Use the formula for percent change discussed earlier in the chapter. To find the *percent change* between two numbers, you need to determine the original number and the difference between the two numbers. The difference between the two scores is 100 − 75 = 25. The original score (Peter's) is 75. $\frac{25}{75} = \frac{1}{3}$, which is approximately 33%.

Circle Graphs (Pie Charts)

Pie charts are useful for comparing different data that, taken together, form a whole. Look at the following chart:

Jeremy's household expenditures as a percentage of monthly income

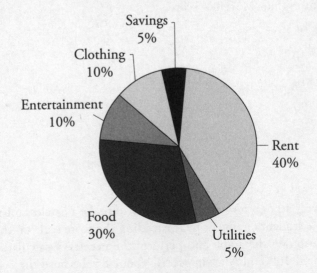

Notice that the sum of the percentages is 100 (40 + 5 + 30 + 10 + 10 + 5 = 100). With a pie chart, the pieces will always add up to a whole. You can expect questions that ask you to compare percentages and read numbers. Try these:

---○---

If Jeremy spent $100 on utilities in a certain month, how much did he spend on clothing?

- ○ $10
- ○ $50
- ○ $100
- ○ $200
- ○ $500

Here's How to Crack It

According to the chart, Jeremy spent 5% of his income on utilities and 10% of his income of clothing. Because 10% is twice 5%, he spent twice as much money on clothing as he did on utilities. He spent $100 on utilities, so he must have spent $200 on clothing. The best answer is (D).

What is Jeremy's monthly income if he spends $720 on food each month?

- ○ $216
- ○ $2,400
- ○ $7,200
- ○ $14,400
- ○ $21,600

Here's How to Crack It

This one's a little tougher, but here's how to tackle it. Food costs constitute 30% of his income, so the answer has to be bigger than $720. Eliminate (A). One way you can approach the problem from here is to say that if 30% of Jeremy's income is $720, then 100% of his income should be a little bit more than 3 times $720. We know that $3 \times 720 = 2,160$, and (B) is a little more than that. Furthermore, all the other choices besides (A) are much larger. Another way to approach the problem is to notice that (C) is $7,200. If $7,200 was Jeremy's total monthly income, $720 would be 10% of it, so (C) must be too large. Because we've already eliminated (A), (B) must be the correct answer.

---○---

If this seems like trickery to you, and you feel that you should be setting up an equation to solve a problem like this, you need to adjust your thinking. While there are some problems on the test that may require algebraic manipulation, this is primarily a test of numerical reasoning rather than mathematical skills. If reasoning can get you to the right answer without tedious calculation, then use reasoning.

Histograms

A **histogram** is similar to a bar graph. It is commonly used to show the **frequency** of different values in a data set.

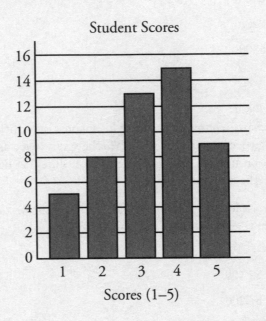

Student Scores

This histogram shows the number of students who achieved each score. (5 students scored 1, 8 students scored 2, and so on.)

If you were asked to find the *average score* from the data shown above, you would need to calculate the total score count, and divide by the total number of students. The data, written as a list, looks like this:

{1, 1, 1, 1, 1, 2, 2, 2, 2, 2, 2, 2, 2, 3, 3, 3, 3, 3, 3, 3, 3, 3, 3, 3, 3, 3, 4, 4, 4, 4, 4, 4, 4, 4, 4, 4, 4, 4, 4, 4, 4, 5, 5, 5, 5, 5, 5, 5, 5, 5}

Written as a table, the data looks like this:

Score	Frequency
1	5
2	8
3	13
4	15
5	9

To find the total more efficiently, use multiplication.

$$1 \times 5 = 5$$
$$2 \times 8 = 16$$
$$3 \times 13 = 39$$
$$4 \times 15 = 60$$
$$5 \times 9 = 45$$

Add the products together:

$$5 + 16 + 39 + 60 + 45 = 165$$

Calculate the total number of students:

$$5 + 8 + 13 + 15 + 9 = 50$$

To find the average, divide the total by the number of students.

$$165 \div 50 = 3.3$$

The average student score is 3.3.

Samples

When we need to gather data about a very large group, it may be difficult or impossible to survey every single member of the group. In these cases, we would use a **sample**—a smaller group of data that is used to form a conclusion about a larger group. For example, before an election, a newspaper might conduct a **survey** to ask a few thousand people whom they intend to vote for. Based on this smaller group of people, the newspaper might conclude that the winner in the survey is likely to be the winner in the real upcoming election.

For a survey to be accurate, it needs to be **random** and not biased. In the example of a national election, it would be necessary to gather results from different people all over the country. If you conducted a survey in a candidate's hometown, for instance, you might find that the residents are disproportionately loyal to that candidate because of their shared hometown. If you surveyed only teachers, you might find that the results are skewed based on the candidate's specific policies on education. The results would not be accurate to predict the outcome of the election.

Look at the following example.

A transportation director wishes to survey bus riders to determine whether improvements are needed for the bus system in the city. Which of the following samples would be the most representative of the director's targeted group?

○ A survey of all riders on a randomly selected full bus on a Monday morning

○ A random sample of all city residents who have ridden the bus at least once

○ A random sample from all bus riders who use the bus for their daily commute

○ A random sample from all bus riders who reported that ride times were too long

○ A random sample from all registered vehicle owners in the city

---

Here's How to Crack It

The director wishes to survey the opinions of bus riders in the city. Use Process of Elimination to get rid of answers that would produce biased results.

Eliminate (A). This sample would be limited to riders on a full bus at a particular time of the week. There would be no useful information about riding conditions at other times, such as weekends. You can also eliminate (C), as this sample would be limited to daily commuters, whose opinions are likely to be different from occasional riders, or those who use the bus for traveling, and so on. Eliminate (D) because this sample would be limited to riders who already have a negative opinion about the bus system. The results are likely to indicate that improvements are necessary, which may not be the case. Finally, eliminate (E) because this sample would be skewed toward people who own vehicles, and are less likely to ride the bus. It would likely exclude the opinions of regular bus riders, such as commuters. The correct answer is (B): this sample would be randomized to target a mixed group of residents who have at least some experience riding the bus. The sample would include some commuters, some occasional riders, and so on, which is likely to be representative of the director's targeted group.

The Praxis Core Math Test covers a broad range of topics. As you continue to study and practice for the exam, it will be helpful to revisit this chapter to make sure you remember important concepts. For now, try the drill on the next page. Use the explanations at the end of the chapter to assess your strengths as well as identify the topics you may need to re-review.

Expanded Explanations, Alternative Approaches

There's usually more than one way to solve a math problem, which is why we created an online supplement filled with alternative approaches to several questions in this book, including practice test questions. Just register your book to download this bonus material!

MATH DRILL

Answers and explanations can be found at the end of the chapter.

What is the difference between 2.5 and .167 ?

- ○ 0.83
- ○ 2
- ○ 2.333
- ○ 2.667
- ○ 4.17

Hugo and Aaron played volleyball for a total of 63 hours in June, and for 89 hours in July. How many more hours did they play in July than the average of hours played in June and July?

- ○ 6 hours
- ○ 13 hours
- ○ 26 hours
- ○ 63 hours
- ○ 89 hours

Dale is flipping a coin. On the first five throws, heads has appeared every time. What is the probability that the next flip will appear as tails?

- ○ $\frac{1}{6}$
- ○ $\frac{1}{5}$
- ○ $\frac{1}{3}$
- ○ $\frac{1}{2}$
- ○ $\frac{5}{6}$

In his programming class, Chris took three tests. He scored a 78 on his first test, and a 90 on his second test. If Chris had an average of 81 in his class, what did Chris score on his third test?

- ○ 75
- ○ 81
- ○ 83
- ○ 90
- ○ 243

$10y - 36 + 4y - 6 + y = 3$. What is the value of y ?

- ○ 3
- ○ 4
- ○ 6
- ○ 10
- ○ 36

Judy owns 387 stickers. If she were to purchase three times that amount, approximately how many stickers would she then own?

- ○ 400
- ○ 1,200
- ○ 1,550
- ○ 2,000
- ○ 3,870

Which of the payments shown below is greatest?

○ 5% of 500

○ 25% of 50

○ 50% of 5

○ 50% of 25

○ 25% of 5% of 500

Candidate	Votes Received
Lyn	150
Jolene	10
Brian	80
Adam	?
TOTAL	300

Using the chart above, which of the following statements is true?

○ Adam received the most votes.

○ Brian received 50 more votes than Adam.

○ Jolene did not receive the smallest number of votes.

○ Adam received 15 more votes than the average number of votes Brian and Jolene received.

○ Adam received 10 less than half the number of votes Lyn received.

MATH DRILL ANSWERS AND EXPLANATIONS

1. **C**   When subtracting decimals, be sure to align the decimals vertically, as shown below:

$$2.500$$
$$-\ \ .167$$
$$=2.333$$

2. **B**   The question requires that you know the average number of hours played in June and July. To find an average, take the total (152 hours), and divide by the number of things (2 months). The average is 76 hours per month. To answer question, subtract 76 from the number of hours played in July (89): $89 - 76 = 13$.

3. **D**   Flipping a coin is an independent event. Prior outcomes do not influence the next event. Dale could have flipped 100 coins that all appear as heads, but that will not change the probability of the next flip (even though this feat is incredibly rare). There are two outcomes—heads or tails, and we want to know one possible event—tails. Therefore, the probably is $\frac{1}{2}$.

4. **A**   Start by finding the total score on all three tests. The average is 81, and there are 3 things, so the total is 243 (beware of (E) as a partial answer). Subtracting the first two test scores from 243 yields 75. Note that is a question you can likely estimate. Before his third test, Chris had an average over 81, so his score must be below 81 on the third test. Choice (A) is the only possible answer choice.

5. **A**   Simplify the equation to get

$$15y - 42 = 3$$
$$15y = 45$$
$$y = 3$$

6. **C**   The question asks you approximately how many stickers Judy would own, so approximate! She has around 400 now. Three times that amount is 1,200. The total amount of stickers is the sum of these two numbers—around 1,600. Choice (C) is the correct answer. Be careful about (B), which is a partial answer.

7. **A**   Try to estimate these types of questions so that you do not waste time doing needless calculations. Choice (C) should be eliminated immediately—it is visibly less than (D), which is the same percentage, but of a larger number. Further, you should spot that (E) is less than (A). Doing the calculations, you will find that (A) = 25, while (B) and (D) equal 12.5.

8. **D**   First, find the total number of votes Adam received. If you subtract 300 from the total of votes listed in the chart, you will find that Adam received 60 votes. From this, you can eliminate (A), (B), and (C) without doing any calculations. The average number of votes Brian and Jolene received is 45 (90 divided by 2). This is 15 less than the number Adam received.

Part III
Praxis Core
Practice Tests

Chapter 6
Reading Practice
Test 1

READING

Praxis Core Academic Skills for Educators

Reading

Time—85 minutes

56 Questions

Thermal maturity is one of the factors that indicates whether or not coal or petroleum have formed from their source rocks. As sedimentary rock layers are laid down, the organic material undergoes heat and pressure. After enough time has passed, and if other conditions are right, the organic material can become coal or petroleum.

According to the statement above, what promotes thermal maturity?

- Petroleum
- Weather conditions
- Age of the materials
- Coal
- Heat and pressure

The American public and the transportation community depend on the National Transportation Safety Board (NTSB) to fulfill its mission, not only in the wake of an accident, but also to be proactive through the Board's advocacy role and by conducting safety studies. Additionally, the NTSB has an important role in assisting victims and their families in the wake of transportation disasters. The NTSB must also keep up with emerging technologies in transportation, which have the potential to dramatically improve safety, but may present challenges, as well.

According to the statement above, the NTSB is responsible for

- investigating ways to prevent transportation disasters
- notifying families of victims about transportation disasters
- cleaning up debris in the wake of an accident
- investigating all transportation accidents nationwide
- creating new technologies that promote safety

The Law Enforcement Torch Run for the Special Olympics raises awareness and funds for the Special Olympics movement. Each year, law enforcement officers and Special Olympics athletes carry the "Flame of Hope" into Opening Ceremonies of local competitions. The Law Enforcement Torch Run began in 1981 in Wichita, Kansas, as a way to involve local law enforcement with Special Olympics. Today, it has grown into the largest grassroots fundraising effort in the worldwide Special Olympics movement. Approximately 97,000 law enforcement officers in 46 countries have raised more than $600 million since its inception.

Which of the following best states the main idea of the statement?

- The Law Enforcement Torch Run is the Special Olympics' only source of revenue.
- The Law Enforcement Torch Run is the oldest Special Olympics charity event.
- The Law Enforcement Torch Run has raised more money in the history of the Special Olympics than any other organization.
- The Law Enforcement Torch Run is an effective fundraiser for the Special Olympics.
- Many important fundraising efforts begin in Wichita, Kansas.

READING

Questions 4-6 refer to the following passage.

From small towns in rural America to the country's bustling metropolitan centers, older Americans are playing an ever-growing role in
Line   shaping the nation's economy through work.
(5)   Whether they work on farms growing produce, in office buildings developing new technologies, or in hardware stores ringing up customers, aging Americans are a critical and expanding share of the nation's workforce every day.

(10)   With advances in public health and medicine, Americans are living longer and working longer, resulting in an unprecedented transformation of the workplace. The number of Americans over age 55 in the labor force is projected to increase from
(15)   35.7 million in 2016 to 42.1 million in 2026, and, by 2026, aging workers will make up nearly one quarter of the labor force. These significant changes will present tremendous opportunities and challenges. The changing face of the average American worker
(20)   will shape preferences about work and retirement, practices implemented by employers, the composition of the economy, and the direction of public policy. Decisions made by employers and policy makers in response to the aging of the labor force will have
(25)   significant implications for all American workers.

4 of 56

According to the passage, why is the number of older Americans in the workforce on the rise?

- There is more of a need for experienced workers in the technology sector.
- There are greater benefits for extended years of employment.
- The life expectancy of Americans is increasing.
- Older Americans no longer have a preference for retirement.
- Significant decisions made by employers provided opportunities for Americans to work longer.

5 of 56

Which of the following best describes the relationship between the two paragraphs in the passage?

- The first paragraph demonstrates an economic reality, while the second paragraph lists reasons for its demise.
- The first paragraph advocates a business practice, while the second paragraph analyzes the ethics of that practice.
- The first paragraph offers a theory, while the second paragraph highlights ways that theory may be tested.
- The first paragraph lays out a problem, while the second paragraph offers potential solutions for the problem.
- The first paragraph describes a phenomenon, while the second paragraph explains its significance.

6 of 56

The author would likely agree with which of the following statements about older employees?

- Wages will increase to accommodate the needs of older employees.
- Workplaces of the future will look different because of the presence of older employees.
- Older employees make better workers than their younger counterparts due to the difference in experience.
- The number of older employees will decrease after peaking in 2026.
- There is little benefit to having an abundance of older employees.

READING

Dark features previously proposed as evidence for significant liquid water flowing on Mars have now been identified as granular flows, where sand
Line and dust move rather than liquid water. These
(5) new findings indicate that present-day Mars may not have a significant volume of liquid water. Scientists analyzed narrow, down-slope trending surface features on Mars that are darker than their surroundings, called Recurring Slope Lineae, or RSL.
(10) These RSL features grow incrementally, fade when inactive and recur annually during the warmest time of year on Mars. The appearance and growth of these features resemble seeping liquid water, but how they form remains unclear.

7 of 56

Which of the following would be an appropriate title for this passage?

- "Previous Evidence of Water on Mars Confirmed to be Granular Flows"
- "Sand and Dust Found on Mars"
- "Recurring Slope Lineae Found on Mars"
- "Cause of Recurring Slope Lineae Confirmed"
- "Water on Mars Found to Exist in the form of Granular Flows"

8 of 56

What does the passage indicate about Mars?

- There is no water on Mars.
- Water once existed on Mars.
- Mars lacks significant water flow.
- Mars contains more RSL than does other planets.
- Mars's RSL can resemble water flow.

9 of 56

It can be inferred from the passage that

- it was once believed that water was observable on Mars during the warmest time of the year
- recurring Slope Lineae is probably formed by water
- down-slope trending surface features typically resemble sand and dust
- features that appear darker than the rest of the surface are actually water
- the argument for the existence of water on Mars has been debunked

10 of 56

The function of the final sentence in the passage is to

- demonstrate the purpose of seeping liquid water
- explain the material composition of Recurring Slope Lineae
- convey that a topic is in need of further research
- clarify how Recurring Slope Lineae form
- offer a theory that life may, in fact, exist on Mars

11 of 56

According to the passage, why were Recurring Slope Lineae mistaken for water?

- They are composed primarily of ice.
- They fade when they are inactive.
- Their appearance is similar to that of liquid streams.
- Granular flows are typically water-based.
- They grow only incrementally.

READING

Questions 12-14 refer to the following passage.

In the United States, the digital economy
has had a staggering impact on jobs and growth.
Virtually all industry sectors, from manufacturing
Line   to financial services, education, agriculture and
(5)   health care, have benefited from the adoption of
digital technologies, applications, and services. This
remarkable expansion of the digital economy in the
U.S. did not happen by chance. On the contrary,
it is a direct result—first and foremost—of the
(10)   ingenuity and inherent entrepreneurial spirit of the
American people. The United States continually
produces the most innovative companies, founded by
the most creative minds in business and engineering.
Yet the success of American entrepreneurship in the
(15)   digital economy was not a foregone conclusion and
did not occur in a vacuum. Indeed, for the digital
economy to thrive, governments, working in concert
with other stakeholders, must create a legal, policy,
and diplomatic environment conducive to creativity,
(20)   competition, and investment.

12 of 56

Which of the following best describes the organization
of this passage?

- ⒶAn outlier is presented; the reason behind it is
  articulated; and an alternative point of view is
  argued.

- ⒷA historical occurrence is explained; counterpoints
  are given; and a resolution is taken into account.

- ⒸA conundrum is laid out; the author presents a
  tangent; and a resolution concludes the passage.

- ⒹA cautionary take is given; possible course of
  action are analyzed; and preventative measures
  are listed.

- ⒺAn achievement is praised; the reasons for it are
  posited; and factors necessary to such a success
  are enumerated.

13 of 56

Which of the following could be substituted for the
phrase "in a vacuum" in line 16 with the least change
in meaning?

- Ⓐcleanly

- Ⓑwithout certain factors

- Ⓒover the course of time

- Ⓓwith skill and determination

- Ⓔwith outside help

14 of 56

According to the passage, which of the following
describes the relationship between government and
"success of American entrepreneurship" (line 14)?

- ⒶThe government funds American entrepreneurs to
  ensure their success.

- ⒷDespite government regulations, American
  entrepreneurship finds a way to thrive.

- ⒸAmerican entrepreneurship is successful when the
  government creates favorable conditions.

- ⒹThe government benefits most from the success
  of American entrepreneurship.

- ⒺAmerican entrepreneurship finds success only
  when the government allows it to.

READING

Amtrak operates the only high-speed rail operation in the United States, the Acela service. Acela can reach an operating speed of up to 150 miles per hour (mph) but due to track curvature and speed restrictions, actually reaches 150 mph for only 28 miles of the Washington, DC to Boston route. Acela falls far short of international high-speed trains, which can average 150 mph, and many nations are upgrading systems to achieve top speeds of 220mph.

Based on the information above, which of the following statements is valid?

- The Acela does not achieve significant speed between Washington, DC and Boston.

- High-speed rail is the most effective method of travel within foreign countries.

- The Acela, if permitted, can move as fast as the international high-speed trains.

- The Acela is expected to have similar upgrades as international high-speed trains.

- International high-speed trains do not experience either the same track curvatures or speed restrictions as the Acela.

Any single skill, behavior, or ability may involve multiple areas of development. For example, as infants gain fine motor skills, they can manipulate objects in new ways and deepen their understanding of cause and effect. As preschoolers gain new verbal skills, they can better manage their emotions and form more complex friendships.

The author would most likely agree with which of the following statements?

- To understand cause and effect, one must develop fine motor skills.

- Acquisition of a skill can yield development in seemingly unrelated areas.

- Object manipulation is useful in forming complex friendships.

- Verbal skills are the most difficult skills for a preschooler to develop.

- The residual effects of behavioral development are narrow.

Patients want access to their own health data, and they should have an easy way to do that. Making sure that patients have access to their own information is also the best way to engage patients in their own healthcare and to improve outcomes. We've come a long way from the time when doctors wrote all of their notes in paper charts and then filed them away until the next visit. But we still have ways to go before we have the kind of interoperable, consumer-friendly system that will make sure that patients can actually see their own information and that will give access to that information to different doctors, hospitals, and other healthcare providers

The tone of the statement above is best described as

- haughty

- ambivalent

- skeptical

- incensed

- adamant

READING

In the first ecosystem-wide study of changing sea depths at five large coral reef tracts in Florida, the Caribbean and Hawai'i, researchers found the
Line sea floor is eroding in all five places, and the
(5) reefs cannot keep pace with sea level rise. As a result, coastal communities protected by the reefs are facing increased risks from storms, waves and erosion. In the Florida Keys, the U.S. Virgin Islands and Maui, coral reef degradation has caused sea
(10) floor depths to increase as sand and other sea floor materials have eroded over the past few decades, the study found. In the waters around Maui, the sea floor losses amounted to 81 million cubic meters of sand, rock and other material—about what it would
(15) take to fill up the Empire State Building 81 times, the researchers calculated.

18 of 56

The function of the reference to the Empire State Building (line 15) is

● to give a false impression of the severity of erosion

● to demonstrate the enormity of sea floor erosion

● to offer an explanation for the loss of sea floor material

● to account for previously unknown factors

● to exaggerate the significance of a problem

19 of 56

This passage is primarily concerned with

● offering alternate explanations for the findings in a new study

● critiquing the methods of a scientific experiment

● downplaying the impact of a natural phenomenon

● advocating that people change their behavior in light of a new study

● informing readers about the findings of a new study

Based on the information provided, which of the following would be most vulnerable to storms?

● Coral reefs

● Coastal communities

● The Empire State Building

● The sea floor

● The waters around Maui

READING

Questions 21-24 refer to the following passage.

Entrepreneurship, or small business ownership, is an increasingly attractive option to young people as well as adults who are striving to find careers that are exciting to them and offer the potential
(5) for personal and financial success. In recent years, the majority of new jobs in both professional and technical areas have been in the small business sector. In addition, over half of the U.S. private work force is employed in small businesses. Low-
(10) income populations, at-risk youth, and women are especially attracted to entrepreneurial ventures as they offer an opportunity to apply creativity, risk-taking inclinations, and complex life experience to educational and career endeavors that have the
(15) potential to deliver them from poverty, uncertainty, and conflicts they experience in their current environments. For these populations, and for all students who are motivated to be self-employed, career and technical education (CTE) can provide
(20) the help they need to prepare for success as small business owners and operators.

21 of 56

The author mentions "low-income populations, at-risk youth, and women" (lines 9–10) in order to

- counter an assumption made in a previous sentence
- list groups who currently benefit most from entrepreneurship
- give context to a general claim
- illustrate examples of people who might interested in a particular type of career
- advocate for a change in policy

22 of 56

As used in line 13, "inclinations" most nearly means

- goals
- challenges
- decisions
- stunts *trick*
- tendencies

23 of 56

The passage suggests that one can best be trained for entrepreneurship through which of the following?

- Financial studies
- Professional environments
- Personal successes
- Complex life experiences
- Career and technical education

24 of 56

What connection does the author make between the "private work force" (lines 8–9) and entrepreneurship?

- Most of the private work force is employed by entrepreneurial enterprises.
- The private workforce trains people for entrepreneurship.
- The private workforce and entrepreneurship both rely on low income populations.
- Nearly all of the private workforce began as entrepreneurs.
- The private workforce applies creativity to entrepreneurship.

READING

Language is variable. Two individuals of the same generation and locality, speaking precisely the same dialect and moving in the same social
Line circles, are never absolutely at one in their speech
(5) habits. A minute investigation of the speech of each individual would reveal countless differences of detail—in choice of words, in sentence structure, in the relative frequency with which particular forms or combinations of words are used, in the pronunciation
(10) of particular vowels and consonants and of combinations of vowels and consonants, and in all those features, such as speed, stress, and tone, that give life to spoken language. In a sense they speak slightly divergent dialects of the same language
(15) rather than identically the same language.

25 of 56

Which of the following best states the main idea of the passage?

- Sentence structure varies between speakers of the same language.
- No two people speak a language in the exact same way.
- People in the same social circle cannot ever truly understand one another.
- The speed, stress, and tone individuals use when speaking a language is unique.
- Language is consistent and largely unchanging.

26 of 56

In line 14, "divergent" most nearly means

- foreign
- incomprehensible
- opposing
- different
- relatable

27 of 56

The author discusses "choice of words," "sentence structure," and "the relative frequency with which particular forms or combinations of words are used" (lines 7–9) to illustrate

- ways that a spoken language can vary
- the most important components of spoken language
- a counter example to the author's main point
- the limits of spoken language
- what speakers of the same language have in common

READING

Bitcoin has exploded in value, though its future as a viable currency remains questionable. While there are many who would gladly exchange goods and services for bitcoins, in order to be taken seriously, the currency would need to have a marketplace in which sellers are confident in bitcoin's stability. Currently, the bitcoin is far too volatile for the majority of merchants to accept them. Currency, after all, needs to be a store of value, in which people know that it will be worth the same amount in the future as it is now. Bitcoin simply cannot offer this assurance at the present time.

According to the statement, Bitcoin will be seen as legitimate in the mainstream market place when

- ● it can be exchanged for goods and services
- ● more businesses begin to accept it
- ● it becomes certified as an official currency
- ● the market accepts its volatility
- ● it can demonstrate the stability of its value

While many Americans lament the two-party system, it may, in fact, be the case that such a political condition is inevitable. French political scientist Maurice Duverger posited in the mid-20th century that plurality systems of elections typically yield two-party systems. If Americans would like to see a movement toward multiple viable parties, perhaps they should amend their constitution to incorporate proportional representation, as is seen in much of Europe.

Which of the following can be inferred from the statement?

- ● Maurice Duverger advocated a system of proportional representation.
- ● Plurality systems are not found in Europe.
- ● Proportional representation does not tend to promote a two-party system.
- ● Multi-party systems did not exist until the mid-20th century.
- ● The American Constitution prohibits multiple parties.

READING

Amphibians—the big-eyed, swimming-crawling-jumping-climbing group of water and land animals that includes frogs, toads, salamanders
Line and worm-like caecilians—are the world's most
(5) endangered vertebrates. One-third of the planet's amphibian species are threatened with extinction. Now, these vulnerable creatures are facing a new foe: the *Batrachochytrium salamandrivorans* (Bsal) fungus, which is the source of an emerging
(10) amphibian disease that caused the die-off of wild European salamander populations. The Bsal fungus has not yet appeared in U.S. salamander populations. However, scientists caution that without preventive measures, the fungus is likely to emerge
(15) via the international pet trade or through other human activities.

30 of 56

According to the passage, European salamanders are currently different from American ones in that unlike American species,

- European salamanders are considered amphibians
- European salamanders are among the world's most endangered vertebrates
- European salamanders have completely died off
- European salamanders have had to contend with Bsal
- European salamanders are vulnerable to the international pet trade

31 of 56

The passage suggests that worm-like caecilians are

- threatened by human activities
- capable of swimming
- endangered
- dying off in Europe
- susceptible to Bsal

32 of 56

According to the passage, experts are concerned about the international pet trade because

- it could lead to the spread of Bsal to the United States
- it is illegal
- it focuses on salamanders
- it preys on vulnerable creatures
- one-third of animals on the market are threatened with extinction

READING

Questions 33-38 refer to the following pair of passages.

Passage 1

The communities of King Cove and Cold Bay are located at the far west end of the Alaskan Peninsula. King Cove is especially remote, linked to
Line   the outside world by a small gravel airstrip and a
(5)   harbor. In the winter, harsh weather conditions and gale-force winds routinely ground planes and prohibit sea travel, preventing the community of nearly 1,000 from accessing hospitals and other emergency services. This has resulted in a number of fatal
(10)   accidents over the years, with evacuation from King Cove sometimes taking days due to the extreme weather. As a result, the residents of King Cove seek a public road to the larger, more modern airport twenty miles away in Cold Bay.

Passage 2

(15)   The U.S. Army Corps of Engineers published a report in 2015 outlining "non-road alternatives" for transportation between King Cove and Cold Bay. That report determined that suitable options exist, including an ice-capable marine vessel, construction
(20)   of a new airport and the addition of a heliport. As early as 1996, U.S. Fish and Wildlife Service advised against construction of the road, citing both the potential damage to refuge resources and the availability of alternative transportation options.
(25)   Construction of the road has been exhaustively evaluated by numerous federal agencies and each evaluation has concluded that the road would do irreparable damage to the ecological resources of the refuge.

As used in line 3, "remote" most nearly means

Ⓟ lacking any modes of transportation

Ⓟ uninhabited by people

Ⓟ not given a significant chance for success

Ⓑ controlled by forces on the mainland

Ⓟ lacking much connection to the outside world

Which of the following best characterizes how the author of Passage 2 views the plan for a road between King Cove and Cold Bay?

Ⓒ The plan would be unacceptably disruptive to biological habitats.

Ⓓ The plan would be supported by U.S. Fish and Wildlife Service.

Ⓒ The plan would fail to gain government approval.

Ⓒ The plan would only benefit King Cove, but not Cold Bay.

Ⓒ The plan would be acceptable if it included an ice-capable marine vessel.

Which of the following best describes the relationship between Passage 1 and Passage 2 ?

Ⓟ Passage 1 offers a proposal that Passage 2 dismisses out of hand.

Ⓟ Passage 1 introduces a theory that Passage 2 connects to corroborates.

Ⓟ Passage 1 lays out a solution that is further developed in Passage 2.

Ⓟ Passage 1 introduces a plan that Passage 2 calls into question.

Ⓟ Passage 1 delivers an unorthodox method that is defended by Passage 2.

Which of the following, if true, would most weaken the argument in Passage 2 regarding transportation between King Cove and Cold Bay?

- The federal studies were conducted before most of the wildlife between King Cove and Cold Bay permanently migrated northward.

- Severe weather incidents have increased in King Cove.

- Heliports are more cost-effective than building new roads.

- Rising sea levels have altered the amount of available land to develop into usable road ways.

- Ice-capable marine vessels are more readily available in King Cove than they had been in years.

Both passages would agree with which of the following statements about King Cove?

- King Cove is long overdue for a new public road.

- It is necessary for residents of King Cove to connect with Cold Bay.

- The construction of a heliport would provide King Cove sufficient contact with Cold Bay.

- Ecological concerns should halt any effort to develop more thoroughfares in King Cove.

- King Cove experiences harsher weather than any other place in Alaska.

The authors' arguments differ in that the author of Passage 2

- expresses the availability of alternate forms of transportation, while the author of Passage 1 finds support in the U.S. Army Corps of Engineers

- cites federal agencies, while the author of Passage 1 references meteorological conditions

- advocates the construction of a road to a more modern airport, while the author of Passage 1 claims residents can rely on the small gravel airstrip

- consistently mentions the weather in King Cove, while the author of Passage 1 uses statistics

- relies on emotional appeal, while the author of Passage 1 offers data on travel accidents.

The Republic of the Marshall Islands is a sovereign nation. While the government is free to conduct its own foreign relations, it does so under the terms of the 1983 Compact of Free Association with the United States. The United States has full authority and responsibility for security and defense of the Marshall Islands, and the government of the Marshall Islands is obligated to refrain from taking actions that would be incompatible with these security and defense responsibilities.

It can be inferred from the passage above that the 1983 Compact of Free Association

- forces the Marshall Islands to run all foreign policy decisions by the United States

- disallows the Marshall Islands from defending itself

- permits the United States to oversee the Marshall Islands' trade practices

- prevents the Marshall Islands from undermining the defense efforts of the United States

- is obligated to refrain from the seeking input of the United States in matters of foreign policy

That the author of the best nonsense writing in the language should be a professional mathematician and logician, is not a paradox but a sequence. A gymnast cannot divert us by pretending to lose his balance unless perfectly able to keep his balance. Actors who counterfeit insanity must be acutely sane. But Lewis Carroll's 'Alice in Wonderland' is closer to their creator's intellectual being even than this. A very slight glance at its matter and mechanism shows that it is the work of one trained to use words with the finest precision, to teach others to use them so, to criticize keenly any inconsistency or slovenliness in their use, and to mock mercilessly any vagueness or incoherence in thought or diction. The fantastic framework and inconsequent scenes of this wonder-story mask from the popular view the qualities which give it its superlative rank and enduring charm.

According to the statement above, Carroll's use of "nonsense-writing" can best be attributed to his

- careful use of logic and word choice

- balance and insanity

- vagueness and incoherence in thought

- superlative rank and enduring charm

- inconsistency and slovenliness

READING

In an updated study evaluating threats to the long-term persistence of polar bears, scientists found that aggressive greenhouse gas mitigation could greatly reduce the chance of a substantial decline in the worldwide polar bear population. The polar bear, a species listed as threatened because of Arctic sea ice loss, depends on the ice over the biologically productive continental shelves of the Arctic Ocean as a platform for hunting seals. Declining sea ice conditions, affected by rising global temperatures, are the most influential factors in determining the future of the polar bear population. In the new study, models show that if atmospheric greenhouse gas concentrations continue to rise at current rates, polar bear population sizes will greatly decrease by the end of this century.

Which of the following, if true, would most seriously undermine the conclusion drawn in the statement above?

- Sea ice conditions are actually rising in several areas near Antarctica.

- Other marine-based animals could provide alternative food sources to polar bears.

- Polar bears cannot swim for extended periods.

- Current greenhouse gas levels are already too high to reverse ice deterioration.

- Migration patterns are drawing polar bears away from the continental shelves of the Arctic Ocean.

Questions 42-46 refer to the following passage.

Professional sports leagues generate billions of dollars, thousands of jobs, and critical economic activity in multiple industries. The Super Bowl is, in
(5) fact, the highest rated event on television, and the NFL playoffs have in the past collectively accounted for the ten most-watched sporting events of an entire year. Most of these games were carried on free over-the-air television. Sports fans power this media and merchandising juggernaut by purchasing
(10) tickets and merchandise, watching games on TV, and supporting their teams through thick and thin.

Sadly, in return, fans and the public are often treated like a fumbled football, sometimes even a kicked football. When places like Buffalo, New York
(15) fail to sell out its 74,000-person stadium, the Bills game is blacked out for local fans. When powerful cable companies and broadcasters fail to reach an agreement, it is often the threat of holding sports programming hostage that is used to negotiate
(20) higher fees. When fans live too close to their favorite baseball team, but not close enough to actually watch them on television, they face online blackouts that force them to drive to the next city to catch a game. These blackouts are loathed
(25) by fans, hated by consumers, and even reviled by most of the industry stakeholders in the business of television.

As used in line 9, "juggernaut" most nearly means

- a televised product

- a dishonest corporation

- a wide-reaching company

- a for-profit organization

- a controversial sport

READING

Which of the following describes the organization of the passage?

Ⓐ A successful product is described, and a criticism of that product is laid out.

Ⓑ An altruistic endeavor is outlined, and reasons for its success are given.

Ⓒ A business practice is articulated, and a controversial issue is resolved.

Ⓓ An organization flaw is discussed, and its ramifications are analyzed.

Ⓔ The benefits of a sport are highlighted, and its ulterior motives are exposed.

The passage suggests that blackouts occur due to

Ⓐ fans living too close to their favorite teams

Ⓑ threats of holding sports programming hostage

Ⓒ illegal online broadcasts of games

Ⓓ cable companies and broadcasters reaching an agreement

Ⓔ the failure of teams to sell all of its tickets

The passage is primarily concerned with

Ⓐ offering solutions to a perceived problem

Ⓑ contrasting customer loyalty with a business practice

Ⓒ attracting potential customers to a product

Ⓓ explaining the sports industry

Ⓔ defending an industry

The function of the final sentence in the passage is

Ⓐ to list advocates of a business practice

Ⓑ to give voice to those who typically are not heard

Ⓒ to hold responsible parties accountable

Ⓓ to offer a point of view contrary to the author's

Ⓔ to demonstrate that a wide spectrum of opposition exists

READING

Questions 47-49 refer to the following.

Sydney teachers four sections of a biology class and calculates student grades based on five tests throughout the semester. Below is a chart showing the average grades for each class on the five unit tests.

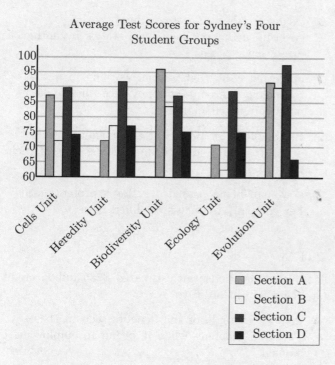

Average Test Scores for Sydney's Four Student Groups

- ☐ Section A
- ☐ Section B
- ☐ Section C
- ☐ Section D

47 of 56

On which unit test did Section B have the greatest change in its class average from the previous test?

- Ⓐ Cells Unit
- Ⓑ Heredity Unit
- Ⓒ Biodiversity Unit
- Ⓓ Ecology Unit
- Ⓔ Evolution Unit

How do the results of the Evolution Unit test compare to the results of the Ecology Unit test?

- Ⓐ Most class sections saw a decrease in their scores on the Evolution Unit test.
- Ⓑ The average score among the four class sections, taken as a whole, increased for the Evolution Unit test.
- Ⓒ The Evolution Unit test had more test takers than did the Ecology Unit test.
- Ⓓ The Evolution Unit test was graded on a curve to equally distribute scores, whereas the Ecology Unit test was not.
- Ⓔ The four class sections, taken as a whole, had the same average on both tests.

49 of 56

Which of the following statements is best supported by the information provided?

Select all that apply.

- ☐ With only one exception, Section B experienced consistent growth across the tests.
- ☐ Students in all four sections found the Ecology Unit test to be the most challenging.
- ☐ The Biodiversity Unit test was the only case in which Section C did not outscore Section A.

READING

Questions 50-53 refer to the following passage.

All countries stand to benefit from women's
increased economic participation. But the potential
gains are particularly great across the developing
Line world, due to the extent of the constraints that so
(5) many women face on their ability to own property,
their ability to access financial services, or work
outside the home. Consider that women in more
than half the world's countries face limits on their
ability to own or manage property, while women-
(10) led small- to medium-size firms in developing
countries face an estimated $285 billion credit gap.
As renowned Peruvian economist Hernando de Soto
explained, one of the primary sources of stagnant
growth and unrest in developing economies is a
(15) lack of property rights, and the resulting exclusion
of workers, including women, from the formal
economy. These constraints directly harm women
by preventing them from working, from saving, and
from controlling their own future. But they also
(20) harm economic growth and they harm stability. In
fact, a multitude of studies project huge gains of
global GDP from increases in women's economic
participation. Perhaps that is why, after de Soto
helped reform the customary laws in his native
(25) Peru to make it easier for Peruvian women to work
and to own property, women's formal labor force
participation increased by 15 percent in that country.
As a result, Peru became one of the fastest-growing
economies in Latin America.

50 of 56

It can be inferred from the passage that making work
and property ownership more accessible to women in
developing nations would

- create $285 billion dollars in revenue
- prevent women from saving for their future
- contribute to stagnant growth
- yield significant GDP increases
- lead to even greater economic gains than the
  ones seen in Peru

51 of 56

Which of the following best illustrates the
"constraints" mentioned in line 17 ?

- the lack of a right for women to vote, as dictated
  by their country's constitution
- excessive inheritance taxes paid to the
  government, as outlined by a state's byzantine
  excise laws
- operating costs that women working in a
  technology start-up company face due to the
  male-dominated market
- the inability for people of a particular ethnic
  group to own land according to the laws of their
  country
- a woman being passed over for a promotion at
  her company by a less qualified man

52 of 56

The author mentions "an estimated $285 billion credit
gap" (line 11) in order to

- give an example of the benefits seen in the
  Peruvian economy when it began to employ more
  women
- illustrate that the economic challenges facing
  women in developing nations go beyond property
  rights
- compare economic opportunities of women in
  developing nations with their counterparts in the
  developed world
- demonstrate that the problem of women's
  economic participation is not limited to
  developing countries
- show the potential windfall global companies
  would experience by increasing female hires

READING

According to the passage, Hernando de Soto demonstrated that

Ø while Peru's system of property rights impacted many women directly, it had little effect on the economy as a whole

Ø a 15% increase in women's participation in the workforce would lead to a change in the customary laws of Peru

Ø Peru's economic situation was unique in its treatment of women

Ø financial services in Peru were equally available to both men and women

Ø a lack of economic opportunities for women has consequences at both the micro and macro level

At the time of NASA's founding, astronomers were using balloons, sounding rockets, and airplanes to carry their instruments to altitudes between 8.5 and 70 miles above the surface of Earth. All of these airborne methods allow instruments to overcome atmospheric obstructions, such as dust and water vapor, at many (but not all) wavelengths, including parts of the infrared spectrum. The only way to eliminate the interference caused by the atmosphere, especially in the infrared, is to get above it. Instruments on balloon and rocket flights were further constrained by an inability to view a celestial object long enough or accurately enough to make a satisfactory observation. Placing an instrument on board a satellite in low Earth orbit (typically 200–800 miles in altitude) would allow for better observation of sources that often appear faint.

According to the statement above, which of the following must be true?

There are some wavelengths at which instruments attached to sounding rockets cannot properly function.

Placing instruments on board satellites solves all problems related to image obstruction.

Balloons are not adequate to overcome atmospheric obstructions.

Instruments on airplanes typically view a celestial image for a sufficient amount of time.

Objects in low Earth orbit are too low to be affected by dust and water vapor.

In the aftermath of the problems of political succession at the later stages of the Mao Zedong era and the domestic social turmoil of the Cultural Revolution of the 1960s and 1970s, Deng Xiaoping emerged as China's paramount leader. In February 1979, fewer than two years after he assumed his role as Vice Premier, and only months after normalizing relations with the United States, Deng's government decided to wage a limited war against Vietnam. China used Vietnam's 1978 invasion into Cambodia as a *jus ad bellum*, thus prompting China to conduct a cross-border invasion of its own in order to aid its political ally in Cambodia.

As used in the statement above, *jus ad bellum* most nearly means

the end of a revolution

to give political aid

an establishment of diplomatic negotiations

a lost cause

a reason to go to war

High blood pressure is a risk factor for multiple diseases, including heart disease, stroke, and kidney disease. In 2011–2014, about 29% of U.S. adults had hypertension. Adults with hypertension who are undiagnosed and unaware of their hypertension will not be treated, and their blood pressure may remain above normal levels with damaging effects. Therefore, diagnosis and awareness of hypertension are essential for blood pressure management and control.

The author's attitude toward awareness of hypertension can best be described as

nonplussed surprise & confuse

vigilant alert

nonchalant little care

melodramatic overly emotional

dismissive something not worthy

Chapter 7
Reading Practice
Test 1: Answers and
Explanations

READING PRACTICE TEST 1 ANSWER KEY

1.	E	29.	C
2.	A	30.	D
3.	D	31.	B
4.	C	32.	A
5.	E	33.	E
6.	B	34.	A
7.	A	35.	D
8.	E	36.	A
9.	A	37.	B
10.	C	38.	B
11.	C	39.	D
12.	E	40.	A
13.	B	41.	D
14.	C	42.	C
15.	E	43.	A
16.	B	44.	E
17.	E	45.	B
18.	B	46.	E
19.	E	47.	E
20.	B	48.	B
21.	D	49.	A, C
22.	E	50.	D
23.	E	51.	D
24.	A	52.	B
25.	B	53.	E
26.	D	54.	A
27.	A	55.	E
28.	E	56.	B

READING PRACTICE TEST 1 EXPLANATIONS

1. **E** The text states that *the organic material undergoes heat and pressure,* which, after enough time, becomes coal or petroleum. That process is the thermal maturity. Therefore, heat and pressure are necessary to promote thermal maturity. Choice (E) is correct. Coal and petroleum undergo thermal maturity, but they are not the catalyst for the process. Eliminate (A) and (D). Weather conditions and the age of materials are not mentioned in the text, so you can also eliminate (B) and (C).

2. **A** The statement notes that *the NTSB must also keep up with emerging technologies in transportation, which have the potential to dramatically improve safety.* This is most closely related to (A) because the focus on improving safety is synonymous with preventing disasters. Also, note that (E) is incorrect because, according to the statement, the NTSB does not create the new technologies, but rather keeps up with them. While the statement mentions that the NTSB assists families after accidents, it does not say that they notify the family. Eliminate (B). The statement does not indicate that the NTSB investigates *all* accidents nationwide, so (D) is incorrect. There is no reference to cleaning up debris after an accident, so eliminate (C).

3. **D** The topic of this statement is in the first sentence (the Torch Run raises money for the Special Olympics), which, combined with the final sentence (the amount of money raised), makes it clear that (D) is the correct answer. Choices (A) and (B) are incorrect, as the extreme language used in them (*only* and *oldest*) is not supported by the text. Eliminate (C) because the passage does not compare the fundraiser to any other organizations. Choice (E) is incorrect because it is too broad and off topic.

4. **C** The passage states that due to *advances in public health and medicine, Americans are living longer and working longer, resulting in an unprecedented transformation of the workplace.* This reference to life expectancy best supports (C). While the passage mentions that older Americans participate in creating new technologies, it does not indicate that there is a need for such workers or that it has anything to do with experience. Choice (A) is incorrect. Benefits are not mentioned, so eliminate (B). The passage mentions that the changing workforce *will shape preferences about work and retirement,* but it does not mention that there is no longer a desire for retirement; (D) is incorrect. The mention of employers' decisions relates how they will react to the changing workforce, not how they caused it. Eliminate (E).

5. **E** The purpose of the first paragraph is to discuss the wide-ranging presence of older workers. The purpose of the second paragraph is to give numbers supporting the scope of the issue, while claiming that employers will have to respond to this change. This is best described by (E). There is no discussion of a demise, so eliminate (A). The first paragraph describes the reality of older workers in the workplace, not business practice or a theory. Choices (B) and (C) are incorrect. Choice (D) is also incorrect because the second paragraph does not give any solutions, but rather discusses the urgency of employers reacting to the changing workforce.

6. **B** The second paragraph indicates that employers will need to react to the increasing presence of older employees in the workforce, so the author would clearly agree that the workforce of the future will look different because of the presence of older employees. Choice (B) is correct. The author does not offer any particular recommendations, so (A) is incorrect. Be skeptical of answer choices that make comparisons: (C) is incorrect, as the author makes no such comparison. The author notes that older workers are *critical* to the workforce, so (E) is incorrect. While 2026 is mentioned in the passage, (D) is incorrect because it does not accurately describe how the author uses that date.

7. **A** The passage describes how lines that scientists once hypothesized were water are actually made up of sand and dust. This supports (A), which would be the title of such a passage. Choices (B), (C), and (D) are incorrect because they miss the key component of the passage that scientists once thought the lines were evidence of water. Eliminate (E) because the scientists noted that the granular flows meant that the RSL were not comprised of water.

8. **E** The text states that the RSL features *resemble seeping liquid water*, which almost directly aligns with (E). Be careful to not take what the author says too far. While the RSL are not evidence of water, there is nothing in the text that would indicate that there is no water on Mars. Eliminate (A) and (C). Likewise, there is no evidence in the text that water does or did exist on Mars. Eliminate (B). Be skeptical of answer choices that offer direct comparisons. The comparison made in (D) does not occur anywhere in the text. Eliminate it.

9. **A** The passage states that the RSL become visible during the warmest time of the year on Mars. Since scientists once thought of these lines as water, the conclusion in (A) is consistent with the passage. The passage does not report any relationship between RSL and water, so (B) is incorrect. Scientists long thought the down-slope trending surface features were water, not sand and dust. Eliminate (C). Choice (D) is incorrect because the purpose of the passage is to report that the features are not actually water. Choice (E) is incorrect because it makes a conclusion that is not supported by the passage—the lines were confirmed to not be water, but the presence of water *anywhere* on Mars has not been debunked by this finding.

10. **C** The final sentence mentions that it remains unclear how the features formed. This indicates that it is a topic that could be studied further. Choice (C) is correct. There is no mention of the purpose of seeping liquid water, only that the Recurring Slope Lineae can appear similar to water. Eliminate (A). The material composition of Recurring Slope Lineae (sand and dust) occurs in the first sentence, not the final one. Eliminate (B). Choice (D) is incorrect because the final sentence tells you that scientists do not yet know how Recurring Slope Lineae are formed. Choice (E) is incorrect because the final sentence does not mention life on Mars.

11. **C** The final sentence states that *the appearance and growth of these features resemble seeping liquid water*, which lines up consistently with (C). Eliminate (A) since the passage does not mention ice. The passage does mention that the RSL fade when inactive, but this is unrelated to why they might be mistaken for water. Eliminate (B). The text notes that granular flows are composed of sand and

dust, not water, so (D) is incorrect. Eliminate (E) because the rate of growth is unrelated in this text to how RSL can be mistaken for water.

12. **E** Focus on how the answer choices address the opening sentence. The passage begins by discussing the achievement of the digital economy's impact on jobs and growth. This is consistent with (E). This statement is not an outlier, a conundrum, or a caution. Eliminate (A), (C), and (D). Choice (B) is also incorrect, as there are no counterpoints offered.

13. **B** The phrase *did not occur in a vacuum* is used to convey the idea that American entrepreneurship in the digital economy required assistance, examples of which are listed in the following sentence. Choice (B), *without certain factors,* captures this idea well. Choice (E) can be eliminated because it is the opposite of not requiring assistance. Saying that the digital economy did not occur with *skill and determination* would undermine the laudatory tone that the author uses to describe the entrepreneurs. Eliminate (D). The word *cleanly* is not specific enough to be a proper word choice, so (A) is incorrect. The time it took to develop the digital economy is irrelevant, so eliminate (C).

14. **C** The final sentence of this passage states that in order for the digital economy to thrive, the government must take certain steps. The sentence goes on to say that these steps will be *conducive* to the factors that will lead to success (creativity, competition, and investment). This is consistent with the creation of *favorable conditions,* as mentioned in (C). The answer choice words *ensure* and *only* are too strong since the text does not mention a guarantee of success. Eliminate (A) and (E). Since the government is described as helpful to the digital economy, (B) is incorrect. The text makes no mention about how the government might benefit from this relationship. Choice (D) is incorrect.

15. **E** According to the statement, both the Acela and the international trains are capable of hitting 150 mph (the international trains can go even faster). The text states that the Acela normally does not go that fast due to speed restrictions and track curvature. Since the international trains average 150 mph, they must not face a combination of these same two restrictions. Choice (E) is correct. Since the text states that Acela can reach 150 mph, (A) is incorrect. Be wary of answer choices that make comparisons: (B) gives a comparison that does not exist in the passage. We do not know the full speed of international high-speed trains, so (C) is not a statement that can be proven by the text. There is no indication about what the future holds for Acela, so eliminate (D).

16. **B** The text states that *any skill…may involve multiple areas of development,* meaning that skill acquisition is not isolated to one area. This, combined with the example given in the statement, makes it clear seemingly unrelated areas can both experience development due to learning a new skill. Choice (B) is correct. Choice (E) is incorrect because it contradicts this information. Choice (A) is incorrect because, while developing fine motor skills deepens the understanding of cause and effect, the word *must* in the answer choice misrepresents the original statement. Choice (C) is incorrect because it mixes the two examples given. Be wary of answer choice that make comparisons: (D) gives a comparison that does not exist in the passage.

17. **E** The author wants to ensure that all patients have access to their medical information (he even says it is the *best* way to engage patients in their own healthcare). The author's insistence on this happening creates an *adamant* tone. Choice (E) is correct. Accordingly, his tone is not *ambivalent*, which would imply that he has no clear interest in what happens; eliminate (B). *Haughty* implies arrogant, a tone that is not present in this text. Eliminate (A). The author does not seem to express doubt in any particular idea, so (C), *skeptical*, is incorrect. An *incensed* tone would convey anger, which is not present in the text. Eliminate (D).

18. **B** The author mentions the Empire State Building in the final sentence to make a connection with the reader about what the 81 million cubic meters of eroded sea floor material looks like. Since this is used to show the largeness of the erosion, (B) is correct. The use of a specific number (81 million) tells us that this is a precise accounting of the problem rather than a false impression or an exaggeration. Eliminate (A) and (E). The number simply shows the scale of the erosion; it does not account for the cause. Eliminate (C). The reference to the Empire State Building also does not bring up anything about previously unknown factors, so (D) is incorrect.

19. **E** The first sentence states that this is the first study of its kind, while the rest of the passage explains the findings of the study. Therefore, (E) is correct. No explanations for the erosions are given, so eliminate (A). The methods are not discussed, let alone critiqued, so (B) is incorrect. The passage highlights the seriousness of the findings, so (C) is also incorrect. Finally, there is no recommendation about people changing their behavior, so eliminate (D).

20. **B** The only mention of storms in the passage is *coastal communities protected by the reefs are facing increased risks*. Choice (B) best aligns with this statement. Be careful with the other choices. Even though that sentence mentions coral reefs, it does so by stating that they protect coastal communities, not that they are vulnerable to storms (they may be, but the text does not state it!). Eliminate (A). While the sea floor is eroding, particularly in the waters around Maui, the passage does not discuss storms in that sentence. Eliminate (D) and (E). The Empire State Building is mentioned only as a point of reference for the scale of how much the sea floor is eroding. It has nothing to do with being vulnerable to storms. Eliminate (C).

21. **D** The text mentions that these groups *are especially attracted to entrepreneurial ventures*. This is consistent with (D), which is correct. Eliminate (B) because the passage does not state that the groups currently benefit from entrepreneurship. The sentence in question actually adds support to the previous sentence, not counters it. Eliminate (A). While this sentence does support the general claim of the passage, its purpose is not to give context to any particular claims. Choice (C) is incorrect. The passage advocates for an existing career path, but does not argue for a change in policy. Eliminate (E).

22. **E** Cross out the word *inclinations* in the passage and write your own word choice in. You may come up with something such as "motivations" or "orientations." These words would not match *goals*. Eliminate (A). They are also not the same as *challenges* or *decisions*, so (B) and (C) are incorrect. *Stunts* does not mean the same as "motivations" or "orientations," so (D) is incorrect. Choice (E), *tendencies*, is correct because it is closest.

23. **E** The final sentence states *career and technical education (CTE) can provide the help they need to prepare for success.* Choice (E) is correct. The passage mentions *professional and technical areas* are growing, but not that they provide training. Choice (B) is incorrect. The passage tells you that small businesses offer people the opportunities for financial and personal success, but does not point to finance specifically or personal success on its own as a method of training. Eliminate (A) and (C). According to the text, people with complex life experiences are typically drawn to entrepreneurship, but there is no indication that such experiences provide the best training. Choice (D) is incorrect.

24. **A** The text states that *over half of the U.S. private work force is employed in small businesses.* The first sentence establishes that the author uses entrepreneurship synonymously with small business ownership. Therefore, it would be accurate to state that most (over 50%) of the private work force comes from entrepreneurship. Choice (A) is correct. Choice (B) is incorrect because the only training the passage discusses is CTE, not the private workforce itself. The text notes that low-income populations are drawn to entrepreneurship, but not that the private workforce and entrepreneurship rely on this group. Eliminate (C). There is no information in the text about how members of the private workforce began their careers, so (D) is incorrect. Creativity is mentioned only as a quality of those drawn to entrepreneurial ventures, not as a way to connect the workforce and entrepreneurship. Choice (E) is incorrect.

25. **B** The second sentence tells you that *two individuals…are never absolutely at one in their speech habits.* This best supports (B), that no two people speak a language in the exact same way. Be careful to not choose an answer that gives a supporting detail rather than the main idea; for this reason eliminate (A) and (D). Choice (E) is incorrect because it contradicts the main point of the passage. Lastly, (C) is incorrect because it extends the main idea too far to a conclusion that is not supported.

26. **D** Cross out the word *divergent* and write your own word in, based on the sentence's context clues. You might come up with something like "separate." This is closest to (D), *different.* Eliminate (A), (B), and (E) because they are not similar to separate. While *opposing* can mean "separate," it does not fit the context of the sentence, since *opposing* implies that the dialects compete against one another. Eliminate (C).

27. **A** The point of the passage is that two speakers of the same language can speak in slightly different ways. *Choice of words, sentence structure,* and *the relative frequency with which particular forms or combinations of words are used* are supporting details for this claim because they explain the ways that language can differ from person to person. Choice (A) is therefore correct. Since these words support rather than undermine the main point, (C) is incorrect. Be wary of extreme answer choices: (B) is incorrect because the passage does not state what the most important components of spoken language are. Eliminate (E) because the purpose of this sentence is that these components show how dialects can differ. Choice (D) is incorrect because it is not discussed in the passage.

28. **E** The statement tells you that currency *needs to be a store of value, in which people know that it will be worth the same amount in the future as it is now.* Therefore, you should look for an answer that deals with currency being worth the same amount over the course of time. This describes stability, as mentioned in (E). This also means that the currency would need to avoid volatility, so eliminate (D). There is no mention of Bitcoin being certified as official currency, so eliminate (C). Choice (B) may seem correct at first, but it does not match the specific reasoning previously mentioned as well as (E). Eliminate (B). Bitcoin currently can be exchanged for goods and services, but it is not seen as legitimate in the mainstream market, so (A) is incorrect.

29. **C** The text states that the two-party system may go away if Americans switch to a proportional representation system. This implies that such a system would not promote a two-party rule. Choice (C) is correct. There is no mention of Duverger promoting a particular system, only that he published his observations. Eliminate (A). While the final sentence implies that Europe has something other than plurality representation, it does not go so far as to say that none are found in Europe. Eliminate (B). Choice (D) is incorrect because it takes the mention of the 20th century out of context to make a claim that is not supported by the text. There is no evidence in the text that the American Constitution prohibits multiple parties, so eliminate (E).

30. **D** Although the passage mentions that the Bsal fungus has harmed the European salamander population, it states that the *Bsal fungus has not yet appeared in U.S. salamander populations.* This is the key difference between the two populations. Choice (D) is correct. The passage does not indicate that any salamander species are not amphibians, so (A) is incorrect. The first sentence supports the idea that amphibians as a whole, though not exclusively European salamanders, are the world's most endangered vertebrates. Therefore, (B) is incorrect. Choice (C) is too extreme: the text states only that the fungus has caused a *die-off* in the wild population, but does not mention extinction. Eliminate it. Choice (E) is incorrect because it takes the phrase *international pet trade* out of context.

31. **B** *Worm-like caecilians* are mentioned in the first sentence when the passage defines and lists amphibians. One part of that definition is that amphibians, and therefore caecilians, are swimmers. Choice (B) is correct. The phrase *human activities* is taken out of context, as the final sentence does not state that human activities are a threat. Eliminate (A). While amphibians are the world's most endangered vertebrates, according to the first sentence, there is no indication as to which specific species are endangered. Choice (C) is incorrect. European salamanders, not caecilians, are described as dying off. Eliminate (D). According to the passage, Bsal is a threat to salamanders, not caecilians. Choice (E) is incorrect.

32. **A** The passage notes that the fungus has not arrived in U.S. salamander populations yet, but that preventative measures are required lest *the fungus is likely to emerge via the international pet trade.* Therefore, the international pet trade could spread the fungus to the U.S. Choice (A) is correct. There is no mention of the international pet trade being illegal or of which animals it primarily exploits. Choices (B), (C), and (D) are incorrect. Choice (E) is incorrect because the phrase

one-third is taken out of context. In the passage, *one-third* refers to the number of amphibian species that are threatened with extinction.

33. **E** Passage 1 states that King Cove is remote because it is *linked to the outside world by only a small gravel airstrip and a harbor.* Choice (E) is correct. This statement contradicts (A), which claims there is no mode of transportation. Choice (B) is also incorrect because Passage 1 begins by mentioning the *communities of King Cove.* Therefore, it is inhabited by people. There is no information in Passage 1 that would support (C) and (D), so eliminate those choices.

34. **A** The author of Passage 2 concludes by stating that the road *would do irreparable damage to the ecological resources of the refuge.* Therefore, the author believes that it would disrupt biological habitats. Choice (A) is correct. Choice (B) is incorrect because the text states that U.S. Fish and Wildlife Service *advised against the construction of the road.* While the agency advised against it, there is no indication of whether the government would ultimately approve the road. Eliminate (C). The author of the passage almost exclusively discusses the ecological problems with the road and does not go into which communities might benefit from it. Eliminate (D). The author argues that the ice-capable vessel would be a good alternative to the road, not work in conjunction with the road. Therefore, (E) is also incorrect.

35. **D** The plan to build a road, which is offered by the author of Passage 1, is seen as problematic by the author of Passage 2 due to the ecological impact of such a project. Choice (D) is correct because the author of Passage 2 questions the implementation of the proposal in Passage 1. Since the author of Passage 2 gives reasons for opposition to the plan, it is not dismissed out of hand. Choice (A) is incorrect. Since the author of Passage 2 disagrees with the proposal in Passage 1, it would be incorrect to say that the ideas are corroborated, defended, or further developed in Passage 2. Eliminate (B), (C), and (E).

36. **A** The author of Passage 2 cites evidence that constructing the road will disrupt wildlife in the area. If, hypothetically, the wildlife were no longer there, this would not be a reasonable concern. Choice (A) is correct. Since Passage 2 deals with wildlife, not weather, the amount of severe weather incidents would be irrelevant to the author's argument. Eliminate (B). Helicopters would be an option supported by the author of Passage 2 (he mentions heliports as a viable alternative plan). Therefore, this would not weaken the argument. Eliminate (C). Since the author advocates alternatives to roads, the statement in (D) does not affect his argument in a meaningful way. Eliminate it. The author claims that ice-capable marine vessels are a wise alternative to a road. Therefore, (E) would support the author's argument and can be eliminated.

37. **B** Both authors are seeking solutions to the difficulty of connecting the residents between the two towns. Choice (B) correctly states this. The author of Passage 2 clearly does not support the construction of a road, as that is the primary argument of the text. Eliminate (A). Only the author of Passage 2 advocates a heliport. The author of Passage 1 is fine with constructing a new road, so (C) is incorrect. Only the author of Passage 2 seems to be concerned about ecological disturbances; the

author of Passage 1 does not bring up this issue, so eliminate (D). There is no comparison between the weather in King Cove and other places in Alaska. Choice (E) is incorrect.

38. **B** Choice (B) is a true statement because the author of Passage 2 references U.S. Fish and Wildlife Service, a federal agency, which the author of Passage 1 does not. However, the author of Passage 1 brings up the weather, which the author of Passage 2 does not. Choice (B) is the correct answer. The author of Passage 1 does not discuss the U.S. Army Corps of Engineers, so eliminate (A). Passage 2 argues against a road; therefore, (C) is incorrect. The author of Passage 1 never mentions the weather, so (D) is incorrect. There is no actual data given about travel accidents in Passage 1 (only a claim), so you can eliminate (E).

39. **D** The text states that, according to the compact, the Marshall Islands is *obligated to refrain from taking actions that would be incompatible with* the United States' *security and defense responsibilities.* This aligns with (D). The text also states that the Marshall Islands is *free to conduct its own foreign relations,* which undermines (A) and (B). Eliminate them. The compact is about security and defense, not commerce. Choice (C) is incorrect. Since the United States has authority and is responsible for the Marshall Islands' security, it would stand to reason that the nation is free to seek input from the United States on matters of foreign policy. Choice (E) is incorrect.

40. **A** The passage states that Carroll's writing is *the work of one trained to use words with the finest precision* and that the author of nonsense-writing could be a logician. Therefore, (A), *careful use of logic and word choice,* is supported by the text. Choice (B) is incorrect because it takes words from the author's analogies (*balance* and *insanity*), which do not have literal relationships to the craft of writing. The text states that one who writes like Carroll is likely a person trained *to criticize keenly any inconsistency or slovenliness* in the use of words and *to mock mercilessly any vagueness or incoherence in thought or diction.* Therefore, (C) and (E) are incorrect. The phrase *superlative rank and enduring charm* is taken out of context. In the final sentence, this phrase refers to Carroll's writing, not the author himself. Eliminate (D).

41. **D** The first sentence claims that *aggressive greenhouse gas mitigation could greatly reduce the chance of a substantial decline in the worldwide polar bear population.* However, if current levels are so high that they are irreversible, mitigation would not reduce the decline. Choice (D) is the best answer. Choice (A) is incorrect because this would be evidence that greenhouse gas mitigation efforts have been effective. While other animals could provide food sources for polar bears, there is no guarantee that those animals would continue to survive in deteriorating Arctic conditions. Eliminate (B). Choice (C) is incorrect because it supports why declining ice is bad for polar bears. Choice (E) shows that polar bears are leaving their natural habitat, which would not undermine the conclusion. Rather, it would be evidence of the crisis polar bears are facing. Eliminate it.

42. **C** After using the word *juggernaut,* the final sentence of the first paragraph lists the ways that sports leagues make money off its customers. These varying revenue sources support the idea that the sports industry is wide reaching. Choice (C) is correct. Since television is not the only merchandising and media outlet mentioned, (A) is incorrect. While the passage is critical of the sports indus-

try, it does not accuse any organization of being dishonest. Choice (B) is incorrect. The idea of a *juggernaut,* as used in the passage, implies more than just a for-profit organization. It implies its size and scale. Eliminate (D) because it is not specific enough. The sentence that mentions *juggernaut* is not concerned with controversy. Therefore, (E) is not supported.

43. **A** The first paragraph of this passage discusses the amount of attention (ratings) and revenue sources of sports leagues. The second paragraph begins the discussion of a criticism *(Sadly, in return, fans and the public are often treated like a fumbled football).* Choice (A) best describes this organization. There is no altruism (charity or selflessness) mentioned in the first paragraph, so (B) is incorrect. Since the second paragraph issues criticisms without resolving them, you can eliminate (C), which says the controversial issue is resolved. The first paragraph describes the successes of the NFL and does not bring up flaws quite yet. Therefore, (D) is incorrect. Be careful with (E), while you may try to reason that they have *ulterior motives* for the blackouts, this does not capture the issue as well as (A). Further, even though they both have positive connotations, the word *benefits* is not synonymous with *successes.* Choice (E) is therefore incorrect.

44. **E** The passage lists several reasons that blackouts occur. One of those reasons is mentioned when the author states that *places like Buffalo, New York fail to sell out its 74,000-person stadium, the Bills game is blacked out for local fans.* This best aligns with (E). Be careful not to pick (A), as it takes information *(fans live too close to their favorite baseball team, but not close enough to actually watch them on television)* out of context. Choice (B) is incorrect because while it offers an alternative way to describe blackouts, it does not actually give a reason for them. Choice (C) is not mentioned in the text, so eliminate it. Finally, (D) is incorrect because the opposite is true—it is the *inability* of cable companies and broadcasters to reach an agreement that would lead to a blackout.

45. **B** The passage uses the first paragraph to describe how much fans support the product and the second paragraph to argue they are not treated well in return. This best aligns with (B), since the paragraphs create a contrast. The passage does not offer any solutions, only criticisms. Eliminate (A). The passage does not seek to attract customers, so eliminate (C). The passage has too narrow a focus (blackouts) to explain the entire sports industry, so (D) is incorrect. Further, since the author is leveling a criticism and not defending the organization, (E) is incorrect.

46. **E** By listing fans, customers, and television industry stakeholders, the author makes it clear that opposition to this policy is widespread. Choice (E) best supports this idea. Since this list contains only opponents of the practice of blacking out games, (A) is incorrect. The final sentence lists those who are opposed to the practice of blackouts, but not necessarily those who do not have their voices heard (it would be a stretch to think that the television industry is voiceless). Eliminate (B). Those mentioned in the sentence are not those to be held accountable, so (C) is incorrect, and they would agree with the author's point, not hold a contrary view. Eliminate (D).

47. **E**   On this question, compare Section B from test to test by subtracting. The increase from the Ecology Unit to the Evolution Unit is a jump from 62 to 90, which is 28 points. This is the greatest increase, so (E) is correct. Section B does not experience an increase on the Cells Unit because it is the first test of the curriculum, so eliminate (A). The Heredity Unit shows an increase of only 5 points, so (B) is incorrect. The increase on the Biodiversity Unit is only slightly larger, about 6 points. Eliminate (C). Section B saw a decrease in their average test scores on the Ecology Unit, so (D) is incorrect.

48. **B**   Evaluate each statement separately in order to determine which one is actually supported by the data. If you don't trust your eyes, the statement in (B) can be supported by averaging the four sections on the Ecology test and on the Evolution test. The average of the four sections on the Ecology test is 74.25, while the average for the Evolution test is 89. Choice (B) is correct. This also makes it clear that the claim in (E), that the averages were equal on both tests, is incorrect. Only one section—D— saw a decrease in the average score for the Evolution test. Eliminate (A). The number of test takers is impossible to know because there are only average scores per section. Choice (C) is therefore incorrect. Further, there is no information given that the instructor ever used a curve, so eliminate (D).

49. **A, C**

   This is a "select all that apply" question, so it is important to consider each answer choice knowing that more than one may be correct. Section B increased its average score on each test, except for the Ecology test. Therefore, (A) is correct; keep it. Even though the Ecology test produced the lowest average score for a couple of the sections, there is no data that records the students' opinions of the relative difficulty of each test. Therefore, (B) cannot be supported; eliminate (B). The Section C line is consistently higher than the Section A line, with the one exception of the Biodiversity test. Choice (C) makes just that claim, so keep (C). You are left with (A) and (C) as your answers.

50. **D**   The passage defines economic participation as working and owning property. The passage also claims that *a multitude of studies project huge gains of global GDP from increases in women's economic participation.* Therefore, economic participation should yield increases in global GDP. This best aligns with (D). It also would stand to reason from this evidence that (C) is incorrect, because the GDP would not be considered stagnant if it were growing. The number $285 billion dollars in (A) is taken out of context to say something completely different from the text. Eliminate it. The passage states that preventing women from having property rights stands in the way of women controlling their own future. Increasing property rights would seemingly allow women to save for the future. Eliminate (B). Be skeptical of answer choices that offer direct comparisons. The comparison made in (E) does not occur anywhere in the text, so eliminate it.

51. **D**   The passage states that *these constraints directly harm women by preventing them from working.* The specific constraints should therefore be enumerated in the previous sentence, which says *a lack of property rights, and the resulting exclusion of workers, including women, from the formal economy.* This information aligns closely with the example about an ethnic group being denied property rights in (D), which is the correct answer. Choice (A) is incorrect because the text deals with

economic participation, not democratic participation. Being taxed would indicate that an individual participates in the economy; however, the constraints mentioned in the text were such that women were not able to participate in the economy. Eliminate (B). The term *constraints* covers barriers to economic participation, but does not cover operating costs or hiring practices, so (C) and (E) are also incorrect.

52. **B** This quote arises in a sentence about constraints in women's ability to own property. The sentence goes on to say that *women-led small- to medium-size firms in developing countries face an estimated $285 billion credit gap.* In other words, even the women who do have the opportunity to participate in the economy face significant challenges, in particular the ability to build credit. Choice (B) is correct because it mentions that the problems women face go beyond property rights. This sentence comes before the mention of the Peruvian example, so (A) is incorrect. Be skeptical of answer choices that offer direct comparisons. The comparison made in (C) does not occur anywhere in the text. Eliminate it. The sentence that contains the quote in question clearly states that the women-led firms are in developing nations. Eliminate (D). The $285 billion figure is about a credit gap, not a windfall of money. Choice (E) is incorrect.

53. **E** Hernando de Soto's work found that *one of the primary sources of stagnant growth and unrest in developing economies is a lack of property rights, and the resulting exclusion of workers, including women, from the formal economy.* This information directly supports (E), that the lack of opportunities has consequences. It also contradicts (A), which claims that Peru's system had little effect on the economy as a while. Eliminate it. Choice (B) is also incorrect: it takes the 15% figure out of context. The text says that Peru saw a 15% increase in women's participation in the labor force, not the other way around, as the answer choice states. The text states that other developing countries have the same restrictions on women in the economy. Therefore, Peru was not unique in this regard. Eliminate (C). There is no evidence in the text that financial services were as available to women as they were to men. In fact, it mentions that developing countries, such as Peru, had a $285 billion credit gap. Eliminate (D).

54. **A** The text tells you that the devices can bring instruments high enough to overcome atmospheric obstructions *at many (but not all) wavelengths.* Therefore, there are at least some wavelengths that still cause trouble. Choice (A) is correct. A key problem with (B) is that the word *all* makes it too extreme. Such words typically ruin an answer choice, so eliminate it. The first sentence tells you that the balloons can overcome atmospheric obstructions, so (C) is incorrect. Airplanes, along with the other older airborne methods mentioned in the first sentence, are limited in their *inability to view a celestial object long enough.* So, to say that they view a celestial image for a sufficient amount of time would be incorrect. Eliminate (D). It is clear from the passage that dust and water vapor are obstructions at least at some altitudes. It is not clear as to when they cease to be obstructions, if ever. Therefore, you are unable to verify (E), so eliminate it.

55. **E**   In case you haven't brushed up on your Latin, use context clues to figure out *jus ad bellum*. The text mentions that China "uses" Vietnam's invasion of Cambodia for something. Then we read that China conducts a cross-border invasion to attach Vietnam. It would assume that "something" would be a justification to go to war (perhaps the "jus" in *jus ad bellum* is related to the English word "justification"). Choice (E) is therefore correct. There is no reference to a revolution, so (A) is not supported. Eliminate it. China wants to go to war with Vietnam in this passage, so it would not be reasonable that China either wants to give political aid or establish diplomacy. Therefore, you can eliminate (B) and (C). The text does not support any claim that the invasion was a lost cause for China. Eliminate (D).

56. **B**   The author sees awareness of hypertension as an urgent matter. This can be supported in the final sentence when the author writes, *awareness of hypertension [is] essential for blood pressure management and control.* Since the author sees awareness as essential, it can be concluded that he is vigilant, or alert, about the matter. Choice (B) is correct. *Nonplussed* means surprised and confused, which does not describe the author's attitude. Eliminate (A). The author is adamant about being aware of hypertension; therefore, he cannot be described as *nonchalant*, which means with little care, or *dismissive*, which means feeling that something is not worthy of consideration. Eliminate (C) and (E). However, as much as the author cares about the issue, he cannot be described as *melodramatic*, or overly emotional, as that would be an extreme interpretation of what the text says. Therefore, (D) is incorrect.

Chapter 8
Reading Practice
Test 2

READING

1 of 56

A recent study found dozens of contaminants within the protected areas of Congaree National Park in South Carolina. The study examined whether contaminants are commonly found within protected areas. The contaminants found were detected at levels below any considered to pose a risk to the health of park visitors who might drink or come in contact with waters in the backcountry. Additional research would need to take place to determine if the present levels or mixture of contaminants could cause adverse health impacts to aquatic organisms.

According to the statement above, which of the following must be true?

- Ⓧ Contaminants are harmful to the health of aquatic organisms.

- Ⓐ Park visitors will benefit from drinking the water in protected areas of the park.

- Ⓧ South Carolina's parks are free from contaminants that could harm humans.

- Ⓧ Not all organisms are affected by contaminants in the same way.

- Ⓧ Contaminants in unprotected areas of the park will yield the same results.

2 of 56

Army art from the Vietnam War is unlike Army art from any other period. In striking contrast to the more conventional artistic approaches of the world wars, the Vietnam period is characterized by a wide stylistic diversity with many artists working in bright, vibrant colors and an expressive manner. Some artists preferred quick sketches or watercolors, with figures and landscape elements defined by only a few swift brushstrokes. Figures are often thin or ghost-like and are sometimes dwarfed by the landscape or war machines surrounding them.

As used in the statement above, "dwarfed" most nearly means

- Ⓠ simplified

- Ⓐ overwhelmed

- Ⓠ shrunken

- Ⓠ featured

- Ⓠ haunted

3 of 56

A distinguished thinker, Mr. Guglielmo Ferrero, has found the charm of Fogazzaro in the deep seriousness of the historic and social setting of his novels. This setting (save perhaps in 'Piccolo Mondo Antico') is suggested rather than described. It too is implicit in character portrayal rather than explicit in plot. It reveals its presence, rather than in social criticism, in an undertone of earnest civic purpose fundamental in all of Fogazzaro's extremely rich and complicated lyric moods. These moods, when most intense and most characteristic, rise usually from the conflict in individuals between higher spiritual ideals and the natural impulses of human nature.

It can be inferred from the statement above that "Piccolo Mondo Antico" would most likely be characterized by

- Ⓟ explicit descriptions

- Ⓟ high spirituality

- Ⓟ impulsive conflict

- Ⓟ humorous insights

- Ⓟ implicit character portrayal

READING

Communication technologies have the power to transform our lives in many positive ways. When technology is accessible for people with disabilities,
Line it can bridge gaps, opening doors to jobs, education,
(5) recreation, and the commercial marketplace. By way of example, accessible broadband technologies can help level the playing field for people who cannot see, hear, or easily get around, and thereby break down not only physical, but attitudinal barriers for
(10) people with disabilities. However, when accessibility is forgotten or ignored, and physical or technical barriers create obstacles to technological innovations, the consequences can be dire. Without access, people with disabilities are prevented from having
(15) the tools they need to improve their productivity and self-sufficiency. Opportunities for growth and independence are cut off, access to Internet commerce is denied, and even exercising one's civic responsibilities can become a challenge.

4 of 56

Which of the following would be an example of "physical or technical barriers" (lines 11–12)?

- A voice-controlled device that operates household appliances
- A smartphone with small, nonadjustable font
- A streaming video service that offers closed captioning
- A computer with "sticky keys" that create sequential keystrokes by pressing a single button
- A flexible, adjustable computer monitor

It can be inferred from the passage that making technology accessible to people with disabilities could

- be a challenge
- revolutionize commerce
- present obstacles
- create career opportunities
- require civic responsibilities.

6 of 56

Which of the following could be substituted for the phrase "level the playing field for" in line 7 with the least change in meaning?

- give the benefit of the doubt to
- give a second chance to
- extend an olive branch to
- lower the standards for
- provide equal access to

READING

Discipline rates (out-of-school suspension and expulsion rates) at District of Columbia (D.C.) charter schools dropped from school years 2011-12
Line through 2013-14. However, these rates remained
(5) about double the rates of charter schools nationally, slightly higher than D.C. traditional public schools, and disproportionately high for some student groups and schools. Specifically, during this period, suspension rates in D.C. charter schools dropped
(10) from about 16 percent of all students to about 13 percent, and expulsions, which were relatively rare, went down by about a half percent. Absent a coordinated plan to continue progress in reducing discipline rates in charter schools, as well as
(15) clarified roles, responsibilities, and authorities of D.C. agencies with respect to oversight of discipline in charter schools, continued progress may be slowed.

The author's attitude about the drop in out-of-school suspensions and expulsion rates is best understood as

- dispassionately informative
- playfully naïve
- enthusiastically laudatory
- cautiously optimistic
- callously disapproving

The author mentions Washington, D.C. "traditional public schools" (line 6) in order to

- offer a point of comparison
- give a model of an ideal system
- show an example of a system with a higher discipline rate
- present the data more objectively
- call attention to possible anomaly

How do the discipline rates in charter schools around the country compare to Washington, D.C. charter schools?

- Discipline rates in charter schools around the country are 16%, while those in D.C. are 13%.
- Unlike charter schools in D.C., there is no data on charter schools around the country.
- Discipline rates in charter schools around the country are roughly equal to those in D.C.
- Discipline rates in charter schools around the country are significantly higher than those of D.C. charter schools.
- Discipline rates in charter schools around the country are half that of D.C. charter schools.

The passage is primarily concerned with

- advocating the status quo
- criticizing a conclusion
- analyzing data
- exploring underlying causes
- uncovering multiple explanations

The author includes the final sentence of the passage in order to

- resolve a conflict
- encourage continuing a previous plan
- explain a new issue
- recommend a course of action
- undermine a conclusion

READING

A new study providing an unprecedented regional view of the earth's crust beneath Yellowstone National Park will begin with a
Line helicopter electromagnetic and magnetic (HEM)
(5) survey. Scientists hope to distinguish zones of cold fresh water, hot saline water, steam, clay and unaltered rock from one another to understand Yellowstone's myriad hydrothermal systems. These observations, combined with existing geophysical,
(10) geochemical, geological and borehole data, will help close a major knowledge gap between the surface hydrothermal systems and the deeper magmatic system. For example, research shows that the hot water spurting from Yellowstone's geysers
(15) originates as old precipitation, snow and rain that percolates down into the crust, is heated and ultimately returns to the surface. This process takes hundreds if not thousands of years. Little, however, is currently known about the paths taken by the
(20) waters.

According to the passage, the deepest hydrothermal systems contain

- cold fresh water
- magma
- hot saline water
- snow and rain
- steam

As used in the passage, "percolates" (line 16) most nearly means

- filters
- cleans
- encapsulates
- wavers
- changes

Which of the following can be inferred from the passage about surface hydrothermal systems?

- They exist primarily in Yellowstone National Park.
- They represent a gap in scientists' knowledge.
- Old precipitation is heated in them.
- They are composed of magma.
- Scientists have a solid understanding of them.

READING

The summer smog season, also known as the ozone season, is a powerful reminder of how important it is to have clean air to breathe. Smog-causing air pollution from dirty power plants, automobiles, and other sources is linked to serious health problems, like asthma, strokes, heart attacks, and even early deaths.

The author would most likely agree with which of the following statements?

- More people die during the smog season than during any other time of the year.
- The ozone season is correlated with strokes.
- Dirty power plants and automobiles are the two largest contributors to smog.
- Summer provides cleaner air than any other season of the year.
- Asthma primarily occurs in the summer.

There are 4,000 people who lose their lives to large truck accidents each year, and over 100,000 people are injured. There's a 4.4 percent increase in accidents from 2014 to 2015. The numbers represent a truck crash each week in America. It is paramount that Congress works in a deliberative way, having a discussion on what is one of the monumental areas in which people are dying in America.

The author's tone in the statement above can best be described as

- conciliatory *Pacifying*
- tentative *unsure*
- glib *Insincere*
- insistent
- resigned

Of the major American novelists, Mark Twain derived least from any literary, or at any rate from any bookish, tradition. Hawthorne had the example of Irving, and Cooper had that of Scott, when they began to write; Howells and Henry James instinctively fell into step with the classics. Mark Twain came up into literature from the popular ranks, trained in the school of newspaper fun-making and humorous lecturing, only gradually instructed in the more orthodox arts of the literary profession.

Which of the following can be inferred from the statement?

- Mark Twain is not to be considered a major American novelist.
- Newspaper fun-making is part of the orthodox arts of the literary profession.
- Henry James has experience in humorous lecturing.
- Hawthorne was unfamiliar with the popular ranks.
- Irving and Scott are indicative of the literary tradition.

READING

Scientists recently reconstructed the skin of endangered green turtles, marking the first time that skin of a non-mammal was successfully engineered in a laboratory. In turn, the scientists were able to grow a tumor-associated virus to better understand certain tumor diseases. In an international collaboration, scientists engineered turtle skin in order to grow a virus called chelonid herpesvirus 5, or ChHV5. The scientists used cells from tumors and normal skin from turtles to reconstruct the complex three-dimensional structure of turtle skin, allowing growth of ChHV5 in the lab. Growing the virus gave scientists an opportunity to observe virus replication in unprecedented detail, revealing bizarre systems such as sun-shaped virus replication centers where the viruses form within cells.

Line (5)

(10)

(15)

18 of 56

The function of the second sentence in the above passage is

- ⓐ to reveal the motivation behind an action
- ⓑ to offer opposing evidence to a previous claim
- ⓒ to define a term mentioned in the first sentence
- ⓓ to give the author's opinion
- ⓔ to introduce a controversial viewpoint

19 of 56

According to the passage, how was ChHV5 used by scientists?

- ⓐ It was turned into a complex three-dimensional structure.
- ⓑ It was maintained as a control in an experiment on another virus.
- ⓒ It was given to turtles to help treat tumors.
- ⓓ It was manipulated to engineer turtle skin.
- ⓔ It was grown in the lab in order to observe how the virus reproduces.

Which of the following best describes the organization of this passage?

- ⓐ A hypothesis is offered, methods to test it are laid out, and data from the experiment are provided.
- ⓑ An experiment is introduced, its details are explained, and the purpose for the experiment is conveyed.
- ⓒ A routine procedure is discussed, problems with the procedure are analyzed, and real-world implications are noted.
- ⓓ A scientific breakthrough is reported, its significance is celebrated, and criticisms of the breakthrough are answered.
- ⓔ A new approach is uncovered, its fallacies are investigated, and a new area of research is presented.

READING

Questions 21-24 refer to the following passage.

Childhood obesity continues to be a local, state, and national problem affecting not only children, but their families, schools, employers, and
Line communities. Obesity affects approximately 12.5
(5) million (17%) US children and adolescents aged 2 to 19 years, with higher levels among some groups of children, including those living in low-income households. Obesity can have harmful effects during childhood. Children who have obesity are more likely
(10) to have high blood pressure and high cholesterol, which are risk factors for cardiovascular disease. They are more likely to have asthma, sleep apnea, fatty liver, insulin resistance, and type 2 diabetes. Obesity is also related to psychosocial problems in
(15) children, such as anxiety, depression, low self-esteem, and social problems such as bullying and stigma. To address obesity, the National Academy of Medicine, among other groups, has called for interventions to alter nutrition and physical activity environments
(20) and promote behavior change in multiple settings to reach adults and children.

21 of 56

Which of the following best states the main idea of the passage?

- Psychosocial problems can arise from childhood obesity.

- Childhood obesity is the most significant public health issue in the United States.

- 12.5 million children are in danger of becoming obese.

- Childhood obesity can lead to a number of serious health consequences.

- There are several ways to address childhood obesity.

22 of 56

The author lists "asthma, sleep apnea, fatty liver, insulin resistance, and type 2 diabetes" (lines 12–13) in order to

- inform the reader of some possible consequences of childhood obesity

- further a stigma around the issue of childhood obesity

- cast doubt on the harmfulness of childhood obesity

- provide possible alternative treatments to childhood obesity

- offer a list of health concerns that inevitably result from childhood obesity

23 of 56

The author of the passage establishes a correlation between obesity and which of the following?

- Age
- Poverty
- Family
- School
- Behavior

24 of 56

Why does the author of the passage mention the National Academy of Medicine?

- To give evidence of experts who doubt the significance of childhood obesity

- To contradict findings presented earlier in the passage

- To give possible behavioral changes that will lower the risk of obesity.

- To call for interventions in how the group conducts its studies

- To offer a plan that will guarantee positive health outcomes

READING

Any type of psychology that treats *motives*, thereby endeavoring to answer the question as to *why* men behave as they do, is called a *dynamic*
Line *psychology*. By its very nature it cannot be
(5) merely a descriptive psychology, content to depict the *what* and the *how* of human behavior. The boldness of dynamic psychology in striking for causes stands in marked contrast to the timid, "more scientific," view that seeks nothing else than
(10) the establishment of a mathematical function for the relation between some artificially simple stimulus and some equally artificial and simple response. If the psychology of personality is to be more than a matter of coefficients of correlation, it too must be
(15) a dynamic psychology, and seek first and foremost a sound and adequate theory of the nature of human dispositions.

Dynamic psychology is a field that seeks to

Ⓐ understand nature

Ⓑ be more scientific

Ⓒ establish mathematical functions

Ⓓ determine reasons for human behavior

Ⓔ develop a descriptive perspective

The passage is primarily concerned with

Ⓐ defining the theories within dynamic psychology

Ⓑ discussing the various fields of psychology

Ⓒ exposing the flaws of psychology

Ⓓ explaining the origins of a field of psychology

Ⓔ distinguishing one approach to psychology from another

How does the author characterize the "more scientific view" described in line 9?

Ⓐ Disjointed

Ⓑ Engaging

Ⓒ Without merit

Ⓓ Fascinating

Ⓔ Dull

READING

The Spanish city of Barcelona is the home of Catalans, a people of the northeastern region of Spain. Many are surprised to know that the Catalan language is not a dialect of Spanish, but rather an entirely different language. While both are considered Romance languages, Catalan differs from Spanish in some substantial ways. For instance, the cluttering of consonants in Catalan more resembles Portuguese than it does Spanish. However, a trip to Barcelona will not leave a Spanish speaker unable to communicate: most Catalans in Barcelona speak Spanish, as well.

Which of the following best describes the structure of the statement above?

- An argument is given, counterarguments are introduced, and supporting details for each side are developed.

- A topic is introduced, related facts are given, and it concludes with a historical argument.

- An argument is given, supporting details are laid out, and it concludes with a statement of compromise.

- A topic is introduced, a surprising distinction is made, and details about that distinction are explored.

- A fact is put forth, alternate explanations for that fact are listed, and one explanation is declared to be the true one.

The popular use of computer-driven cars is not as far off as one might expect, yet the benefits of such technology are still not widely accepted. Motorists will benefit from self-driving technology in two substantial ways: efficiency and safety. Clogged streets and frustrating traffic jams will be a thing of the past as cars will be able to communicate with one another and work in tandem to effectively move commuters to their desired destination. Further, automobile accidents caused by drug and alcohol inebriation will sharply decline since there will be less of a need for intoxicated individuals to operate their vehicles.

The author's attitude toward computer-driven cars can best be described as

- patronizing

- sarcastic

- scornful

- skeptical

- supportive

READING

The announcement of Edward Bok's retirement came as a great surprise to his friends. Save for one here and there, who had a clearer vision, the feeling was general that he had made a mistake. He
Line
(5) was fifty-six, in the prime of life, never in better health, with "success lying easily upon him"—said one; "at the very summit of his career," said another—and all agreed it was "queer," "strange,"— unless, they argued, he was really ill. Even the most
(10) acute students of human affairs among his friends wondered. It seemed incomprehensible that any man should want to give up before he was, for some reason, compelled to do so. A man should go on until he "dropped in the harness," they argued.

What does the passage suggest about retirement?

Ⓐ It should not come about by choice.

Ⓑ It is the greatest period of a person's life.

Ⓒ It is strange.

Ⓓ It is generally seen as a mistake.

Ⓔ It is advisable only when one first saves enough money.

How does the passage characterize people's opinions of Bok's decision?

Ⓐ They met the decision with full admiration.

Ⓑ They perceived the decision to be abnormal.

Ⓒ They openly opposed the decision.

Ⓓ They cautiously supported the decision.

Ⓔ They found the decision to be unremarkable.

What is the function of the final sentence of this passage?

Ⓐ To use a famous saying as a means of persuasion

Ⓑ To offer words of advice in support of Bok's decision

Ⓒ To introduce a new topic with a thought-provoking cliché

Ⓓ To support a previous statement with an idiom

Ⓔ To give context by appealing to the subject's wisdom

READING

Questions 33-38 refer to the following pair of passages.

Passage 1

Clean energy demand continues to grow
worldwide, with an investment of nearly $400 billion
in 2015 and 2016. Many governments see investment
Line in this technology as important to transforming
(5) energy markets and claim the additional benefits
from those investments, for example, stronger heavy
industry sector, maintaining and growing jobs, and
avoiding the health consequences of pollution. In a
global clean energy market, the U.S. is considering
(10) how to best invest in the power, transportation, and
industrial energy sectors as they change nationally
and globally. In this context, carbon capture, use,
and storage (CCUS) remains a critically important
and under-supported sector in the clean energy
(15) industry. CCUS includes carbon capture and storage,
CO_2 enhanced oil recovery, CO_2 conversion and
use, and even carbon removal from the atmosphere.
These different pathways provide real commercial
and environmental opportunities for companies,
(20) communities, and governments.

Passage 2

Before America ever sees the deployment of
a commercial solar fuel system, a lot of discovery
science must be accomplished. For the solar fuel
process, also known as artificial photosynthesis, new
(25) materials and catalysts will need to be developed
through research. If this research yields the right
materials, scientists could create a system that could
consolidate solar power and energy storage into one
cohesive process. This would potentially remove the
(30) intermittency of solar energy and make it a reliable
power source for chemical fuels production. That is a
game-changer.

33 of 56

Which of the following best describes the relationship
between Passage 1 and Passage 2 ?

- Ⓐ Passage 1 proposes a specific type of clean energy
  production, while Passage 2 strongly opposes that
  type.
- Ⓑ Passage 1 argues the economic importance
  of clean energy, while Passage 2 argues the
  environmental importance.
- Ⓒ Passage 1 opposes the movement toward clean
  energy, while Passage 2 supports it.
- Ⓓ Passage 1 advocates one form of clean energy
  development, while Passage 2 advocates a
  different form.
- Ⓔ Passage 1 casts doubt on a form of renewable
  energy described in Passage 2.

34 of 56

As used in line 30, "intermittency" most nearly means

- Ⓐ imprecision
- Ⓑ toxicity
- Ⓒ expense
- Ⓓ unreliability
- Ⓔ plausibility

35 of 56

Both passages would agree with which of the following
statements about energy production?

- Ⓐ Alternative energy sources will create jobs.
- Ⓑ It is possible to more efficiently capture and
  store energy sources.
- Ⓒ Solar energy is a cleaner form of energy
  production than carbon capture.
- Ⓓ American investment in energy is key to its
  economic success.
- Ⓔ Demand for clean energy is experiencing global
  growth.

READING

Which of the following best characterizes what the author of Passage 2 advocates in terms of the future of energy production?

Ⓐ The collection and storage of solar energy should become a singular process.

Ⓑ Solar energy should be supplemented with other renewable sources.

Ⓒ Carbon capture is capable of creating new opportunities for industry.

Ⓓ Solar energy needs to be discovered through research.

Ⓔ Carbon capture is key to chemical fuels production.

Which of the following, if true, would most weaken the argument in Passage 1 regarding the use of CCUS?

Ⓐ Jobs in CO_2 conversion and use have seen dramatic growth.

Ⓑ Environmental advocacy groups pressure companies to use clean energy.

Ⓒ The $400 billion-dollar investment increased by 20% in the following year.

Ⓓ CCUS remained under-supported in the clean energy industry into 2017.

Ⓔ Non-carbon-based energy sources are given tax incentives due to their perceived cleanliness.

Unlike the author of Passage 2, the author of Passage 1

Ⓐ describes a technology that has yet to be fully realized

Ⓑ uses scientific terminology

Ⓒ describes the economic benefits of alternative energy

Ⓓ outlines multiple examples of alternative energy sources

Ⓔ speculates on potential research

READING

Some avian influenza, or bird flu, viruses that are able to enter North America from other continents through migrating birds can be deadly to poultry and can infect waterfowl populations. Scientists analyzed the genes, or genome, of the avian flu viruses that spread in the United States during 2014-2015. This outbreak resulted in more than $3 billion in losses to the United States poultry industry. The study found that even though the viruses likely evolved in Asia, they easily infected and spread among North American wild birds. The viruses were also able to spread between domestic and wild birds, in a process called spillover. However, this study found that the rate of spillover was minor, and the poultry outbreak was able to persist without further transmission from wild birds.

According to the statement, which of the following is true about spillover?

Ⓐ Spillover is unique to North American birds.

Ⓑ Spillover actually had little effect on the spread of bird flu.

Ⓒ Spillover is not necessary for domestic bird populations to be infected.

Ⓓ Spillover was responsible for most cases of bird flu in North America.

Ⓔ Spillover involved the transmission of the virus from domestic birds to wild birds.

There are two main types of electrical charging that lead to lightning during a volcanic eruption: 1) "frictional charging" from colliding particles of volcanic ash and 2) "ice charging" from the freezing and growth of ice and hail. The first happens during all types of explosive eruptions, because there are always ash particles colliding with each other, especially close to a volcano's vent. However, "ice charging" occurs only when the hot ash plume reaches high into the freezing-cold parts of the atmosphere. When this happens, the electrification becomes much more intense, and more like a regular thunderstorm.

Based on the information above, which of the following statements is a valid conclusion?

Ⓐ Thunderstorms tend to originate from frictional charging in volcanoes.

Ⓑ Regular thunderstorms involve the interaction of hot and cold air.

Ⓒ Volcanic eruptions have only two types of electrical charging that lead to lightning.

Ⓓ Frictional charging is rare compared to ice charging.

Ⓔ Ash particles do not collide during ice charging.

In the isolation and chaos of the 9th and 10th centuries, European leaders no longer attempted to restore Roman institutions, but adopted whatever would work. The result was that Europe developed a relatively new and effective set of institutions, adapted to a moneyless economy, inadequate transportation and communication facilities, an ineffective central government, and a constant threat of armed attack by raiders, such as the Vikings, Magyars, and Saracens. The most well-known of the institutions was manorialism (the organization of peasants), monasticism (the organization of churchmen), and feudalism (the institution of the aristocracy).

It can be inferred from the passage that feudalism was

Ⓐ the primary reason for an ineffective central government

Ⓑ possible at least in part due to the lack of a moneyed economy and effective transportation

Ⓒ one of only three institutions from the 9th and 10th centuries

Ⓓ introduced by Vikings, Magyars, and Saracens

Ⓔ a successfully restored Roman institution

Questions 42-46 refer to the following passage.

In the year when President Garfield died, New York saw the unusual sight of two young "silk-stockings," neither of whom had ever been in politics
Line before, running for office in a popular election. One
(5) was the representative of vast inherited wealth, the other of the bluest of the old Knickerbocker blood: William Waldorf Astor and Theodore Roosevelt. One ran for Congress, pouring out money like water, contemptuously confident that so he could
(10) buy his way in. The newspapers reported his nightly progress from saloon to saloon, where "the boys" were thirstily waiting to whoop it up for him, and the size of "the wad" he left at each place, as with ill suppressed disgust he fled to the next.

(15) The other, nominated for the State Legislature on an issue of clean streets and clean politics, though but a year out of college, made his canvass squarely upon that basis, and astounded old-time politicians by the fire he put into the staid residents
(20) of the brownstone district, who were little in the habit of bothering about elections.

As used in line 13, "the wad" most nearly means

Ⓐ a series of lies

Ⓑ a sum of money

Ⓒ campaign promises

Ⓓ a crowd of people

Ⓔ feelings of disgust

Which of the following describes the organization of the passage?

Ⓐ Two politicians are introduced, and their divergent approaches are summarized.

Ⓑ Two elected officials are celebrated, and their plans to improve New York are analyzed.

Ⓒ Two politicians are criticized, and a defense for each man is offered.

Ⓓ Two leaders are endorsed, and the reasons for each endorsement are laid out.

Ⓔ Two politicians are juxtaposed, and their merits are called into question.

READING

It can be inferred from the passage that Theodore Roosevelt

- furiously spent money on the campaign trail
- was advanced in age when he first ran for office
- won his first election
- was a resident of the brownstone district
- inspired even non-regular voters to support him

The passage is primarily concerned with

- the political stances of two famous candidates
- informing the reader of the history of New York politics
- contrasting the political strategies of two individuals from similar backgrounds
- the outcome of two elections
- creating a picture of New York at the time of President Garfield's death

The author mentions "silk-stockings" (lines 2–3) in order to

- suggest the men had crooked motives
- criticize the men's fashion senses
- make the candidates' socioeconomic standings evident
- make the men more relatable to the common man
- convey the adversity each man had overcome

READING

Questions 47-49 refer to the following.

Maren is the CEO of a tech company with offices in four cities around the country: Seattle, Los Angeles, Chicago, and Dallas. In order to ensure smooth operations, Maren travels extensively among the four offices, discussing an array of topics. Below is her schedule for October:

Monday	Tuesday	Wednesday	Thursday	Friday
		1 **Meeting topic:** Budget **Location:** Seattle	**2** **Meeting topic:** Research and development **Location:** Seattle	**3** **Meeting topic:** Research and development **Location:** Seattle
6 **Meeting topic:** Employee relations **Location:** Dallas	**7** **Meeting topic:** Marketing **Location:** Chicago	**8** **Meeting topic:** Budget **Location:** Chicago	**9** **Meeting topic:** Budget **Location:** Los Angeles	**10** **Meeting topic:** Corporate partnerships **Location:** Los Angeles
13 **Meeting topic:** Corporate partnerships **Location:** Dallas	**14** **Meeting topic:** Budget **Location:** Dallas	**15** **Meeting topic:** Research and development **Location:** Seattle	**16** **Meeting topic:** Budget **Location:** Seattle	**17** **Meeting topic:** Budget **Location:** Chicago
20 **Meeting topic:** Research and development **Location:** Los Angeles	**21** **Meeting topic:** Corporate partnerships **Location:** Los Angeles	**22** **Meeting topic:** Corporate partnerships **Location:** Los Angeles	**23** **Meeting topic:** Marketing **Location:** Seattle	**24** **Meeting topic:** Employee relations **Location:** Seattle
27 **Meeting topic:** Budget **Location:** Chicago	**28** **Meeting topic:** Research and development **Location:** Chicago	**29** **Meeting topic:** Marketing **Location:** Dallas	**30** **Meeting topic:** Marketing **Location:** Dallas	**31** **Meeting topic:** Corporate partnerships **Location:** Dallas

D - 6

READING

Which of the following statements is best supported by the information on the calendar?

Ⓐ The Chicago and Seattle offices do not employ corporate partnership specialists.

Ⓑ Maren will conduct the first employee relations meeting of the year on the 6th of the month.

Ⓒ Maren will attend twice as many budgeting meetings as marketing meetings.

Ⓓ The Los Angeles office employs the most people.

Ⓔ Maren will conduct most of her October meetings in Dallas.

In which offices did Maren have at least two marketing meetings?

Select **all** that apply.

☐ Seattle

☐ Chicago

☐ Dallas

Which of the following claims about research and development is best supported by the information on the calendar?

Ⓐ Research and development meetings take longer than any other type of meeting.

Ⓑ Research and development occupies the most meeting days for the first half of the month.

Ⓒ The company's research and development efforts have been on the rise.

Ⓓ The office in Dallas lacks research and development facilities and personnel.

Ⓔ It is essential for the company to have a meeting on research and development at least once per week.

READING

Questions 50-53 refer to the following passage.

Black lung disease is caused through the inhalation of coal mine dust, and it leads to severe breathing complications. It is found mostly in central
Line Appalachia, in particular the states of Pennsylvania,
(5) West Virginia, Kentucky, and Virginia. According to the Department of Labor, black lung disease contributed to the deaths of over 75,000 miners from 1968 to 2007. While overall rates have dropped since 1968, research shows that there has been a
(10) spike since the early 1990s, particularly in the most severe, fast progressing type of black lung disease, which has increasingly affected younger miners. Last October, the Center for Public Integrity and ABC News released findings from a year-long investigation
(15) examining how coal industry doctors and lawyers helped defeat and delay benefit claims from the growing number of miners suffering from black lung disease and their grieving survivors, who have been consistently denied or delayed justice from
(20) a system that seems increasingly stacked against them. According to data from the Department of Labor, black lung claimants are waiting an average of 429 days just for their cases to be assigned to an administrative law judge and an additional 90
(25) to 120 days after assignment before their cases are heard in court.

50 of 56

Which of the following would be an appropriate title for this passage?

 "Black Lung Disease Relief Slowed by Coal Industry"

 "Causes of Black Lung Disease"

 "Black Lung Disease on the Decline in Coal Country"

 "Coal Industry Successfully Fights for the Health of Former Employees"

 "Black Lung Disease: The Silent Killer"

51 of 56

It can be inferred from the passage that the coal industry

🅐 has been effective in helping those afflicted with black lung disease

🅑 has delivered benefits to black lung disease claimants within an average of 429 days

🅒 is viewed by a number of coal miners as legally responsible for their illness

🅓 has spiked since the early 1990s

🅔 has been found guilty in a criminal trial

52 of 56

Which of the following best illustrates the "system" mentioned in line 20?

🅐 Construction workers contracting illness due to years of breathing asbestos on jobsites

🅑 The auto industry being forced to install airbags to maximize safety

🅒 A doctor prescribing a less effective medication because he was pressured by a pharmaceutical representative

🅓 Coal companies conspiring to overcharge for energy

🅔 The tobacco industry using its deep resources to avoid payment to lung cancer victims

53 of 56

According to the passage, the Center for Public Integrity and ABC News demonstrated that

🅐 black lung disease is worse than originally thought

🅑 the coal industry has lost in court when cases have been heard

🅒 the coal industry dedicates more resources to lawyers than it does to coal miners

🅓 cases of black lung disease are increasing

🅔 the coal industry has worked diligently to avoid paying out benefits

READING

How a wind energy facility is designed can influence the behavior of animal predators and their prey. Scientists placed motion-activated cameras facing the entrances of 46 active desert tortoise burrows in a wind energy facility near Palm Springs, California. Video recordings showed that visits to burrows from five predators—bobcats, gray foxes, coyotes, black bears and western spotted skunks—increased closer to dirt roads, and decreased closer to wind turbines. Results suggest that infrastructure associated with wind energy facilities, such as dirt roads or culverts, may create movement corridors through disturbed habitat that some animals prefer. Dirt roads may act as funnels for predators because they are potential corridors through the wind energy facility.

The word "funnels" in the final sentence most nearly means

(A) areas to be avoided

(B) wind tunnels

(C) passageways

(D) decoys

(E) hiding places

There can be no doubt that the early appearance of Russian armies in East Prussia in September 1914 diverted the energies and attention of the Germans from their first victorious drive upon Paris. The sufferings and deaths of scores of thousands of ill-led Russian peasants saved France from complete overthrow in that momentous opening campaign, and made all Western Europe the debtors of that great and tragic people. But the strain of the war upon this sprawling, ill-organized empire was too heavy for its strength. The Russian common soldiers were sent into battle without guns to support them, without even rifle ammunition; they were wasted by their officers and generals in a delirium of militarist enthusiasm.

According to the statement, who are the "great and tragic people"?

(A) Germans

(B) French

(C) Russians

(D) Western Europeans

(E) East Prussians

Chronic absenteeism is widespread—about one out of every seven students missed three weeks or more of school in 2013–14. That translates to approximately 98 million school days lost. Research suggests the reasons for chronic absenteeism are as varied as the challenges our students and families face—including poor health, limited transportation, and a lack of safety—which can be particularly acute in disadvantaged communities and areas of poverty. Whatever its causes, chronic absenteeism can be devastating: Children who are chronically absent in preschool, kindergarten, and first grade are much less likely to read at grade level by the third grade. Students who cannot read at grade level by the end of third grade are four times more likely than proficient readers to drop out of high school.

Which of the following best states the main idea of the statement?

(A) 98 million school days are lost per year due to chronic absenteeism.

(B) Chronic absenteeism is caused by factors such as poor health, limited transportation, and a lack of safety.

(C) Communities of poverty tend to be more affected than other communities by chronic absenteeism.

(D) There exists an array of long-term consequences associated with chronic absenteeism.

(E) Chronic absenteeism may lead one to drop out of high school.

Chapter 9
Reading Practice
Test 2: Answers and
Explanations

READING PRACTICE TEST 2 ANSWER KEY

1.	D		29.	E
2.	B		30.	A
3.	A		31.	B
4.	B		32.	D
5.	D		33.	D
6.	E		34.	D
7.	D		35.	B
8.	A		36.	A
9.	E		37.	E
10.	C		38.	C
11.	D		39.	C
12.	B		40.	B
13.	A		41.	B
14.	E		42.	B
15.	B		43.	A
16.	D		44.	E
17.	E		45.	C
18.	A		46.	C
19.	E		47.	A
20.	B		48.	C
21.	D		49.	D
22.	A		50.	A
23.	B		51.	C
24.	C		52.	E
25.	D		53.	E
26.	E		54.	C
27.	E		55.	C
28.	D		56.	D

READING PRACTICE TEST 2 EXPLANATIONS

1. **D** While the contaminants were found to be *at levels below any considered to pose a risk to the health of park visitors,* the text also mentions that further study would be required to see whether the contaminants were dangerous to aquatic organisms. In other words, just because humans are not harmed by the contaminants, there is not certainty that other organisms would be. Choice (D) best aligns with this information. Since additional research has not yet been conducted, it is not clear whether contaminants would be harmful to aquatic organisms. Choice (A) is incorrect. While the study found that the water is not harmful for humans to drink, there is no evidence that the water is beneficial. Eliminate (B). Be wary of answer choices that take what the text says too far: the study focused only on Congaree National Park's protected areas, not its unprotected parts and definitely not all of South Carolina's parks. Eliminate (E) and (C).

2. **B** Look for your own word to replace *dwarfed*. The final sentence tells you that the figures are *thin* and *ghost-like* in comparison to the landscapes and war machines that surround them. The figures in the images are therefore *overwhelmed* by their surroundings, (B). Eliminate (D) because *featured* is the opposite of what you are looking for; the figures are not the primary focus of the images. Eliminate (E) because *haunted* is unrelated to *dwarfed*. The landscape cannot *simplify* or *shrink* the figures, so (A) and (C) are incorrect. Choice (B) is correct.

3. **A** Ferrero's novels are *suggested rather than described* and implicit, not explicit. Because the second sentence tells you that Piccolo Mondo Anticó is the exception to Ferrero's trends, you can conclude that this particular work is described and explicit. This matches (A) very closely. Spirituality in (B) is taken out of context, as the last sentence uses the term *spiritual* to describe the internal conflicts of Ferrero's characters. Eliminate (B). Likewise, the reference to conflict in that sentence is also taken out of context. Eliminate (C). There is no reference in the text to humor, so (D) is incorrect. Choice (E) is incorrect as it describes Ferrero's normal writing, not his portrayal in Piccolo Mondo Antico.

4. **B** The text notes that physical or technical barriers occur when *accessibility is forgotten.* Therefore, look for an answer choice that describes a lack of accessibility for a person with a disability. Choice (B) is correct because small, nonadjustable font would provide a barrier to a person with a visual impairment. Choices (A), (C), (D), and (E) each describe accommodations that technologies can make for people with disabilities. Therefore, none of those is an appropriate answer.

5. **D** The text states that when technology is accessible for people with disabilities, it can open *doors to jobs.* This best aligns with (D). Choices (A) and (E) are incorrect because they take the final sentence out of context. Choice (C) is incorrect because making technology more accessible would remove, not present, obstacles. There is no evidence of the impact that accessible technology has on the economy as a whole, so (B) is not supported. Eliminate it.

6. **E** Later in this sentence, the author states that accessible broadband technologies can *break down… barriers for people with disabilities.* This best aligns with (E). Choices (A), (B), (C), and (D) do not mean to remove barriers, so those choices can be eliminated.

7. **D** The author describes that suspension and expulsion rates have dropped (a good thing), but cautions that without a coordinated plan, this progress may slow down (a bad thing). This can be described as *cautiously optimistic.* Choice (D) is correct. The author is not entirely dispassionate, as an opinion is offered to the reader. Eliminate (A). The author cannot be described as playful or naïve, as there is close attention paid to the seriousness of the issue. Eliminate (B). Since the author offers some cautions at the end of the text, his or her attitude cannot be described as *enthusiastically laudatory* (praising). Eliminate (C). The author does see progress being made, so (E) can be eliminated as well.

8. **A** The author focuses on Washington, D.C. charter schools, so connections to charter schools nationwide or traditional schools in Washington, D.C. are meant as points of comparison. Choice (A) is therefore correct. The traditional schools are not presented as ideal since they are only slightly lower than the charter schools described in this passage. Eliminate (B). Since the traditional schools are slightly lower in discipline rates, not higher, (C) can be eliminated. The comparison does not affect the objectivity of the data or present an outlier. It shows only a comparable system to give context. Therefore, you can eliminate (D) and (E).

9. **E** The text states that the discipline rates in Washington, D.C. charter schools are *double the rates of charter schools nationally.* Therefore, the claim in (E), that rates in charter schools around the country are half that of D.C., is accurate. Since there is data on both Washington, D.C. charter schools as well as charter schools nationwide, (B) is incorrect. Be careful not to take numbers out of context. Choice (A) is incorrect because it pulls numbers from D.C. charter school's declining discipline rates and applies them to schools nationwide. Finally, since the text makes it clear that discipline rates in D.C. charter schools are higher than discipline rates nationwide, you can eliminate the answer choices with contradictory claims—(C) and (D).

10. **C** The author presents data, compares it to other pieces of data, and makes a recommendation on how to continue a trend. The author therefore evaluates, or analyzes, the data. Choice (C) is correct. Since the author wants some things to change, it cannot be said that the author advocates the status quo. Eliminate (A). The author presents the findings of the study but does not criticize its conclusion, so (B) is incorrect. The passage does not delve into the causes of the disciplinary rates, nor attempt to offer multiple explanations for the data. Eliminate (D) and (E).

11. **D** The author cautions that discipline rates are not likely to continue to drop without a coordinated effort to continue the decline. This is a recommendation, which makes (D) the best answer. Since the author recommends some changes, eliminate (B). There is no conflict presented in the passage that needs to be resolved, so (A) is incorrect. The author does not present a new issue in the final sentence. It continues to focus on decreasing disciplinary rates. Eliminate (C). Finally, since the

author uses the conclusion of the data to recommend a new course, there is no effort to undermine the conclusion of the data. Choice (E) is incorrect.

12. **B** The passage states that the study *will help close a major knowledge gap between the surface hydrothermal systems and the deeper magmatic system.* Accordingly, the deep portions contain magma. Choice (B) is correct. Cold fresh water, hot saline water, and steam are all mentioned earlier in the passage as other components of the hydrothermal system. Be sure not to read those items out of context. Eliminate (A), (C), and (E). Finally, (D) is incorrect, as the passage mentions only snow and rain as *old precipitation,* which seeps through the surface down into the crust.

13. **A** Snow and rain are described as percolating down into the crust and returning to the surface once heated. Without looking at the answer choices, think of a replacement word for *percolating.* "Seeps," which means to slowly flow through a material, would be a good option for a replacement word. This matches (A), *filters,* very closely. The remaining answer choices do not mean seep or imply slowly leaking through a material.

14. **E** You learn from the text that scientists hope to *close a major knowledge gap between the surface hydrothermal systems and the deeper magmatic system.* The knowledge gap tells us that there is much knowledge about one part, but not about the other. Later, the passage states that scientists do not know much *about the paths taken by the waters.* So while they understand the surface part of the process, the deeper, underground process is still unclear. This information best supports (E). While the study is focusing on Yellowstone National Park, there is no information to suggest that this is the only place this phenomenon occurs. Eliminate (A). Choice (B) can also be eliminated because it takes a phrase out of context—it is the deeper hydrothermal systems, not the surface ones, that scientists do not understand. You also learn from the passage that old precipitation is heated deeper below the surface, so (C) is incorrect. Finally, the magma is positioned far below the surface, so (D) can be eliminated as it is contradicted by the text.

15. **B** The ozone season is also the smog season, and the pollution that contributes to smog is linked with health problems, one of which is stroke. Therefore, (B) is correct. Be wary of answer choices that make comparisons: the claims made in (A), (C), and (D) do not exist in the statement. Eliminate them. While asthma can occur during the summer smog season, you do not have any information about how this compares to other seasons. Eliminate (E).

16. **D** The author states that it is *paramount,* or of the utmost importance, for Congress to address the issue of large truck accidents. Therefore, the best answer is (D), *insistent.* The author sees this issue as significant, so *conciliatory* (pacifying), *tentative* (unsure), *glib* (insincere), and *resigned* (accepting, though not thrilled about it) would not accurately describe the tone. Eliminate (A), (B), (C), and (E).

17. **E** The first sentence states that Mark Twain derived little from tradition, whereas two authors (who you can assume are more traditional by contrast) follow the example of Irving and Scott. Therefore, Irving and Scott are indicative of the literary tradition. Choice (E) is correct. Twain was instead

influenced by elements such as *newspaper fun-making,* which is not included in the *orthodox arts of the literary profession*—he later transitioned to that tradition. Eliminate (B). The first sentence opens with *Of the major American novelists, Mark Twain...,* which tells you that Twain is indeed a major American novelist. Choice (A) is incorrect. Since Henry James *fell in step with the classics,* you have no reason to associate him with the less-traditional influences of Twain, such as humorous lecturing. Therefore, (C) is incorrect. There is no indication that Hawthorne was not familiar with the popular ranks, just that he was influenced by a more classic tradition. Eliminate (D).

18. **A** The second sentence states that *scientists were able to grow a tumor-associated virus to better understand certain tumor diseases.* This was the purpose, or motivation, for reconstructing the skin of endangered green turtles. Therefore, (A) is correct. There is no previous claim given, so (B) is incorrect. The second sentence does not define any terms. Eliminate (C). The sentence does not offer a viewpoint or opinion, just a reason for why the experiment was conducted. Eliminate (D) and (E).

19. **E** You learn in the final sentence that the experiment *gave scientists an opportunity to observe virus replication in unprecedented detail.* Therefore, (E), which states that it was grown in order to observe how the virus reproduces, is correct. The turtle skin, not the ChHV5, was turned into a complex three-dimensional structure. Eliminate (A). There is no other virus mentioned in the passage, so (B) is incorrect. The passage does not say that the virus was given to turtles. Choice (C) is incorrect. Further, you can eliminate (D) because the virus was grown on the turtle skin, not the other way around.

20. **B** The first sentence tells you what occurred. The passage also covers how this process was done, and finishes by describing what scientists want to do with this new finding. This best aligns with (B). There is no hypothesis given, so (A) is incorrect. Since replicating turtle skin was done for the first time, it cannot be described as routine. Eliminate (C). There are no criticisms or fallacies discussed in the text, so (D) and (E) are incorrect.

21. **D** After stating how widespread a problem childhood obesity is, the passage gives an array of health risks associated with the condition. Therefore, the main idea of the passage is that childhood obesity is linked to a variety of health problems. This best aligns with (D). When looking for the main idea, try not to get trapped by supporting details. Choices (A), (C), and (E) offer supporting details, not the main idea, so eliminate them. Be suspicious of superlative language. While the passage would support the claim that childhood obesity is a major issue, nowhere in the passage does it state that childhood obesity is the *most* significant public health issue in the United States. Eliminate (B).

22. **A** The author mentions that those who have childhood obesity are more likely to have the symptoms listed. Therefore, the correct answer is (A). These symptoms are not stigmas, but actual consequences associated with childhood obesity. Eliminate (B). The author considers childhood obesity a serious issue, so (C) is incorrect. The items in the list are not treatments, but rather the results of a condition. Eliminate (D). Be wary of overly binding language, such as *inevitably* in (E). These are possible symptoms, not unavoidable consequences. Eliminate (E).

23. **B** The passage states that childhood obesity has *higher levels among some groups of children, including those living in low-income households.* This makes (B), *poverty,* the correct answer. Age is not a factor here, since, by definition, all people experiencing childhood obesity are children. Eliminate (A). Family, school, and behavior are not specifically mentioned as factors in the text. Schools and families are mentioned only as being affected *by* childhood obesity. Eliminate (C), (D), and (E).

24. **C** In the final sentence, the author references the National Academy of Medicine in order to call for interventions in the epidemic of childhood obesity. This best aligns with (C). The National Academy of Medicine, in giving recommendations to curb the epidemic, does not doubt the significance of it nor does it contradict the findings presented earlier. Eliminate (A) and (B). There is no criticism offered in how the National Academy of Medicine conducts studies, so eliminate (D). Finally, be wary of overly binding language, such as *guarantee* in (E). Eliminate it.

25. **D** The first sentence tells you that a field of psychology that is interested in answering *the question as to* why *men behave as they do, is called a* dynamic psychology. This best aligns with (D), *determine the reasons for human behavior.* There is no evidence in the text about understanding nature, so eliminate (A). The phrases *more scientific* in (B) and *mathematical functions* in (C) are taken out of context. Eliminate those. The text states that dynamic psychology is not *merely a descriptive psychology,* so (E) is not supported by the passage and can be eliminated.

26. **E** The passage attempts to define dynamic psychology by differentiating it from descriptive psychology. Therefore, (E), which states that the passage distinguishes one approach to psychology from another, is correct. The passage does not delve into specific theories within the field of dynamic psychology, so (A) is incorrect. Choice (B) is also incorrect, as it is too broad, claiming that the passage discusses other fields of psychology, which it does not. The passage does not point out any particular flaws of psychology, so you can eliminate (C). Finally, while the passage discusses a field of psychology, you do not learn about its origins in this passage. Eliminate (D).

27. **E** The author contrasts dynamic psychology with the *more scientific* approach that the author characterizes as *timid* and seeking *nothing else than the establishment of a mathematical function for the relation between some artificially simple stimulus and some equally artificial and simple response.* In other words, the author sees the *more scientific* approach as somewhat dry. Choice (E), *dull,* best aligns with "dry." Accordingly, the author does not find the *more scientific* approach engaging or fascinating, so eliminate (B) and (D). That said, the *more scientific* approach is not characterized as disjointed or without merit, so (A) and (C) can be eliminated.

28. **D** The passage introduces its topic (the Catalans), puts forth a distinction (that Catalan is not a dialect of Spanish) and explores that distinction with some details. This process is best described by (D). There is no argument given, so (A), (B), and (C) are incorrect. Further, there are no alternative explanations given, so eliminate (E).

29. **E** The author gives a series of benefits for computer-driven cars; therefore, the author can be described as supportive of the idea. Choice (E) is correct. The author is not *patronizing,* which

means condescending, or *sarcastic*, so eliminate (A) and (B). Since you know the author has a positive tone toward the idea of computer-driven cars, you can eliminate (C) and (D), *scornful* and *skeptical*.

30. **A** The passage states that *it seemed incomprehensible that any man should want to give up before he was, for some reason, compelled to do so.* So, according to the author, one should not retire until he or she has to. This best aligns with (A). The author seems to look down on retirement, so the answer should not have a positive connotation. Eliminate (B). Be careful not to take words out of context. The text states that retiring by choice was strange, not that retirement itself is strange. It also claims that Bok's *choice* was a mistake, not retirement itself. Eliminate (C) and (D). Finally, there is no mention of saving for retirement, so (E) is incorrect.

31. **B** According to the passage, people *agreed it was "queer," "strange"* for Bok to choose to retire. This best matches (B). Since it was strange to the people, their reaction cannot be characterized as *unremarkable*. Eliminate (E). They also didn't support or oppose it—they simply found it to be out of the ordinary. Therefore, (C) and (D) are incorrect. The final sentence of the passage implies that a man should work until he dies. Therefore, they likely don't admire Bok's decision to retire. Eliminate (A).

32. **D** The final sentence uses an idiom, or saying (*dropped in the harness*), to imply that a person should work until he dies. This builds upon the previous sentence that claims no one would want to retire until he was *compelled to do so.* Therefore, (D) is the best answer. The aim of the passage is not to persuade, so (A) is incorrect. The author certainly is not giving support to Bok's decision to retire by offering this idiom, so you can eliminate (B). A new topic is not introduced; rather, the author closes out the discussion with this saying. Eliminate (C). Finally, (E) is incorrect because the author uses the entirety of the text to show that many felt Bok's decision to be unwise.

33. **D** Passage 1 puts forth the benefits of a process known as carbon capture (CCUS), while Passage 2 advocates solar power. Both claim they are clean energy sources. Therefore, (D) is correct. Passage 2 does not address CCUS, so (A) is incorrect. Passage 1 mentions both economic and environmental importance of CCUS, and Passage 2 discusses the possibility of a commercial solar fuel system. Therefore, you can eliminate (B). You can also eliminate (C) because Passage 1 supports a form a clean energy. Finally, eliminate (E), as the passages do not discuss the same form of renewable energy.

34. **D** The second-to-last sentence of the passage states that a goal in the solar energy field is to *remove the intermittency of solar energy and make it a reliable power source.* Therefore, *intermittency* should be the opposite of *reliable*. Choice (D), *unreliability,* is the best match. *Imprecision, toxicity, expense,* and *plausibility* do not mean *reliable,* so eliminate (A), (B), (C), and (E).

35. **B** Since both authors put forth alternative energy solutions, it can logically be concluded that both authors think it is possible to more efficiently capture and store energy. Choice (B) is correct. Eliminate (A) because only Passage 1 discusses job growth. Neither author compares his preferred form

of energy to others, so (C) is unsupported. Only Passage 1 discusses the importance of energy investment to a country's overall economic success, so eliminate (D). Finally, only Passage 1 brings up demand for clean energy, so (E) is incorrect.

36. **A** The author of Passage 2 writes that, if research yields the proper results, *scientists could create a system that could consolidate solar power and energy storage into one cohesive process*. Therefore, the author of Passage 2 advocates turning energy collection and storage into a singular process. Choice (A) is correct. The author of Passage 2 does not mention other energy sources, so (B), (C), and (E) are incorrect. The author writes with an awareness that solar power has already been discovered, so eliminate (D).

37. **E** The author of Passage 1 claims that there are plenty of economic benefits of carbon capture. Therefore, you should look for an answer choice that shows there are economic drawbacks not mentioned in the passage. Choice (E) is correct because it claims that there are tax incentives (savings) for energy sources that are not carbon based. Choices (A) and (C) should be eliminated because they strengthen the claim that CCUS is economically effective. Since the author of Passage 1 claims that CCUS is a clean energy source, (B) would not weaken the argument. Eliminate it. Finally, eliminate (D) because the fact that CCUS is under-supported is unrelated to whether or not the process has economic benefits.

38. **C** While the author of Passage 1 describes the economic benefits of energy production, the author of Passage 2 does not discuss this matter. Choice (C) is therefore correct. You can eliminate (A) because Passage 2, not Passage 1, describes an unrealized technology (perfecting solar power storage). The author of Passage 2 also uses scientific terminology (artificial photosynthesis), so (B) is incorrect. The author of Passage 1 discusses only one form of energy—carbon capture. Eliminate (D). The author of Passage 2 focuses primarily on potential research—how to convert solar power capture and energy storage into one cohesive process. Eliminate (E).

39. **C** Spillover occurs when wild birds transmit the disease to domestic birds. However, the text states that *the rate of spillover was minor, and the poultry outbreak was able to persist without further transmission from wild birds*. Therefore, since domesticated birds still contracted the virus without spillover, (C) is the best option. There is no evidence in the text that spillover occurs only in North America. Eliminate (A). Although the passage states that the rate of spillover in North America was minor, you should not take this to mean that spillover has little effect on the spread of bird flu, so (B) is incorrect. Since the rate of spillover was minor, (D) is incorrect. Finally, eliminate (E) because it reverses the direction of spillover to say that domestic birds infect wild birds.

40. **B** The passage states that *ice charging* occurs when hot ash interacts with the cold atmosphere, creating an electrification like a regular thunderstorm. Therefore, regular thunderstorms involve the interaction of hot and cold air. Choice (B) is correct. This statement involves lightning during a volcanic eruption, not all thunderstorms. Eliminate (A). Be wary of overly binding language, such as *only* in (C). The first sentence tells you that there are two main types of electrical charging. This

implies that there are other types besides the two mentioned in this text. Eliminate (C). The text mentions that frictional charging happens during all types of explosive eruptions, so it is not particularly rare. Choice (D) is incorrect. Choice (E) is also incorrect, as the text states that *there are always ash particles colliding with each other.*

41. **B** The text states that in the 9th and 10th centuries, Europe was characterized by a *moneyless economy* and *inadequate transportation*. The new institutions that developed to adapt to these conditions included feudalism. Therefore, (B) is the best answer. The ineffective government was one of the reasons for the *new* institutions of the Middle Ages, not the other way around. Eliminate (A). Be wary of overly binding language, such as *only* in (C). The list at the end of the text is not an exhaustive one. Eliminate (C). Choice (D) is incorrect, as it takes the phrase *Vikings, Magyars, and Saracens* out of context. The first sentence states that the European leaders did not try to restore Roman institutions, so eliminate (E).

42. **B** The previous sentence states that Astor was *pouring out money like water* and wanted to *buy his way in* to the government. Therefore, the newspapers were reporting on the size of the sum of money he left at the saloons. Choice (B) is correct. There is no evidence that he lied and/or made campaign promises during the saloon visits; therefore, (A) and (C) are incorrect. While there may have been a crowd of people in the saloons, it wouldn't make much sense to say that Astor left a crowd of people at each place. Choice (D) is incorrect. The passage does mention that he felt disgust about visiting the saloons, but that is mentioned after the reference to the wad. Eliminate (E).

43. **A** While the opening sentence describes that two wealthy men ran for office, the rest of the passage focuses how each candidate took his own approach to attempting political success. Choice (A) best aligns with this description. The passage does not discuss plans to improve New York, nor do they take a particularly celebratory tone toward Astor. Eliminate (B). The passage describes Roosevelt in a positive light, not a critical one, so (C) is incorrect. The author is a historian, not a contemporary advocating for either man, so there is no endorsement given. Eliminate (D). The author does not call Roosevelt's merits into question, so (E) is incorrect.

44. **E** The second paragraph discusses Roosevelt. It says that he put *fire* into those *who were little in the habit of bothering about elections* to become involved. This aligns with (E). The text tells you that it is the former of the two—Astor—who spent large amounts of money on the campaign trail. Eliminate (A). Both candidates mentioned in the text are described as young, so (B) is incorrect. The text states only that Roosevelt was nominated for the State Legislature, but we do not know the results of that race. Eliminate (C). While Roosevelt campaigned in the brownstone district, the passage does not say where he resided, so (D) is incorrect.

45. **C** The first paragraph discusses one candidate who spent money recklessly, while the second paragraph discusses the other candidate who used his time on the campaign trail to motivate non-regular voters to support him. These two approaches are juxtaposed to highlight the differences in approach. Therefore, (C) is correct. The passage does not delve into the stances of the candidates,

so (A) is incorrect. Choices (B) and (E) are incorrect because the scope of the passage is about only two candidates, not all of the history of New York politics or New York at the time of Garfield's death. We also don't learn the outcomes of the elections, so eliminate (D).

46. **C** The text tells you that one politician inherited wealth, while the other was a blue blood (an old term for an aristocrat). This information helps define *silk-stockings* as wealthy people, which best aligns with (C). The passage does not give evidence that the men are crooked, so eliminate (A). Their fashion senses are not brought up, so (B) is incorrect. Since the passage emphasizes their wealth, the men, particularly Astor, are not portrayed as terribly relatable to the common man. Eliminate (D). Neither man is described as having gone through adversity, so (E) is incorrect as well.

47. **A** Neither the Chicago nor the Seattle office hosts a corporate partnership meeting. Therefore, the claim in (A) can be supported by the information given in the calendar. While October 6 will be the first employee relations meeting of the month, there is no data for the earlier months of the year, so (B) cannot be substantiated. Eliminate it. Maren will attend four marketing meetings and seven budgeting meetings. Therefore, she will fall just barely short of attending twice as many budgeting meetings. Eliminate (C). The calendar offers no data about how many employees work at each office, so eliminate (D). Maren conducts only six meetings in Dallas, which, out of 23 meetings in the month, is not nearly a majority of them. Eliminate (E).

48. **C** Maren conducts a total of four marketing meetings in October. One is in Chicago, one is in Seattle, and two are in Dallas. Therefore, you can eliminate (A) and (B). Choice (C), Dallas, is the only correct answer.

49. **D** All of the research and development meetings are in Seattle, Los Angeles, or Chicago. Dallas does not host any meetings, which is consistent with the claim made in (D). There is no information about how long meetings take or about the success of research and development efforts, so (A) and (C) are incorrect. Choice (B) is incorrect because while there are three research and development meetings between October 1 and October 15, there are more (four) budgeting meetings in that time span. Finally, you can eliminate (E) because the week of October 6 does not have a research and development meeting, which implies that it is not essential to schedule at least one per week.

50. **A** This question is really a main idea question in disguise. The passage focuses on the difficulty for coal miners who contracted black lung disease to get the help they need from their former employers. The phrase *coal industry doctors and lawyers helped defeat and delay benefit claims* provides the main idea of the passage; therefore, the most appropriate title is (A). The main idea does not focus on the disease itself, so (B) and (E) are incorrect. You learn in the passage *that there has been a spike since the early 1990s*, so (C), which claims that the disease is on the decline, is incorrect. Finally, eliminate (D) because the point of the passage is that the coal industry is attempting to avoid paying for the healthcare of its former employees.

51. **C** The passage mentions that former workers have filed claims for the coal industry to cover the health expenses brought on by black lung disease. Therefore, you can infer that they view the coal industry as responsible. Choice (C) is correct. Choices (A) and (B) are incorrect because they contradict the main point of the passage. Choice (D) is incorrect because it takes a phrase out of context (the spike has to do with cases of black lung disease, not the coal industry). Choice (E) is incorrect because there is no evidence that a criminal trial ever took place.

52. **E** The *system* is described as being *increasingly stacked against* the coal miners who contracted black lung disease. You want to find an answer choice with a similar situation: a powerful industry that victims have difficulty fighting against. The clearest example of this is the nearly identical example of the tobacco industry avoiding paying for the healthcare of smokers who contracted lung cancer. Choice (E) is correct. While *construction workers who breathed asbestos* seems similar, this answer choice does not contain the element of a company avoiding paying for healthcare. Choice (A) is incorrect. Choice (B) does not fit the situation either, since it describes a company complying with a regulation to benefit people. Choices (C) and (D) are also incorrect, as there is no company avoiding payment in those situations.

53. **E** The text states that *coal industry doctors and lawyers helped defeat and delay benefit claims.* This information best aligns with (E). There is no reference to how bad experts originally thought black lung disease was, so eliminate (A). The text does not reveal the outcomes of any court cases, so (B) is incorrect. Be wary of any answer choice with a comparison. The comparison in (C) is not in the text, so eliminate it. While the text tells you that cases of black lung disease are increasing, this information is given before the mention of the Center for Public Integrity and ABC News are mentioned. Therefore, this is not the information those organizations uncovered. Eliminate (D).

54. **C** The key word in the final sentence is *corridors*, which are like hallways—narrow passages. Given this, (C), *passageways,* is the best option.

55. **C** The text states that *scores of thousands of ill-led Russian peasants saved France.* Therefore, the people of Western Europe were indebted to the Russians (referred to as *great and tragic people*). Choice (C) is correct. The Germans are described as the aggressors in this text, and the French are described as the people who needed saving. Choices (A) and (B) are incorrect. East Prussia and Western Europe are mentioned in the passage, though not in reference to a *great and tragic people*. Choices (D) and (E) are incorrect.

56. **D** While the opening sentence states that absenteeism is widespread, the final sentence deals with a different, yet related issue: the likelihood of students who cannot read at grade level to drop out of high school. Think about the connection between the two ideas. The path this passage takes is to explain how chronic absenteeism can lead to negative outcomes. Choice (D) best aligns with this idea. Choices (A), (C), and (E) are supporting details rather than main ideas, so they can be eliminated. Choice (B) is incorrect because it reverses the cause-and-effect relationship described in the passage.

Chapter 10
Writing Practice
Test 1

WRITING

Questions 1 to 19:

Each of the following questions consists of a sentence that contains four underlined portions. Read each sentence and decide whether any of the underlined parts contains an element that would be considered incorrect or inappropriate in carefully written English. The error or concern may be in grammatical construction, word use, or an instance of incorrect or omitted punctuation or capitalization. If so, select the underlined portion that must be revised to produce a correct sentence. If there are no errors in the sentence as written, select "No error." **No sentence has more than one error.**

1 of 40

Fred, <u>well aware</u> of his <u>parents'</u> dislike of football,
      A   B

had no <u>allusion</u> that they <u>would allow</u> him to play.
       C   D

<u>No error</u>
  E

2 of 40

Despite her efforts <u>to persevere</u>, Christine, who
            A

<u>was suffering</u> from a <u>ghastly</u> flu, got <u>hardly no work</u>
   B   C   D

done that morning. <u>No error</u>
            E

3 of 40

Jack and Susie were <u>utterly mortified</u> when Ms. Jones,
              A

their <u>hot-tempered</u> <u>spanish</u> teacher, scolded them
      B   C

<u>in front of</u> the entire class. <u>No error</u>
   D   E

4 of 40

The <u>second-grade</u> students were all running around
    A

the classroom yelling loudly until the teacher raised

his voice <u>;</u> <u>abashed</u>, the children quickly took their
      B   C

<u>seat.</u> <u>No error</u>
 D   E

5 of 40

The <u>long-suffering</u> <u>principal</u> of the local junior high
     A   B

school <u>;</u> has been steadfastly working in that capacity
     C

for nearly thirty-two <u>highly eventful</u> years. <u>No error</u>
                D   E

6 of 40

<u>Given</u> the animosity <u>among</u> Bob and his siblings, <u>his</u>
 A   B   C

going to visit them at the family reunion this past

October <u>was</u> surprising. <u>No error</u>
     D   E

7 of 40

Linda, who greatly enjoys reading, studying, and even

<u>doing her homework,</u> <u>could not be</u> more <u>different than</u>
     A   B   C

her sister, who <u>rarely ever</u> picks up a book. <u>No error</u>
          D   E

WRITING

<u>Although</u> there was heavy rainfall during the holiday
   A
picnic this past Saturday, <u>that</u> didn't negatively <u>affect</u>
               B   C
any of us; everyone <u>has</u> a great time. <u>No error</u>
                 D   E

The delightfully graceful ballet <u>dancer's</u>
                         A
<u>were all leaping into</u> the air <u>like</u> gazelles. <u>No error</u>
  B   C   D   E

When <u>traveling</u> in a foreign <u>Country</u>, <u>it's</u> best to keep
     A   B   C
<u>your</u> passport with you at all times. <u>No error</u>
 D   E

<u>Today's</u> athlete <u>may feel</u> such intense pressure
 A   B
<u>to succeed</u> that <u>they begin</u> taking steroids at an early
 C   D
age. <u>No error</u>
    E

The worshiping of extremely rich A-list celebrities,
some of <u>whom</u> earn millions of dollars for <u>each</u> of
       A   B
<u>their</u> movies, <u>are</u> very disturbing to many Americans.
 C   D
<u>No error</u>
 E

The influence of baseball <u>on</u> American life <u>during</u> the
                     A   B
<u>Great Depression</u> years <u>were</u> profound. <u>No error</u>
   C   D   E

The college newspaper will print the <u>contestants</u>
                                      A
<u>who</u> win prizes for essays and short stories <u>;</u> poetry,
 B   C
however, will not be <u>accepted</u> for publication.
                   D
<u>No error</u>
 E

Mary not only ate three enormous helpings of
macaroni and cheese, <u>and also</u> <u>greedily devoured</u> a
                   A   B
<u>huge slice of</u> chocolate cake for <u>dessert</u>. <u>No error</u>
   C   D   E

The trick <u>to becoming</u> popular, gaining <u>others'</u>
          A   B
respect <u>,</u> and having many friends <u>are</u> to be nice and
     C   D
helpful to everybody. <u>No error</u>
                E

whose

The elderly woman <u>who's</u> purse I found on the
                 A
subway was extremely grateful <u>to get</u> her property
                           B
back <u>;</u> she thanked me <u>repeatedly</u>. <u>No error</u>
   C   D   E

<u>Whichever</u> of the two candidates <u>wins</u> a majority of
 A   B
the electoral votes is <u>going to be</u> the future <u>governor</u>.
                   C   D
<u>No error</u>
 E

WRITING

The <u>infamous</u> Tower of London, one of <u>England's</u>
    A   B

most popular tourist destinations, <u>having</u> been
                             C

<u>associated with</u> violence and intrigue for centuries.
     D

<u>No error</u>
    E

Questions 20 to 30:

In each of the following questions, part of the sentence or the entire sentence is underlined. Beneath each sentence are five ways of writing the underlined part. The first of these repeats the original, but the other four are all different. If you think the original sentence is better than any of the suggested changes, you should select the first answer choice; otherwise you should select one of the other choices. This is a test of correctness and effectiveness of expression.

In choosing answers, follow the requirements of standard written English; that is, pay attention to acceptable usage in grammar, diction (choice of words), sentence construction, and punctuation. Choose the answer that expresses most effectively what is presented in the original sentence; this answer should be clear and exact, without awkwardness, ambiguity, or redundancy.

Canada is known for having very <u>cold weather, they get a great deal</u> of snow each winter.

- ○ cold weather, they get a great deal
- ○ cold weather; they get a great deal
- ○ cold weather, with them getting a great deal
- ⊙ cold weather; the country gets a great deal
- ○ cold weather, the country gets a great deal

When going hiking, you must take a map, plenty of extra food and <u>water, and you should have</u> a first-aid kit in case of injury.

- ○ water, and you should have
- ○ water, and having
- ○ water, and one should have
- ○ water, but one should have
- ⊙ water, and

<u>Running down the street frantically to catch the bus, Linda's</u> lovely handmade scarf blew off and then landed in the dirty street.

- ○ Running down the street frantically to catch the bus, Linda's
- ○ Running down the street frantically to catch the bus; Linda's
- ⊙ As Linda was running down the street frantically to catch the bus, her
- ○ As Linda has been running frantically down the street to catch the bus, her
- ○ Linda had been running run down the street frantically to catch the bus, until her

Jeremy and Margaret will surely do well in the spelling contest on <u>Monday; their among the best spellers</u> in the class.

- ○ Monday; their among the best spellers
- ○ Monday, their among the best spellers
- ○ Monday, they're being among the best spellers
- ⊙ Monday; they're among the best spellers
- ○ Monday. Their among the best spellers

WRITING

Leonard had been one of the first employees at the plant <u>demanding that all workers be tested for the harmful effects</u> of radiation.

- ○ demanding that all workers be tested for the harmful effects
- ◉ to demand that all workers be tested for the harmful effects
- ○ to have been demanding that all workers be tested for the harmful effects
- ○ to demand that all workers be tested for the harmful affects
- ○ to demand that all workers are being tested for the harmful affects

Some women fought in the Civil War by <u>wearing men's clothes and they were using</u> false names.

- ○ wearing men's clothes and they were using
- ○ wearing mens' clothes and using
- ○ wearing men's clothes but also they were using
- ◉ wearing men's clothes and using
- ○ wearing men's clothes; and they were using

When it was announced that school would end early because of the snowstorm, the children <u>cheered and were clapping;</u> the teachers were secretly happy too.

- ○ cheered and were clapping;
- ◉ cheered and clapped;
- ○ were cheering and were clapping;
- ○ cheered and clapped,
- ○ cheered and then were clapping;

Jack was extremely upset with his brother, <u>since he had taken his car</u> without permission.

- ○ since he had taken his car
- ◉ who had taken Jack's car
- ○ since he took his car
- ○ being that he had taken his car
- ○ the reason being that the brother had taken Jack's car

Everyone <u>needs to bring their own</u> cooking supplies to my house for the barbecue on Saturday.

- ○ needs to bring their own
- ○ is needing to bring their own
- ◉ needs to bring his or her own
- ○ needs to be bringing their own
- ○ needs to bring his own cooking supplies or her own

Josie was ecstatic because <u>her first-semester grades were better than her sister</u>.

- ○ her first-semester grades were better than her sister
- ◉ her first semester grades were better than those of her sister
- ○ her first-semester grades were better than the first-semester grades of her sister
- ○ her first-semester grades were better than her sisters' grades
- ○ her first semester grades was better than her sister's

WRITING

Shakespeare, <u>an author who wrote many memorable plays, is</u> also admired for his poetry.

- ◉ an author who wrote many memorable plays, is
- ○ an author that wrote many memorable plays, is
- ○ being an author who wrote many memorable plays, is
- ○ an author that wrote many memorable plays is
- ○ an author who wrote many memorable plays is,

Questions 31-36 refer to the following passage:

(1) In recent years the popularity of farmers' markets, at which local produce and various homemade items are sold, has risen dramatically. (2) Many consumers view the farmers' market as a healthful alternative to grocery store fruits and vegetables, which are usually mass-produced, stored and shipped for relatively lengthy periods, and then purchased wholesale by retailers. (3) However, since many of the agricultural products sold in grocery stores are imported, many consumers fear that these items are more likely to have been contaminated or exposed to dangerous pesticides. (4) Other mass-produced foods sold in grocery stores, such as baked goods and jams, often contain chemical preservatives and other undesirable ingredients as well. (5) In contrast, the various foods sold at farmers' markets are presumed to be fresher, tastier, and more nutritious than their grocery store counterparts. (6) This is a common presumption.

(7) Despite the obvious allure of the farmers' market, shopping regularly at this type of local establishment may not offer as many health benefits as is commonly believed. (8) There is evidence that a disturbing percentage of farmers' market vendors do not actually grow their produce themselves, but rather buy the food from large distributors and resell it as their own. (9) Relying upon the assurance that the market sells only locally grown fruits and vegetables and homemade edibles, they buy it and never know the difference. (10) The degree and quality of regulation vary greatly from place to place, but some dishonest vendors may never be exposed. (11) Moreover, with virtually no threat of criminal penalty for this type of false advertising in some areas, there may often be no real deterrent to farmers' market fraud. (12) Store-bought pies and jams may also be sold in this deceptive manner by simply transferring the items into containers that bear the vendor's brand name. (13) Even when market vendors are honest about the products they sell, however, buying one's groceries at farmers' markets still may not be the best option for a healthy lifestyle. (14) Because customers believe homemade items to be pure and nutritious, they are apt to purchase sugary and high-fat items more freely.

WRITING

Which is the best version of the underlined portion of sentence 9 (reproduced below)?

Relying upon the assurance that the market sells only locally grown fruits and vegetables and homemade edibles, they buy it and never know the difference.

- ○ (As it is now)

- ○ they buy it and do not ever know the difference.

- ○ consumers buy it and never even know the difference.

- ○ they buy the food but don't know the difference.

- ◉ consumers buy the food and never know the difference.

Which is the best way to revise and combine the underlined portion of sentences 5 and 6 (reproduced below)?

In contrast, the various foods sold at farmers' markets are presumed to be fresher, tastier, and more nutritious than their grocery store counterparts. This is a common presumption.

- ○ are presumed to be fresher, tastier, and more nutritious than their grocery store counterparts and this is a common presumption.

- ○ are presumed to be fresher, tastier, and more nutritious than their grocery store counterparts; this being a common presumption.

- ○ are presumed to be fresher, tastier, and more nutritious than their grocery store counterparts; this is a common presumption.

- ◉ are commonly presumed to be fresher, tastier, and more nutritious than their grocery store counterparts.

- ○ are presumed to be commonly fresher, tastier, and more nutritious than their grocery store counterparts.

Where would the following sentence best be inserted?

Just because food is made entirely of natural ingredients doesn't necessarily mean that it's good for you.

- ○ Immediately after sentence 3

- ○ Immediately after sentence 4

- ◉ Immediately after sentence 9

- ○ Immediately after sentence 11

- ◉ Immediately after sentence 14

What is the best way to deal with sentence 3 (reproduced below)?

However, since many of the agricultural products sold in grocery stores are imported, many consumers fear that these items are more likely to have been contaminated or exposed to dangerous pesticides.

- ○ Change "dangerous" to "hazardous."

- ◉ Change "however" to "moreover."

- ○ Change the comma after "however" to a dash.

- ○ Change "agricultural" to "agriculture."

- ○ Change "are imported" to "are being imported."

What is the best way to deal with sentence 12 (reproduced below)?

Store-bought pies and jams may also be sold in this deceptive manner by simply transferring the items into containers that bear the vendor's brand name.

- ○ Leave it where it is.

- ◉ Place it immediately after sentence 8.

- ○ Place it immediately after sentence 10.

- ○ Place it immediately after sentence 14.

- ○ Delete it from the passage.

WRITING

In context, which of the following revisions of sentence 10 (reproduced below) is most needed?

The degree and quality of regulation vary greatly from place to place, but some dishonest vendors may never be exposed.

- ○ Change "vary greatly" to "greatly vary."
- ○ Change "may" to "might."
- ○ Delete the comma.
- ◉ Change "but" to "so."
- ○ Insert "the" before "quality."

Which one of the following sources is **LEAST** relevant to a research paper about the Kennedy assassination?

- ○ A documentary about alleged governmental conspiracies to replace President Kennedy with Vice President Johnson through violent means
- ○ A published doctoral dissertation detailing the evidence and prevailing theories surrounding the deaths of every U.S. president who was assassinated
- ○ A scholarly journal article presenting a psychological case study of Lee Harvey Oswald, Kennedy's presumed assassin
- ◉ A book about Kennedy's childhood and early life experiences growing up in Massachusetts
- ○ The Zapruder film, the only known footage of the Kennedy assassination

One might find an abstract

- ○ at the end of a book about the Civil War
- ◉ at the beginning of a scholarly journal article about schizophrenia
- ○ immediately preceding a poem in a poetry magazine
- ○ on the cover of a book of short stories
- ○ immediately following a bibliography

Johnson, O.M. (2003). The effects of birth order on sibling autonomy. *Psychology, Sociology, and the Family, 47(2)*, 47-58.

The work cited above is most likely a

- ○ book
- ○ internet blog
- ◉ journal article
- ○ documentary
- ○ newspaper

Which of the following would be a secondary source for a report about Queen Victoria?

- ◉ A recently published best-selling biography
- ○ Copies of letters written by Victoria to her children
- ○ Victoria's personal memoirs
- ○ The transcript of a speech Victoria made before Parliament during the first year of her reign
- ○ A well-known photograph of Victoria that was taken shortly before her death

WRITING

You will have a total of 30 minutes to plan and write an argumentative essay on the topic presented in the following section. The essay should be based on your own reading, experience, and observations.

Read the topic carefully. DO NOT WRITE ON A TOPIC OTHER THAN THE ONE SPECIFIED. Essays on topics of your own choice are not acceptable. In order for your test to be scored, your response must be in English.

The essay questions are included in this test to give you an opportunity to demonstrate how well you can write. You should consider the topic, organize your thoughts, and take care to write clearly and effectively, using specific examples where appropriate. How well you write is much more important than how much you write; however, to cover the topic adequately, it is suggested that you write more than one paragraph.

Read the opinion stated below.

"To address the problem of chronic truancy, schools should fine the parents of students who are frequently absent from school."

Discuss the extent to which you agree or disagree with this point of view. Support your position with specific reasons and examples from your own experience, observations, or reading.

WRITING

You will have a total of 30 minutes to read two short passages on a topic and to plan and write an essay on that topic. The essay should be an informative essay based on the two sources provided.

Read the topic carefully. DO NOT WRITE ON A TOPIC OTHER THAN THE ONE SPECIFIED. Essays on topics of your own choice are not acceptable. In order for your test to be scored, your response must be in English.

The essay questions are included in this test to give you an opportunity to demonstrate how well you can write. You should consider the topic, organize your thoughts, and take care to write clearly and effectively, using specific examples where appropriate. How well you write is much more important than how much you write; however, to cover the topic adequately, it is suggested that you write more than one paragraph.

Directions:

The following assignment requires you to use information from two sources to discuss the most important concerns that relate to a specific issue. When paraphrasing or quoting from the sources, cite each source by referring to the author's last name, the title, or any other clear identifier.

Assignment:

Both of the following sources address the issue of how modern technology allows large amounts of information to be accumulated about individuals and then used for commercial or other purposes. Read the two passages carefully and then write an essay in which you identify the most important concerns regarding this issue, explaining why these concerns are important. Your essay must draw on information from BOTH of the sources. In addition, you may draw upon your own experience, observations, or reading. Be sure to CITE the sources, whether you are paraphrasing or directly quoting.

Source 1:

Adapted from:

McFarland, Michael. "Ethical Implications of Data Aggregation." *Markkula Center for Applied Ethics*, Santa Clara University, 1 June 2012.

One powerful new capability the computer gives us is the ability to compile large amounts of data from disparate sources to create a detailed composite picture of a person or to identify people who meet some criterion or stand out in some way. This has numerous uses and abuses. One application of this is with what David Burnham calls "transaction data." Now that many ordinary daily activities, such as making a telephone call, purchasing an item with a credit card, and renting a video, are computerized, the details of all of these transactions are recorded and saved. There are legitimate reasons for collecting this information: billing, inventory, predicting future needs and so on. But out of this mass of seemingly innocent details, an enterprising sleuth can assemble a revealing portrait of a person and his or her activities.

The capability the computer gives of being able to assemble these seemingly innocent and insignificant facts into a comprehensive personal profile and to make it widely available gives that information a different significance. Even though limited groups of people may have legitimate reasons to have access to some of these facts for specific purposes, when the facts are all put together into a dossier they become much more personal and invasive. They thus present many of the dangers of other invasions of privacy. The information can be used for purposes other than those for which it was intended. For example information provided for billing purposes can reveal a person's movements, whereabouts and habits. The subject loses control of who knows what about him or her and what they do with it. And strangers can get a much more intimate look at the person's life than the person would allow if consulted.

WRITING

Source 2:

Adapted from:

Naylor, Brian. "Firms Are Buying, Sharing Your Online Info. What Can You Do about It?" *All Tech Considered.* NPR, 11 July 2016.

There are some big companies out there that you've probably never heard of, that know more about you than you can imagine. They're called data brokers, and they collect all sorts of information—names, addresses, income, where you go on the Internet and who you connect with online. That information is then sold to other companies. There are few regulations governing these brokers.

Data brokers have been around for a long time, collecting information about your magazine and newspaper subscriptions. They know whether you prefer dogs or cats. From public records they can tell if you drive a Ford or a Subaru or if you've declared bankruptcy. But the Internet upped the ante considerably. Think of all that personal data you share on Facebook, or your online shopping. According to Julie Brill, who recently stepped down as a commissioner on the Federal Trade Commission, these companies share just about everything. "It's what Web pages we visit, where we're shopping, who we're interfacing with on social media—all of that information is available to be collected by entities that park themselves on the various websites," Brill said. Once these companies collect the information, the data brokers package and sell it—sometimes to other brokers, sometimes to businesses—that then use the information to target ads to consumers...

When the FTC studied data brokers two years ago, it found that brokers take the information they gleaned about consumers and use it to put us into categories. Some of the categories are innocuous—pet owner, or winter sports enthusiast. But Brill says others were more problematic, like "single mom struggling in an urban setting" or "people who did not speak English and felt more comfortable speaking in Spanish" or "gamblers." "And so the concern is not only the fact that these profiles are being created, but how are they being used," Brill said.

Chapter 11
Writing Practice
Test 1: Answers and
Explanations

WRITING PRACTICE TEST 1 ANSWER KEY

1.	C		21.	E
2.	D		22.	C
3.	C		23.	D
4.	D		24.	B
5.	C		25.	D
6.	E		26.	B
7.	C		27.	B
8.	D		28.	C
9.	A		29.	B
10.	B		30.	A
11.	D		31.	E
12.	D		32.	D
13.	D		33.	E
14.	A		34.	B
15.	A		35.	B
16.	D		36.	D
17.	A		37.	D
18.	C		38.	B
19.	C		39.	C
20.	D		40.	A

WRITING PRACTICE TEST 1 EXPLANATIONS

Multiple-Choice Questions

1. **C**   The use of the word *allusion* in this instance is a diction error. An *illusion* is a false belief or impression; an *allusion* is an indirect or casual reference.

2. **D**   The phrase *hardly no work* contains a double negative. *Hardly any work* is the correct phrase.

3. **C**   The word *Spanish* is a proper name (the name of a language) and must be capitalized accordingly.

4. **D**   Stating that the children *took their seat* suggests that all of the children piled together into the one seat that they were sharing. *Took their seats* is the correct phrase.

5. **C**   The comma presents an unnecessary and illogical break between subject and verb in this case.

6. **E**   This sentence contains no errors in grammar or usage.

7. **C**   The phrase *different than* in this instance is unidiomatic and therefore incorrect. *Different from* is the correct phrase.

8. **D**   The sentence discusses a picnic that took place the previous Saturday. The use of the present tense verb *has* is therefore illogical. The verb should be *had*.

9. **A**   The word *dancer* is pluralized by simply adding an *s;* adding an apostrophe and an *s* indicates possession (e.g., the dancer's shoe).

10. **B**   The word *country* in this sentence is simply a common noun and does not need to be capitalized.

11. **D**   *Athlete* is a singular noun and requires a singular pronoun; the plural nominative pronoun *they* is therefore incorrect. *He begins* or *she begins* would be acceptable substitutes, as would *he or she begins* (although the *he or she* construction can be awkward when used repeatedly).

12. **D**   The subject of this sentence is *the worshipping of extremely rich A-list celebrities;* the gerund *worshipping* is singular and requires the singular verb *is*. The parenthetical information does not make the subject plural.

13. **D**   The singular subject *influence of baseball* requires the singular verb *was*. The presence of plural nouns in between the subject and verb does not make the subject plural.

14. **A**   This sentence indicates that the newspaper will publish the *contestants themselves*, as opposed to publishing the contestants' work.

15. **A**   The phrase *and also* is not idiomatic in this instance and is therefore incorrect. *Not only* requires the corresponding *but also* construction.

16. **D** The singular subject *trick* requires the singular verb *is*. The presence of plural nouns in between the subject and verb does not make the subject plural.

17. **A** The possessive pronoun *whose* is required here to indicate that the purse belonged to the woman. *Who's* is simply a contraction of the words *who* and *is* or *who* and *has* (e.g., she is the woman who's looking for her purse) and does not signify possession.

18. **C** The phrase *going to be the future governor* is redundant, as both *going to be* and *future* refer to an event that has not yet occurred.

19. **C** The use of the word *having* here, as opposed to the present perfect tense (*has been*), creates a sentence fragment with no verb.

20. **D** The first problem with this sentence is that two independent clauses (clauses that can stand on their own) are joined by a comma (a comma splice). The second problem is that the singular noun *Canada* is replaced by the plural pronoun *they*; only (D) corrects both errors.

21. **E** Items in a list should be in parallel grammatical form. The first two items in this list of necessary hiking supplies are simply stated without any additional words (*a map* and *plenty of extra food and water*). The *and you should bring* construction does not conform to this structure, nor do any of the answer choices except for (E).

22. **C** This sentence is obviously meant to convey the idea that Linda's scarf blew off while she was running down the street. However, grammatically, the sentence states that the scarf (which is the subject and is performing the action) was running down the street trying to catch the bus (a highly unlikely scenario)! Only (C) corrects this misplaced modifier without introducing an additional error. Choice (D) illogically introduces the present perfect *has been running* construction, which suggests that Linda is still performing the action. Choice (E) changes the meaning of the sentence by stating that Linda had been running down the street *until* her scarf blew off (the past perfect tense). This construction indicates that she stopped running when she lost the scarf (a scenario not presented by the original sentence).

23. **D** This sentence contains a diction error. The possessive pronoun *their* is incorrectly used to mean *they're* (which is a contraction of the words *they* and *are*). Choices (C) and (D) both correct this error, but the former introduces two new errors. Choice (C) incorrectly replaces the semicolon with a comma (a "comma splice") and adds the redundant word *being* (*they are being among*).

24. **B** The word *demanding* creates an awkward and incorrect construction; the simple infinitive *to demand* is appropriate here. Choice (B) corrects this error without introducing additional ones. Choice (C) presents an unwarranted and awkward change in tense (*to have been demanding*), while (D) and (E) incorrectly substitute the word *affects* for *effects*. The word *affect* is a verb when used in this sense, while *effect* is a noun; for example, the *effects* of radiation are terrible in that it *affects* the human body horribly. Choice (E) also presents an illogical change in tense (*to demand that all workers are being tested*).

25. **D** The parallel grammatical structure is violated by the addition of the words *they were;* only (B) and (D) present parallel constructions (*wearing* and *using* without additional words). However, (B) incorrectly forms the possessive by adding an *s* followed by an apostrophe (*men's* is correct instead).

26. **B** The principle of parallelism requires that both verbs (*cheer* and *clap*) be in the same form in this case, as the actions apparently occurred together. Choice (C) corrects this error but is repetitive and wordy. Choice (D) presents verbs in parallel form but incorrectly replaces the semicolon with a comma, creating a comma splice. Choice (E) not only fails to correct the nonparallel structure, but also indicates that the clapping occurred *after* the cheering, which the sentence does not suggest.

27. **B** This construction is problematic because the pronouns *he* and *his* are ambiguous. Who took whose car without permission? One might assume that the brother took Jack's car, but the sentence as written does not clearly express what happened. Choices (B) and (E) both resolve the ambiguity, but (E) is awkward and wordy, while (B) is succinct.

28. **C** The pronoun *everyone* is singular and therefore the plural possessive pronoun *their* is incorrect here. Choices (C) and (E) both correct this error, but (E) is extremely wordy. There is no need to use the phrase *own cooking supplies* more than once.

29. **B** This sentence states that Josie was ecstatic because her first-semester grades were better than her *sister*, not better than her *sister's grades* (which is obviously the intended meaning). Choice (B) corrects this problem without introducing other errors. Choice (C) is unnecessarily repetitive and wordy. Choice (D) incorrectly forms the possessive by adding an *s* followed by an apostrophe (*sisters' grades*), which is the plural form and would mean that there is more than one sister. Choice (E) incorrectly uses the singular verb *was* with a plural noun *(grades was)*.

30. **A** There are no errors in grammar or usage in this sentence.

31. **E** The underlined portion of this sentence contains two errors. First, the pronoun *they* is ambiguous, as it has no identifiable antecedent (*who* buys it?). Only (C) and (E) correct this error. Second, the singular pronoun *it* appears to be replacing the noun phrases *locally grown fruits and vegetables and homemade edible items* (which contain all plural nouns). Choice (E) corrects this error by using the phrase *the food* instead, thus eliminating the need for the pronoun.

32. **D** The second sentence is largely repetitive; it adds no additional information apart from the fact that the previously mentioned presumption is a common one. Choice (C) is equally repetitive, simply using a semicolon to join the two sentences. Choice (B) is repetitive and grammatically incorrect, with a semicolon followed by an awkward sentence fragment. Choice (D) inserts the adverb *commonly* before the word *presumed* and thus expresses the idea succinctly. Choice (E) is similarly succinct but incorrectly inserts the word *commonly* before *fresher;* the presumption is common here, not the freshness of the food.

33. **E** This additional statement would best be inserted at the end of the passage. The final paragraph discusses how, even when vendors are honest about what they are selling, shopping at farmers' markets may not be good for one's health. Specifically, consumers believe farmers' market food to be healthful, so they freely purchase homemade pies and jams (which are high in fat and sugar). The statement that *just because food is made entirely of natural ingredients doesn't necessarily mean that it's good for you* expands logically upon that thought.

34. **B** Sentence 2 discusses how farmers' markets are thought to be a healthful option and lists some presumably negative information about produce sold in grocery stores (it's mass-produced, stored for lengthy periods, etc.). Sentence 3 then explains how agricultural products in grocery stores, which are more likely to be imported, are thought to have a greater chance of contamination and exposure to dangerous pesticides. Since sentence 3 continues to discuss the downside of shopping at grocery stores, the transition word *however* is illogical, and *moreover* would be an appropriate substitute.

35. **B** The placement of sentence 12 in the passage as written is illogical and confusing; sentence 12 should be placed immediately after sentence 8, which means (B) is correct. Sentence 8 discusses how some vendors buy produce from distributors and then fraudulently pass it off as their own at farmers' markets. Sentence 12 expands on this idea by stating that vendors also fraudulently sell store-bought pies and jams by simply switching the containers. However, sentences 9, 10, and 11 go on to talk about how consumers are duped, the extent of farmers' market regulation, the likelihood that fraud will be detected, and possible criminal penalties. Information about how the fraud occurs should logically occur earlier, so (A), (C), and (D) can be eliminated. Choice (E) is wrong because sentence 12 should not be deleted, as it contains information relevant to the passage.

36. **D** The sentence *the degree and quality of regulation vary greatly from place to place, but some dishonest vendors may never be exposed* is confusing. The first clause simply states that the level of regulation varies; it does *not* suggest that exposure is likely. Accordingly, the transition word *but* is inappropriate, as it signifies contrast or a change in direction. The word *so* should be used here instead, conveying the idea that some dishonest vendors may never be exposed *because* regulation varies from place to place.

37. **D** Note that you are looking for the source that is LEAST relevant. Information about alleged governmental conspiracies to replace President Kennedy through violent means would certainly be relevant to a paper about the assassination, about which numerous conspiracy theories exist and are continually revisited; eliminate (A). A psychological case study of the presumed assassin would also be highly relevant, as would video footage of the assassination itself; (C) and (E) can be eliminated. A dissertation outlining the theories and evidence surrounding the murders of every U.S. president who has been assassinated would contain material irrelevant to the Kennedy assassination (i.e., the portions dealing with the other presidents), but the part dealing with President Kennedy would be extremely relevant. Eliminate (B). However, a book about Kennedy's childhood and early life would be unlikely to contain information relevant to his assassination as president, which occurred decades later. Therefore, (D) is the least relevant source and the correct answer.

38. **B** An abstract is a brief summary of an article, text, or other document that typically appears at the beginning of the work. Choices (A), (D), and (E) can be eliminated. An abstract would not precede a poem or similar piece of creative writing, so (C) is incorrect as well. Choice (B) is the right answer.

39. **C** This citation follows APA format for a journal article in print: author's last name, author's initials, year of publication, title of article, title of publication (in italics), volume and issue (in italics), and page numbers.

40. **A** Primary sources are contemporaneous sources that provide firsthand information about a person, thing, or event. In contrast, secondary sources provide indirect information through evaluation, analysis, or interpretation of primary sources. Private letters, memoirs, speeches, and photographs would all be considered primary sources, while a biography written a century after the subject's death would be a secondary source. Therefore, (A) is correct.

Argumentative Essay

"To address the problem of chronic truancy, schools should fine the parents of students who are frequently absent from school."

Sample of an Essay with a Score of 6

The following essay displays a high level of competence, despite having a few minor errors. It states the thesis clearly, is organized, and has well-developed ideas. The essay demonstrates a facility with language and is generally free of errors.

There is no doubt that such chronic truancy and tardiness have an impact on the success of students in school. It is very difficult for students to stay on top of school curricula if they miss any significant time. I fully support initiatives designed to reduce the amount of chronic truancy within schools. However, I strongly disagree that the proper way to address the problem is through financial measures. Fining parents when their children are absent from school can have unintended negative consequences, and will create an adversarial relationship between parents and schools: two parties that increasingly need to work in collaboration to further the development of children.

The proposal to charge parents for their child's truancy assumes that financial penalties correct the problem. However, I believe that the problem of truancy stems from underlying reasons that cannot easily be fixed through the addition of financial pressure. For example, if a child is frequently sick and therefore misses significant time in school recovering at home, how will a fine help the child or family? If anything, the additional fine could keep the child out of school longer, if such a time were to cause low-income families not to spend money on healthcare treatment. On the other hand, some families are so wealthy that a financial charge would not likely drive any behavioral changes. What's an extra $60 to someone that has millions?

In addition to sickness, another reason for chronic truancy is the belief from certain parents that a child's schedule should revolve around the parent's schedule, and not the school schedule. My neighbors frequently remove their children from school for two weeks per year to take a family vacation. This vacation takes place right in the middle of the school year, as the father cannot take any time off during the summer. I don't think that a fine would change their behavior. Instead, the parents would need to understand how such actions are putting their children at an educational disadvantage.

In summary, truancy is a serious problem that deserves attention from schools and parents. There are many possible reasons for chronic truancy, and in order to truly serve the child, teachers and parents must work together to identify the unique challenges and potential solutions for each specific child. Additional financial pressure could further complicate matters, causing more harm than good.

Sample of an Essay with a Score of 3

The following essay does display some competence but it is also clearly flawed. The ideas presented are not well-developed, and analysis of the issue is superficial. There is an accumulation of errors in grammar, usage, and mechanics.

Finally, someone has a great idea. If parents are ever going to learn the importance of sending their kids to school, they'll understand when they have to pay for it. Money talks, and this is no exception.

The average student misses 12 days per year. Let's say that whenever a child misses more than 10 days per year, the parents are fined $100. The money generated will go to schools that are already lacking budgets. This way, parents will always think twice about having there kids absent for a day when they really don't need to. If a child has missed like seven days, and their parents want to travel with them, they'll think about it twice because if they take that time off than there is no room for sick days that may occur during the remainder of the year. So there you go, a policy that has a definite impact.

My only recommendations to make a strong impact would be to charge parents different amounts based on how much money they make each year. You want each parent to feel the impact on there truant child, but you don't want to penalize the poor or give breaks to those that are rich.

Sample of an Essay with a Score of 1

The following essay is fundamentally inadequate. The ideas presented are undeveloped, and there are serious and persistent writing errors.

I remember when I was in school, and it really bothered me when other kids were not there and I was told by my mom that I had to be. That type of double-standard really bothers me, how some people get to do something different from others for no epparent reason. That's why when I have kids I'm not sure how I'm gonna answer them when they ask me for the day off of school cause there friends are taking the day off as well. You want to be a good parent, but it is hard to say things like your parents did to you, when you vowed that you would always be different then them.

Source-Based Essay

Sample of an Essay with a Score of 6

The following essay, while not perfect, is good enough to earn the highest score of 6. Both sources are skillfully incorporated into the essay and are cited appropriately, and the essay explains why the issues that are discussed are important. The essay is organized logically, has well-developed ideas, and includes appropriate examples. There is a variety of sentence structure and, while the essay contains a few errors, it is generally well written.

The modern technological ability to accumulate large amounts of information about people presents a major issue—one of individual privacy! As Brian Naylor says in the "All Tech Considered" article, businesses and other entities have always collected information about people for various reasons (they just weren't as efficient at it before computers were around). In the "Ethical Implications" article, Michael McFarland notes that there are often legitimate reasons for doing this. These might include serving customers better by keeping their purchase history handy or stocking up on items that customers like. However, as Naylor explains, the Internet has "upped the ante" and now the tremendous amount of data collected about people is really an invasion of privacy. Privacy is a basic human right; even the United States Supreme Court has declared that all Americans have a basic right to privacy, even though that's not actually stated in the Constitution (Roe vs. Wade). The basic element of privacy rights is choice: people should be able to choose (within reason) whether or not to reveal personal information. If I choose to "reveal" to a store that I like political documentaries through my act of purchasing one, that doesn't mean that I want that information combined with every other bit of "transaction data" (McFarland) and sold to businesses and political groups so that they can target me! Those "choices" are qualitatively different, and the second situation is a violation of my privacy.

Another major concern regarding data accumulation is discrimination and abuse against vulnerable people. As Naylor explains, "profiles" collected by "data brokers" are used to put us into groups such as "Spanish-speaking person" or "struggling single mother in the city". These profiles can be used to target people based on ethnicity or socioeconomic status, which violates our American societal values. Spanish-speakers might fall victim to scam artists who assume that they are easy prey because they don't understand English and are less culturally savvy. "Struggling single mothers" may also be seen as vulnerable "easy targets" because they're alone and poor and, in extreme cases, might become victims of stalking or other crimes! As McFarland warns: "information provided for billing purposes can reveal a person's movements, whereabouts and habits." The government is supposed to protect its citizens safety and privacy, so regulations need to be enacted to safeguard against these types of abuses.

Sample of an Essay with a Score of 3

The following essay demonstrates some competence, but also displays obvious flaws. Both sources are cited but they are inadequately incorporated into the essay. Moreover, the essay never really explains why the various issues are important and the reasoning and ideas are poorly developed. The author does not provide helpful examples or details and mostly just paraphrases the passages. There is also an accumulation of errors in grammar, usage, and mechanics.

I believe privacy is the most important concern when it comes to modern technology and businesses getting everybodys information. According to McFarland, nowadays companies accumulate transaction data which means nearly everything we do is recorded. A person cant buy a plane ticket or even make a phone call without it being recorded and this information can be used against you (Michael McFarland). Company's collect it and make up a file on you with all your information, this is a total invasion of privacy (as McFarland said). You're information isnt in your control anymore but instead its in the control of people who might want to harm you (or at least use it against you). Companies have always been collecting information about us (what car we drive, etc) but with computers its so much easier to collect a lot of it, so this has become a much bigger problem in the modern age (Michael McFarland).

As Brian Naylor argued, today there are data brokers that collect all your information from google and Facebook and sell it (Brian Naylor). These companies exploit us all and make money by basically spying on our lives on the internet. The government doesn't really do anything about it (Naylor), but they should. Its bad enough that they collect our information, but the worst part is they put is in categories that can be used to discriminate against people. Why do they care that somebody is a "single mother struggling in an urban community" or speaks spanish? How do they plan to use that information? (Naylor). It cant be anything good. In conclusion, the most important concern about transaction data and data brokers is privacy. The government needs to step in and come up with regulations to stop these abusive behaviors.

Sample of an Essay with a Score of 1

The following essay is fundamentally deficient. Neither of the two sources is cited. Moreover, while some issues similar to the ones presented in the passages are discussed, the authors' specific ideas are not incorporated into the essay. The essay is undeveloped and poorly organized; there are also serious and persistent errors in grammar, usage, and mechanics.

It seems like every time I buy any thing at the store these days I get ads on my computer for the very thing that I bought. Its like somebody (or some thing) is keeping track of my purchases and knows exactly what I like and want. Every store has a "savings card" that customers use for discounts, this is one of the ways they keep track of what were buying. Also when I do a google search on something its like their all sharing the information about me which is a total invasion of privacy!

Some things I dont care about – like what toothpaste I use – but some things are more personal (and even things like toothpaste might be personal for people who are more sensitive and private than me). It would be great if everybody refused to use the card but they wont because its cheaper to use them. I think the government should definetely step in and protect peoples privacy because today its toothpaste but tomorrow, who know what "big brother" will be spying on us all about?

Chapter 12
Writing Practice
Test 2

WRITING

Questions 1 to 19:

Each of the following questions consists of a sentence that contains four underlined portions. Read each sentence and decide whether any of the underlined parts contains an element that would be considered incorrect or inappropriate in carefully written English. The error or concern may be in grammatical construction, word use, or an instance of incorrect or omitted punctuation or capitalization. If so, select the underlined portion that must be revised to produce a correct sentence. If there are no errors in the sentence as written, select "No error." **No sentence has more than one error.**

1 of 40

My <u>next-door neighbor</u>, Ms. Jones, was
       A
<u>kind and gracious enough</u> to give my <u>sister and I</u> a
       B   C
ride to the store <u>last evening</u>. <u>No error</u>
                D   E

2 of 40

Meryl, an <u>exquisite</u> ballerina , <u>danced so good</u> in the
       A   B   C
annual recital that she <u>easily won</u> the admiration of
                   D
the entire audience. <u>No error</u>
            E

3 of 40

President Abraham Lincoln, who led the nation

<u>so ingeniously</u> during the <u>calamitous</u> Civil War,
   A   B
<u>was ruthlessly assassinated</u> by John Wilkes Booth
          C
<u>in the year</u> 1865. <u>No error</u>
   D   E

4 of 40

While smaller and less aggressive <u>than</u> <u>its</u> formidable
                    A   B
cousin, the crocodile, the alligator <u>is most definitely</u> a
                        C
creature <u>to be feared</u>. <u>No error</u>
        D   E

5 of 40

Bobby was <u>conscious</u> of the fact that he
         A
<u>had been gaining weight</u> recently , so he <u>didn't eat</u>
   B   C   D
neither the ice cream nor the cake at the party.

<u>No error</u>
   E

6 of 40

The blue sports car that <u>Bill's parents</u> generously
               A
bought him for his <u>twenty-first</u> birthday , was ,
            B   C   D
unfortunately, totaled. <u>No error</u>
           E

7 of 40

When <u>approached by</u> an aggressive bear, you should
     A
<u>raise</u> your arms and wave <u>them</u> wildly in the air
   B   C
<u>for appearing</u> larger than you really are. <u>No error</u>
   D   E

8 of 40

Ted is typically careful not to eat <u>to</u> much spicy food
                      A
right before bedtime ; otherwise , he <u>is apt</u> to have
              B   C   D
nightmares. <u>No error</u>
        E

WRITING

Kevin was so <u>horribly</u> depressed after <u>receiving</u> an "F"
.........A...B
in English, which <u>had been</u> his favorite subject, that
...........................C
he didn't talk to <u>nobody</u> for three full days. <u>No error</u>
..........................D..E

The teachers were eager to get a glimpse of <u>their</u> new
....A
<u>principal</u> <u>,</u> <u>whom</u> they had never seen before. <u>No error</u>
....B........C....D..E

While conversing with the foreign exchange students,

<u>whose</u> <u>English</u> was <u>poor</u>, the bus driver spoke very
...A.........B.................C
<u>slow</u> so that they could understand. <u>No error</u>
...D..E

The chocolate cupcakes <u>that</u> <u>Charles's</u> mother baked
.................................A.......B
for him were absolutely delicious <u>,</u> he <u>ate them all</u> in
....C..........D
one sitting. <u>No error</u>
.................E

Linda <u>has lived</u> abroad for more <u>than</u> ten years,
...........A............................B
<u>thoroughly enjoying</u> European culture, until she
...........C
became homesick a few years ago and moved back to

<u>the</u> United States. <u>No error</u>
...D..........................E

No member of the student advisory board <u>should vote</u>
....A
against the proposal if <u>their</u> <u>conscience</u> forbids <u>it</u>.
.............................B........C..................D
<u>No error</u>
...E

The <u>Johnsons</u> are not sure where they want to go for
........A
<u>their vacation</u> <u>;</u> they want either to go to Florida to
.....B.............C
scuba dive, <u>but maybe</u> to visit New York to see a
.....................D
Broadway play. <u>No error</u>
..............................E

My aunt, <u>whose</u> opinion I value <u>greatly</u>, gave my
.................A.............................B
sister and <u>me</u> some good advice about <u>choosing</u> a
.................C......................................D
college. <u>No error</u>
.................E

Dave knew that his parents <u>would give him</u> a
....A
graduation present <u>;</u> <u>however</u>, a new car was an
........................B.......C
<u>unexpected</u> surprise. <u>No error</u>
...D.............................E

Paul and Joan were appalled by the offensive tone of

last <u>week's</u> staff meeting; they <u>voiced</u> their concerns
........A...D
and <u>have left</u> the conference room before the meeting
.........C
<u>ended</u>. <u>No error</u>
...D..........E

The best part of eating an ice cream sundae <u>are</u>
....A
the delicious toppings <u>,</u> <u>such as</u> hot fudge sauce <u>and</u>
...............................B.....C...........................D
whipped cream. <u>No error</u>
...............................E

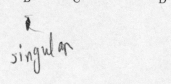

WRITING

In each of the following questions, part of the sentence or the entire sentence is underlined. Beneath each sentence are five ways of writing the underlined part. The first of these repeats the original, but the other four are all different. If you think the original sentence is better than any of the suggested changes, you should select the first answer choice; otherwise you should select one of the other choices. This is a test of correctness and effectiveness of expression.

In choosing answers, follow the requirements of standard written English; that is, pay attention to acceptable usage in grammar, diction (choice of words), sentence construction, and punctuation. Choose the answer that expresses most effectively what is presented in the original sentence; this answer should be clear and exact, without awkwardness, ambiguity, or redundancy.

20 of 40

The elderly gentlemen all <u>removed their hat when the ladies entered</u> the room.

- ○ removed their hat when the ladies entered
- ◉ removed their hats when the ladies entered
- ○ removed their hats when the ladies' entered
- ○ removed their hat when the ladies were entering
- ○ removed their hat when the lady's entered

21 of 40

Startled by the loud noise, <u>the phone dropped from John's hand</u> while he was speaking with his wife.

- ○ the phone dropped from John's hand
- ○ the phone dropped from Johns hand
- ◉ John dropped the phone
- ○ John dropped the phone from his hand
- ○ John's hand dropped the phone

22 of 40

<u>Unlike Europeans, the desserts served in American restaurants are typically huge.</u>

- ○ Unlike Europeans, the desserts served in American restaurants are typically huge.
- ○ Unlike Europeans, the deserts served in American restaurants are typically huge.
- ◉ American restaurants typically serve huge desserts, unlike those served in Europe.
- ○ Unlike European restaurants, the desserts served in American restaurants are typically huge.
- ○ Unlike European restaurants, the deserts served in American restaurants are typically huge.

23 of 40

<u>If you're going to invite Karen and me</u> to the movies, be sure to invite Jeffrey as well.

- ◉ If you're going to invite Karen and me
- ○ If your going to invite Karen and me
- ○ If you're going to invite Karen and I
- ○ If you're going to invite Karen, as well as me,
- ○ If you are going to invite Karen and I

24 of 40

The movie star was mortified <u>to read the unauthorized biography of her life.</u>

- ○ to read the unauthorized biography of her life.
- ○ to read the biography of her life that she had not authorized.
- ○ to have been reading the unauthorized biography of her life.
- ○ to read that her biography was unauthorized.
- ◉ to read her unauthorized biography.

WRITING

Our supervisor does not <u>permit us eating lunch at our desks.</u>

- ○ permit us eating lunch at our desks.
- ◉ permit us to eat lunch at our desks.
- ○ permit us to eat lunch at our desk.
- ○ permit us to be eating at our desks.
- ○ permit that lunch be eaten by us at our desk.

<u>The most delicious meal of all: meat loaf,</u> mashed potatoes, and peas!

- ○ The most delicious meal of all: meat loaf,
- ○ The most delicious meal of all: meat loaf
- ○ The most delicious meal of all; meat loaf,
- ○ The most delicious meal of all: is meat loaf,
- ◉ This is the most delicious meal of all: meat loaf,

With only three hours left until summer vacation, Jill was extremely <u>eager to put her books away, join her friends at the beach, and be enjoying the sunshine.</u>

- ○ eager to put her books away, join her friends at the beach, and be enjoying the sunshine.
- ◉ eager to put her books away, join her friends at the beach, and enjoy the sunshine.
- ○ eager to be putting her books away, be joining her friends at the beach, and be enjoying the sunshine.
- ○ eager to put her books away, join her friends at the beach, and to be enjoying the sunshine.
- ○ eager to put her books away, to join her friends at the beach, and to enjoy the sunshine.

Lou adores animals, <u>except for snakes, spiders, and the alligator.</u>

- ○ except for snakes, spiders, and the alligator.
- ○ with an exception for snakes, spiders, and the alligator.
- ○ except for the snakes, the spiders, and the alligators.
- ◉ except for snakes, spiders, and alligators.
- ○ with an exception being snakes, spiders, and alligators.

<u>While reading a story about medieval knights, my cat Dolly lay</u> on top of the book and refused to move.

- ○ While reading a story about medieval knights, my cat Dolly lay
- ○ While reading a story about medieval knights, my cat Dolly laid
- ◉ While I was reading a story about medieval knights, my cat Dolly lay
- ○ While I was reading a story about medieval knights, my cat Dolly laid
- ○ During the time that I was reading a story about medieval knights, my cat Dolly lay

After the university admissions officer interviewed <u>all the prospective students, she began to review their</u> respective files.

- ◉ all the prospective students, she began to review their
- ○ all the prospective students, she began to review there
- ○ all the perspective students, she began to review their
- ○ all the perspective students; she began to review their
- ○ all the prospective students, she had begun to review their

WRITING

(1) Many Americans believe that the line that separates the criminal justice system from the entertainment world is becoming increasingly blurred. (2) Once a mere curiosity, television shows that feature video footage of police officers in action are now a staple of pop culture. (3) Around-the-clock programming, the multitude of channels and videotape options available, and the worldwide prevalence of the Internet have created a seemingly insatiable demand for police video. (4) But what effect do the cameras have on the officers? (5) Some fear that the desire for ratings might put pressure on the police to create drama through shocking or dramatic confrontation. (6) However, even if most officers are not negatively affected by the cameras, the civilians who are filmed may suffer negative consequences. (7) Experiencing a crisis is unpleasant enough for them, and so they don't need millions of people watching. (8) Cynics may argue that, at least in some cases, the officer's mere knowledge that he or she might appear on television could lead to posturing and overzealousness.

(9) Americans' desire to be entertained by real-life crime affects the court system as well. (10) Many judges now allow cameras in the courtroom, and comprehensive "gavel to gavel" coverage of criminal trials is not uncommon. (11) While courthouses in the United States have traditionally been open to the public, never before have millions of people effectively had a front seat in the courtroom. (12) Lawyers and judges may behave differently when the cameras are rolling, as impression management may outweigh important professional concerns. (13) Moreover, witnesses may be reluctant to testify candidly about personal matters when the media are present. (14) Jurors are not typically shown on camera in the courtroom, they may nonetheless feel compelled to render verdicts in accordance with popular opinion in cases that are closely scrutinized.

Where would the following sentence best be inserted?

The fact that many witnesses appear in court involuntarily, having been compelled by subpoena, makes it even worse to broadcast sensitive testimony.

○ Immediately after sentence 10

○ Immediately after sentence 11

○ Immediately after sentence 12

◉ Immediately after sentence 13

○ The sentence cannot fit logically into the passage.

Which is the best version of the underlined portion of sentence 7 (reproduced below)?

Experiencing a crisis is unpleasant <u>enough for them, and so they don't need</u> millions of people watching.

○ (As it is now)

◉ enough without

○ enough for these civilians, and so they don't need

○ enough for them; and so they don't need

○ enough for them, and they don't need

What is the best way to deal with sentence 8 (reproduced below)?

Cynics may argue that, at least in some cases, the officer's mere knowledge that he or she might appear on television could lead to posturing and overzealousness.

○ Leave it where it is.

○ Place it immediately after sentence 3.

◉ Place it immediately after sentence 5.

○ Place it immediately after sentence 6.

○ Delete it from the passage.

WRITING

In context, which of the following revisions of sentence 14 (reproduced below) is most needed?

Jurors are not typically shown on camera in the courtroom, they may nonetheless feel compelled to render verdicts in accordance with popular opinion in cases that are closely scrutinized.

- ⬤ Add "While" at the beginning of the sentence.

- ○ Change "may" to "might."

- ○ Delete the comma.

- ○ Change "typically" to "usually."

- ○ Change "in the courtroom" to "courtrooms."

What is the best way to deal with sentence 2 (reproduced below)?

Once a mere curiosity, television shows that feature video footage of police officers in action are now a staple of pop culture.

- ⬤ Leave it as it is.

- ○ Delete the comma.

- ○ Insert a comma after the word "action."

- ○ Move it to the end of the first paragraph.

- ○ Delete it from the passage.

Which of the following sentences would best conclude the passage?

- ○ It is therefore critically important that police officers be careful not to let the cameras affect their behavior.

- ○ For this reason, cameras should only be allowed in courtrooms when there is a high-profile defendant on trial.

- ○ So allowing cameras in the courtroom is actually much worse than using police videos for entertainment purposes.

- ○ In conclusion, although filming police and courtroom activity can be problematic, the entertainment value of these videos outweighs any negative considerations.

- ⬤ Consequently, some criminal defendants may not get the fair trial that they deserve.

Five high school seniors in a criminal justice class are working on a group paper about Americans' attitudes towards capital punishment. Which of the following would be most relevant?

- ⬤ The results of a credible nationwide survey indicating that 65% of Americans currently favor the death penalty because they believe it has a deterrent effect

- ○ Transcripts of interviews in which the students' family members discuss how they feel about the death penalty

- ○ Copies of official records listing the names of all persons currently on death row in the United States

- ○ A list of the states that currently impose the death penalty

- ○ A copy of a document outlining the official United Nations policy on capital punishment

Jenkins, Maria. *The History of Modern Art.* Random House, 2014. Print

The citation above would be appropriate for

- ○ a website

- ○ an electronic book

- ○ a magazine article in print

- ○ a doctoral dissertation published online

- ⬤ a book in print

A ninth grader checks out a book entitled *The American Civil War: Four Bloody Years* to use as his main source for a research paper on the Battle of Gettysburg. Relying primarily on this book would most likely

- ○ narrow the topic

- ⬤ broaden the topic

- ○ neither narrow nor broaden the topic

- ○ yield no information relevant to the topic

- ○ yield inaccurate information

WRITING

Which of the following is a primary source?

- ◉ A photograph of President Nixon leaving the White House after his resignation (for a book about the Nixon presidency)

- ○ A fictional short story, published in 1977, about a Victorian lady (for a book about the Victorian era)

- ○ A television documentary about the Revolutionary War (for a magazine article about the life of Revolutionary War soldiers)

- ○ The transcript of a television interview with the author of a novel set in ancient Rome (for a book about ancient Rome)

- ○ A journal article in which a lawyer analyzes all the known evidence surrounding a crime that took place a century earlier

WRITING

Argumentative Essay

30 minutes

You will have a total of 30 minutes to plan and write an argumentative essay on the topic presented in the following section. The essay should be based on your own reading, experience, and observations.

Read the topic carefully. DO NOT WRITE ON A TOPIC OTHER THAN THE ONE SPECIFIED. Essays on topics of your own choice are not acceptable. In order for your test to be scored, your response must be in English.

The essay questions are included in this test to give you an opportunity to demonstrate how well you can write. You should consider the topic, organize your thoughts, and take care to write clearly and effectively, using specific examples where appropriate. How well you write is much more important than how much you write; however, to cover the topic adequately, it is suggested that you write more than one paragraph.

Read the opinion stated below.

"All schools should have school uniforms."

Discuss the extent to which you agree or disagree with this point of view. Support your position with specific reasons and examples from your own experience, observations, or reading.

WRITING

Source-Based Essay

30 minutes

You will have a total of 30 minutes to read two short passages on a topic and to plan and write an essay on that topic. The essay should be an informative essay based on the two sources provided.

Read the topic carefully. DO NOT WRITE ON A TOPIC OTHER THAN THE ONE SPECIFIED. Essays on topics of your own choice are not acceptable. In order for your test to be scored, your response must be in English.

The essay questions are included in this test to give you an opportunity to demonstrate how well you can write. You should consider the topic, organize your thoughts, and take care to write clearly and effectively, using specific examples where appropriate. How well you write is much more important than how much you write; however, to cover the topic adequately, it is suggested that you write more than one paragraph.

Directions:

The following assignment requires you to use information from two sources to discuss the most important concerns that relate to a specific issue. When paraphrasing or quoting from the sources, cite each source by referring to the author's last name, the title, or any other clear identifier.

Assignment:

Both of the following sources address the issue of how online education compares with traditional classroom education and discuss some advantages and disadvantages of each. Read the two passages carefully and then write an essay in which you identify the most important concerns regarding this issue, explaining why these concerns are important. Your essay must draw on information from BOTH of the sources. You may also draw upon your own experience, observations, or reading. Be sure to CITE the sources, whether you are quoting from the passage or simply paraphrasing.

Source 1:

Adapted from:

Richardson, Kelly. "Interpersonal Aspects of Online Education." *Modern Pedagogy*, vol. 42, no. 3, 2016, pp.134-137.

Recent years have seen a steady increase in the popularity of online higher education. Viewed by many as a cheaper and more convenient alternative to the traditional classroom experience, many students are now eschewing the brick-and-mortar universities that were the focal point of their parents' college years. From an interpersonal perspective, however, online education poses unique issues and challenges.

According to many college graduates, the most beneficial aspect of their education was not the information they were given, but rather the professors and instructors whom they came to know. The opportunity to be guided by an older and more experienced person during one's transition to adulthood can be an invaluable experience, and both students and teachers place considerable importance on mentoring relationships. However, the opportunity for online instructors to mentor their students is limited. It is difficult for a student to truly get to know a teacher whom he or she has never met in person. Moreover, the fact that online instructors typically have many more students than traditional instructors do makes mentorship all the more difficult, impractical, and unlikely.

The lack of physical proximity and in-person communication among students can similarly detract from one's interpersonal experiences of college. Friendships are harder to develop, as is a sense of community with one's peers. However, while modern technology does, in a sense, erect barriers between students, it also brings them closer in many ways. The relative convenience and affordability of online classes allows many more people to participate than would be able to attend traditional classes. The result is a larger and more diverse group of students. No longer insulated by geographical area, age, affluence, or lifestyle choices, students can have meaningful exchanges and even bond with others with whom they might otherwise never interact.

WRITING

Source 2:

Adapted from:

Stevenson, Frederick. "Traditional Universities Vs. Online Colleges: An Analysis of the Respective Advantages of In-Person and Computer-Based Higher Education." *The International Journal of Technology and Education*, vol. 11, no. 2, 2015, pp. 217-223.

The most obvious virtue of online classes is the ease and convenience with which people can now educate themselves. No longer does the new parent have to forego a degree because of childcare responsibilities, or the family breadwinner have to commit to spending virtually all waking hours away from home in an effort to better the family's prospects. Now fewer people have to choose between a livelihood (or any other time-consuming preoccupation) and an education, as online courses can accommodate virtually anybody's schedule and idiosyncratic needs. Moreover, ordinary people can now avail themselves of opportunities that were once reserved for the super-rich—such as an American taking a class with an esteemed instructor who teaches exclusively in Europe. Remote access to people and places one would not otherwise ever dream of encountering has allowed millions of twenty-first century students to expand their intellectual horizons and elevate their status in society.

Remote access has proved, however, to be a highly troublesome two-edged sword. How can an online instructor ever truly know whether his student, "John Smith," is actually John Smith's wife who has expertise in the course material beyond that of her husband? Similarly, how can one ascertain whether an ostensibly brilliant student actually wrote her thesis herself, as opposed to purchasing it from the many opportunistic individuals who thrive on the inability of online instructors to detect plagiarism? The idea of widespread cheating is disturbing enough when dealing with humanities coursework, but the idea of, for example, a pharmacological student fraudulently obtaining his credentials is positively frightening. Indeed, it is this lack of quality control that leads many traditional universities to reject online education altogether. Many unfortunate students study for years in online classes only to discover that their credits and degrees will never be accepted by prestigious institutions of learning

Chapter 13
Writing Practice
Test 2: Answers and
Explanations

WRITING PRACTICE TEST 2 ANSWER KEY

1.	C	21.	C
2.	C	22.	C
3.	D	23.	A
4.	E	24.	E
5.	D	25.	B
6.	C	26.	E
7.	D	27.	B
8.	A	28.	D
9.	D	29.	C
10.	E	30.	A
11.	D	31.	D
12.	C	32.	B
13.	A	33.	C
14.	B	34.	A
15.	D	35.	A
16.	E	36.	E
17.	D	37.	A
18.	C	38.	E
19.	A	39.	B
20.	B	40.	A

WRITING PRACTICE TEST 2 EXPLANATIONS

Multiple-Choice Questions

1. **C**   The objective pronoun *me* is required here. Just as it would be correct to state *give me a ride to the store* (not *I*) in this context, the fact that the sister is included does not change the grammatical structure of the sentence.

2. **C**   An adverb is required here to modify the word *dance*. *Good* is an adjective and *well* is an adverb.

3. **D**   The phrase *in the year 1865* is redundant (1865 is a year). The words *the year* are unnecessary because omitting them does not change the meaning of the sentence or result in a grammatical error.

4. **E**   This sentence contains no errors in grammar or usage.

5. **D**   This is a double negative. The *neither...nor* construction is negative, as is the contraction *didn't*. The correct wording is *he ate neither the ice cream nor the cake*.

6. **C**   The comma is unnecessary here and creates an illogical break between the subject and the verb.

7. **D**   The *for appearing* construction is awkward and unwarranted here; the simple infinitive *to appear* is correct.

8. **A**   This sentence contains a diction error. The adverb *too* is needed here which (when used in this sense) indicates excessiveness: *He is too old for toys*. In contrast, the word *to* usually functions as a preposition: *I go to the store*. These words are not interchangeable. Example: *If the jeans are **too** small for you, give them **to** your sister*.

9. **D**   This sentence contains a double negative. The contraction *didn't* (did not) and the word *nobody* are both negative. *He didn't talk to anybody* or *he talked to nobody* are both correct in this case.

10. **E**   This sentence contains no errors in grammar or usage.

11. **D**   The adverb *slowly* should be used here to modify the verb *spoke*; the word *slow* is an adjective and is therefore incorrect.

12. **C**   This is a comma splice: two clauses that could each stand alone as sentences (i.e., two independent clauses) are joined by a comma. A semicolon is correct here.

13. **A**   The use of the present perfect *has lived* here is incorrect. The action (living in Europe) ended at a specified time in the past, so the past perfect (*had lived*) is required.

14. **B**   The singular noun *member* requires a singular pronoun. Therefore, *no member...should vote against the proposal if his or her conscience forbids it* would be correct here. The singular pronouns *his* and *her* are both grammatically correct as well, although their use might be confusing if the group

consists of males and females. (The traditional use of *his* to refer to both males and females is increasingly discouraged as sexist.)

15. **D** The *either...but maybe* construction is unidiomatic and incorrect. *Either...or* is the correct construction: they want *either* to go to Florida to scuba dive, *or* to visit New York.

16. **E** This sentence contains no errors in grammar or usage.

17. **D** *Unexpected surprise* is redundant. Surprises are, by definition, unexpected.

18. **C** There is no reason to use the present perfect *have left* construction here. The simple past tense *left the conference room* is correct.

19. **A** The subject of this sentence is *the best part of eating an ice cream sundae*; the noun *part* is singular so the singular verb *is* is required.

20. **B** This sentence is obviously meant to convey that each of the gentlemen removed his hat when the ladies entered. However, the phrase *removed their hat* suggests that the gentlemen had only one hat among them and were somehow all wearing it (an unlikely scenario)! Only (B) and (C) correct this error. Choice (C), however, incorrectly uses the plural possessive *(ladies')* when the simple plural *(ladies)* is required.

21. **C** The error here is a misplaced modifier. The sentence is obviously meant to convey that John was startled by a loud noise and dropped the phone. However, the phone is actually the subject of the sentence (as it is written) because the phone is the only entity performing action. Accordingly, the sentence indicates that *the phone* was startled by the noise. Only (C) and (D) correct this error by making John the subject of the sentence. Choice (E) introduces another misplaced modifier by making John's hand the subject. Choice (D), however, is unnecessarily wordy (it is generally understood that one holds a phone in one's hand) while (C) is succinct.

22. **C** There is a comparison error in this sentence. Instead of comparing the desserts served in American restaurants with the desserts served in European restaurants, the huge American desserts are compared with the Europeans themselves (implying that European *people* are small)! Choice (B) does not correct this error. Choices (D) and (E) introduce a similar error, comparing the American desserts to the European *restaurants*. Choices (B) and (D) also introduce a diction error by substituting the word *desert* (an arid region). Only (C) properly compares American desserts with European desserts (and does not introduce additional errors).

23. **A** The original sentence properly uses the objective pronoun *me*, unlike (C) and (E), which are wrong. Choice (B) introduces a diction error by using the possessive pronoun *your* instead of *you're* (the contraction of *you* and *are*). For example: *If you want to succeed, **you're** going to have to change **your** attitude.* Choice (D) is awkward and wordy and therefore does not improve upon the original sentence.

24. **E** The phrase *biography of her life* is redundant; by definition, a biography is the story of a person's life; eliminate (A), (B), and (C). Choice (D) changes the meaning of the sentence, indicating that the movie star was mortified by the fact that her biography was unauthorized, not by the biography itself.

25. **B** The gerund *eating* is incorrect, as the simple infinitive *to eat* is called for here. Choices (B) and (C) correct this error, but (C) introduces another error by changing *desks* to *desk*, implying that all the individuals who work for this supervisor share one desk. Choices (D) and (E) are wordy and awkward.

26. **E** This sentence incorrectly has a colon after a sentence fragment. Choices (A), (B), and (D) fail to correct this error (and introduce other errors as well). Choice (C) replaces the colon with a semicolon, which cannot properly follow a fragment either. Only (E) correctly has a complete sentence before the colon.

27. **B** The principle of parallelism requires that all the verbs in this list of actions be in the same form; the words *be enjoying* deviate from the pattern. Only (B) and (C) are parallel, but (C) is wordy and repetitive, while (B) is succinct.

28. **D** The items in this list should be in parallel form—that is, they should all be plural. *The alligator* deviates from the pattern. Choices (C), (D), and (E) are all parallel, but (C) is wordy and repetitive, and (E) is wordy and awkward.

29. **C** This sentence contains a misplaced modifier. The sentence is meant to convey that while the speaker, *I*, was reading a story about medieval knights, the cat lay down on the book. Because the cat, Dolly, is the subject here, the sentence actually states that the cat was reading the book (an unlikely scenario)! Choices (C), (D), and (E) correct this error, but (E) is too wordy. Choice (D) introduces another error by substituting *laid* for *lay*. The past tense of the verb *lie* (to recline) is *lay*. A correct use of this verb is *I don't need to **lie** down now because I **lay** down earlier to rest.*

30. **A** This sentence is correct as written. Choices (C) and (D) introduce a diction error by substituting the word *perspective* ("mental view") for the word *prospective* ("potential"). For example: *From my **perspective**, all the **prospective** jurors would be good choices.* Choice (B) introduces a different diction error by substituting the word *there* ("in or at that place") for the possessive pronoun *their* ("belonging to them"). For example: *Tell them to put **their** books over **there**.* Choice (E) incorrectly changes the verb tense.

31. **D** The only logical place to insert this sentence would be immediately after sentence 13, which introduces the issue of filming witnesses. Sentence 13 states that witnesses may be reluctant to testify on camera about sensitive matters. The new sentence elaborates on this idea by acknowledging that many witnesses do not testify willingly, which makes the invasion of privacy worse.

32. **B** Sentence 7 is wordy and awkward, and (B) is the only revision that expresses the idea succinctly.

33. **C**   Sentence 8 is out of place in the passage as written and should be placed immediately after sentence 5. Sentence 4 rhetorically asks what affect cameras have on the police, and sentence 5 suggests that filming negatively affects officers' conduct. Sentence 6 then transitions from discussing police officers to the issue of witnesses by stating that, even if most officers are *not* adversely affected, civilians may be. The discussion of additional negative effects on police officers at the end of the paragraph (i.e., sentence 8) indicates a disorganized passage.

34. **A**   Sentence 14 has a comma splice (two independent clauses are joined by a comma). Adding *While* at the beginning of the sentence corrects this error.

35. **A**   Sentence 2 contains no errors in grammar or usage and fits logically where it is. Moreover, it is relevant to the passage, so it should not be deleted; (E) is incorrect.

36. **E**   Choice (A) would not logically conclude the passage because the second paragraph deals entirely with the courts, not the police. Choice (B) would not make sense because it contradicts the passage. The second paragraph expresses concern that jurors might feel coerced by popular opinion in trials that receive a great deal of attention. Therefore, cameras should *not* be permitted when there is a high-profile defendant. Choice (C) is wrong because the passage makes no comparison between the downside of filming the police and the downside of filming trials. Choice (D) is clearly wrong because the passage never suggests that the entertainment value of crime-related video outweighs the negative effects (the opposite is strongly implied). Choice (E) is correct because it elaborates on the issue of jurors feeling pressured by the cameras to render popular verdicts.

37. **A**   A credible nationwide survey that shows that 65% of Americans favor capital punishment (and why) would be highly relevant to a paper about how Americans feel about the death penalty. Interviews with the students' family members would be mildly relevant (assuming they are Americans), but the opinions of a handful of people would not offer insight into how Americans feel about the issue in general. Choice (B) is incorrect. Neither a list of death row inmates nor a list of states that impose the death penalty would offer much insight into Americans' feelings about this issue, so (C) and (D) are incorrect. United Nations policy would not be relevant to the issue of how *Americans* feel about capital punishment, so (E) can be eliminated as well.

38. **E**   This citation follows the MLA format for a book: the author's name, the book title, the city of publication, the publisher, and, finally, the year of publication. Eliminate (A), (C), and (D). The word *print* at the end indicates the medium, so eliminate (B) as well.

39. **B**   The Battle of Gettysburg was one incident in the Civil War, so relying on a book that covers the entire war would broaden the topic; eliminate (A) and (C). Choice (D) is wrong because the book would almost surely contain *some* information about Gettysburg. There is no reason to believe that the Civil War book would be inaccurate, so eliminate (E).

40. **A** The photograph of President Nixon leaving the White House would be the only example of original source material. Primary sources are contemporaneous sources that provide firsthand information about a person, thing, or event. The other answer choices feature secondary sources; in each case the source's subject matter belongs to an earlier historical period.

Argumentative Essay

"All schools should have school uniforms."

Sample of an Essay with a Score of 6

The following essay is not perfect, but it is good enough to earn a score of 6. The thesis is supported by a fairly well-developed analysis. Moreover, the essay is organized and demonstrates good overall writing skills.

I strongly agree with the belief that all schools, even public schools, should have school uniforms. A common dress code, with limited apparel selection, will help to minimize the often apparent socio-economic differences present among children. The amount of time and energy spent by children on their dress can be redirected towards learning. Further, a common dress code will allow students to develop socially based on factors outside of the clothing they wear.

I came from a relatively poor family, and attended a school where the median household income was well more than $250,000. Many of the girls at school would brag about the new clothes they purchased, often at outrageous prices. I immediately felt left out because I could not wear the same things they could. I became bitter towards my parents at their inability to provide for me the same things other girls would receive whenever they wanted. In addition to impacting my relationship with my parents, I was very tentative at school. I never raised my hand or volunteered; in part, perhaps, because I did not want to call attention to myself, often clothed in hand-me-downs from my older sister.

Many critics of a universal uniform policy criticize the financial costs of such a program. I do not think this is a valid argument. Parents should be asked to pay for the basic set of clothing required for school. In theory, parents can use the money allocated for school clothes for the school year, and focus those dollars towards the uniforms. For some parents, however, I understand that there is not always a sufficient "school clothes" budget to cover the cost of uniforms. In that case, these families should receive a subsidy for uniforms. Schools have already shown the ability to execute these programs—the free lunch program is widely praised for its fair approach and ease of execution.

In the final analysis, I think the benefits of a school uniform policy far outweigh any deficits. Children need not worry about the pressures of "looking cool" or fitting in with those of different financial backgrounds. Instead, students can focus on expressing their individuality through their education, a positive effect for all involved.

Sample of an Essay with a Score of 3

The following essay states a position and supports it with relevant examples, but the analysis is weak and the ideas are not well-developed.

It sounds very easy—give children the same clothes to wear at school, and things will be great. Well I'm not so sure. The belief is that school uniforms will allow children to focus more and not worry about what they wear. In fact, they'll just find other ways to differentiate themselves, which may be worse or more extreme than if they could wear what they wanted in the first place.

My niece goes to a private school, which has uniforms. Because the kids can't express themselves through their clothes, they do it through other ways. One girl has her ear pierced seven times. Another one has dyed her hair purple. Would these extreme measures be necessary if they didn't have a uniform policy? I don't think so. I'm worried about these kids going too far trying to be recognized or different from their peer groups.

In conclusion, uniforms are not a very good idea. They just lead to more extreme behaviors, as I have shown above.

Sample of an Essay with a Score of 1

The following essay is clearly deficient. The ideas are undeveloped, the examples provided are extremely limited, and there is virtually no analysis. There are also persistent errors in grammar, punctuation, and usage.

I went to school were there was a uniform policy, and man it was no fun. Their were only five shirts you could wear—a blue button down, a yellow button down, a button down that was white, one of those white golf shirts, and the fifth one was a blue golf shirt. As for pants, we could where any type of khaki that we wanted. Shoes were no fun to wear either—no tennis shoes, only on free dress days. Unless students want to be as miserable as me back then, I don't think their should be a uniform policy anywhere.

Source-Based Essay

Sample of an Essay with a Score of 6

The following essay, while not perfect, is good enough to earn the highest score of 6. Both sources are skillfully incorporated into the essay and are cited appropriately, and the essay explains why the issues that are discussed are important. The essay is organized logically, has well-developed ideas, and includes appropriate examples. There is a variety of sentence structure and, while the essay contains a few errors, it is generally well written.

Both online and traditional classes have many advantages and disadvantages. One of the most important concerns about choosing which school to attend, however, is the issue of diversity. Education isn't just about getting information; it's about interacting with many different kinds of people and getting as many different perspectives about life as possible! As Frederick Stevenson explains in Source 2, the convenience of online classes allows all sorts of people with different lifestyles to attend school and participate in the dialogue. He further states that, with remote access, even people who live in different countries and come from very different cultures can go to school together and learn from each other. It's true that the diverse group of online students may not be able to get to know each other as well as if they attended traditional classes together, as Kelly Richardson discusses in Source 1. However, with modern technology like email, texting, and Skype, students can actually form pretty normal friendships with people who live far away. Richardson explains that, with online classes, barriers like wealth and age are torn down because more people can participate; this really increases diversity! One of the best parts of going to (traditional) college for me was actually being mentored by some much older students! As Richardson wisely says: "The opportunity to be guided by an older and more experienced person during one's transition to adulthood can be an invaluable experience…"

Unfortunately, however, having a wonderfully diverse student body isn't enough – students need to receive a quality education! Ultimately we are all in school to learn and to receive the best education possible in order to become successful – that is the chief priority. Traditional universities have a major advantage in this regard and, as Stevenson explains, some don't even accept credits from online schools. Stevenson's idea of remote access as a "highly troublesome two-edged sword" in that people can easily cheat in online classes is very true! If your online degree isn't worth much because nobody knows if you actually learned anything or if you cheated, then the best teachers wont teach online and will only associate themselves with the more prestigious traditional programs. The quality of online education just goes downhill from there. Moreover, as Richardson explains, because many more students can enroll online, the teacher can only give each student so much attention. The learning experience just can't be as rich or rewarding when the teacher doesn't even know your name. Online schools may have some advantages, but I don't think they will ever be as good or prestigious as traditional colleges.

Sample of an Essay with a Score of 3

The following essay demonstrates some competence, but also displays obvious flaws. One source is cited, but the second source is not. Moreover, the essay inadequately explains why the various issues are important and the reasoning and ideas are poorly developed. The essay, while coherent, is somewhat poorly organized in that it contains only one paragraph. There is also an accumulation of errors in grammar, usage, and mechanics.

The most important issue about online vs. regular college is that online students can cheat which isn't fair to everybody else (Stevenson). How can you really know if the student did their own work, or whether they paid somebody to write it for them or got a family member to do it? (Stevenson). College students work hard and it isnt fair for people to pass somebody elses work off as there own. Its also really scary for people to do that if, say, their going to be a doctor or a pharmicist or something, "a pharmacological student fraudulently obtaining his credentials is positively frightening". (Stevenson). I dont want some doctor working on me, that cheated on all his online tests! But students being able to remotely access everything is also a good thing. (Stevenson). Otherwise only rich people get to do things like take courses by european teachers and poor people and people with families cant have any education at all cause they don't have the money or the time. (Stevenson). On line courses do have advantages because people can elevate their status and expand their horizons, when with regular courses they wouldn't be able to. (Stevenson). I think fairness is extremely important. On line classes are fair because they allow everybody to have the opportunity for an education but also unfair because some people (not everybody) can cheat on line. (Stevenson). So in conclusion on line has both advantages and disadvantages.

Sample of an Essay with a Score of 1

The following essay is fundamentally deficient. Neither source is cited, nor are the ideas that are presented in the passages incorporated into the essay. The essay is undeveloped and there are serious and persistent errors in grammar, usage, and mechanics.

I wanted to take only online classes cause it was cheaper (which is a pretty big factor!) but my parents wanted me to go to a regular college cause thats what they did. Im really glad that I listened! I joined a fraternity and made alot of really good friends that I still talk to today. I think if I had went with the online college I never would never have had such a good experence or had so much fun. I would definetely advice anybody who is thinking of going to college to stay away from online schools! Just because their cheap doesnt mean they will pay off in the end. The quality of the experience is what matters most of all, I look back on my college days with hardly no regret.

Chapter 14
Math Practice
Test 1

MATH

Praxis Core Academic Skills for Educators

Mathematics

Time—85 minutes

56 Questions

Directions: For each question, select the best answer or answers from the choices given for selected-response questions, or provide an answer by typing in the answer box. Remember to read the directions for each question carefully, as you may be asked to respond in a variety of ways, including selecting one answer choice from a list, checking multiple checkboxes, or typing your answer into an answer box.

Which of the following contains the three numbers in order from smallest to largest?

○ 3.092, 3.5, 3.52

○ 3.092, 3.52, 3.5

○ 3.5, 3.52, 3.092

○ 3.52, 3.5, 3.092

○ 3.5, 3.092, 3.52

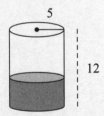

A cylindrical water tank has a radius of 5 feet and a height of 12 feet. If 250 cubic feet of water is placed into the tank, what is the height of the water in the tank? Round your answer to the nearest hundredth.

Note: The value of pi is approximately 3.14.

 feet

Click on the box and type in a number.
Backspace to erase.

A vending machine contains 42 items. There are 13 candy bars, 14 bags of pretzels, and 15 packs of gum. After recess, there are 11 items remaining in the vending machine.

In order to calculate the total value of the items not sold during recess, what additional information would be needed?

○ The cost of a bag of pretzels, the cost of a candy bar, and the cost of a pack of gum

○ The number of candy bars left in the vending machine after recess

○ The number of bags of pretzels left in the vending machine after recess

○ All of the above

○ None of the above

MATH

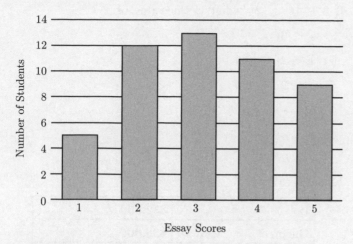

Essay Scores

Kathleen graded essays on a scale from 1 to 5 for her 50 students. The students' scores are shown in the bar chart above. What is the mean score for the essays?

○ 3.0

○ 3.04

○ 3.14

○ 3.24

○ 4.0

Population Distribution in Town C

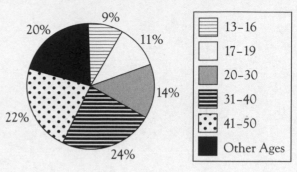

Suppose there are 7,840 people in Town C who are in the age group 20–30. How many people are in the age group 41–50 ?

○ 6,160

○ 11,200

○ 12,320

○ 13,440

○ 56,000

Suppose there are 125,000 people in Town C. Given this additional piece of information, which of the following statements CANNOT be solved from the chart above?

○ The percent of the total population of adults over 50

○ The number of people between the ages of 20 and 50, inclusive

○ How many more 31–40 year olds there are than 41–50 year olds

○ The percent of the total population that are teenagers

○ The number of 20–30 year olds

MATH

In the number 345.678, what is the sum of the digit in the hundreds place and the digit in the tenths place?

- ○ 7
- ○ 8
- ○ 9
- ○ 10
- ○ 11

x	y
0	–6
2	0
4	6
5	9

Which of the following formulas expresses the relationship between x and y in the table above?

- ○ $y = 3x - 6$
- ○ $y = x + 6$
- ○ $y = -6$
- ○ $y = 4x + 6$
- ○ $y = 2x - 1$

$$(10)(25) + (35)(10) + (27.5)(10)$$

Which of the following calculations will lead to the same result as the statement above?

- ○ $(10)(25 + 35 + 27.5)$
- ○ $(30)(25 + 35 + 27.5)$
- ○ $(35)(45)(37.5)$
- ○ $(10)(10)(10) + (25)(35)(27.5)$
- ○ $(1,000)(87.5)$

If $3 - 6x < 12y$, what is the value of x ?

- ○ $x < 3$
- ○ $x < 2y + 0.5$
- ○ $x > 2y + 0.5$
- ○ $x > -2y + 0.5$
- ○ $x > -2y - 0.5$

Bob	$32,000
Gurpreet	$36,000
Huang	$34,000
Roland	$33,000
Maria	$35,000
Alice	$32,000

The table above shows the salaries of the six employees at Company Y. Suppose two new employees are hired, whose salaries are $34,000 and $38,000. Which statement is true about the **new** mean of the eight employee salaries at Company Y ?

- ○ The mean would increase.
- ○ The mean would remain the same.
- ○ The mean would decrease.
- ○ The mean would double.
- ○ The mean would halve.

A student makes a building model that is 21 inches wide. In the model, $\frac{1}{3}$ inch represents an actual length of 3 feet. What is the width, in inches, of the building represented by the model?

[_____] inches

Click on the box and type in a number.
Backspace to erase.

MATH

If $3A \div 7 = B$, then $6A \div 14 =$

○ B

○ $2B$

○ $B \div 2$

○ $3B \div 7$

○ 2

Brett works 35 hours per week and used to earn $12.50 per hour. His employer gave him a raise that increases his weekly gross pay to $480.00. What is the increase in Brett's weekly gross pay?

○ $37.50

○ $42.50

○ $47.50

○ $48.00

○ $50.00

A triangle has a side that is 6 units long and a side that is 4 units long. Which of the following could be the length of the third side of the triangle?

Select **all** that apply.

☐ 12

☐ 10

☐ 8

☐ 6

☐ 4

Steve is throwing a standard six-sided die. If he throws a 4 on his first throw, what is the probability that his next throw will NOT be a 4 ?

○ $\frac{1}{6}$

○ $\frac{1}{3}$

○ $\frac{1}{2}$

○ $\frac{2}{3}$

○ $\frac{5}{6}$

In the month of April, Jasleen ran 6 miles. In the month of July, she ran 9 miles. If Jasleen's running progress continues in a linear trend, how many miles will she run in October?

○ 10

○ 11

○ 12

○ 13

○ 14

$$2m + 3n + 4 = 0$$

The relationship between m and n is expressed by the equation above. If n increases by 2, what happens to the value of m ?

○ m increases by 2.

○ m increases by 3.

○ m decreases by 2.

○ m decreases by 3.

○ m remains the same.

MATH

Triangle ABC is a right triangle at angle B. If $\overline{AB}$ is 6, and $\overline{BC}$ is 8, what is the length of $\overline{AC}$?

- ○ 7
- ○ 8.5
- ○ 10
- ○ 14
- ○ 28

Julie can grade 20 spelling tests per hour. If she starts grading tests at 9:00 A.M., which of the following is the best estimate as to when she will be finished grading 134 tests?

- ○ 12:30 P.M.
- ○ 1:30 P.M.
- ○ 2:00 P.M.
- ○ 3:30 P.M.
- ○ 5:00 P.M.

If 3 less than 8 times a number is 37, what is the number?

- ○ 34
- ○ 29
- ○ 21
- ○ 5
- ○ 4

How many times greater than $\frac{1}{4}$ is $\frac{1}{2}$?

- ○ $\frac{1}{2}$
- ○ 2
- ○ 4
- ○ 6
- ○ 8

On a recent test, Valerie answered 2 questions correctly for every 3 questions she missed. If the test had a total of 80 questions, how many questions did Valerie answer correctly on the test?

- ○ 5
- ○ 32
- ○ 48
- ○ 80
- ○ 160

Helen, Anna, and Emily want to go to the baseball game together. They agree to combine their money. Helen has $11.00; Anna has $15.00; and Emily has $16.00. Admission to the game is $21.00 per person. How much more money will they each need to obtain, on average, in order for everyone to be able to go to the game together?

- ○ $5.00
- ○ $6.00
- ○ $7.00
- ○ $14.00
- ○ $21.00

What is 20 percent of 30 ?

A student tries to answer the question above. Which of the following calculations would produce the correct result?

Select **all** that apply.

- ☐ 0.2×30
- ☐ $\dfrac{(20 \times 30)}{100}$
- ☐ $\dfrac{(20 \times 100)}{30}$
- ☐ $20 \div 0.3$

MATH

Connie owns a laundry service. She charges $3.50 for a small load of laundry, and $4.25 for a large load. One day, Octavio brings her 7 small loads and 4 large loads. Assuming no tax is charged, how much will Connie charge Octavio for this laundry order?

○ $35.00

○ $38.75

○ $41.50

○ $47.25

○ $54.25

x	y
5	17
2	11
8	23
6	19
12	31

Which of the following graphs best represents the relationship between x and y ?

○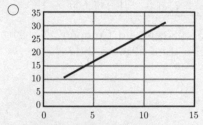

○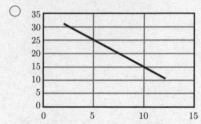

○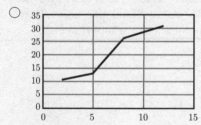

○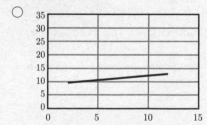

○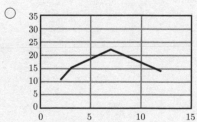

MATH

Sales for Company X		
Product	2016 Sales	2017 Sales
Product A	200,000	250,000
Product B	150,000	150,000
Product C	30,000	60,000
Product D	145,000	160,000
Product E	75,000	65,000

By approximately what percent did Company X increase in product sales from 2016 to 2017 ?

○ 14%

○ 25%

○ 33%

○ 45%

○ 85%

Howard wants to raise his weekly gross pay to $168 per week, and currently makes $8.00 per hour. How many additional hours must he work per week?

○ 4 hours

○ 5 hours

○ 6 hours

○ 7 hours

○ It cannot be determined from the information given.

> If Kyle finishes his homework,
> he will get ice cream for dessert.

Given the statement above, which of the following must be true?

○ Kyle did not get ice cream for dessert, so he did not do his homework.

○ Kyle did not finish his homework, so he did not get ice cream.

○ If Kyle ever gets ice cream, it is because he finished his homework.

○ Sometimes Kyle does not finish his homework.

○ Kyle can only have ice cream for dessert.

Ben's garden has a collection of roses, tulips, and carnations, in a ratio of 3:2:1. If Ben has a total of 72 flowers in his garden, how many roses are in his garden?

○ 6 roses

○ 12 roses

○ 24 roses

○ 36 roses

○ It cannot be determined from the information given.

If the value of y is between .00268 and .0339, which of the following could be y ?

○ 0.00175

○ 0.0134

○ 0.0389

○ 0.268

○ 2.6

MATH

$3x + 12 = 7x - 16$. What is x ?

○ 3

○ 7

○ 12

○ 16

○ 28

Laura is scheduled to perform 24 surgeries this week. If she performs 4 surgeries on Monday, how many surgeries must she perform each day, on average, to finish by Friday?

○ 2

○ 3

○ 4

○ 5

○ 6

It is 260 miles between Santa Escuela and Santa Novia. Mr. Lewis drives 40 miles per hour. Assuming he takes a direct route between the two cities, how many hours will it take Mr. Lewis to drive from Santa Escuela to Santa Novia?

○ 5 hours

○ 5.5 hours

○ 6 hours

○ 6.5 hours

○ 7 hours

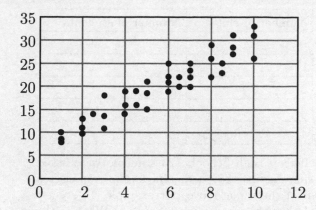

Which of the following statements best describes the trend between x and y ?

○ As x increases, y increases.

○ As x increases, y decreases.

○ As x increases, y remains constant.

○ Both x and y remain constant.

○ There is no trend between x and y.

Kathleen bought a new suit at 25 percent off the regular price of $400.00. She had an additional coupon, which saved her an additional 15 percent off the sale price. What price did she pay for the suit?

○ $85.00

○ $112.50

○ $240.00

○ $255.00

○ $285.00

MATH

Number of clubs	Number of students
0	19
1	28
2	36
3	24
4	16

At Jefferson High School, 123 students were asked how many clubs they had joined. The responses are shown in the table above (for example, 19 students stated that they had joined 0 clubs). What is the average number of clubs per student, to the nearest tenth?

[_____] clubs per student

Click on the box and type in a number.
Backspace to erase.

List of Television Shows		
Television Show	Start Time	End Time
Show A	9:30	
Show B	10:15	10:45
Show C	11:00	11:20
Show D	12:00	12:45
Show E		2:30

If Show A is 20 minutes longer than Show C, what time does Show A end?

○ 9:50

○ 10:10

○ 10:20

○ 10:30

○ 11:40

Stem	Leaf
2	2 3 3 4 7 8
3	2 2 3 4 5 6 7 7 9
4	1 2 4 5 6

In a book club, the ages of the members are listed in the stem-and-leaf plot above. What is the median age of the members?

○ 32.5

○ 33

○ 33.5

○ 34

○ 34.5

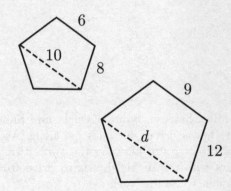

In the figure above, the two pentagons are similar. What is the length of diagonal d ?

$d =$ [_____]

Click on the box and type in a number.
Backspace to erase.

MATH

$$3x + 2 > 8 - 5x$$

Solve for x in the inequality above.

○ $x < -3$

○ $x > 3$

○ $x > \dfrac{3}{4}$

○ $x < \dfrac{4}{3}$

○ $x > \dfrac{1}{2}$

Arlene, Benjamin, and Cristiano have a total of 35 board games. If Benjamin has twice as many games as Arlene, and Cristiano has three more games than Arlene, how many games does Arlene have?

○ 8

○ 9

○ 10

○ 11

○ 12

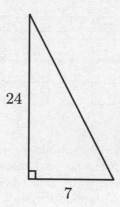

Silvia is constructing a fenced garden in the shape of a right triangle, as shown. What is the perimeter of the fence?

○ 31

○ 44

○ 47

○ 56

○ 58

If $4a + \left(\dfrac{2}{3}\right)b = 26$ and $b = 9$, what is the value of a ?

$$a = \boxed{}$$

Click on the box and type in a number.
Backspace to erase.

MATH

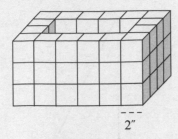

2"

A rectangular structure is built from play blocks, as shown. 48 blocks are used, and the structure is 6 blocks long, 4 blocks wide, and 3 blocks high. If each block is a cube with a side length 2 inches, what is the volume of the space **inside** the structure?

○   24 cubic inches

○   48 cubic inches

○   72 cubic inches

○   144 cubic inches

○   192 cubic inches

In a class of 22 students, the students had earned an average of $34 in the winter candy fundraiser. The principal decides to purchase a candy bar from each student, adding $3 to each of their sales. What is the new total amount of money raised, after the principal's contribution?

Total amount of money raised = $ ☐

Click on the box and type in a number.
Backspace to erase.

An opera theater sells two types of tickets: balcony tickets are $120 each, and mezzanine tickets are $70 each. If the theater sold a total of 910 tickets in one night, and made a total of $68,200, how many of the tickets sold were balcony tickets?

○   90

○   120

○   420

○   540

○   820

A costume designer needs to cut a circle of fabric, with a radius of 16 inches. The fabric supplier sells fabric in only rectangular shapes. What is the minimum area, in square inches, of fabric that the designer must purchase?

○   256

○   512

○   804

○   1,024

○   2,048

$$y = 3x - 4$$

The equation above is graphed as a line. Which of the following points lies **above** the line?

Select **all** that apply.

☐ (0, –6)

☐ (1, –1)

☐ (2, 4)

☐ (3, 2)

☐ (4, 11)

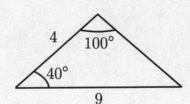

In the figure above, what is the perimeter of the triangle?

Perimeter = ☐

Click on the box and type in a number.
Backspace to erase.

MATH

In one summer, Keith read k books. Keith read twice as many books as Luanne, and then read five more. In terms of k, how many books did Luanne read?

○ $2k - 5$

○ $2k + 5$

○ $\dfrac{(k - 5)}{2}$

○ $\dfrac{(k + 5)}{2}$

○ $2k - 10$

If $6 < m < 10$ and $20 < n < 30$, then the value of $\dfrac{m}{n}$ must be between which of the following?

○ $\dfrac{1}{3}$ and $\dfrac{1}{2}$

○ $\dfrac{3}{10}$ and $\dfrac{1}{2}$

○ $\dfrac{1}{4}$ and $\dfrac{1}{3}$

○ $\dfrac{1}{5}$ and $\dfrac{1}{3}$

○ $\dfrac{1}{5}$ and $\dfrac{1}{2}$

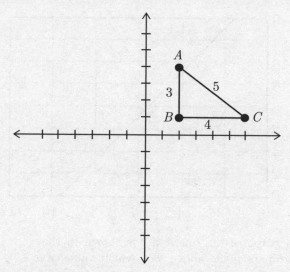

In the figure above, the triangle is plotted in the standard xy-plane, with point A at coordinate $(2, 4)$ and point B at coordinate $(2, 1)$. If the figure is translated 3 units up and 6 units to the right, what are the new coordinates of point C?

○ $(12, 4)$

○ $(12, 7)$

○ $(8, 4)$

○ $(8, 7)$

○ $(7, 4)$

MATH

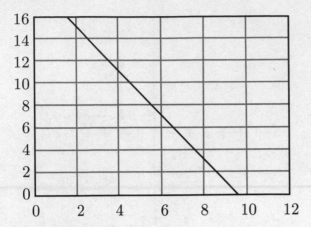

The graph of the function f is shown in the coordinate plane above. For which value of x is $f(x) = 7$?

- ○ 2
- ○ 3
- ○ 5
- ○ 6
- ○ 7

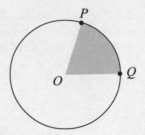

The circle with center O has a radius of 5. If the length of minor arc PQ is 2π, what is the measure of the central angle x ?

- ○ 36°
- ○ 72°
- ○ 108°
- ○ 144°
- ○ 216°

Chapter 15
Math Practice
Test 1: Answers and Explanations

MATH PRACTICE TEST 1 ANSWER KEY

1.	A	29.	E	
2.	3.18 feet	30.	A	
3.	D	31.	D	
4.	C	32.	B	
5.	C	33.	B	
6.	A	34.	D	
7.	C	35.	D	
8.	A	36.	A	
9.	A	37.	D	
10.	D	38.	1.9	
11.	A	39.	B	
12.	189	40.	E	
13.	A	41.	15	
14.	B	42.	C	
15.	8, 6, and 4	43.	A	
16.	E	44.	D	
17.	C	45.	5	
18.	D	46.	E	
19.	C	47.	$814	
20.	D	48.	B	
21.	D	49.	D	
22.	B	50.	C, E	
23.	B	51.	17	
24.	C	52.	C	
25.	A, B	53.	E	
26.	C	54.	A	
27.	A	55.	D	
28.	A	56.	B	

MATH PRACTICE TEST 1 EXPLANATIONS

1.　**A**　You might notice that each answer choice has the same three numbers in a different order: 3.092, 3.5, and 3.52. To compare them, it might help to line them up by decimal place:

3.092

3.5

3.52

Start by comparing the leftmost digits. In each case, the ones digit is 3, so the ones digits don't affect the order. Next, compare the tenths digits. The tenths digits are 0, 5, and 5. Since 0 is the smallest, so you know that 3.092 is the smallest number. Eliminate (C), (D), and (E). Next, compare the hundredths digits for (3.5) and (3.52). The hundredths digits are 0 and 2, so 3.52 is larger than 3.5. Select (A), which has the numbers in the correct order: 3.092, 3.5, and 3.52.

2.　**3.18 feet**

The volume of a cylinder is the product of the height and the area of the base. The base is a circle, whose area is $\pi \times r^2$. Therefore, the volume is $(\pi \times r^2 \times h)$.

We are solving for the *height* of the water in the tank, so h is the unknown. Plug in the known *volume* (250) and the known *radius* of the tank (5), and solve for h using the formula for volume.

$$\text{volume} = (\pi \times r^2 \times h)$$

$$250 = (\pi \times 5^2 \times h)$$

$$250 = (\pi \times 25 \times h)$$

$$\frac{250}{25} \text{ ft} = (\pi \times h)$$

$$10 = \pi \times h$$

$$\frac{10}{\pi} = h$$

$$3.18 \approx h$$

3.　**D**　In order to calculate the value of the items not sold during recess, you need to know the cost of each item, and the number of items sold. Choice (A) would tell you the cost of the items. Choices (B) and (C) would tell you how many candy bars and pretzels (respectively) were sold. With this information from (B) and (C), you could also derive the number of packs of gum sold, as well as find how many of each item was *not* sold. To find the value of all the items *not* sold, you need the information from (A), (B), and (C). Select (D).

4.   **C**   To find the mean, you must first find the sum of the scores for *all 50* students. You can use multiplication to make this easier.

$1 \times 5 = 5$
$2 \times 12 = 24$
$3 \times 13 = 39$
$4 \times 11 = 44$
$5 \times 9 = 45$

Sum: $5 + 24 + 39 + 44 + 45 = 157$

To calculate the mean, divide the sum by the number of students. (Note that the number of students is stated in the problem.)

$$\text{Mean: } \frac{157}{50} = 3.14$$

The mean score for the essays is 3.14.

Note: It is not correct to simply find the mean of {1, 2, 3, 4, 5}. This is because the scores aren't evenly distributed among the 50 students. In other words, each bar in the chart has a different height (quantity), so the mean and median are not equal.

5.   **C**   The chart indicates that 14% of people are in the age group 20–30. To solve this question, you can first find the total number of people in Town C. To find the unknown in a percent problem, you can use an equation like whole × percent = part. (Make sure to use the decimal or fraction value of the percent).

$$\text{whole} \times 0.14 = 7{,}840$$

$$\text{whole} = \frac{7{,}840}{0.14}$$

$$\text{whole} = 56{,}000$$

Next, find the number of people in the age group 41–50. The chart indicates that this is 22% of the population.

$$\text{whole} \times \text{percent} = \text{part}$$

$$56{,}000 \times 0.22 = \text{part}$$

$$12{,}320 = \text{part}$$

Another way to solve this question is with a proportion comparing the two age groups.

$$\frac{14}{7,840} = \frac{22}{x}$$

$$14x = 22 \times 7,840$$

$$x = \frac{(22 \times 7,840)}{14}$$

$$x = 12,320$$

6. **A** The category "other ages" includes any "missing" categories from the legend. The legend includes age groups from 13 to 50. Therefore, the "other ages" category includes children under 13, as well as adults over 50. You cannot determine how many adults over 50 are in Town C. Select (A), since this information cannot be determined. The other choices refer to calculating the *number* of people in each age group, which is possible if we know the total. This information is given in the question, so (B), (C), (D), and (E) can be eliminated.

7. **C** The hundreds place is 3, and the tenths place is 6. The sum of these two numbers is 9.

8. **A** To solve this question, you can plug in values from the table. Start with the pair $(0, -6)$. Plug in to each answer choice:

(A) $y = 3x - 6$
    $-6 = 3(0) - 6$
    $-6 = 0 - 6$
    $-6 = -6$ True. Keep $y = 3x - 6$, for now.

(B) $y = x + 6$
    $-6 = 0 + 6$
    $-6 = 6$ False. Eliminate $y = x + 6$.

(C) $y = -6$
    $-6 = -6$ True. However, you might notice that not all of the table values have $y = -6$. This allows you to eliminate $y = -6$.

(D) $y = 4x + 6$
    $-6 = 4(0) + 6$
    $-6 = 0 + 6$
    $-6 = 6$ False. Eliminate $y = 4x + 6$.

(E) $y = 2x - 1$
    $-6 = 2(0) - 1$
    $-6 = -1$?   False. Eliminate $y = 2x - 1$.

The correct answer is therefore (A).

9. **A** This question is testing the use of the Distributive Property, which states $ab + ac = a(b + c)$. Each term in the original expression contains a 10, so the 10 can be factored. $(10)(25) + (35)(10) + (27.5)(10) = (10)(25 + 35 + 27.5)$. This matches (A). Choices (B), (C), (D), and (E) violate more or one rules in combining terms. You can also solve this question by calculating the value of each expression, but that will take quite a bit more time. For this type of question, try to look for common factors, or use other number properties (such as the Associative Property).

10. **D** You can solve this question using algebra. You need to solve for x, so try to get x by itself.

$$3 - 6x < 12y$$

$-6x < 12y - 3$	Subtract 3 from both sides.
$-x < \dfrac{(12y - 3)}{6}$	Divide both sides by 6.
$x > \dfrac{(12y - 3)}{-6}$	Divide both sides by –1. Flip the inequality sign!
$x > -2y + \dfrac{1}{2}$	Use the Distributive Property to divide both terms by –6.

This matches (D).

11. **A** To solve the problem, you need to calculate and compare the old and new averages. The average of the old salaries is 33,666.66. To calculate, find the sum of all of the salaries and then divide by the number of employees (6).

Old sum: $32,000 + 36,000 + 34,000 + 33,000 + 35,000 + 32,000 = 202,000$
Old average: $202,000/6 = 33,666.66$

New sum: $202,000 + 34,000 + 38,000 = 274,000$
New average: $274,000/8 = 34,250$

Note that the new sum is divided by 8, since you are counting the two new employees. The new average is higher than the old average, so the mean increased. Choose (A).

12. **189**

To solve this question, use a proportion. $\dfrac{1}{3}$ of an inch represents 3 feet; you can use the ratio $\dfrac{1}{3}$ in.:3 ft. The other ratio is 21 in.:x ft, with x being the width of the "real" building.

$\dfrac{\left(\dfrac{1}{3}\right)}{3} = \dfrac{21}{x}$	
$\left(\dfrac{1}{3}\right) \times x = 3 \times 21$	Cross-multiply.
$x = 3 \times 21 \times 3$	Multiply both sides of the equation by 3.
$x = 189$	

13. **A** You don't have to isolate a variable to compare these expressions. Look closely, and notice that the second expression is equal to the first expression $\times \left(\dfrac{2}{2} \right)$.

$$\left(\dfrac{3A}{7} \right) \times \left(\dfrac{2}{2} \right) = \dfrac{6A}{14}$$

Note: It might be tempting to think that the expression was merely doubled. However, that would double only the numerator, not the denominator.

Since the value of the expression was multiplied by $\left(\dfrac{2}{2} \right)$, or (1), then the value of B does not change. Select (A).

14. **B** First, find Brett's weekly gross pay, from his former rate of $12.50 per hour.

$$35 \times \$12.50 = \$437.50$$

Brett's weekly pay before his raise is $437.50. The new weekly pay is $480.00, so subtract these values to find the difference:

$$\$480.00 - \$437.50 = \$42.50$$

15. **8, 6,** and **4**

To solve this question, use the Triangle Inequality Theorem: the length of the third side of a triangle must be greater than the difference, but less than the sum, of the other two side lengths. In other words, *(difference of two known sides) < (third side) < (sum of two known sides)*. The difference of the two known side lengths is 2, and their sum is 10. The third side must be greater than 2 and less than 10.

16. **E** Throws of a die are independent events: the second outcome is not affected by the first. You can ignore the fact that "he throws a 4 on his first throw." There are 5 desired outcomes that are "not a 4": 1, 2, 3, 5, and 6, out of a total of 6 possible outcomes. The probability is $\dfrac{5}{6}$.

17. **C** If you were to plot Jasleen's progress as coordinates, you would plot (April, 6 miles) or (4, 6), and then (July, 9 miles) or (7, 9). Notice that the distance increased by 1 mile per month. Since the question states that her progress will follow a linear trend, the miles should continue increasing 1 mile per month through October.

$$(7, 9) \ (8, 10) \ (9, 11) \ (10, 12)$$

The distance ran in October will be 12 miles.

18. **D** You can plug in a number to solve this question. Since you are told to increase the value of n, plug in a number for n, and solve for m. Next, you'll increase n by 2 to see how that changes the value of m.

$$n = 4$$
$$2m + 3(4) + 4 = 0$$
$$2m + 12 + 4 = 0$$
$$2m = -16 \qquad \text{Subtract } (12 + 4), \text{ or } 16, \text{ from both sides.}$$
$$m = -8$$

Now, increase n by 2, and solve for m once more.

$$n = 6$$
$$2m + 3(6) + 4 = 0$$
$$2m + 18 + 4 = 0$$
$$2m = -22 \qquad \text{Subtract } (18 + 4), \text{ or } 22, \text{ from both sides.}$$
$$m = -11$$

m changed from -8 to -11, so it decreased by 3. This matches (D).

You can also solve this problem by substitution. First, solve the equation for m:

$$2m + 3n + 4 = 0$$
$$2m = -3n - 4 \qquad \text{Subtract } (3n + 4) \text{ from both sides.}$$
$$m = \frac{-(3n - 4)}{2}$$

If we substitute $(n + 2)$ for n,

$$m_2 = \frac{(-3(n + 2) - 4)}{2}$$

$$m_2 = \frac{(-3n - 6 - 4)}{2}$$

$$m_2 = \frac{(-3n - 10)}{2}$$

Using the Distributive Property, compare the expressions $\dfrac{-(3n - 4)}{2}$ and $\dfrac{(-3n - 10)}{2}$. The first expression is equal to $\left(\dfrac{-3n}{2}\right) - 2$, and the second expression is equal to $\left(\dfrac{-3n}{2}\right) - 5$. The difference between them is 3, so the original value of m is decreased by 3.

19. **C** The triangle is a right triangle, so use the Pythagorean Theorem. The triple 6-8-10 is a common Pythagorean Triple, so you might quickly recognize that the third side is 10. You can use the Pythagorean Theorem to confirm:

$$6^2 + 8^2 = c^2$$
$$36 + 64 = c^2$$
$$100 = c^2$$
$$10 = c \qquad \text{Find the square root of both sides.}$$

The third side of the triangle is 10.

20. **D** Julie must grade 134 tests, and she can grade 20 tests per hour.

$$\frac{134}{20} = 6.7 \text{ hours}$$

6.7 is a little more than $6\frac{1}{2}$ hours. If she starts at 9:00 A.M., she will finish a little after 3:30. (9:00 + 3 hours = 12:00; 12:00 + $3\frac{1}{2}$ hours is 3:30). Since this is an "estimate" question, choose (D) .

21. **D** You can solve by making an equation.

3 less than 8 times a number is 37 *a number* is an unknown, so use a variable like *n*.

is means =, and *times* means ×

3 less than $8 \times n = 37$ *3 less than* means subtract 3.
$8 \times n - 3 = 37$ $3 - 8 \times n$ is incorrect!

Now solve for *n*:

$8 \times n - 3 = 37$
$8 \times n = 37 + 3 \qquad \text{Add 3 to both sides.}$
$8 \times n = 40$
$n = 40 \div 8 \qquad \text{Divide both sides by 8.}$
$n = 5$

How can you solve by Plugging In? See your Student Tools to learn more about this question!

22. **B** The question can be written as an equation:

$$\left(\frac{1}{4}\right) \times n = \left(\frac{1}{2}\right)$$
$$n = \left(\frac{1}{2}\right) \div \left(\frac{1}{4}\right)$$
$$n = \left(\frac{1}{2}\right) \times 4$$
$$n = \frac{4}{2}$$
$$n = 2$$

23. **B** To solve this question, use a proportion. But first, make sure that your proportion correctly uses corresponding parts. The ratio 2:3 is the ratio of *questions correct : questions missed*. We need the ratio of *questions correct : total questions*, so use the ratio 2:(2 + 3), or 2:5.

Now, you can solve a proportion:

$$\frac{2}{5} = \frac{x}{80}$$

$2 \times 80 = 5 \times x$ Cross-multiply.

$160 = 5 \times x$

$\frac{160}{5} = x$ Divide both sides by 5.

$32 = x$

Valerie answered 32 questions correctly.

24. **C** Together, the three have $42.00, and need a total of $63.00. Together, they need an additional $21.00, which works out to an average of $7.00 per person.

25. **A, B**

To solve 20 percent of 30, multiply $0.2 \times 30 = 6$. Compare the answer choices.

(A) $0.2 \times 30 = 6$

This choice produces the correct result, so select 0.2×30.

(B) $\frac{20 \times 30}{100} = \frac{600}{100} = 6$

This choice produces the correct result, so select $\frac{20 \times 30}{100}$.

(C) $\frac{20 \times 100}{30} = \frac{2,000}{30} = 66\frac{2}{3}$

This choice does not produce the correct result, so eliminate $\frac{20 \times 100}{30}$.

(D) $20 \div 0.3 = 66\frac{2}{3}$

This choice does not produce the correct result, so eliminate $20 \div 0.3$.

26. **C** The total cost can be found by multiplying 3.50×7, and 4.25×4. These totals are $24.50 and $17.00, respectively. Then add: $24.50 + $17.00 = $41.50.

27. **A** It might at first seem like the numbers have no apparent trend. However, if you notice that the x-values are not in order, then you should write the table in order to see the trend more clearly.

x	y
2	11
5	17
6	19
8	23
12	31

Now you can see that the y-values increase as the x-values increase. Eliminate (B) and (E), since these do not follow an increasing trend. Next, you can inspect the graphs and see which graph contains the coordinates from the table. The first coordinate is (2, 11), which seems like it might fit in each of the three remaining choices. The next coordinate is (5, 17), which seems to fit in graph (A), but not in graphs (C) or (D). This leaves only (A). You can also confirm that the other coordinates (6, 19), (8, 23), and (12, 31) lie in graph (A).

28. **A** To find percent increase, use the formula *percent change* $= \dfrac{difference}{original}$. Find the total in product sales for 2005 and 2006. The totals are 600,000 and 685,000, respectively. The difference is 85,000. The "original" number is 600,000, since we are finding the percent *increase*. The value of $\dfrac{85,000}{600,000}$ is approximately 0.14, or 14%. Select (A).

29. **E** You know that Howard makes $8.00 per hour, but you do not know the number of hours he currently works. Therefore, you cannot compare his current weekly gross pay (undetermined) with his desired weekly gross pay ($168). Select (E): it cannot be determined from the information given.

30. **A** This is a logic question that follows the "If A, then B" construction. The only true statement that always applies is "If not B, then not A." Choice (A) retains that structure and is therefore correct.

31. **D** You're asked to compare the number of roses to the total number of flowers, so set up a proportion:

$$\frac{3}{3+2+1} = \frac{x}{72}$$

$$\frac{3}{6} = \frac{x}{72}$$

$$3 \times 72 = 6 \times x$$

$$216 = 6 \times x$$

$$\frac{216}{6} = x$$

$$36 = x$$

There are 36 roses in the garden.

32. **B** The tenths place of the answer must be a zero, so you can eliminate (D) and (E). Choice (A) is too small, while (C) is larger than .0339.

33. **B** You can solve this question using algebra:

$3x + 12 = 7x - 16$

$12 = 4x - 16$	Subtract $3x$ from both sides.
$28 = 4x$	Add 16 to both sides.
$7 = x$	Divide both sides by 4.

34. **D** With 24 surgeries to complete, and 4 completed on Monday, there are 20 surgeries remaining with 4 days left. Divide 20 by 4 to get the average of 5 surgeries per day.

35. **D** Divide the total number of miles (260) by the miles driven per hour (40). This total is 6.5 hours.

36. **A** You can sketch an approximate best fit line, which would show the trend of y increasing along with x. Although the points don't all fall on a line, the positive correlation exists between x and y. Eliminate (B), since it indicates a negative correlation, and (C), since it indicates a horizontal trend. Choice (D) does not agree with the concept of a scatter plot containing many points. Choice (E) is incorrect because there is a positive correlation between x and y. (Choose "no trend" if the points are scattered all over the graph, and not grouped about a line of best fit.)

37. **D** First, find the price after the 25% discount:

$$\$400 \times 0.25 = \$100$$

This is the amount of the first discount. *Subtract* this discount from the original price.

$$\$400 - 100 = \$300$$

Next, the coupon gives an additional 15% off the sale price (NOT the original price).

$$\$300 \times 0.15 = \$45$$
$$\$300 - \$45 = \$255$$

38. **1.9** To find the average, we need to find the *total* number of clubs for all the students and then divide by the *total* number of students. You can use multiplication to make finding the sum easier:

$$0 \times 19 = 0$$
$$1 \times 28 = 28$$
$$2 \times 36 = 72$$
$$3 \times 24 = 72$$
$$4 \times 16 = 64$$

Sum of the products = 236

Total number of students: 123 (this is given in the problem).

$\frac{236}{123} = 1.9186\ldots$. Rounded to the nearest tenth, the average is 1.9.

39. **B** Show C runs for 20 minutes (11:00 to 11:20), so Show A runs for a total of 40 minutes (20 minutes longer than Show C). 9:30 plus 40 minutes is 10:10.

40. **E** A stem-and-leaf plot shows data grouped by initial digits. The data values for this plot are:

{22, 23, 23, 24, 27, 28, 32, 32, 33, 34, 35, 36, 37, 37, 39, 41, 42, 44, 45, 46}

There are 20 members, which is an even number, so the median will be the average of the middle two members. Find the middle two members, which are 34 and 35. (There are nine values on either side of 34 and 35.) The median is $\frac{(34 + 35)}{2}$, or 34.5.

41. **15** The two figures are similar, so you can use a proportion. You can use the corresponding sides 6:9 or 8:12, and make a proportion with 10:d.

$$\frac{6}{9} = \frac{10}{d}$$
$$6d = 90$$
$$d = \frac{90}{6}$$
$$d = 15$$

42. **C** You can solve the inequality algebraically:

$3x + 2 > 8 - 5x$
$8x + 2 > 8$ Add $5x$ to both sides.
$8x > 6$ Subtract 2 from both sides.
$x > \frac{6}{8}$ Divide both sides by 8.
$x > \frac{3}{4}$

You can also solve this problem by Plugging In. Check out your Student Tools for an alternate approach to this problem!

43. **A**   This problem can be solved algebraically. Be careful to avoid mistakes!

$B = 2A$
$C = A + 3$

$$A + B + C = 35$$
$$A + 2A + A + 3 = 35$$
$$4A + 3 = 35$$
$$4A = 32$$
$$A = 8$$

You can also solve by Plugging In. Check out your Student Tools for the alternate approach to this problem!

44. **D**   To find the perimeter, you'll need to find the length of the hypotenuse. Use the Pythagorean Theorem.

$$7^2 + 24^2 = c^2$$
$$49 + 576 = c^2$$
$$625 = c^2$$
$$25 = c$$

Add the three sides to find the perimeter: $7 + 24 + 25 = 56$.

45. **5**   The value of b is given, so substitute the value into the equation:

$$4a + \left(\frac{2}{3}\right) b = 26$$

$$4a + \left(\frac{2}{3}\right) 9 = 26$$

Simplify, and solve for a:

$$4a + 6 = 26$$
$$4a = 20$$
$$a = 5$$

46. **E**   The space *inside* the structure is bound by a length of 4 blocks, width of 2 blocks, and height of 3 blocks. Note that each block has a length of 2 inches. It may be a good idea to convert the blocks to inches first.

$$V = 4 \times 2 \times 3 \text{ blocks}$$
$$V = 4(2) \times 2(2) \times 3(2) \text{ in.}^3$$
$$V = 8 \times 4 \times 6 \text{ in.}^3$$
$$V = 192 \text{ in.}^3$$

You can also find the volume in blocks first and then convert to inches:

$$4 \times 2 \times 3 \text{ blocks} = 24 \text{ blocks}$$

Each block is 2 × 2 × 2 inches.

$$V = 24 \text{ blocks} \times (2 \times 2 \times 2 \text{ inches})$$
$$V = 24 \times 8 \text{ in.}^3 = 192 \text{ in.}^3$$

47. **$814**

Before the principal's contribution, the students had earned $34 × 22, or $748. After the principal's contribution, the average increased from 34 to 37, so they earned $37 × 22, or $814. You can also think about it by adding the principal's total contribution. The principal added $3 for each of the 22 students, so he added $66. The older total $748 plus the $66 from the principal equals $814. Note that the problem indicates an "average." Recall that an average is equal to the total sum, divided by the total number of members. So, we can find the total sum by multiplying the average by the number of members. In this case, the average earnings is multiplied by the number of students.

48. **B** This problem can be solved algebraically:

$b + m = 910$	Equation for the number of tickets.
$120b + 70m = 68,200$	Equation for the total revenue.

Solve by substitution:

$120b + 70(910 - b) = 68,200$	Substitute $(910 - b)$ for the value of m.
$120b + 63,700 - 70b = 68,200$	Simplify.
$120b - 70b = 4,500$	
$50b = 4,500$	
$b = 90$	Divide both sides by 50.

It's a good idea to check the value in the original equations.

$b + m = 910$	
$90 + m = 910$	Substitute 90 for b.
$m = 820$	
$120b + 70m = 68,200$	
$120(90) + 70(820) = 68,200$	Substitute 90 for b and 820 for m.
$10,800 + 57,400 = 68,200$	True. $b = 90$

You can also solve by Plugging In. Check out your Student Tools for the alternate approach to this problem!

49. **D** If the radius of the circle is 16 inches, then the diameter is 32 inches. The minimum *rectangular* size to fit the circle would be 32 inches by 32 inches.

Calculate: 32 × 32 = 1,024.

50.   **C, E**

If the line is $y = 3x - 4$, then the points *above* the line will satisfy the inequality $y > 3x - 4$. You can Plug In the Answers to find which coordinate(s) make the inequality true.

$$y > 3x - 4$$

(A) (0, −6)

$$-6 > 3(0) + 4$$
$$-6 > 0 + 4$$
$$-6 > 4 \qquad \text{False. Eliminate (0, −6).}$$

(B) (1, −1)

$$-1 > 3(1) - 4$$
$$-1 > 3 - 4$$
$$-1 > -1 \qquad \text{False. Eliminate (1, −1).}$$

(C) (2, 4)

$$4 > 3(2) - 4$$
$$4 > 6 - 4$$
$$4 > 2 \qquad \text{True. Select (2, 4).}$$

(D) (3, 2)

$$2 > 3(3) - 4$$
$$2 > 9 - 4$$
$$2 > 5 \qquad \text{False. Eliminate (3, 2).}$$

(E) (4, 11)

$$11 > 3(4) - 4$$
$$11 > 12 - 4$$
$$11 > 8 \qquad \text{True. Select (4, 11).}$$

51. **17** You can determine that the triangle is isosceles. Since two angles are known, find the measure of the third angle:

$$180° = 100° + 40° + x°$$
$$180° = 140° + x°$$
$$40 = x°$$

Since two angle measures are congruent (40°), the triangle is isosceles. This means that two sides are congruent, and the unknown side length must be 4.

Add the side lengths to find the perimeter:

$$9 + 4 + 4 = 17$$

52. **C** You can solve this question algebraically:

$k = 2l + 5$ *Keith read twice as many books as Luanne, and then read 5 more.*

$k - 5 = 2l$ Subtract 5 from both sides.

$\dfrac{(k-5)}{2} = l$ Divide both sides by 2.

The number of books Luanne read is $\dfrac{(k-5)}{2}$. You can also solve by Plugging In. Check out your Student Tools for another approach to this problem!

53. **E** When a question has expressions with variables in a range, it's a good idea to test all the combinations of the numbers shown in the problem. In this case, we'll test the expression $\dfrac{m}{n}$, for the values $m = 6$, $m = 10$, $n = 20$, and $n = 30$.

$m = 6$, $n = 20$ $\dfrac{6}{20} = \dfrac{3}{10}$

$m = 6$, $n = 30$ $\dfrac{6}{30} = \dfrac{1}{5}$

$m = 10$, $n = 20$ $\dfrac{10}{20} = \dfrac{1}{2}$

$m = 10$, $n = 30$ $\dfrac{10}{30} = \dfrac{1}{3}$

Put the results in numerical order:

$\dfrac{1}{5} = 0.2$ $\dfrac{3}{10} = 0.3$ $\dfrac{1}{3} = 0.333$ $\dfrac{1}{2} = 0.5$

You can also use common denominators to compare. In this case, the lowest common denominator is 60.

$\dfrac{1}{5} = \dfrac{12}{60}$ $\dfrac{3}{10} = \dfrac{18}{60}$ $\dfrac{1}{3} = \dfrac{20}{60}$ $\dfrac{1}{2} = \dfrac{30}{60}$

The smallest result was $\dfrac{1}{5}$, and the greatest result was $\dfrac{1}{2}$. That means the value of $\dfrac{m}{n}$ must be between $\dfrac{1}{5}$ and $\dfrac{1}{2}$. Select (E).

54. **A** The figure is a right triangle. This is determined by the Pythagorean Theorem, or by recognizing the triple 3-4-5. Since it is a right triangle, you can determine that point C is at coordinate $(6, 1)$ in the figure. (It is 4 units to the right of point B, which is at $(2, 1)$. If the figure moves 3 units up and 6 units to the right, the new coordinate for point C will be $(12, 4)$.

55. **D** To evaluate a function from its graph, inspect the graph at the given input or output value. In this case, you are given the output value $f(x) = 7$, which means $y = 7$ at the indicated point on the graph. Inspect the graph where $y = 7$. The x-value at this coordinate appears to be 6.

You can also check the other closest answer choices to confirm that they can be eliminated. At $x = 5$, the y-coordinate appears to be 9. This does not equal 7, so you can eliminate (C). At $x = 7$, the y-coordinate appears to be 5. This does not equal 7, so you can eliminate (E). Choose (D).

56. **B** To solve a question about arcs, use a proportion from the following relationships:

$$\frac{(arc\ length)}{(circumference\ of\ circle)} = \frac{(area\ of\ sector)}{(area\ of\ circle)} = \frac{(measure\ of\ central\ angle)}{360°}$$

We have the arc length, and the central angle. Use this proportion:

$$\frac{(arc\ length)}{(circumference\ of\ circle)} = \frac{(measure\ of\ central\ angle)}{360°}$$

$$\frac{2\pi}{circumference} = \frac{x}{360°}$$

We'll also need the circumference of the circle, which we can calculate from the given radius (5).

$$C = 2\pi r$$
$$C = 2\pi(5)$$
$$C = 10\pi$$

$\dfrac{2\pi}{10\pi} = \dfrac{x}{360°}$

$\dfrac{2}{10} = \dfrac{x}{360°}$ Cancel π from the fraction.

$360(2) = 10(x)$ Cross-multiply.

$720 = 10(x)$

$72 = x$ Divide both sides by 10.

The central angle is 72°.

Chapter 16
Math Practice
Test 2

MATH

Praxis Core Academic Skills for Educators

Mathematics

Time—85 minutes

56 Questions

Directions: For each question, select the best answer or answers from the choices given for selected-response questions, or provide an answer by typing in the answer box. Remember to read the directions for each question carefully, as you may be asked to respond in a variety of ways, including selecting one answer choice from a list, checking multiple checkboxes, or typing your answer into an answer box.

Percent of Colored Balloons at Party

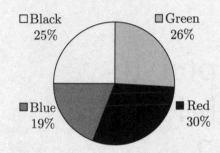

☐ Black   ☐ Green
  25%   26%

■ Blue   ■ Red
  19%   30%

The pie chart above shows the percent of different colored balloons at a party. If there are a total of 300 balloons at the party, how many more red balloons are there than blue balloons?

- ○ 33
- ○ 57
- ○ 75
- ○ 78
- ○ 90

Sarah earns $1,300 per month. If she pays $520 per month for her student loans, which of the following shows the percent of Sarah's earnings that is used to pay student loans?

- ○ $\dfrac{\$1,300}{(\$1,300 - \$520)}$

- ○ $\dfrac{\$520}{(\$1,300 - \$520)}$

- ○ $\dfrac{\$520}{(\$1,300 \times \$100)}$

- ○ $\dfrac{\$520}{(\$1,300 - \$520)} \times 100$

- ○ $\dfrac{\$520}{1,300} \times 100$

Nine students took a test, and received the following scores: 27, 83, 45, 81, 22, 34, 9, and 22. What is the average score on the test?

- ○ 22
- ○ 38
- ○ 38.25
- ○ 45
- ○ 342

MATH

> The drawing contained only rectangles, but no squares.

If the above statement is true, which of the following statements must also be true?

○ Some of the rectangles contained four sides of equal length.

○ Triangles were present in the drawing.

○ There were no right angles in the drawing.

○ None of the rectangles have four sides of equal length.

○ Some of the rectangles were of different sizes.

Currently, Lisa has 3 dogs and 5 turtles. What fraction represents the number of dogs she has?

○ $\frac{3}{2}$

○ $\frac{2}{5}$

○ $\frac{3}{5}$

○ $\frac{3}{8}$

○ $\frac{5}{8}$

Adam arrived at school at 9:45 A.M. and left school 11 hours and 15 minutes later. What time did Adam leave school?

○ 6:15 P.M.

○ 7:45 P.M.

○ 8:00 P.M.

○ 8:30 P.M.

○ 9:00 P.M.

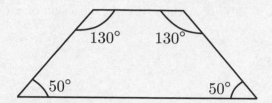

The figure above is which of the following?

Select **all** that apply.

☐ parallelogram

☐ rhombus

☐ quadrilateral

☐ square

☐ rectangle

☐ trapezoid

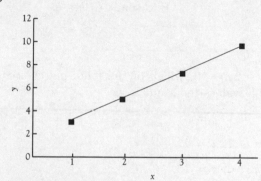

Which of the following is true about the graph above?

○ As x increases, y increases.

○ As x increases, y decreases.

○ As x decreases, y increases.

○ As x increases, y remains the same.

○ As x decreases, y remains the same.

MATH

If 300 is 60% of z, then what is the value of z ?

- ○ 30
- ○ 125
- ○ 200
- ○ 260
- ○ 500

Terry rolls two standard six-sided number cubes. What is the probability that the two numbers rolled will have a sum of 8 ?

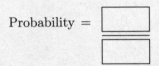

Probability =

Click on the box and type in a number.
Backspace to erase.

If $8x + 2z = 10$, which of the following choices are possible values for x and z ?

- ○ $x = 1, z = 5$
- ○ $x = 1, z = 1$
- ○ $x = 0, z = 10$
- ○ $x = 3, z = 7$
- ○ $x = 4, z = -10$

The price of strawberries is one crate for $4, or three crates for $10. What is the minimum cost to buy exactly 20 crates?

- ○ $68
- ○ $70
- ○ $74
- ○ $80
- ○ $84

If $4x + 6 = 2(y - 3)$, then $y =$

- ○ $2x$
- ○ $2x - 6$
- ○ $3x + 12$
- ○ $x + 12$
- ○ $2x + 6$

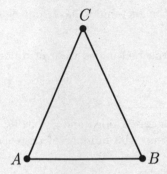

In the figure above, triangle ABC is to be plotted in the standard coordinate plane, with point A at (3, 0) and point B at (7, 0). If the triangle is isosceles with base $\overline{AB}$, and the height of the triangle is 6, what is the coordinate of point C ?

- ○ (5, 6)
- ○ (6, 5)
- ○ (7, 6)
- ○ (3, 6)
- ○ (4, 5)

If $x + 4$ is a multiple of 5, which of the following could be the value of x ?

- ○ 45
- ○ 46
- ○ 55
- ○ 63
- ○ 67

MATH

Brian has ridden 31 miles of his daily 50-mile bike ride. How many more miles has he left to ride?

- ○ Less than half the ride remaining
- ○ More than half the ride
- ○ Less than one quarter of the ride
- ○ Just over 20 miles of the ride
- ○ Just under 15 miles of the ride

For every two apple pies that Kathleen bakes, she gets paid $26. How much money will she earn if she works for 6 hours?

- ○ $13
- ○ $32
- ○ $52
- ○ $78
- ○ It cannot be determined from the information given.

Multiplying a number by $\frac{3}{4}$ is the same as dividing that number by

- ○ $\frac{9}{16}$
- ○ $\frac{3}{4}$
- ○ 1
- ○ $\frac{4}{3}$
- ○ 4

At a school supplies store, the price of a blackboard is reduced from $70.00 to $56.00. By what percent is the price of the blackboard decreased?

- ○ 10%
- ○ 14%
- ○ 20%
- ○ 56%
- ○ 86%

At his office, Adam did a survey on what his employees wanted for lunch—sandwiches or pizza. Adam received 34 more votes for pizza than sandwiches. If Adam received a total of 76 votes, how many votes did he receive for sandwiches?

- ○ 21
- ○ 40
- ○ 42
- ○ 84
- ○ 110

What is the altitude of an equilateral triangle whose sides each have a length of 4 ?

- ○ $2\sqrt{2}$
- ○ $2\sqrt{3}$
- ○ $4\sqrt{2}$
- ○ $4\sqrt{3}$
- ○ $4\sqrt{5}$

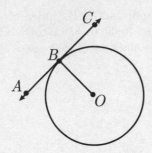

In the figure above, the line $\overline{AC}$ is tangent to the circle at point B, and OB is a radius of the circle. What is the measure of angle $\angle OBC$?

 degrees

Click on the box and type in a number.
Backspace to erase.

While planning an office barbecue, an assistant determines that she must purchase at least 163 hot dogs. The bulk food store sells hot dogs only in packages of 12. What is the minimum number of packages the assistant must purchase?

Click on the box and type in a number.
Backspace to erase.

If two sides of a rectangle are 11 and 6, what is the perimeter of the rectangle?

- ○ 10
- ○ 17
- ○ 22
- ○ 23
- ○ 34

A rectangular water tank has side lengths of 10 cm and 18 cm and a height of 16 cm. What is the capacity of the tank, in liters?

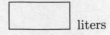 liters

Click on the box and type in a number.
Backspace to erase.

$14p - 16 + 3(p - 4) + p = 16$. What is the value of p ?

- ○ $\dfrac{2}{3}$
- ○ $1\dfrac{1}{9}$
- ○ $1\dfrac{1}{5}$
- ○ $2\dfrac{4}{9}$
- ○ $4\dfrac{2}{5}$

Seventy-one percent is between

- ○ $\dfrac{1}{2}$ and $\dfrac{3}{5}$
- ○ $\dfrac{3}{5}$ and $\dfrac{3}{4}$
- ○ $\dfrac{3}{5}$ and $\dfrac{7}{10}$
- ○ $\dfrac{3}{4}$ and $\dfrac{7}{8}$
- ○ $\dfrac{1}{7}$ and $\dfrac{7}{10}$

MATH

David walked 485 yards from class to the cafeteria. How many feet did David walk?

- ○ 40 feet
- ○ 161 feet
- ○ 1,455 feet
- ○ 2,100 feet
- ○ 5,820 feet

At a high school, 2 out of every 5 students plan to go to Butterick College. If there are 240 students, how many are expected to go to Butterick College?

- ○ 24 students
- ○ 96 students
- ○ 120 students
- ○ 144 students
- ○ 180 students

> If Jed scores a goal,
> then his team will win.

If the sentence above is true, which of the following statements must also be true?

- ○ Jed's team can win only if he scores a goal.
- ○ If Jed does not score, his team will lose.
- ○ Jed is the best player on the team.
- ○ Only Jed can score on his team.
- ○ If Jed's team lost, he did not score a goal.

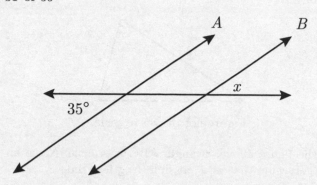

In the figure above, if lines A and B are parallel, what is the measure of angle x ?

- ○ 35°
- ○ 45°
- ○ 70°
- ○ 145°
- ○ It cannot be determined from the information given.

The surface area of a sphere is given by the formula *surface area* $= 4\pi r^2$, where r is the radius. What is the radius of a sphere whose surface area is 25π ?

- ○ 25
- ○ 6.25
- ○ 5
- ○ 2.5
- ○ 1.25

MATH

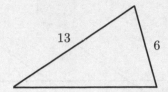

Figure not drawn to scale.

In the figure above, triangle ABC is scalene. Name an integer value that is a possible length of side x.

Click on the box and type in a number.
Backspace to erase.

Shareholders in Company W	
Shareholder	Shares of Stock Owned
Lyn	150
Jolene	10
Adam	80
Brian	60

What is the average number of shares owned by each shareholder?

○ 60

○ 65

○ 70

○ 75

○ 80

Number of pets	Number of students
0	24
1	32
2	21
3	19
4	14
5 or more	8

For the above chart, a group of students reported the number of pets that they had at home. They were then asked to estimate the probability that a student has 4 or more pets. Which of the following is the closest estimate?

○ $\frac{1}{7}$

○ $\frac{3}{8}$

○ $\frac{1}{6}$

○ $\frac{1}{8}$

○ $\frac{2}{7}$

Select **all** numbers that have a value less than –12.

☐ –22

☐ –14

☐ –9

☐ 0

☐ 10

☐ 14

MATH

If x is 4 more than 5 times y, which of the following expresses the value of y in terms of x ?

○ $\dfrac{x}{5} + 4$

○ $\dfrac{4x}{5}$

○ $\dfrac{x}{5} - 4$

○ $\dfrac{x - 4}{5}$

○ $\dfrac{x + 4}{5}$

If the area of a triangle is 24, and the height of the triangle is 6, then the base of the triangle is

○ 3

○ 4

○ 6

○ 8

○ 12

If $p = 5$, what is the value of $-20 \div p + 3(p + 7)$?

○ 11

○ 18

○ 26

○ 32

○ 40

A student correctly answered 80% of 90 science questions. How many science questions did she answer incorrectly?

○ 8

○ 9

○ 18

○ 71

○ 72

$$24 \div 8 \times 3 = \underline{\quad}$$

A student attempted the above equation, and answered **1**. What mistake did the student most likely make?

○ The student performed the multiplication first, and the division second.

○ The student did not correctly apply the Distributive Property.

○ The student performed subtraction instead of division.

○ The student performed addition instead of multiplication.

○ The student did not reduce his or her answer.

What is the slope of the line with the equation

$$\dfrac{y}{2} - 5 = 6x \ ?$$

○ $\dfrac{1}{12}$

○ $\dfrac{1}{3}$

○ 3

○ 6

○ 12

MATH

$$x + 2 = \sqrt{(x + 4)}$$
$$(x + 2)^2 = x + 4$$
$$x^2 + 4x + 4 = x + 4$$
$$x^2 + 4x = x$$
$$x^2 + 3x = 0$$
$$x(x + 3) = 0$$
$$x = 0, \ x = -3$$

A student performs the steps above, and arrives at the two solutions shown: $(x = 0, \ x = -3)$. Regarding extraneous solutions in this equation, which of the following statements is true?

○ 0 is an extraneous solution.

○ −3 is an extraneous solution.

○ Both 0 and −3 are extraneous solutions.

○ 0, −3, and 5 are all extraneous solutions.

○ Neither 0 nor −3 is an extraneous solution.

$$y = 3x - 4$$
$$y = -2x + 5$$

Which of the following graphs represents the system of equations shown above?

○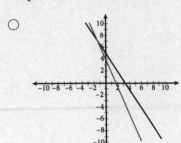

○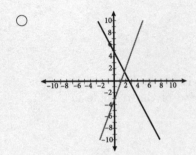

○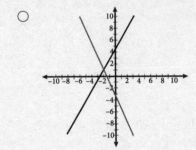

○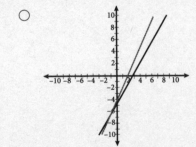

○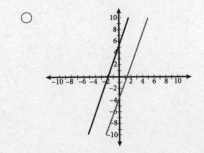

MATH

$$2(x + 1) < 3x + 4 \leq x - 5$$

Which of the following graphs represents the inequality shown above?

○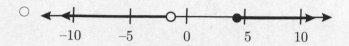

○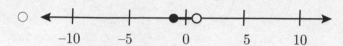

○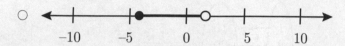

○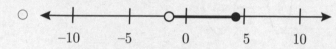

○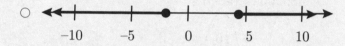

A student writes a table of values for the function $f(x) = 3(x + 4)^2$. Which table shows the correct output values for the x-values $\{0, 1, 2, 3, 4\}$?

○

0	48
1	27
2	12
3	3
4	0

○

0	48
1	75
2	108
3	147
4	192

○

0	0
1	12
2	48
3	108
4	192

○

0	48
1	12
2	0
3	12
4	48

○

0	144
1	225
2	324
3	441
4	576

MATH

A linear function contains the values $f(2) = -13$ and $f(5) = -25$. What is the value of $f(-3)$?

$$f(-3) = \boxed{}$$

Click on the box and type in a number.
Backspace to erase.

Which of the following coordinate(s) is a solution to the inequality $y < 3x - 8$?

Select **all** that apply.

- ☐ $(-4, -20)$
- ☐ $(-2, -12)$
- ☐ $(0, -10)$
- ☐ $(2, -2)$
- ☐ $(4, 2)$

Which of the following diagrams does NOT represent a function?

○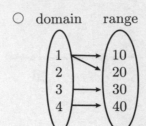

○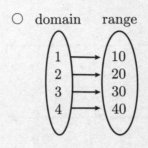

○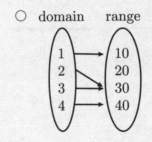

○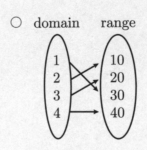

○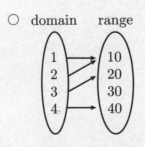

MATH

Snickers is three years older than Princess's. If Princess's age is twice Roxie's age, which of the following represents Roxie's age in terms of Snickers's age?

(Let p, r, and s represent the ages of Princess, Roxie, and Snickers, respectively.)

○ $2s + 3$

○ $s - 3$

○ $\dfrac{(s - 3)}{2}$

○ $s + \dfrac{3}{2}$

○ $2(s - 3)$

A freelance writer has different rates for different types of jobs. She spends 16 hours writing sports articles for $15 per hour, 27 hours writing social media posts for $12 per hour, and 32 hours editing technical documents for $18 per hour. What is the mean hourly rate that the writer earned for all of these jobs?

○ $15.00

○ $15.20

○ $15.50

○ $16.00

○ $16.80

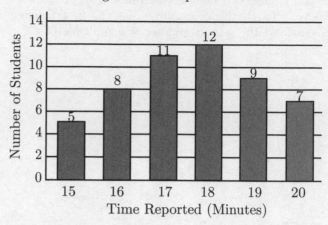

Jog-A-Thon Reported Times

At a school Jog-A-Thon, 52 students participated and jogged 1 mile. Each student recorded the time it took to complete 1 mile (rounded to the nearest minute). The results are shown in the chart above (for example, 5 students reported that it took 15 minutes). What was the median time to run 1 mile?

○ 17.0

○ 17.2

○ 17.5

○ 17.6

○ 18.0

Maribel uses a computer program to randomly generate a two-digit number from 00 to 99. If she runs the program twice, and the first outcome does not affect the second outcome, what is the probability that both numbers generated are less than 50 ?

○ 0.24

○ 0.25

○ 0.37

○ 0.5

○ 0.75

MATH

$$\{1, 2, 3, 4, 5, 6, 7, 8, 9, 10, 11, 12\}$$

If you choose two numbers at random from the set above, what is the probability that the first number is odd and the second number is a multiple of 4 ?

○ $\frac{1}{8}$

○ $\frac{1}{6}$

○ $\frac{3}{8}$

○ $\frac{1}{2}$

○ $\frac{3}{4}$

If a basketball team has 12 players, how many different ways can 5 players be chosen to play a drill?

☐ ways

Click on the box and type in a number.
Backspace to erase.

In a small survey in Town X, $\frac{2}{7}$ of people reported that they would vote "yes" on a new tax bill. If the survey is representative of the population, and there are 10,675 voters in Town X, how many people would be expected to NOT vote "yes" on the tax bill?

○ 3,050

○ 4,270

○ 4,575

○ 7,625

○ 14,945

Chapter 17
Math Practice
Test 2: Answers and
Explanations

MATH PRACTICE TEST 2 ANSWER KEY

1.	A	29.	B
2.	E	30.	E
3.	B	31.	A
4.	D	32.	D
5.	D	33.	Any of the values in set {8, 9, 10, 11, 12, 14, 15, 16, 17, 18}
6.	E		
7.	trapezoid, quadrilateral	34.	D
8.	A	35.	C
9.	E	36.	−22, −14
		37.	D
10.	$\dfrac{5}{36}$	38.	D
		39.	D
11.	B	40.	C
12.	A	41.	A
13.	E	42.	E
14.	A	43.	B
15.	B	44.	B
16.	A	45.	D
17.	E	46.	B
18.	D	47.	7
19.	C	48.	C, E
20.	A	49.	A
21.	B	50.	C
22.	90	51.	B
23.	14	52.	E
24.	E	53.	B
25.	2.88	54.	A
26.	D	55.	792
27.	B	56.	D
28.	C		

MATH PRACTICE TEST 2 EXPLANATIONS

1. **A** To solve this problem, first find the number of red balloons and the number of blue balloons.

    $$\text{Red balloons: } 30\% \times 300 = 90$$

    $$\text{Blue balloons: } 19\% \times 300 = 57$$

    Find the difference: $90 - 57 = 33$. There are 33 more red balloons than blue balloons.

2. **E** To find a percent, divide the *part* by the *whole*. This produces a fractional or decimal value. To convert it to a percent, multiply by 100. This matches the steps shown in (E). If you were to calculate this percent, you would divide $\frac{520}{1,300} = 0.4$. Then multiply by 100 to find the percent: 40%.

3. **B** To find the average, find the total sum of the scores, and divide by the number of scores.

    $$\text{Sum: } 27 + 83 + 45 + 81 + 22 + 34 + 9 + 22 = 342.$$

    $$\text{Average: } \frac{342}{9} = 38$$

    If you chose (A), be careful; the question asks for the average, not the mode.

4. **D** A rectangle has four sides and four right angles. A square is a rectangle whose side lengths are all equal. The statement tells us that the drawing contained *no squares*. Therefore, it's true that *none of the rectangles have four sides of equal length*. Eliminate (A), because it can't be true that *some of the rectangles contained four sides of equal length*. Those would be squares. Eliminate (B), because the statement indicates that the drawing contained "only rectangles." Therefore, it had no triangles. Eliminate (C) because you know that the drawing contained rectangles (therefore, it contained right angles). Eliminate (E). The rectangles *could* have been different sizes, but it's not true that they *must be* different sizes. Be careful on "must be" questions!

5. **D** Fraction means $\frac{part}{whole}$. When the question asks "what fraction of her animals," that means the "whole" is the *total* number of animals. The total number of her animals is $3 + 5$, or 8. She has 3 dogs, so the $\frac{part}{whole}$ is $\frac{3}{8}$.

6. **E** The time starts at 9:45 A.M. and ends 11 hours 15 minutes later. 11 hours after 9:45 A.M. is 8:45 P.M. Add 15 minutes to that, and you get 9:00 P.M. Alternatively, 11 hours 15 minutes is the same as 12 hours *minus* 45 minutes. You can add 12 hours to 9:45 A.M., and get 9:45 P.M. Then, *subtract* 45 minutes for 9:00 P.M.

7. **trapezoid, quadrilateral**

    The figure is a *trapezoid*, which has exactly one pair of parallel sides, as well as a *quadrilateral*, which has four straight sides. The figure is NOT a *parallelogram*, which has two pairs of parallel sides; a *rhombus,* which has four congruent sides; a *square*, which has four congruent sides and four right angles; or a *rectangle*, which has four right angles.

8. **A** Since the line has positive slope (that is, it slants upward to the right), this means that *as x increases, y increases*. You can inspect the points on the graph to see this trend: as the *x*-values increase from 1, to 2, to 3, and to 4, the *y*-values increase from 3, to 5, to 7, to 10, respectively.

9. **E** The phrase "300 is 60% of *z*" can be written as a number sentence:

    $$300 = 60\% \times z$$

    Solve for *z*:

    $300 = 0.6 \times z$
    $300 \div 0.6 = z$ Divide both sides by 0.6
    $300 \div 0.6 = 500$

    For similar percent problems, it might help to think of a number sentence that makes sense to you: for example, "4 is 50% of 8" means $4 = 50\% \times 8$. Then, translate the word problem based on your example.

10. $\dfrac{5}{36}$

    Probability means *number of desired outcomes/number of total possible outcomes*. When rolling two number cubes, the combinations that have a sum of 8 are as follows: (2,6), (3,5), (4,4), (5,3), and (6,2). This is 5 combinations. There are 36 total possible combinations ($6 \times 6 = 36$). The probability to roll a sum of 8 is $\dfrac{5}{36}$.

11. **B** You can Plug In the Answers to solve this question.

    $8x + 2z = 10$
    $8(1) + 2(5) = 10$ Substitute the values $x = 1$, $z = 5$ from (A).
    $8 + 10 = 10$
    $18 = 10$ False. Eliminate (A).

    $8x + 2z = 10$
    $8(1) + 2(1) = 10$ Substitute the values $x = 1$, $z = 1$ from (B).
    $8 + 2 = 10$
    $10 = 10$ True. Select (B).

12.   **A**   To find the *minimum cost* for 20 crates, see if you can buy them all at the lowest rate. The lower rate is 3 crates for $10, which is about $3.33 per crate. 20 is not evenly divisible by 3, so the most we can buy for the lower rate (3 crates at a time) is 18 crates. The exact price for the 18 crates is $\left(\dfrac{\$10}{3}\right) \times 18$, which is $60. There are 20 crates total, so you need to purchase 2 more. These 2 crates will have the slightly higher rate of $4 each (since they weren't a group of 3). The 2 crates will cost $4 × 2 = $8. The total cost is $60 + $8 = $68.

13.   **E**   You can solve this question algebraically. Make sure to solve for *y*, not *x*.

$$4x + 6 = 2(y - 3)$$
$4x + 6 = 2y - 6$ Use the Distributive Property.
$4x + 12 = 2y$ Add 6 to both sides.
$2x + 6 = y$ Divide both sides by 2.

Therefore, the answer is (E), $2x + 6$. You can also solve this problem by Plugging In; check out your Student Tools for this alternate solution!

14.   **A**   It might help to sketch and label the known coordinates before you begin. The base of the triangle lies on the *x*-axis (since the *y*-coordinates for *A* and *B* are both 0). If the height of the triangle is 6, the *y*-coordinate of point *C* must be 6. Eliminate (B) and (E). Since the triangle is isosceles, it is symmetrical. This means that if you folded it down the middle through point *C*, you would find the midpoint of *AB*. Point *C* has the same *x*-coordinate as the midpoint of *AB*, which is $\dfrac{(3 + 7)}{2} = 5$. The coordinates for point *C* are (5, 6).

15.   **B**   The answer choices are for the value of *x*, but you have an expression regarding *x* + 4. A good way to organize this problem would be to write the value of *x* + 4 next to each answer choice.

x	*x* + 4
(A) 45	49
(B) 46	50
(C) 55	59
(D) 63	67
(E) 67	71

The question asks, *if x + 4 is a multiple of 5*. Look at the values of *x* + 4 to see if you find a multiple of 5. Choice (B), 50, is a multiple of 5, so it is the correct answer.

To check:

$x = 46$

$x + 4 = 46 + 4$

$46 + 4 = 50$

50 is a multiple of 5.

16. **A** This is a type of estimation question. You are asked how many miles Brian has left to ride. You can calculate $50 - 31 = 19$. However, the answer choices aren't numbers. Read the answers, and eliminate those that are false. Is 19 *less than half the ride*? Half the ride is $\frac{50}{2}$, or 25, so this answer is true. Choice (A) looks like the correct answer. Eliminate (B), which says the opposite: *more than half the ride*. Is 19 *less than one quarter of the ride*? One quarter of the ride would be $\frac{50}{4}$, or 12.5 miles, so this answer is false. Eliminate (C). Since 19 is not *just over 20 miles*, nor *just under 15 miles*, eliminate (D) and (E).

17. **E** The question does not tell us how many pies Kathleen bakes *per hour*, so you cannot determine how many pies she will bake in 6 hours. Note that (D) is a trap answer: if you assumed that she made 6 pies in 6 hours, you would have calculated $\$26 \times 3 = \$78$.

18. **D** $\frac{4}{3}$ is the reciprocal of $\frac{3}{4}$. Multiplying by a number is the same as dividing by the reciprocal of that number.

19. **C** Percent change is $\frac{difference}{original}$. To solve this question, first find the difference between the two numbers: $\$70 - \$56 = \$14$. The original number is 70, as that was the price before the change.

$$\frac{difference}{original} = \frac{14}{70} = 0.2$$

0.2 is the same as 20%.

20. **A** This question can be solved algebraically. Write a system of equations to represent the problem. Let's use p for pizza and s for sandwiches.

$p = s + 34$ Adam received 34 more votes for pizza than sandwiches.
$p + s = 76$ Adam received a total of 76 votes.

Substitute $s + 34$ for p in the second equation.

$p + s = 76$
$s + 34 + s = 76$
$2s + 34 = 76$
$2s = 42$ Subtract 34 from both sides.
$s = 21$ There were 21 votes for sandwiches.

To be thorough, you can substitute $s = 21$ in the first equation to find p.

$p = 21 + 34$
$p = 55$

Check the values in the second equation.

$55 + 21 = 76$ True. $s = 21$, and $p = 55$.

You could have also used Plugging In on this question. Check out your Student Tools to find out how!

21.   **B**   It's a good idea to sketch the figure on your scratch paper. To solve the question, you can divide the triangle into two congruent right triangles with a base of 2. Then, use Pythagorean Theorem to calculate the height.

$$2^2 + b^2 = 4^2$$
$$4 + b^2 = 16$$
$$b^2 = 12$$
$$b = \sqrt{12}$$
$$b = 2\sqrt{3}$$

22.   **90**   The question states that the line AC is tangent to the circle. Therefore, from the definition of *tangent* you know that the line AC is perpendicular to the radius BO. Angle OBC must be 90°.

23.   **14**   If you divide 163 by 12, the result is approximately 13.58. You cannot purchase fractional packages of hot dogs, so you must purchase the next greatest whole number amount: 14 packages. Note that 13 packages is not enough. $13 \times 12 = 156$, and the question states that there must be *at least 163 hot dogs*.

24.   **E**   To find the perimeter, add the lengths of all the sides. The two sides given are 11 and 6. Since the shape is a rectangle, you know that the other two sides are also 11 and 6. The perimeter is $11 + 6 + 11 + 6 = 34$.

25.   **2.88**   The tank's side lengths are given in centimeters. Calculate the volume in cubic centimeters: $10 \times 18 \times 16 = 2,880$. Note that the question asks for the tank's capacity *in liters*. There are 1,000 cubic centimeters in 1 liter, so divide the cubic centimeter capacity by 1,000. The capacity of the tank is $2,880 \div 1,000 = 2.88$.

26.   **D**   You can solve this question algebraically:

$14p - 16 + 3(p - 4) + p = 16$
$14p - 16 + 3p - 12 + p = 16$ Use the Distributive Property.
$\quad\quad 18p - 16 - 12 = 16$ Combine the p terms.
$\quad\quad\quad\quad 18p - 28 = 16$ Combine the integer terms.
$\quad\quad\quad\quad\quad\quad 18p = 44$ Add 28 to both sides.

$$p = \frac{44}{18}$$ Divide both sides by 18.

$$p = \frac{22}{9}$$ Reduce.

$$p = 2\frac{4}{9}$$ Convert to a mixed number.

You can also Plug In the Answers to solve this problem. Check out your Student Tools to see how to apply this strategy.

27. **B** 71% written as a decimal is 0.71. To solve this question, you can convert the fractions to decimals (you can do this by dividing on the calculator) to see which answer would fit the value 0.71.

(A) $\frac{1}{2}$ = 0.5 $\frac{3}{5}$ = 0.6

0.71 is larger than both values, so it isn't in this range.

(B) $\frac{3}{5}$ = 0.6 $\frac{3}{4}$ = 0.75

0.71 is larger than 0.6 and smaller than 0.75. This is the correct answer.

(C) $\frac{3}{5}$ = 0.6 $\frac{7}{10}$ = 0.7

0.71 is larger than both values, so it isn't in this range.

(D) $\frac{3}{4}$ = 0.75 $\frac{7}{8}$ = 0.875

0.71 is smaller than both values, so it isn't in this range.

(E) $\frac{1}{7}$ = 0.14 $\frac{7}{10}$ = 0.7

0.71 is larger than both values, so it isn't in this range.

28. **C** This question tests your knowledge of U.S. customary units. To answer correctly, you'll need to remember that 1 yard = 3 feet. You can multiply $3 \times 485 = 1{,}455$. If you weren't sure whether to multiply or divide, use a proportion: $\frac{feet}{yards} = \frac{3}{1} = \frac{x}{485}$.

$$\frac{3}{1} = \frac{x}{485}$$

$3 \times 845 = 1 \times x$ Cross-multiply.

$1{,}455 = x$

29. **B**   To solve this question, you can use a proportion:

$$\frac{2}{5} = \frac{x}{240}$$

$$2 \times 240 = 5 \times x$$

$$480 = 5 \times x$$

$$\frac{480}{5} = x$$

$$96 = x$$

30. **E**   For an if-then logic statement, use the *contrapositive* to form an equivalent statement. For a statement *if A, then B*, the contrapositive is *if not B, then not A*.

If Jed scores a goal, then his team will win.

If (it's not true that) his team will win, then (it's not true that) Jed scores a goal.

Find the answer that paraphrases the contrapositive statement. *If Jed's team lost, he did not score a goal* is the closest.

31. **A**   If two parallel lines are intersected by a third line, then several pairs of congruent angles are formed. In the figure, the marked angles 35° and x° are alternate exterior angles, and they are congruent. If you did not recognize alternate exterior angles in the figure, you can also find the angle using more steps. For instance, if you label the angles in the figure as B and C, you might recognize that angle B is a vertical angle with the original 35° angle, which means that B is 35°. Angle C forms an alternate interior angle with angle B, and is also 35°. This means that the angle x is also 35°, since it is a vertical angle with angle C.

32. **D**   You can solve this question algebraically. Use the formula *surface area* = $4 \times \pi \times r^2$:

$25\pi = 4 \times \pi \times r^2$	Substitute 25π for surface area.
$25 = 4 \times r^2$	Divide both sides by π.
$6.25 = r^2$	Divide both sides by 4.
$2.5 = r$	Take the square root of both sides.

You can also solve by Plugging In the Answers. This alternate approach can be found in your Student Tools!

33.   **Any of the values in the set {8, 9, 10, 11, 12, 14, 15, 16, 17, 18}**

The Triangle Inequality Theorem states that the length of the third side of a triangle must be greater than the *difference*, but less than the *sum*, of the other two side lengths. In this case, that means that x must be greater than 7 (13 – 6 = 7), but less than 19 (13 + 6 = 19). The question states some other restrictions on x. You know that the side length must be an integer, so no fractional values. Additionally, it is stated that the triangle is *scalene*, which means the side lengths are all different. This eliminates 6 and 13 as possible side lengths.

34. **D** To find the average, find the total number of shares of stock owned, and divide by the number of shareholders, 4.

The number of shares is 150 + 10 + 80 + 60 = 300.

Divide by the number of shareholders: $\frac{300}{4}$ = 75.

35. **C** If you were to find the exact probability, you would find the number of students who have 4 or more pets and divide by the total number of students. To find "4 or more pets" in the chart, include the groups "4" and "5 or more." The sum is 14 + 8 = 22. The total number of students is 24 + 32 + 21 + 19 + 14 + 8 = 118. The exact probability, then, is $\frac{22}{118}$. The question asks you to estimate, so you can estimate the fraction as $\frac{20}{120}$, which is $\frac{1}{6}$. Alternatively, if you use the on-screen calculator, you can find that 22 ÷ 118 is approximately 0.186. Of the listed answer choices, 1 ÷ 6 is the closest to this number, as it is approximately 0.167. The answers in numerical order are:

$\frac{1}{8}$ = 0.125, $\frac{1}{7}$ ≈ 0.143, $\frac{1}{6}$ ≈ 0.167, $\frac{2}{7}$ ≈ 0.286, $\frac{3}{8}$ = 0.375.

36. **–22, –14**

To solve this question, it might help to sketch a number line like the one below:

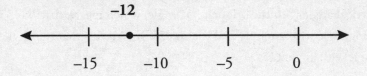

Numbers *less than* –12 would have to be to the *left* of –12 on the number line. From the choices, these values are –14 and –22. All of the remaining choices would be to the *right* of –12 on the number line, and therefore they are greater.

37. **D** Read carefully to translate the statement to an algebraic statement:

x is 4 more than 5 times y

x is 4 more than 5*y*	*Times* means multiply.
x is 4 + 5*y*	*More than* means add.
x = 4 + 5*y*	*Is* means =.

The question asks you to express the value of y. Solve the equation for y.

$x = 4 + 5y$

$x - 4 = 5y$ Subtract 4 from both sides.

$\dfrac{(x - 4)}{5} = y$ Divide both sides by 5.

Therefore, the answer is (D). You can also solve by Plugging In. Check out your Student Tools for this alternate solution.

38.   **D**   The formula for the area of a triangle is $A = \dfrac{1}{2}bh$. Substitute 24 for A, and 6 for B; then, solve for h.

$24 = \dfrac{1}{2}6h$

$4 = \dfrac{1}{2}h$ Divide both sides by 6.

$8 = h$ Multiply both sides by 2.

39.   **D**   To solve this question, substitute 5 for p and evaluate. It's a good idea to substitute before simplifying. That way, you're less likely to make algebra-related mistakes.

$-20 \div p + 3(p + 7)$

$-20 \div 5 + 3(5 + 7)$

$-20 \div 5 + 3(12)$ Evaluate parentheses first.

$-4 + 3(12)$ Perform multiplication and division from left to right.

$-4 + 36$

$= 32$

40.   **C**   The student answered 80% × 90 questions correctly. 0.8 × 90 = 72. Read carefully! The question asks how many questions she answered *incorrectly*. If she answered 72 questions correctly, she answered 18 questions incorrectly (90 − 72 = 18).

41.   **A**   The student performed the multiplication first and the division second. Correct order of operations includes solving multiplication and division together, proceeding from left to right. So the correct solution is:

$$24 \div 8 \times 3 = 3 \times 3 = 9$$

The student should have performed the division first and the multiplication second in order to get 9 as the answer. If you performed the multiplication first, you would get 24 ÷ 8 × 3 = 24 ÷ 24 = 1. This matches the answer indicated in the problem. Choice (B) is not correct; the Distributive Property does not apply in this problem, because there is no addition or subtraction. Choice (C) is not correct; subtraction would have resulted in 24 − 8 × 3 = 24 − 24 = 0. Choice (D) is not correct, as addition would have resulted in 24 ÷ 8 + 3 = 3 + 3 = 6. Finally, (E) is not correct because the correct answer, 9, does not need to be reduced.

42. **E**   To solve this question, you can rewrite the equation in slope-intercept form:

$$\frac{y}{2} - 5 = 6x$$

$$\frac{y}{2} = 6x + 5$$

$$y = 2(6x + 5)$$

$$y = 12x + 10$$

With the equation in slope-intercept form, we can see that the slope is 12.

43. **B**   −3 is an extraneous solution. To check for extraneous solutions, substitute each solution into the *original* equation. Extraneous solutions are solutions derived from algebra, but do *not* make the original equation true.

$$x + 2 = \sqrt{(x + 4)}$$

$$-3 + 2 = \sqrt{(-3 + 4)}$$

$$-1 = \sqrt{(1)}$$

$$-1 = 1 \qquad \text{False.}$$

The statement −1 = 1 is false. Therefore, −3 is an *extraneous* solution.

$$x + 2 = \sqrt{(x + 4)}$$

$$0 + 2 = \sqrt{(0 + 4)}$$

$$2 = \sqrt{(4)}$$

$$2 = 2 \qquad \text{True.}$$

The statement 2 = 2 is true. Therefore, 0 is *not* an extraneous solution.

Note that (D) includes the possible extraneous solution 5. Since 5 is not a solution you would derive from (correct) algebra, it is not an extraneous solution.

44. **B**   Use the slope and *y*-intercept from each equation. You can start by Ballparking: the first equation has a *positive* slope and a *negative y*-intercept. That means that a line should point upward, and cross the lower half of the *y*-axis. Eliminate (A) and (C), as they do not have a line that meets these conditions. The second equation has a *negative* slope, and a *positive y*-intercept. That means that a line should point downward and cross the upper half of the *y*-axis. Eliminate (D) and (E), as they do not have a line that meets these conditions. Choice (B) has a line that fits each equation. One line has a positive slope, and crosses the *y*-axis at −4, which matches the first equation. You can

check the slope by counting units between points: as the line rises by 3, it moves to the right by 1. The other line has a negative slope, and crosses the y-axis at 5, which matches the second equation. You can check the slope by counting the units between points: as the line falls by 2, it moves to the right by 1.

45.   **D**   To solve a compound inequality, break it up into separate inequalities:

$$2(x + 1) < 3x + 4 \qquad \text{and} \qquad 3x + 4 \le x - 5$$

Solve each inequality.

$2(x + 1) < 3x + 4$	
$2x + 2 < 3x + 4$	Use the Distributive Property.
$2x < 3x + 2$	Subtract 2 from both sides.
$-x < 2$	Subtract $3x$ from both sides.
$x > -2$	Divide by -1; flip the inequality sign.

$3x + 4 \le x - 5$	
$3x \le x - 9$	Subtract 4 from both sides.
$2x \le -9$	Subtract x from both sides.
$x \le -4.5$	Divide both sides by 2.

The solution to the compound inequality is $x > -2$ and $x \le 4.5$, or $-2 < x < 4.5$.

Find a graph that shows $x > -2$. The graph needs to have an *open* endpoint symbol at -2 (since the inequality is > and not ≥), and move to the *right* from there. You can eliminate (A) and (E), since each one moves in the wrong direction, and also (B) and (C), since each uses the wrong (closed) endpoint symbol. To inspect the other inequality, look for the graph that shows $x \le 4.5$. The graph needs to have a *closed* endpoint symbol at 4.5, and move to the *left* from there. You can eliminate (A) and (E), since each one moves in the wrong direction. You can also eliminate (B) and (C), since each uses the wrong (open) endpoint symbol.

46.   **B**   To solve this question, you can plug in the values for x.

$$f(x) = 3(x + 4)^2$$

$x = 0$	
$f(0) = 3(0 + 4)^2$	Substitute 0 for x.
$f(0) = 3(4)^2$	Evaluate parentheses first.
$f(0) = 3(16)$	Evaluate powers next.
$f(0) = 48$	Multiply.

When you finish evaluating the function for the x-values {0, 1, 2, 3, 4}, you will have the ordered pairs below:

(0, 48)   (1, 75)   (2, 108)   (3, 147)   (4, 192)

The table that has the correct values is (A). Note that you can use Process of Elimination. For example, you can eliminate (C) and (E) because they do not contain the ordered pair (0, 48).

47.   7   To begin, find the slope of the line containing the coordinates (2, –13) and (5, –25).

$$\frac{(-13 - (-25))}{(2 - 5)} = \frac{12}{-3} = -4$$

You can write the equation in point-slope form, using a point and the slope. Here, you can use the point (2, –13) and the slope (–4):

$$y - (-13) = -4(x - 2)$$
$$y + 13 = -4(x - 2)$$

Now, plug in the value –3 for x:

$y + 13 = -4(x - 2)$

$y + 13 = -4(-3 - 2)$ Substitute –3 for x.

$y + 13 = -4(-5)$ Evaluate parentheses first.

$y + 13 = 20$

$y = 20 - 13$

$y = 7$

48. **C, E**

Substitute the values into the inequality:

(A) (–4, –20)

$-20 < 3(-4) - 8$

$-20 < -12 - 8$

$-20 < -20$ False. Eliminate (–4, –20).

(B) (–2, –12)

$-12 < 3(-2) - 8$

$-12 < -6 - 8$

$-12 < -14$ False. Eliminate (–2, –12).

(C) (0, –10)

$-10 < 3(0) - 8$

$-10 < 0 - 8$

$-10 < -8$ True. Select (0, –10).

(D) (2, –2)

$-2 < 3(2) - 8$

$-2 < 6 - 8$

$-2 < -2$ False. Eliminate (2, –2).

(E) (4, 2)

$$2 < 3(4) - 8$$
$$2 < 12 - 8$$
$$2 < 4 \qquad \text{True. Select (4, 2).}$$

49. **A** The definition of a function states that each value in the input should point to *exactly one* value in the output. The diagrams in the answer choices show the relationships between input values (from the domain) and the output values (from the range). Choice (A) does NOT fit the definition of a function, since the input value 1 points to two output values (10 and 20). Choices (B), (C), (D), and (E) all *do* represent functions, since each input value is matched with only one output value. Note that the reverse can be true—different input values can point to more than one output value.

50. **C** This question can be solved algebraically. Write a system of equations to represent the information in the problem.

$s = p + 3$ Snickers is 3 years older than Princess.

$p = 2r$ Princess's age is twice Roxie's age.

Substitute $2r$ for p in the first equation. Then, evaluate for r.

$$s = 2r + 3$$

$$s - 3 = 2r$$
$$\frac{s - 3}{2} = r$$

How can you solve by Plugging In? See your Student Tools to learn more about this question!

51. **B** To find the mean (average), find the total money earned, and then divide by the total hours worked. To find the total money earned, multiply each rate by the respective hours worked:

$$16 \times 15 = 240$$
$$27 \times 12 = 324$$
$$32 \times 18 = 576$$

Find the sum: $240 + 324 + 576 = 1{,}140$

Find the total hours worked: $16 + 27 + 32 = 75$

Divide the total money by the total hours worked: $1{,}140 \div 75 = 15.20$

Note that it's not correct to simply find the mean of the three rates themselves (which would be $15), since the total and the mean are affected by the hours worked at each rate. The question asked for the average that the writer earned for *all* of the work done.

52.　**E**　To find the median, you have to find the *middle* value when all values are arranged in order. Since there are 52 values, the "middle" will be right between the 26th and 27th value. (Why? Half of 52 is 26. There are 26 values *before* the middle, and 26 values *after* the middle.) You can add the quantity for each bar in order, one at a time, to find where the 26th value is. Think of it as counting each student in each bar, starting from the first:

$$5 + 8 = 13; \text{ keep counting}$$
$$5 + 8 + 11 = 24; \text{ keep counting}$$

After counting all the students in the first three groups, you have two more to reach the median. The median is found in the fourth group: 18 minutes.

53.　**B**　There are 100 total numbers from 00 to 99. Of these, there are 50 numbers less than 50 (00 to 49). That means that the probability of generating a number smaller than 50 is $\frac{50}{100}$, or $\frac{1}{2}$. The probability of doing this twice in a row is $\frac{1}{2} \times \frac{1}{2}$. (Note that these are considered independent events; the first outcome does not affect the second outcome.) $\frac{1}{2} \times \frac{1}{2} = \frac{1}{4}$, or 0.25.

54.　**A**　There are 12 numbers. The probability that the first number is odd {1, 3, 5, 7, 9, 11} is $\frac{6}{12}$, or $\frac{1}{2}$. The probability that the second number is a multiple of 4 {4, 8, 12} is $\frac{3}{12}$, or $\frac{1}{4}$. (Note that these are considered independent events; the first outcome does not affect the second outcome.) The probability that both events happen is $\frac{1}{2} \times \frac{1}{4} = \frac{1}{8}$.

55.　**792**　This is a combination question, as order doesn't matter (in other words, group ABCDE is the same group as BCDEA). To solve, use the multiplication counting principle to find the number of permutations of 5 players there are ($12 \times 11 \times 10 \times 9 \times 8$), and then divide by the duplicate groups ($5 \times 4 \times 3 \times 2 \times 1$). It's probably best to reduce the fraction on paper before multiplying:

$$\frac{12 \times 11 \times 10 \times 9 \times 8}{5 \times 4 \times 3 \times 2 \times 1}$$

$$\frac{12 \times 11 \times \overset{2}{\cancel{10}} \times 9 \times 8}{\cancel{5} \times 4 \times 3 \times 2}$$

$$\frac{12 \times 11 \times 2 \times \overset{3}{\cancel{9}} \times 8}{4 \times \cancel{3} \times 2}$$

$$\frac{12 \times 11 \times 2 \times 3 \times \cancel{8}}{\cancel{4} \times \cancel{2}}$$

The number of combinations is $12 \times 11 \times 2 \times 3$, or 792.

56. **D** If $\frac{2}{7}$ of people would vote "yes," then $\frac{5}{7}$ of people would NOT vote "yes." $(1 - \frac{2}{7} = \frac{5}{7})$ Calculate $\frac{5}{7}$ of 10,675:

$$10,675 \times \frac{5}{7} = 7,625$$

You can also start by calculating $\frac{2}{7}$ of 10,675:

$$10,675 \times \frac{2}{7} = 3,050$$

Then, *subtract* this value from 10,675:

$$10,657 - 3,050 = 7,625$$

Part IV
Praxis Subject Assessments

Chapter 18
Math

MATHEMATICS: CONTENT KNOWLEDGE (5161)

If you are interested in teaching math at the secondary-school level, you may need to take the Math: Content Knowledge Praxis exam. (Before registering for any exam, be sure to check your state's requirements.) This computer-delivered exam is 150 minutes long and contains 60 questions, which include question types like those found on the Praxis Core Math Test: selected-response, select-all-that-apply, and numeric entry, among others.

Approximately 68% of the exam (41 questions) will focus on number theory, algebra, functions, and calculus. The other 32% of the exam (19 questions) will focus on topics in geometry, statistics, probability, and discrete math. We'll go into more detail about each of these content areas later in the chapter, but first let's go over some general test information.

What Score Do I Need to Pass?

Remember that ETS doesn't determine the cutoff for passing scores; individual states do that. Consequently, the number of questions you need to answer correctly varies dramatically from state to state. At the time of publication, the highest cutoff for a passing score is 160. Check www.ets.org/praxis/scores/understand/how/ for the most up-to-date scoring information.

Remember!
The ETS website also provides a scoring bulletin, which can be downloaded from this page: www.ets.org/praxis/scores/understand/.

Manage Your Time and Don't Be Afraid to Guess

You have two-and-a-half minutes per question. Many questions will take only a few seconds to answer; some will take much longer. Read each question carefully, and be sure to read all four answer choices. If you know the correct answer, bubble it in and move on. If you don't, use POE (as discussed in the introduction) to eliminate as many incorrect answers as you can, and then take a guess. An incorrect response carries no penalty, so there's no reason not to guess.

Notations, Definitions, and Formulas
The test will provide you with several pages of notations, definitions, and formulas. You can also find a printable copy in your Student Tools. You may not need to refer to these notations and formulas, but they're there if you need them.

How to Approach the Questions

When working on the multiple-choice questions, remember that there are only four answer choices per question. On the Mathematics: Content Knowledge test, as with all other standardized tests, you will frequently find it easier to eliminate wrong answers than to determine the correct one.

As you read each question, ask yourself the following: *Do I know how to do this?* If the answer is *yes*, then ask yourself: *Is there an easier way?* Compare the answer choices. Sometimes the format of the answer choices will suggest an approach to the problem. For instance, if the answer choices are in decimal format, you'll probably want to work the problem using decimals. If the choices use fractions, you'll probably want to use fractions, too. Remember to eliminate answers that are obviously wrong, and get to work. If the problem involves many steps, stop at the end of each step and determine whether you can eliminate answers based on the work you've done thus far.

If you do not know how to solve this problem, ask yourself: *What answers can I get rid of?* Look at the answer choices to see if any can be eliminated using common sense, basic mathematical reasoning, and/or estimation. Then make your best guess and move on.

Let's try an example.

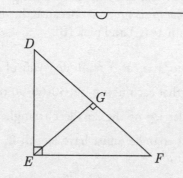

In the figure above, *DEF* is a triangle with a right angle at *E*. $\overline{EG}$ is perpendicular to $\overline{DF}$. If $DG = 3$ and $GF = 1$, then $DE + EF =$

○ $1 + 2\sqrt{2}$

○ $2 + 2\sqrt{3}$

○ $2 + 3\sqrt{2}$

○ $3 + 3\sqrt{3}$

Here's How to Crack It

At first glance, you might assume that the Pythagorean Theorem must come into play because there are three right triangles in the picture. But it may not be obvious how to use it. Ask yourself: *Do I know how to do this?*

Let's assume the answer's *no*. Look at the answer choices. *What can you get rid of?* Remember that $\sqrt{2}$ and $\sqrt{3}$ have numerical values: approximately 1.4 and 1.7, respectively, which means that the answer choices have the following approximate decimal values:

(A) 3.8

(B) 5.4

(C) 6.2

(D) 8.1

That is enough for you to eliminate (A), because you're told that the length $\overline{DF}$ is equal to 4. Therefore, the sum of the lengths of the other two sides must be greater than 4. Similarly, you can eliminate (D) because it's too big. $\overline{DF}$ is the hypotenuse, so the length of each leg must be less than 4. That means the sum of their lengths must be less than 8.

That leaves you with a fifty-fifty chance. Can you do better? Compare the remaining choices. One contains the square root of 3, and the other contains the square root of 2. Which is more likely? The square root of 2 tends to show up in problems involving 45-45-90 triangles. You can trust the drawings on the test unless you're explicitly told that they're *not drawn to scale*. Because the drawing doesn't look like half a square, you can eliminate (C) and pick (B).

Or maybe seeing the square root of 3 reminded you of a 30-60-90 triangle. If you assume for a moment that each figure is a 30-60-90 triangle, then $\overline{FG}$, which has length 1, is the smaller leg of the smallest triangle, meaning that $\overline{EF}$, the hypotenuse of the smallest triangle, must have length 2, and that $\overline{EG}$, the other leg, must have length $\sqrt{3}$.

$\overline{EG}$, in turn, is the shorter leg of triangle DEG, meaning that $\overline{DE}$, the hypotenuse of DEG, must have length $2\sqrt{3}$. So $DE + EF = 2 + 2\sqrt{3}$, and you have further confirmation that (B) is correct.

Granted, the conclusion above relied on the initial assumption that you were dealing with 30-60-90 triangles, which you hadn't proved. If the test asked you to show your work, you'd be in trouble. Fortunately, all you have to do is pick an answer!

Actually, because the triangles all contain right angles, and each of the two smaller triangles shares another angle with the large triangle, they are necessarily similar to each other. Once you know that, you can set up the proportion $\dfrac{3}{x} = \dfrac{x}{1}$, where $x = EG$. Solving that gives you $EG = \sqrt{3}$, proving that all the triangles are 30-60-90 triangles, and the rest of the solution proceeds as above. But don't worry if that didn't occur to you. You can use the answer choices to help you get to the right answer even if you don't know exactly how to do the problem.

The Graphing Calculator

There is an on-screen graphing calculator provided on the test. You are expected to be familiar with its use. The ETS website offers a practice calculator and manual. The calculator includes functions you might expect, such as exponents, logarithms, and trigonometric functions. It also can store values, graph and analyze functions, generate tables for a function, and find solutions for some equations.

On the exam, some numerical answer choices are rounded. Thus, if you use a strategy like Plug In the Answers, the results may be inexact. When using the calculator, you should not round your calculations as you go—use the values provided by the calculator at each step, and round only the final result.

Reminder About Calculator Use
You can check www.ets.org/praxis/test day/policies/calculators/ for the most up-to-date calculator policies.

CONTENT AREAS TO REVIEW

Questions on the Math: Content Knowledge test fall into the following categories: Number and Quantity, Algebra, Functions, Calculus, Geometry, Probability and Statistics, and Discrete Mathematics. Here the topics you should know for each of these content areas.

Praxis Study Companions
ETS offers free study guides on their website for a ton of Praxis exams. You can find more information about the tested content areas on this Subject Assessment by downloading the study companion here: www.ets.org/praxis/prepare/materials/5161.

Number and Quantity

- Properties of exponents
- Properties of rational and irrational numbers, and the interactions between those sets of numbers
- Solving problems by reasoning quantitatively
- The structure of the natural, integer, rational, real, and complex number systems, and performing basic operations on numbers in these systems
- Working with complex numbers when solving polynomial equations and rewriting polynomial expressions
- Performing operations on matrices and using matrices in applications
- Solving problems involving ratios, proportions, averages, percents, and metric and traditional unit conversions
- Analyzing precision and accuracy in measurement situations
- Representing and comparing very large and very small numbers
- Estimating and performing calculations on very large and very small quantities

Algebra

- Writing algebraic expressions in equivalent forms
- Performing arithmetic operations on polynomials
- The relationship between zeros of polynomial functions and factors of the related polynomial expressions
- Using polynomial identities
- Rewriting rational expressions and performing arithmetic operations on rational expressions
- Creating equations and inequalities that describe relationships
- Justifying the process used to solve equations
- Using varied techniques to solve equations and inequalities in one variable
- Using varied techniques to solve systems of equations and inequalities
- Properties of number systems under various operations
- The concept of rate of change of nonlinear functions
- The concepts of intercept(s) of a line and slope as a rate of change
- Finding the zero(s) of functions

Functions

- The function concept and the use of function notation
- Finding the domain and range of a function and a relation
- Analyzing function behavior using different representations
- Using functions and relations to model relationships between quantities
- Obtaining new functions from existing functions
- Differences between linear, quadratic, and exponential models, including how their equations are created and used to solve problems
- Constructing the unit circle and using it to find values of trigonometric functions for all angle measures in their domains
- Modeling periodic phenomena using trigonometric functions
- The application of trigonometric identities
- Interpreting representations of functions of two variables
- Solving equations

Calculus

- Calculating limits of functions, determining when the limit does not exist, and solving problems using the properties of limits
- The derivative of a function as a limit, as the slope of a line tangent to a curve, and as a rate of change
- Showing that a particular function is continuous
- The relationship between continuity and differentiability
- Approximating derivatives and integrals numerically
- Using standard differentiation and integration techniques
- Analyzing the behavior of a function

- Applying derivatives to solve problems
- The foundational theorems of calculus
- Integration as a limit of Riemann sums
- Using integration to compute area, volume, distance, or other accumulation processes
- Determining the limits of sequences, if they exist
- Simple infinite series

Geometry

- Transformations in a plane
- Proving geometric theorems
- Making geometric constructions with a variety of tools and methods
- Congruence and similarity in terms of transformations
- Defining trigonometric ratios in right triangles
- Applying trigonometry to general triangles
- Applying theorems about circles
- Arc length and area measurements of sectors of circles
- Translating between a geometric description and an equation for a conic section
- Using coordinate geometry to algebraically prove simple geometric theorems
- Using perimeter, area, surface area, and volume formulas to solve problems
- Visualizing relationships between two-dimensional and three-dimensional objects
- Applying geometric concepts in real-world situations
- Properties of parallel and perpendicular lines, triangles, quadrilaterals, polygons, and circles, and their use in problem-solving

Probability and Statistics

- Summarizing, representing, and interpreting data collected from measurements on a single variable
- Summarizing, representing, and interpreting data collected from measurements on two variables, either categorical or quantitative
- Creating and interpreting linear regression models
- Understanding and evaluating statistical processes
- Making inferences and justifying conclusions from samples, experiments, and observational studies
- The concepts of independence and conditional probability, and applying these concepts to data
- Computing probabilities of simple events, probabilities of compound events, and conditional probabilities
- Making informed decisions using probabilities and expected values

- Using simulations to construct experimental probability distributions and to make informal inferences about theoretical probability distributions
- Finding probabilities involving finite sample spaces and independent trials

Discrete Mathematics

- Sequences
- Using recursion to model various phenomena
- Equivalence relations
- The differences between discrete and continuous representations (e.g., data, functions), and using each to model various phenomena
- Basic terminology and symbols of logic
- Using counting techniques such as the multiplication principle, permutations, and combinations
- Basic set theory

A review of all of these topics is beyond the scope of this book, but in your Student Tools you can find step-by-step walk-throughs for a bunch of different question types in all of these categories. You can also download a copy of the equations and formulas sheet for the Math: Content Knowledge exam. Be sure to check out the official exam page for even more practice, including a comprehensive study guide and practice test.

Go Online!
Register your book to access study materials for the Math Content Knowledge test, including practice questions and solutions.

MATH DRILL

Answers and explanations can be found at the end of the chapter.

The value of the binomial coefficient $\binom{10}{10}$ is

- ○ 0
- ○ 1
- ○ 10
- ○ undefined

Triangle ABC is inscribed within Circle X, which has a diameter of AB, and center O. Which of the following statements is true?

- ○ $AO = BO = CO$
- ○ $\angle C$ must always be a right angle.
- ○ Both (A) and (B) are true.
- ○ Neither (A) nor (B) is true.

At what coordinates does the graph of $x = t^2 - t - 6$, $y = 2t$, $-5 < t < 5$, cross the y-axis?

- ○ $(-6, 0)$
- ○ $(0, -4)$ and $(0, 6)$
- ○ $(0, 6)$
- ○ $(-2, 3)$

Let $f(x) = x^2 - 3x$, and $g(x) = 3 + x$. What is a simplified formula for $f(g(x))$?

- ○ $x^2 - 3x + 3$
- ○ $x(x + 3)$
- ○ $2x^2 + 3x$
- ○ $(x + 3)(x + 3)$

Using the Mean Value Theorem on the function $F(x) = x^4 - 16x^2 + 2$; $-1 \le x \ge 3$, what are the possible values for x, rounded to the nearest thousandth?

- ○ $x = 0.234, 0.657$
- ○ $x = -0.482, 0$
- ○ $x = 0.382, 2.618$
- ○ $x = 1.428, 2.856$

A student is organizing 5 notebooks from left to right. Each notebook has a distinct color from the other four: red, green, orange, blue, and yellow. When stacking the notebooks from left to right, how many differently ordered color combinations can be created?

- ○ 14
- ○ 25
- ○ 120
- ○ 3,125

$$i^{12} + i^{14} + i^{20} - i^6 =$$

- ○ $-i$
- ○ i
- ○ 1
- ○ 2

In an isosceles triangle, the two equal sides measure 24 meters, and they include an angle of 30 degrees. What is the area of the isosceles triangle, rounded to the nearest square meter?

- ○ 48
- ○ 72
- ○ 144
- ○ 288

MATH DRILL ANSWERS AND EXPLANATIONS

1. **B**   The binomial coefficient can be rewritten as follows: $\begin{pmatrix} N \\ R \end{pmatrix} = \dfrac{N!}{(N-R)!\,R!}$. Therefore, $\dfrac{10!}{0(10!)} = \dfrac{10!}{1(10!)} = 1$. Remember that $0! = 1$.

2. **C**   When a triangle is inscribed in a circle, and one of its sides is the diameter, then the inscribed angle is a right triangle. Statement (A) is true because these are three radii—segments from a point in the triangle to the radius.

3. **B**   The equation is an example of a parametric equation. But the question is a basic graphic question, asking you to find points where the function crosses the y-axis. This is something you will likely be able to graph on your calculator. Or, you can solve for the equations when $x = 0$:

    $$x = (t + 2)(t - 3)$$
    $$0 = (t + 2)(t - 3)$$
    $$t = -2, 3$$

    When $t = -2$, $x = 0$ and $y = 4$; when $t = 3$, $x = 0$ and $y = 6$. Notice that in both examples, t fits within the limits of the function ($-5 < t < 5$).

4. **B**   Solve this composite function problem by taking the value of $g(x)$, and inserting that value as x in the function $f(x)$, as follows:

    $$= (3 + x)^2 - 3(3 + x)$$
    $$= 9 + 6x + x^2 - 9 - 3x$$
    $$= x^2 + 3x$$
    $$= x(x + 3)$$

    Note that (A) gives you the answer for the $g\,(f(x))$. Make sure you work from right to left!

5. **C**   To solve for a function using the Mean Value Theorem, first calculate the quotient for the limits of x:
    $$\frac{f(3) - f(-1)}{3 - (-1)} = \frac{-61 - (-13)}{4} = -12$$

    Next, take the derivative of $f(x)$:

    $$F(x) = 4x^3 - 32x$$

    Equate this with the quotient result above:

    $$4x^3 - 32x = -12$$

    When solving this equation (you can use your calculator!), you will get two answers, which round to 0.382 and 2.618.

6. **C** The answer to this question is the factorial expression 5! In this sequence and order problem, order does matter. How many different notebooks could be used as the first notebook? 5. How many notebooks could be used as the second notebook? 4. The number is 4 because one notebook will have already been used as the first, and you do not have replacement of notebooks. Therefore, the problem can be solved as $5 \times 4 \times 3 \times 2 \times 1$, or 120.

7. **D** The powers of i follow a pattern:

$i^1 = i = \sqrt{-1}$

$i^2 = \sqrt{-1}^2 = -1$

$i^3 = i^2 \cdot i = -i$

$i^4 = i^2 \cdot i^2 = 1$

The pattern repeats for i^5 through i^8, and so on.

Therefore, $i^{12} + i^{14} + i^{20} - i^6 = i^4 + i^2 + i^4 - i^2 = 1 - 1 + 1 - (-1) = 2$.

8. **C** You will need to use trigonometry to solve this problem. The area of $ABC = 0.5bc(\sin A)$:

$= 0.5(24)(24)(\sin 30)$

$= 288(0.5)$

$= 144$

Chapter 19
Social Studies

SOCIAL STUDIES: CONTENT KNOWLEDGE, CONTENT AND INTERPRETATION

There are two key Subject Assessments for Social Studies:

- Social Studies: Content Knowledge (5081)
- Social Studies: Content and Interpretation (5086)

You may need to take one of these tests if you plan to teach social studies at a secondary-school level. Consult your teacher preparation program or state's department of education to determine your testing requirements.

Here is a breakdown of the two tests:

Questions and Time

	Content Knowledge (5081)	Content and Interpretation (5086)
Test Format	130 multiple-choice questions	90 multiple-choice questions 3 short essays
Time	2 hours	2 hours

Content Covered

	Content Knowledge (5081)	Content and Interpretation (5086)
U.S. History	26 questions (20% of test)	18 questions (15% of test)
World History	26 questions (20%)	18 questions (15%)
Government/Civics/Political Science	26 questions (20%)	18 questions (15%)
Economics	19 questions (15%)	13 questions (11%)
Geography	19 questions (15%)	13 questions (11%)
Behavioral Sciences	14 questions (10%)	10 questions (8%)
Short Essays	None	3 (25%)

The key difference between these two exams is that the Content and Interpretation test includes a writing portion. ETS calls this section the "constructed-response questions," short essays that test your ability to understand, analyze, and write about a historical source and its relationship to a historical issue or social studies concept. More on those in a little bit.

Pick Your Battles

If this sounds like an awful lot of material to cover on one two-hour test, you're right—and there's a fair amount of time pressure; you have less than one minute per question. But even ETS admits that it doesn't expect anyone to be able to ace this test. Concentrate on answering the questions that you know you can answer correctly.

What Score Do I Need to Pass?

Your raw score (the number of the 130 questions that you answer correctly) is converted to a scaled score ranging from 100 to 200. ETS doesn't determine the cutoff for passing scores; individual states do that. Consequently, the number of questions you need to answer correctly varies dramatically from state to state. Here's a sampling of states and their passing scaled scores:

State	Passing Score (100–200)
Mississippi	150
Colorado	150
Nevada	152
New Jersey	157
Pennsylvania	157
Connecticut	162

You can find a complete listing of each state's requirements on ETS's website: www.ets.org/praxis/prxstate.html.

Manage Your Time and Don't Be Afraid to Guess

You have a lot of freedom with respect to the number of questions you should spend time answering. Your task is to pick the best of the four answer choices that are in front of you. If you don't like a particular question, use POE to narrow down the possibilities. There's no guessing penalty, so there's no harm in taking a shot in the dark, but you'll probably be able to use your own knowledge to eliminate at least one answer choice on any given question.

Try this sample question:

_____⌒_____

What legal doctrine was established in the Supreme Court's *Plessy v. Ferguson* decision in 1898?

- ○ Right of workers to unionize
- ○ "Separate but equal" laws
- ○ Abolition of slavery
- ○ Sanctity of the flag

Here's How to Crack It

Let's assume that you've never heard of *Plessy v. Ferguson*. Note the date mentioned in the question (1898), and then look at the answer choices.

(A)   Right of workers to unionize

Maybe. Workers' rights might have been an issue at the time.

(B)   "Separate but equal" laws

Maybe. That sounds like something having to do with civil rights and racial issues.

(C)   Abolition of slavery

No. Abolition of slavery happened during the Civil War.

(D)   Sanctity of the flag

No. The Supreme Court doesn't rule on the "sanctity" of anything.

In this case, we were able to eliminate two incorrect answers by knowing a common fact (that slavery ended during the Civil War) and a basic notion about the role of the Supreme Court (that it makes decisions based on legality rather than theology). This leaves only two answers, so we're now down to a fifty-fifty chance of choosing the right one. The right answer happens to be (B). *Plessy v. Ferguson* established the doctrine of "separate but equal," meaning that schools and other public institutions were allowed to be racially segregated. This ruling stood until 1954, when the ruling on *Brown v. Board of Education* overturned it.

_____⌒_____

Other Question Types

While the majority of the questions on the Social Studies tests are selected response (multiple choice), you may see a few question types like select-all-that-apply or "drag and drop," which are generally matching questions. Additionally, the Content and Interpretation Test (5086) includes three short essays, or what ETS calls "constructed-response questions." Let's discuss each of these question types in a little more detail.

Select All That Apply

On certain questions, you are allowed to choose more than one answer. You must select all correct responses—no more, no less—to get credit for one of these questions.

Here's an example:

---○---

Which of the following factors would lead to an increase in demand?

Select **all** that apply.

- ☐ Financial ability to purchase a product
- ☐ A lack of advertising
- ☐ An expectation that the value of a product will decrease in the future
- ☐ Lower price on a product

Here's How to Crack It

An increase in demand comes from the willingness and ability to purchase a product. Both (A) and (D)—having money to spend and finding a less expensive product—point to factors that would make a consumer more likely to purchase. On the other hand, a lack of advertising would make fewer people aware of the product and therefore lower the demand for it. Further, if people expect that the value of an item will decrease, they would be less likely to invest in it. Therefore, (A) and (D) are the correct responses.

---○---

Drag and Drop

These questions require you to drag terms or definitions into appropriate matching categories. As with select-all-that-apply questions, you must match all of these items correctly to get credit for a question.

A drag-and-drop question will look something like this:

Click on a choice and drag it to a box.

From the states listed below, click and drop into the appropriate boxes the choices that correspond with the type of climate that could be found in that region.

Alaska   *Colorado*   *Arizona*   *Florida*

Arid

```
┌──────────┐
│          │
└──────────┘
```

Humid subtropical

```
┌──────────┐
│          │
└──────────┘
```

Subarctic

```
┌──────────┐
│          │
└──────────┘
```

Highland

```
┌──────────┐
│          │
└──────────┘
```

Here's How to Crack It

Think about what kind of weather is common to each region and match it with the climate that would contain that kind of weather. This can be a POE question if you are sure about only two or three of the matches. There are many areas of Arizona that are hot and dry. Match that with *arid,* which means hot and dry. Florida is warm and gets plenty of rain. This is characteristic of *humid subtropical.* Alaska is known for being cold, and close to the Arctic Circle. That can be matched with *subarctic.* This leaves Colorado to be matched with *highland,* which for a state located in the Rocky Mountains, seems quite appropriate.

Constructed-Response Questions (Short Essays)

If you're taking 5081 (Content Knowledge), then feel free to skip this section, as you won't see any constructed-response questions on your test. However, if you're taking 5086 (Content and Interpretation), read on!

A constructed-response question is a fancy term for "short essay." Each of the essays will require you to read and interpret a passage, chart, table, cartoon, photograph, or some other source, and use that source to analyze a larger historical issue or social studies concept. Though the multiple-choice and short-essay sections are not independently timed, it's recommended that you spend 30 minutes in total on the essay section, which works out to 10 minutes per essay.

Each essay is scored on a scale from 0 to 3. To receive a 3, your response needs to

- demonstrate a complete understanding of the source
- completely and accurately answer the question
- provide sufficient analysis of the historical issue or social studies concept
- apply subject knowledge

Your response should also be generally well written and clear, with few grammatical errors or typos.

Let's take a look at a sample question and how you might go about composing your short essay.

Need writing practice? Check out our updated edition of *Writing Smart!*

Read the following speech by Abraham Lincoln.

Four score and seven years ago our fathers brought forth on this continent, a new nation, conceived in Liberty, and dedicated to the proposition that all men are created equal.

Now we are engaged in a great civil war, testing whether that nation, or any nation so conceived and so dedicated, can long endure. We are met on a great battle-field of that war. We have come to dedicate a portion of that field, as a final resting place for those who here gave their lives that that nation might live. It is altogether fitting and proper that we should do this.

But, in a larger sense, we can not dedicate—we can not consecrate—we can not hallow—this ground. The brave men, living and dead, who struggled here, have consecrated it, far above our poor power to add or detract. The world will little note, nor long remember what we say here, but it can never forget what they did here. It is for us the living, rather, to be dedicated here to the unfinished work which they who fought here have thus far so nobly advanced. It is rather for us to be here dedicated to the great task remaining before us—that from these honored dead we take increased devotion to that cause for which they gave the last full measure of devotion—that we here highly resolve that these dead shall not have died in vain—that this nation, under God, shall have a new birth of freedom—and that government of the people, by the people, for the people, shall not perish from the earth.

In your response,

(A) Describe Abraham Lincoln's feelings toward those who fought in the Civil War.

(B) Give two subsequent events that presented a "new birth of freedom" for the United States.

Here's How to Crack It

The constructed-response questions are intended to evaluate your understanding of a social studies concept. This particular prompt asks you about the fallout from the Civil War, using Abraham Lincoln's "Gettysburg Address" as the source material. To obtain a score of a 3 on this question, you must address all parts of the question, while providing specific evidence to use as support. You could successfully do this in four paragraphs.

Introduction: The first, more general part of the question should be answered in your introduction. For this particular prompt, you want to convey the idea that Lincoln has great respect for the men who died in the battle, and that in order for them to not have died in vain, it is necessary to ensure that democracy does not "perish from the earth."

Body Paragraphs: The body paragraphs should provide specific, supporting examples. This will answer the second part of the question. Each body paragraph in the Lincoln question will focus on a specific event that helped the United States rebuild following the Civil War. You may include the 13th Amendment, which ended slavery; the 14th Amendment, which guaranteed equal protection to all people; the Industrial Revolution; or the closing of the West, among other examples for these paragraphs.

Conclusion: Be sure to wrap all of this information up with a smooth conclusion that ties all relevant information together and stays on topic with the prompt.

CONTENT AREAS TO REVIEW

According to ETS, here are the topics and concepts you should be familiar with for the test.

United States History

Native American Peoples

Important political, economic, social, and cultural histories of the following peoples:

- Inuit
- Anasazi
- Northwest Indians
- Plains Indians
- Mound Builders
- Iroquois
- Cherokee
- Seminoles

European Exploration and Colonization

- The major European explorers and the regions each explored
- The reasons for and approaches to colonization of various countries
- Interactions between explorers and Native Americans and consequences thereof
- Different facets of colonial culture (e.g., society, religion, economy) from different perspectives (e.g., wealthy landowners, small farmers, women, slaves)
- Origins of slavery
- The First Great Awakening

Establishing a New Nation (1776–1791)

- Causes of the American Revolution
- Important people and their roles and contributions (e.g., John Adams, Thomas Jefferson, King George III)
- Important events during the Revolutionary War (e.g., the battle of Yorktown, the Treaty of Paris)
- Ideas expressed in the Declaration of Independence
- The first government of the United States under the Articles of Confederation
- The creation and ratification of the United States Constitution
- Federalism and Anti-Federalism
- The Bill of Rights
- How slavery is addressed in the Constitution

Study Guides, Practice Questions, and More
To download the official study guide for this exam, go to www.ets.org/praxis/prepare/materials/5081.

Early Years of the New Nation (1791–1829)

- Early presidential administrations
- The creation and growth of political parties
- The Louisiana Purchase
- The War of 1812
- The Monroe Doctrine

Continued National Development (1829–1850s)

- Slavery's effects on society in the North and South
- "Jacksonian Democracy" (the spoils system, veto of the National Bank, opposition to the Supreme Court)
- Nullification and states' rights
- Westward expansion
- Technological and agricultural innovations and their impact (e.g., cotton gin, steamboat)
- Role of women
- Effects of European immigration
- Treatment of Native Americans (e.g., treaties, Indian Removal Act, "Trail of Tears")
- The Second Great Awakening (e.g., temperance, prison reform)

Civil War Era (1850–1870s)

- Differences between the North and South
- Missouri Compromise and Compromise of 1850
- The abolitionist movement
- The Underground Railroad
- The Women's Movement
- The Fugitive Slave Act
- The Dred Scott decision
- Important people and their roles and contributions (e.g. Abraham Lincoln, Ulysses S. Grant, Jefferson Davis, Robert E. Lee, Frederick Douglass, Harriet Tubman, John Brown)
- Events leading to the Civil War
- Important events during the Civil War (e.g., capture of Fort Sumter, battle of Gettysburg, Lee's surrender, the Gettysburg Address)
- The Emancipation Proclamation
- The 13th, 14th, and 15th Amendments to the Constitution
- Reconstruction
- Jim Crow laws

Emergence of the Modern United States (1877–1900)

- Displacement of Native Americans
- *Plessy v. Ferguson* and segregation
- Federal government's encouragement of business expansion

- Andrew Carnegie, John D. Rockefeller, J. P. Morgan, and their industries
- Sharecropping
- The Industrial Revolution and its impact
- The Labor Movement
- Asian and European immigration
- The Pendleton Act
- The Muckrakers
- Important political and social movements (e.g., Populist movement, Social Darwinism, women's rights, etc.)
- American Imperialism

Progressive Era through the New Deal (1900–1939)
- Direct-ballot
- Mexican immigration
- America's role in World War I
- Isolationism
- The League of Nations
- Important aspects of the 1920s (e.g., the Harlem Renaissance, Prohibition, women's suffrage, mass-production techniques)
- Causes and impact of the Great Depression
- Franklin D. Roosevelt and the New Deal

The Second World War and the Postwar Period (1939–1963)
- America's role in World War II
- The attack on Pearl Harbor
- Battles of Midway, Iwo Jima, and Okinawa
- The invasion of Normandy
- Internment of Japanese Americans
- Decision to drop the atomic bombs on Hiroshima and Nagasaki
- The Marshall Plan
- America's role in the Cold War
- The Korean War
- *Brown v. Board of Education*
- G.I. Bill
- Red Scare and McCarthyism
- Cuban missile crisis

Recent Developments (1960s–Present)
- Causes, events, and results of the Vietnam War
- African American Civil Rights movement
- Martin Luther King, Jr.
- Women's movement and the change in family structure
- The "Great Society" and the "War on Poverty"
- Watergate

- Industrial trends (e.g., deregulation, energy crisis, environmental policy)
- The information revolution and its impact

World History

Human Society to Approximately 3500 B.C.E.
- Human societies during the Paleolithic era
- Human societies during the Neolithic era
- Hunter/gatherer societies
- Agricultural Revolution
- Specialization of tasks
- Tool making

Development of City Civilization (ca. 3500–1500 B.C.E.)
Important characteristics of the following civilizations:

- Mesopotamia
- Egypt
- Indus River Valley
- Early China
- Olmec society in Mesoamerica

Egypt (ca. 1552–1070 B.C.E.)
- Influence of geography
- Pyramids
- Valley of the Kings
- Important advances in art, writing, and architecture

Greece (ca. 2000–300 B.C.E.)
- Influence of geography
- Concepts of citizenship and democracy
- Athens versus Sparta
- Commerce and the city-state
- Persian Wars
- Peloponnesian Wars
- Alexander the Great
- Important advances in drama, art, sports, architecture, mathematics, and science

Rome (ca. 700–500 B.C.E.)

- Influence of geography
- Military domination
- Relative size of the empire at various times
- Republic and empire
- Law and citizenship
- Julius Caesar
- Augustus Caesar
- Pax Romana
- Origin and spread of Christianity
- Constantine
- Important advances in architecture, technology, science, law, and engineering
- Causes of the decline and fall of the Roman Empire

India

- Aryan conquest of the Ganges Valley
- Caste system
- Hinduism
- Buddhism

China

- Imperial government and bureaucracy
- Taoism
- Confucianism
- Buddhism
- Important advances and achievements (e.g., printing, compass, paper, gunpowder)
- China's insularity and its effects

Japan

- Influence of geography
- Shinto
- Buddhism
- Emperor, shoguns, and samurai

Disruption and Reversal (ca. 500–1400 C.E.)

- Nomads including Huns and Mongols
- Byzantine Empire
- Origin and spread of Islam
- Difference between Islam and other faiths
- Influence of Muslim learning
- Present-day influences of Islam

- Feudalism and its effects in Europe and Japan
- The Black Death and its effects
- Mayans
- Aztecs
- Incas
- Trading empires and forest kingdoms in sub-Saharan Africa

Emerging Global Interactions (ca. 1400–1750)
- Transition to market economies
- Navigational advancements and their effects
- Chinese voyages
- European voyages of Magellan, Columbus, and de Gama
- Effects of cultural contact
- The Renaissance
- The Protestant Reformation
- Scientific discoveries of Newton, Galileo, and Copernicus
- The Enlightenment's theoretical basis (e.g., works of Locke, Voltaire, and Rousseau)
- The Enlightenment's effects on the American, French, and Latin American Revolutions

Political and Industrial Revolutions, Nationalism (1750–1914)
- Rise of industrial economies, especially in England
- Effects of rapid scientific and technological change
- The factory system
- Liberalism, socialism, Marxism
- Nationalism and imperialism
- Unifications of Germany and Italy
- European colonies in Africa
- The Meiji Restoration of Japan

Conflicts, Ideologies, and Revolutions in the 20th Century
- Causes and effects of World War I
- Russian, Mexican, and Chinese Revolutions
- Worldwide economic depression
- Rise of communism
- Rise of fascism
- Important figures (e.g., Lenin, Stalin, Mao Zedong, Adolf Hitler, Franklin D. Roosevelt, Mohandas Gandhi, Kwame Nkrumah, Nelson Mandela)
- Causes and effects of World War II
- The Holocaust
- Origin of the Cold War
- NATO
- Warsaw Pact
- European Economic Community

- Organization of African Unity
- OPEC
- SEATO
- Post–World War II China (e.g., the Cultural Revolution)
- Post–World War II Soviet Union (e.g., uprisings in Hungary and Czechoslovakia, perestroika, and glasnost)
- Decolonization in Africa and Asia
- India and Pakistan
- Rise of a global culture and economy
- Major scientific advances (e.g., atomic power, satellites, computers)

Contemporary Trends
- "New Europe"
- Pacific Rim
- Economic and environmental interdependence
- Judaism

Government, Civics, and Political Science

Basic Political Concepts
- Why government is needed
- Major theorists (e.g., Machiavelli, Hobbes, Locke, Marx, Lenin)
- Major concepts (e.g., citizenship, legitimacy, power, justice, authority, liberty, rights and responsibilities, federalism, and sovereignty
- Orientations (e.g., radical, liberal, conservative, and reactionary)

United States Political System
- The Constitution and Bill of Rights, including procedures for interpretation and amendment
- "Separation of powers" among the three branches of government
- Functions and processes in the federal government
- Relationships among federal, state, and local governments
- Regulatory commissions (e.g., Federal Communications Commission)
- Hierarchy of the federal court system
- Landmark Supreme Court decisions (e.g., *Marbury v. Madison*)
- Judicial activism and judicial restraint

Systems of Government/International Politics
- Classical republic
- Liberal democracy
- Federalism
- Absolute monarchy

- Dictatorship
- Parliamentary system
- Autocracy
- Oligarchy
- Theocracy
- Plutocracy

Geography

History Books Galore!
If you're looking for comprehensive content review on any or all of these history topics, consider checking out The Princeton Review's series of AP History titles. Our books on U.S. History, European History, World History, and Human Geography, while focused on the AP exams, will help you prepare for this test as well.

The World in Spatial Terms
- Longitude and latitude
- Geographic features (e.g., continents, oceans, ice caps, mountain ranges)
- Major geographic locations (e.g., seven continents, four oceans)
- General climate patterns for major parts of each continent

Physical Geography of North America
- Physical characteristics and climate patterns of each region
- Main geographic features including mountain ranges, rivers, national parks, etc.

Places and Regions
- Location of major regions, countries, and cities
- Various characteristics of each region

Physical Systems
- Weather patterns, seasons, and climate
- Physical changes (e.g., floods, earthquakes) and their effects

Human Systems
- Causes and effects of settlement patterns
- Population movements
- Difference between developing and industrialized nations

Environment and Society
- Impact of the environment on essentials, transportation, recreation, and economic systems
- Effects of human activity on the environment (e.g., pollution, global warming)
- Renewable and nonrenewable natural resources

Economics

Fundamental Concepts
- Scarcity
- Opportunity cost
- Absolute and comparative advantage
- Command, market, and mixed economies
- Circular-flow model

Microeconomics
- Supply and demand
- Equilibrium price
- Perfect competition
- Monopoly
- Distribution of income

Macroeconomics
- Gross National Product
- Gross Domestic Product
- Inflation
- Unemployment
- Consumer Price Index
- Aggregate supply and aggregate demand models
- The Federal Reserve

International Economic Concepts
- Effects of international trade on domestic economy
- Currency fluctuation
- Protectionism

Current Issues and Controversies
- The balanced-budget amendment
- Protectionism
- Minimum wage
- Government regulation
- Environmental protection
- Fiscal and monetary policy

Behavioral Sciences

Sociology
- Basic concepts (e.g., networks, norms, groups, status, ethnicity)
- Socialization
- Patterns of social organization (e.g., mores, beliefs, social stratification, social mobility)
- Social institutions (e.g., family, faith, clubs, sports)
- Studies of populations
- Multicultural diversity
- Social problems

Anthropology
- Goals of anthropology and archeology
- Human culture including language, learning of roles, and subcultures
- How cultures change (e.g., adaptation, diffusion, assimilation)

FYI
Some of the major theorists listed here are discussed in the next part of this book on the Principles of Learning and Teaching tests. So even if you aren't taking a PLT, you can skim those content review chapters to brush up on some basic psychology concepts for this Social Studies test.

Psychology
- Major theorists (e.g., Freud, Jung, Piaget, Pavlov, Skinner, Erikson)
- Basic concepts (e.g., cognitive development, behavioralism, emotions, motives, values, perception)
- Human development (e.g., physical, cognitive, social, emotional)
- Personality and adjustment (e.g., self-esteem, motivation, assessment)
- Abnormal psychology
- Social psychology

The drill on the next page consists of questions like those you will see on the actual exam. Take the drill and then read the explanations that follow, taking note of which questions you answered correctly and incorrectly. Then, focus your preparation on those areas in which you need more review.

SOCIAL STUDIES DRILL

Answers and explanations can be found at the end of the chapter.

Colonists who were loyal to King George III of England were often known as

- ○ Tories
- ○ Lobsterbacks
- ○ Minutemen
- ○ Patriots

Which group's conquering of Russia in the mid 1200s led to a major change in the rural social structure, which lasted several hundred years?

- ○ Huns
- ○ Mongols
- ○ Turks
- ○ Byzantines

Which of the following is a power of the United States Senate?

Select **all** that apply.

- ☐ The vote to initiate the impeachment of the president.
- ☐ The confirmation of Supreme Court justice nominees
- ☐ The right to impose taxes
- ☐ The power to regulate interstate commerce

Which of the following is NOT an example of spatial diffusion?

- ○ A low-pressure system causing a tornado
- ○ The spread of a wildfire
- ○ The growth of an urban center
- ○ The spread of bubonic plague

An increase in United States imports will most likely lead to which of the following events?

- ○ Increased supply of foreign currency on foreign exchange markets
- ○ A stronger United States dollar compared to other currencies
- ○ A decrease in the supply of United States dollars
- ○ A weaker dollar relative to foreign currencies

Which sociology theory is most concerned with the contribution the various parts of a society make toward the needs of society?

- ○ Functionalism
- ○ Conflict theory
- ○ Interactionism
- ○ Universal interdependence

Click on a choice and drag it to a box.

Match the cause to the correct war.

Missouri Compromise

Intolerable Acts

First Continental Congress

Abolitionist movement

American Revolution   American Civil War

Which United States President completed the Louisiana Purchase?

○ Adams

○ Washington

○ Jefferson

○ Madison

SOCIAL STUDIES DRILL ANSWERS AND EXPLANATIONS

1. **A** Tories were supporters of the king, and many fought for the British during the Revolutionary War.

2. **B** Mongol tribes attacked Russia around the 1230s, and ruled over most of Russia for two and a half centuries. Fearful of attacks, many peasants fled to remote areas of the country. The decision of many peasants to become lifetime laborers of the nobility changed the rural social structure within the country.

3. **B, C,** and **D**

   The Senate has the ability to confirm the president's Supreme Court nominees. Both the House and Senate register votes of impeachment, but impeachment must be initiated by the House. Choices (C) and (D) are fundamental rights granted to the two houses of Congress, which includes the Senate.

4. **A** Spatial diffusion is a concept that discusses how a phenomenon moves through geographic space. This concept seeks to explain the movement of cultures, trends, people, and ideas. The spread of wildfires, the growth of an urban center, and the spread of an infectious disease are all examples of spatial diffusion.

5. **D** In general, an increase in U.S. payments (i.e., U.S. imports, investment income outflows, or more U.S. investment abroad) will lead to an increase in the supply of dollars and thus a weaker dollar relative to foreign currencies.

6. **A** Functionalism originally attempted to explain social institutions as collective means to fill individual biological needs; later it came to focus on the ways social institutions fill social needs, especially social solidarity. Famous functionalists include Malinowski, Durkheim, Parsons, and Radcliffe-Brown.

7. **American Revolution:** Intolerable Acts and First Continental Congress
   American Civil War: Missouri Compromise and Abolitionist Movement

   The Intolerable Acts were created by the British to punish the Massachusetts Bay Colony for the Boston Tea Party, which was an act of rebellion against the British Crown. The First Continental Congress was called to discuss the Patriots' response to the Intolerable Acts. The Civil War was fought over the issue of slavery. The Missouri Compromise helped keep a balance between free states and slave states, while the abolitionists protested the institution of slavery.

8. **C** Acquired from Napoleon in 1803, the Louisiana Purchase marked the beginning of U.S. expansion west of the Mississippi. Thomas Jefferson was president at that time (1803 was in the middle of his first term).

Chapter 20
English Language Arts

ENGLISH LANGUAGE ARTS: CONTENT KNOWLEDGE, CONTENT AND ANALYSIS

There are two Praxis Subject Assessments for English Language Arts: Content Knowledge (5038) and Content and Analysis (5039). Prospective secondary school English Language Arts teachers may need to take one of these exams. Check with your teacher education program or state's department of education to determine which test you should take.

These two exams focus on concepts in the following categories:

1. Reading, including:
   - the study of literature (stories, drama, and poetry)
   - informational texts (literary nonfiction like essays, biographies, speeches)
2. Use of the English language, including:
   - conventions of standard English
   - vocabulary development
3. Writing, speaking, and listening

The key difference between the two tests is the inclusion of two constructed-response (short essay) questions on the Content and Analysis (5039) exam. The first short essay will ask you to analyze the main idea and key literary elements of a prose or poetry excerpt. The excerpt may be from United States, British, or world literature of any time period. The second short essay will require you to read an excerpt from a literary essay and then analyze the central idea as well as the rhetorical strategies and techniques used to build an argument.

This chapter goes into a little more detail about both of these tests so you know what to expect.

English Language Arts: Content Knowledge (5038)

The English Language Arts: Content Knowledge test is 150 minutes long and consists of 130 selected-response (multiple-choice) questions. Like other Praxis exams, it is computer based. While most questions on the exam will likely be traditional multiple-choice questions (four answer choices and you choose one), you may also see a few of any of the following question types:

- Select all that apply
- Ordering/matching
- Table/grid
- Select in passage
- Audio stimulus
- Video stimulus

The following table gives an approximate breakdown of questions across the three main categories covered on the test—reading; language use and vocabulary; and writing, speaking, and listening:

Content Area (5038)	Approximate # of Questions	Approximate Percentage of Test
Reading	49	38%
Language Use and Vocabulary	33	25%
Writing, Speaking, and Listening	48	37%

What Score Do I Need to Pass?

At the time of publication, the passing scores for the states below are as follows. You should check the ETS website regularly for the most up-to-date scoring information.

State	Passing Score (100–200)
Alaska	167
Alabama	147
Colorado	167
Washington D.C.	167
Delaware	167
Hawaii	167
Indiana	167
Kansas	162
Maine	167
Mississippi	167
Montana	167
Nevada	167
New Jersey	167
North Carolina	167
North Dakota	167
Pennsylvania	167
South Dakota	167
Tennessee	167
Virginia	167
West Virginia	167
Wisconsin	167
United States Territory	
American Samoa	152
Guam	167
Northern Mariana Islands	167
Virgin Islands	167

Why Are States Missing from This List?
If the state in which you live or intend to teach is not listed here, that may be because the test is not required in that state. Be sure to check the ETS website for state-by-state testing requirements: www.ets.org/praxis/states.

English Language Arts: Content and Analysis (5039)

The English Language Arts: Content and Analysis test is 3 hours long and computer based. Like the Content Knowledge exam, this test is comprised of 130 selected-response questions. However, this test also has two constructed-response (short-essay) questions. You will have 150 minutes to answer the 130 selected-response questions, and 30 minutes for the constructed-response section. The multiple-choice questions are worth 75% of your total score, and the constructed-response questions are worth 25%. Points earned for the constructed response questions are reported separately from the multiple-choice questions.

While most questions on the multiple-choice section will likely be traditional single-selection questions (four answer choices and you choose one), you may also see a few of any of the following question types:

- Select all that apply
- Ordering/matching
- Table/grid
- Select in passage
- Audio stimulus
- Video stimulus

The following table gives an approximate breakdown of questions across the three main categories covered on the test—Reading; Language Use and Vocabulary; and Writing, Speaking, and Listening:

Content Area (5039)	Approximate # of Questions	Approximate Percentage of Test
Reading	48 multiple-choice questions; 1 constructed response	40%
Language Use and Vocabulary	33 multiple-choice questions	19%
Writing, Speaking, and Listening	49 multiple-choice questions, 1 constructed response	41%

What Score Do I Need to Pass?

At the time of publication, the passing scores for the states below are as follows. You should check the ETS website regularly for the most up-to-date scoring information.

State	Passing Score (100–200)
Alaska	168
Arkansas	168
Connecticut	168
Iowa	164
Kentucky	168
Louisiana	168
Maryland	168
Nebraska	168
New Hampshire	168
Rhode Island	168
South Carolina	168
Utah	162
Vermont	168
Wyoming	168
United States Territory	
Northern Mariana Islands	168

Don't see your state listed here? Go to www.ets.org/praxis/states to determine the testing requirements for the state in which you intend to teach.

CONTENT REVIEW FOR BOTH EXAMS

The English Language Arts Subject Assessments measure three content areas of English: Reading; Language Use and Vocabulary; and Writing, Speaking, and Listening. Questions from each of these appear randomly throughout the test.

Reading questions test your knowledge of canon literature (fiction, poetry, and drama) and analysis of informational texts (literary nonfiction, biographies, essays, speeches, and advertisements). Language Use and Vocabulary questions test your knowledge of standard English and vocabulary development. Writing, Speaking, and Listening questions ask you to understand modes of writing, identify best research practices, and understand the components of effective oral presentations. For all types of questions, you will be asked to identify teaching practices.

Reading

The first major test category is Reading. Reading questions test your knowledge of canon literature (fiction, poetry, and drama) and analysis of informational texts (literary nonfiction, biographies, essays, speeches, and advertisements).

What You Need to Know: Authors, Works, and Historical Periods

Authors

The following is a non-exhaustive list of authors that may appear on the English Language Arts Subject Assessment:

- Maya Angelou
- Jane Austen
- William Blake
- Ray Bradbury
- Charlotte Bronte
- Willa Cather
- Geoffrey Chaucer
- Samuel Coleridge
- Stephen Crane
- Charles Dickens
- Emily Dickinson
- Ralph Ellison
- Ralph Waldo Emerson
- F. Scott Fitzgerald
- Anne Frank
- Robert Frost
- Nathaniel Hawthorne
- Ernest Hemingway
- Zora Neale Hurston

- John Keats
- Harper Lee
- C. S. Lewis
- Christopher Marlowe
- Herman Melville
- Toni Morrison
- George Orwell
- Sylvia Plath
- Edgar Allen Poe
- J. D. Salinger
- William Shakespeare
- Mary Shelley
- Percy Bysse Shelley
- John Steinbeck
- Amy Tan
- J. R. R. Tolkien
- Mark Twain
- Alice Walker
- Walt Whitman

Study Tip

To remember the authors, write down two to three of their best-known works, determine the historical period and/or styles of the writing or dates of their life, and note a few ways in which you may identify their works, such as a subject, writing style, or memorable line(s).

For example:

Author: Herman Melville

Titles: *Moby Dick, Billy Budd*

Historical period: American Renaissance / (b. 1819 – d. 1891)

Identifying factors: Writes about the sea (nautical subject), uses allegory

Book quotes: "Call me Ishmael."

Author: Jane Austen

Titles: *Pride and Prejudice, Sense and Sensibility, Emma*

Historical period: Literary realism (during the time of Romanticism) /
(b. 1775 – d. 1817)

Identifying factors: Writes about society and romantic relationships; uses irony and humor

Book quotes: "It is a truth universally acknowledged, that a single man in possession of a good fortune, must be in want of a wife."

Historical Periods

Note that there are many ways to categorize historical literary periods. The following is a non-exhaustive list of historical periods that may appear on the English Language Arts Subject Assessment:

- Old English
- Middle English
- Renaissance
- British Neoclassical
- British Romanticism
- American Colonialism
- American Renaissance
- American Naturalism (also, Realism)
- British and/or American Modernism
- British and/or American Postmodernism

You will also be tested on specific **literary movements** or **literary schools of thought.** They include the following:

- Metaphysical Poets (Donne, Marvel, Herbert)
- British Romantics (Keats, Shelley, Byron)
- Transcendentalists (Emerson, Thoreau)
- Bloomsbury Group (Woolf, Forster)
- Harlem Renaissance (Hughes, Hurston)

Study Tip

To remember the historical periods and literary movements, write down the dates of each, characteristics of the style, and authors and works associated with each. For example:

Movement: Harlem Renaissance

Dates: c. 1918–1937

Authors: Zora Neale Hurston, Langston Hughes, Richard Wright

Works: *Their Eyes Were Watching God, Native Son*

Defining characteristics: Black American experience, urbanity, and high/low social culture

Sample Author/Work Identification Questions

The tests will likely ask you to identify a work or author based on a short passage, or match a title to an author name. You may need to put a group of historical periods in chronological order. Below are a few variations of identification questions.

An identification question may match the author to the novel. For example:

Drag the novel in the second column to the box beside the author who wrote it.

Identification questions
may also ask you to place
literary works in the order
in which they
were written.

Sylvia Plath		*All the King's Men*
Jack Kerouac		*Catch-22*
Joseph Heller		*On the Road*
Robert Penn Warren		*The Bell Jar*

Here, you would drag *The Bell Jar* to Plath; *On the Road* to Kerouac; *Catch-22* to Heller; and *All the King's Men* to Robert Penn Warren.

An identification question may also ask you to select all answers that apply, like this one:

Which of the following first lines are paired with the correct novel?

Select **all** that apply.

- ☐ "It was the best of times, it was the worst of times..." —*Hard Times*

- ☐ "It was a bright, cold day in April, and the clocks were striking thirteen." —*A Clockwork Orange*

- ☐ "Mother died today. Or maybe, yesterday; I can't be sure." —*The Stranger*

- ☐ "He was an old man who fished alone in a skiff in the Gulf Stream and he had gone eighty-four days now without taking a fish." —*Moby Dick*

- ☐ "It was love at first sight. The first time Yossarian saw the chaplain he fell madly in love with him." —*Catch-22*

- ☐ "All children, except one, grow up." —*The Little Princess*

How did you do? The answers here are (C) and (E). Choice (A) is from *A Tale of Two Cities;* (B) is from *1984;* (D) is from *The Old Man and the Sea;* and (F) is from *Peter Pan.*

The test could also offer a description of the work or a sample passage and ask the test taker to determine the name of the novel based on that information. Try the next example.

Read the following passage and identify the work from which it is derived.

> And therewithal he muste his leve take,
> And caste his eye upon hir pitously,
> And neer he rood, his cause for to make,
> To take hir by the honed al sobrely.
> And lord, so he gan weepen tendrely,
> And he ful softe and sleighly gan hir seve,
> "Now holde your day, and do me not to deye."

- ○ *Beowulf*
- ○ *Troilus and Cressida*
- ○ *Romeo and Juliet*
- ○ *Duchess of Malfi*

Here's How to Crack It

You can use Process of Elimination (POE) to determine the correct answer on identification problems. Figure out what is wrong with other answers until only the correct one is left. Use both the language and the subject.

Read the passage. The first thing you will note is that the language in the passage is not contemporary. Mark anything else that is immediately clear to you, such as the subject of the work. Then quickly go to the answers.

Choice (A) is *Beowulf.* The language of *Beowulf* is Old English, and you may not see the distinction between Old English and Middle English immediately. The subject in *Beowulf* is the killing of Grendel. While the passage also seems to be written in verse, it is not concerned with battle but with love. Eliminate (A). Choice (C) is *Romeo and Juliet,* which is a verse drama about love. The passage concerns two people who seem to be expressing emotion. However, the language is different; it is closer to contemporary English. Eliminate (C). Choice (D) is a head scratcher. *Duchess of Malfi* may not be a play you have heard of or read. However, the word "Duchess" is written in contemporary English. Keep the answer as a weak "maybe" and move to (B).

The language in the passage is not contemporary. If you have read *The Canterbury Tales,* you may have identified a similar style of spelling and turn of phrase. This passage is indeed written by the same author—Geoffrey Chaucer. While you may not have read *Troilus and Cressida,* you may have heard that the work concerns two star-crossed lovers. The language, though difficult to read, does show that the male is crying "he gan weepen tendrely" and mentions dying "do me not to deye" to a "hir" (her). "And lord, so he gan weepen tendrely" has a similar cadence and writing style to the line "And smalle fowles maken melody" from Chaucer's *Canterbury Tales.* The answer is (B).

The test writers want to be sure they select a passage that shows the subject of the whole, or a tell-tale symbol that people who have read the work can easily identify. Test writers must be able to explain why an answer is absolutely right and may be determined from the information given. Pick your answer accordingly.

What You Need to Know: Types of Fiction, Poetry, Drama, and Nonfiction

You should be familiar with the following genres and forms.

Fiction Genres

- Allegory
- Anecdote
- Bildungsroman
- Dystopian fiction
- Epistolary fiction
- Fable
- Fairy tale
- Folk tale
- Frame tale
- Historical fiction
- Horror
- Legend
- Literary fiction
- Mystery
- Myth
- Novel
- Parable
- Roman à clef
- Satire
- Science fiction
- Short story

Poetic Forms

- Ballad
- Cinquain
- Concrete poem
- Elegy
- Epic
- Epigram
- Found poem
- Free verse
- Haiku
- Limerick
- Lyric
- Palindrome
- Pantoum
- Pastoral poem
- Sonnet
- Villanelle

Dramatic Forms

- Comedy
- Farce
- Greek tragedy
- Romantic comedy
- Shakespearean tragedy
- Tragedy

Sample Literary Form Identification Questions

The following is an example of a type of question you may see asking you to identify a literary form, based on a passage.

Read the poem and identify its poetic form.

> I met a traveller from an antique land,
> Who said—"Two vast and trunkless legs of stone
> Stand in the desert. . . . Near them, on the sand,
> Half sunk a shattered visage lies, whose frown,
> And wrinkled lip, and sneer of cold command,
> Tell that its sculptor well those passions read
> Which yet survive, stamped on these lifeless things,
> The hand that mocked them, and the heart that fed;
> And on the pedestal, these words appear:
> My name is Ozymandias, King of Kings;
> Look on my Works, ye Mighty, and despair!
> Nothing beside remains. Round the decay
> Of that colossal Wreck, boundless and bare
> The lone and level sands stretch far away."

Percy Blysse Shelley, "Ozymandias"

The poem is written in which of the following poetic forms?

○ Sonnet

○ Villanelle

○ Ballad

○ Elegy

Here's How to Crack It

Process of Elimination (POE) can help you with this question. After you have read or skimmed the poem, review the answer choices. What do you know?

Look at (A). You may remember that a *sonnet* often has 14 lines and vary in rhyme schemes. The poem does have 14 lines but uses an atypical rhyme scheme (ababa cdcedefef). Keep (A) for now and review the other answer choices. You may not know the definition of *villanelle,* so keep (B) and go back later. A *ballad* is more about nature or love. Eliminate (C). An *elegy* is written when someone dies. And though the poem contains references to a "wreck" and "despair," it is not exclusively about one person or death. Remember that the correct answer must be absolutely, provably correct. Eliminate (D). Now you are down to (A) and (B). You do not know the term villanelle, (B). However, you do know the test makers must justify their choices. A sonnet is generally 14 lines, regardless of the unusual rhyme scheme. Since you can logically argue that choice, you should choose (A) as the correct answer—and it is.

What You Need to Know: Literary and Informational Text Terms

You should be familiar with the following literary terms and rhetorical modes, as well as the terms related to informational texts.

Figurative Language

- Alliteration
- Allusion
- Analogy
- Cliché
- Dialect
- Diction
- Euphemism
- Euphony
- Foreshadowing
- Hyperbole
- Imagery
- Metaphor
- Onomatopoeia
- Oxymoron
- Paradox
- Personification
- Simile
- Slang
- Symbolism
- Verbal irony

Literary Elements

- Action
  - Falling
  - Rising
- Character
  - Antagonist
  - Anti-hero
  - Dynamic
  - Flat
  - Foil
  - Hero
  - Ingenue
  - Narrator
  - Protagonist
  - Round
  - Static
  - Stock
- Characterization
- Climax
- Denouement
- Figurative meaning
- Literal meaning
- Mood
- Plot
- Point of view
  - First
  - Second
  - Third
  - Third omniscient
- Realism
- Setting
- Theme
- Tone
- Tragic flaw
- Voice

Poetry Terms

- Assonance
- Blank verse
- Closed form
- Consonance
- Couplet
- Free verse
- Iamb
- Iambic pentameter
- Internal rhyme
- Meter
- Open form
- Quatrain
- Repetition
- Rhyme scheme
- Rhythm
- Slant rhyme
- Spondee
- Stanza
- Trochee
- Verse

Drama Terms

- Act
- Chorus
- Drama dialogue
- Monologue
- Scene
- Soliloquy
- Stage directions

Informational Text Terms

- Advertisement
- Argument
- Chart
- Claim
- Critical thinking
- Fact
- Graph
- Inference
- Logical fallacy
  - Ad hominem
  - Bandwagon
  - Hasty generalization
  - Red herring
  - Scapegoating
  - Slippery slope
  - Straw man
- Organization
  - Cause-effect order
  - Chronological order
  - Order of importance
  - Problem-solution order
  - Sequential order
- Purpose
  - Entertain
  - Inform
  - Persuade
- Rhetoric
- Rhetorical appeals
  - Ethos
  - Logos
  - Pathos
- Rhetorical strategies
  - Hyperbole
  - Satire
  - Understatement
- Technical language
- Testimonial
- Text features
  - Footnotes
  - Glossary
  - Headings
  - Index
  - Visual aid

Here's an example of a question you might see that tests your knowledge of literary and informational text terms. This one is about **fallacies.**

Identify the fallacious reasoning in the following text.

"Drivers who routinely do not wear seatbelts are more prone to have automobile accidents than drivers who do. If people do not take the quick, preventative measure to protect themselves by putting on a seatbelt, they may fail to take other precautions when driving, such as stopping at a red light."

○ Red herring

○ Straw man

○ Slippery slope

○ Bandwagon

Here's How to Crack It

The answer is (C), *slippery slope*. A slippery slope argument is one that means if you do one small evil, you are more likely to do even greater crimes. A *red herring*, (A), is something that misleads or detracts from the main issue. A *straw man*, (B), sets up and then refutes another argument, but this new argument does not prove the original issue. In a *bandwagon* fallacy, (D), the majority opinion is always correct.

What You Need to Know: Teaching Strategies and Literary Theories

Finally, you should have an understanding of each of the following pedagogical strategies, practices, and theories as they relate to the teaching of literature.

Student Reading Strategies

- Active reading
- Annotating
- Constructing meaning
- Finding textual evidence
- Making inferences
- Making predictions

- Metacognition
- Previewing
- Reflection
- Setting a purpose
- Summarization
- Synthesizing

Teaching Strategies

- Metacognitive practice
- Modeling
- Pre-reading strategies
- Questioning strategies
- Spiraling
- Targeted review

Literary Theories

- Deconstructionist theory
- Feminist theory
- Formalism
- Marxist theory
- New criticism
- Queer theory
- Reader-response theory
- Structuralism

Language Use and Vocabulary

Language Use and Vocabulary questions test your knowledge of standard English and vocabulary development. They also test your knowledge of reference materials and ways of supporting diverse students' language skills.

What You Need to Know: Grammar and Syntax

You may see questions related to the following parts of speech and syntax, so be sure to study each of these terms. You may want to create flash cards with the term on the front, and the definition and an example on the back.

**Test Category #2:
Language Use and
Vocabulary**

Parts of Speech

- Adjectives
- Adverbs
- Conjunctions
- Interjections
- Nouns
- Prepositions
- Pronouns
  - Demonstrative
  - Indefinite
  - Intensive
  - Interrogative
  - Personal
  - Possessive
  - Reflexive
  - Relative
- Verbs
  - Helping
  - Imperative
  - Indicative
  - Linking
  - Subjunctive

Syntax

- Clauses
  - Adjective clause
  - Adverb clause
  - Dependent clause
  - Independent clause
  - Noun clause
- Phrases
  - Absolute phrase
  - Appositive phrase
  - Gerund phrase
  - Infinitive phrase
  - Noun phrase
  - Participial phrase
  - Prepositional phrase
  - Verb phrase
- Sentence structure
  - Complex sentence
  - Compound sentence
  - Compound-complex sentence
  - Simple sentence

Here's an example of a question on sentence structure.

> *The tall, proud girl won the race, but she would not accept the trophy.*
>
> The sentence above can best be classified as
>
> ○ complex
>
> ○ compound
>
> ○ compound-complex
>
> ○ simple

Choice (B) is correct. A compound sentence joins two full independent clauses. A complex sentence, (A), joins an independent clause with a dependent or subordinate clause. A compound-complex sentence, (C), joins a compound sentence with a subordinate or dependent clause. Note that *tall* and *proud* are adjectives that modify the main subject of the sentence (*girl*); these words do not create a full clause. A simple sentence, (D), has only one independent clause.

What You Need to Know: Punctuation, Usage, and Common Errors

Know how to use the following punctuation correctly. Pay special attention to the correct uses of the comma.

> ### Punctuation
>
> - Apostrophe
> - Brackets
> - Comma
> - Ellipses
> - Em dash
> - En dash
> - Parentheses
> - Terminal punctuation
> - Colon
> - Exclamation point
> - Period
> - Question mark
> - Semicolon

Look at the next example question on punctuation.

Identify the punctuation marks needed in the following sentence.

Violets short story The Wolves in Winter contained the following vocabulary words perspicacious, illuminating and itinerant.

○ Violet's short story "The Wolves in Winter" contained the following vocabulary words: perspicacious, illuminating and itinerant.

○ Violets short story, "The Wolves in Winter", contained the following vocabulary words: perspicacious, illuminating and itinerant.

○ Violet's short story, "The Wolves in Winter," contained the following vocabulary words: perspicacious, illuminating, and itinerant.

○ Violets short story The Wolves in Winter contained the following vocabulary words perspicacious, illuminating, and itinerant.

Here's How to Crack It

You can start by using Process of Elimination. You know that Violet owns the story, so you will need an apostrophe between *Violet* and *s*. Eliminate (B) and (D).

Then look for similarities and differences between the two remaining answers. Both use the colon after *words*, so the use of the colon is correct. Choice (A) does not have a comma after *story* or one after *Winter*"—(C) uses a comma after both. If you are uncertain which is correct based on that knowledge, look at the differences in the list of vocabulary words. Choice (A) does not have a comma after *illuminating*, but (C) does. It is correct to use the final comma in a list. Choice (C) is correct.

You should also be familiar with a handful of usage conventions and common errors.

Usage Conventions

- Active voice
- Parallelism
- Passive voice
- Pronoun-antecedent agreement
- Subject-verb agreement

- Verb tense
- Future
- Past
- Perfect
- Present
- Progressive

Common Word Errors

- Affect, effect
- Allusion, illusion
- Among, between
- Elicit, illicit
- Fewer, less
- Good, well

- Its, it's
- Principal, principle
- Reason, why
- To lie, to lay
- Who, whom

Common Grammatical Errors

- Adjective/adverb confusion
- Agreement errors
- Comma splice
- Faulty parallelism

- Inconsistent verb tense
- Misplaced modifier
- Sentence fragments
- Sentence run-ons
- Split infinitive

Try the next question on common errors.

Place a mark in the column next to each sentence that accurately names the type of error contained in the sentence.

For each sentence, select one error.

Sentence	Comma Splice	Faulty Parallelism	Misplaced Modifier	Subject-Verb Agreement
Running down the street, a brick fell on my head.				
The dog ate his food in large gulps, he was tired and hungry.				
The faculty go out together on Friday evenings.				
Sarah enjoyed playing with her brother, singing in the choir, and also to go shopping.				

For the first sentence, you should have selected *misplaced modifier*. The second sentence contains a *comma splice*. The problem in the third sentence is *subject-verb agreement*. And the fourth sentence contains *faulty parallelism*.

What You Need to Know: Vocabulary

To prepare for the vocabulary section, we recommend learning common affixes (prefixes and suffixes) in order to determine the meaning of a word. The following is a non-exhaustive list of common word roots.

- *a* (without)
  Examples: amoral, atheist, atypical, apathy, anomaly

- *ab / abs* (off, away from, apart, down)
  Examples: abduct, abolish, abnormal, abdicate, abstinent, abscond

- *ac / acr* (sharp, bitter)
  Examples: acid, acute, acerbic, acrid

- *ag* (to drive, to force, to lead)
  Examples: agent, agile, agitate

- *ad / al* (to, toward, near)
  Examples: adapt, adjacent, addict, admire, adhere, adjoin, advocate, allure, alloy

This is an abridged word root list. Check out the longer list in your Student Tools!

- *al / ali / alter* (other, another)
  Examples: alternative, alias, alibi, alien, alter ego

- *am* (love)
  Examples: amorous, enamored, amity, paramour, amiable, amicable

- *amb* (to go, to walk)
  Examples: ambitious, amble, ambulance, ambulatory

- *amb / amph* (around; both, more than)
  Examples: amphitheater, ambience, ambivalent, ambidextrous

- *anim* (life, mind, soul, spirit)
  Examples: animosity, equanimity, magnanimous

- *annu / enni* (year)
  Examples: annual, anniversary, centennial, annuity, perennial, millennium

- *ante* (before)
  Examples: anterior, antecedent, antebellum, antediluvian

- *apt / ept* (skill, ability)
  Examples: adapt, aptitude, apt, inept

- *bel / bell* (war)
  Examples: rebel, belligerent, antebellum

- *ben / bon* (good)
  Examples: benefit, beneficiary, beneficent, bonus, bona fide

- *card / cord / cour* (heart)
  Examples: cardiac, courage, concord, accord, cordial

- *chron* (time)
  Examples: synchronize, chronicle, anachronism

- *cis* (to cut)
  Examples: scissors, incision, concise

- *cre / cresc / cret* (to grow)
  Examples: creation, increase, crescendo

- *dem* (people)
  Examples: democracy, epidemic, demographics

- *dic / dict / dit* (to say, to tell, to use words)
  Examples: dictionary, predict, edict, diction

- *doc / dac* (to teach)
  Examples: doctrine, indoctrinate, docile, didactic

- *dur* (hard)
  Examples: endure, durable, obdurate

- *equ* (equal, even)
  Examples: equation, equivalent, equity, equivocal

- *eu* (good, well)
  Examples: euphoria, euphemism, eulogy, euphony

- *fid* (faith, trust)
  Examples: confide, diffident, perfidy

- *flu, flux* (to flow)
  Examples: fluid, influence, fluent, influx, effluence

- *gen* (birth, creation, kind)
  Examples: generous, generate, engender, progeny)

- *greg* (herd)
  Examples: congregation, aggregation, gregarious

- *hyper* (over, excessive)
  Examples: hyperactive, hyperbole

- *im / in* (not, without)
  Examples: inactive, indifferent, impartial

- *inter* (between, among)
  Examples: interstate, interloper, intervene

- *join / junct* (to meet, to join)
  Examples: junction, adjoin, rejoinder

- *jur* (to swear)
  Examples: jury, perjury, abjure

- *loc / log / loqu* (word, speech)
  Examples: dialogue, eloquent, elocution, colloquial

- *luc / lum / lus* (light)
  Examples: illuminate, luminescent, lucid, lackluster

- *mag / maj / max* (big)
  Examples: magnify, major, maximum, majestic

- *mal / male* (bad, ill, evil, wrong)
  Examples: malodorous, malign, malignant, malediction

- *min* (small)
  Examples: minute, miniature, diminish

- *mor / mort* (death)
  Examples: immortal, morbid, morgue

- *nat / nas / nai* (to be born)
  Examples: natural, native, cognate, nascent

- *nom / nym / noun / nown* (name)
  Examples: synonym, pseudonym, nomenclature, misnomer

- *ob / oc / of / op* (toward, to, against, completely, over)
  Examples: object, obstruct, obscure, obfuscate

- *omni* (all)
  Examples: omnipresent, omniscient, omnipotent

- *pac / peace* (peace)
  Examples: appease, pacify, pact

- *pan* (all, everywhere)
  Examples: panorama, pantheon, pandemic

- *para* (next to, beside)
  Examples: paraphrase, parallel, parable

- *ped / pod* (foot)
  Examples: pedal, pedestrian, podiatrist

- *que / quis* (to seek)
  Examples: acquire, conquest, inquisitive

- *rog* (to ask)
  Examples: interrogate, prerogative, arrogate

- *sanct / sacr / secr* (sacred)
  Examples: sacred, sanctify, sacrament

- *sci* (to know)
  Examples: science, conscious, omniscient

- *scribe / scrip* (to write)
  Examples: describe, ascribe, manuscript, circumscribe

- *sens / sent* (to feel, to be aware)
  Examples: sense, sensory, sentiment, dissent

- *spec* (to look, see)
  Examples: perspective, circumspect, perspicacious

- *sub / sup* (below)
  Examples: submissive, subjugate, subversive, suppress

- *tain / ten / tent / tin* (to hold)
  Examples: contain, detain, abstention, tenure, pertinent

- *trans* (across)
  Examples: transfer, transaction, transcendent, transient

- *us / ut* (to use)
  Examples: abuse, usage, utensil, utility

- *ver* (truth)
  Examples: verdict, verify, aver

- *vi* (life)
  Examples: vivid, vicarious, viable

- *vid / vis* (to see)
  Examples: evident, visage, survey

What You Need to Know: Resources and Teaching Diverse Learners

Know when you should use each of the following resources.

Resources

- Acting
- Dictionary
- Glossary
- Spell checker
- Style manual
- Thesaurus

Teaching Diverse Learners

- Content area standards
- Content objectives
- Differentiation
- Discipline based inquiry
- Language diversification
- Language objectives
- Regional and social dialects
- Scaffolding
- Sociolinguistics

Teaching Strategies

- Activating prior knowledge
  - Asking what students know before content introduction
  - Brainstorm
  - Use of vocabulary before content
  - Use of visual aids such as outlines and diagrams
- Cognitive strategies
  - Comprehension
  - Problem solving
  - Reasoning
  - Self monitoring
  - Writing
- Metacognitive strategies
  - Debrief
  - Identifying what is known
  - Journal
  - Plan
  - Self-evaluation

Try the following example.

> Which of the following learning strategies will help students make connection to what they already know?
>
> ○ Organizing
>
> ○ Reasoning
>
> ○ Brainstorming
>
> ○ Problem solving

The correct answer is (C). When students brainstorm, they make connections to what they already know about the subject.

❸

Test Category #3: Writing, Speaking, and Listening

Writing, Speaking, and Listening

Writing, Speaking, and Listening questions ask you to understand modes of writing, identify best research practices, and understand the components of effective oral presentations. In the Reading section, you should also review Nonfiction Genres and Informational Text Terms.

What You Need to Know: Writing

Modes of Writing

- Argumentative
- Explanatory
- Informative
- Narrative

Writing Process

- Prewriting
  - Planning
  - Outlining
- Drafting
- Revising
- Editing and proofreading
- Publishing

Here's an example of a writing question you might see.

Which of the following correctly identifies the sequence of stages in the writing process?

○ Prewriting, drafting, editing, revising, publishing

○ Drafting, writing, publishing, revising, proofreading

○ Prewriting, drafting, revising, editing, publishing

○ Drafting, revising, editing, proofreading, publishing

The answer is (C). The process of writing is: prewriting, drafting, revising, editing, and publishing.

You should also understand and be able to identify the following concepts related to coherent writing, organizational patterns, ethical research, and assessments.

Coherent Writing

- Details and examples that develop a main idea
- Varied and effective transitions
- Clear organization with an introduction, body paragraphs, and a conclusion

Organizational Patterns

- Cause and effect
- Chronological order
- Compare and contrast
- Problem and solution
- Spatial sequence

Ethical Research

- Citation
- Credibility
- Paraphrase
- Source material
  - Common knowledge
  - Plagiarism
  - Source integration
- Summary

Assessments

- Anecdotal record
- Formative assessment
- Holistic scoring
- Observation
- Peer review
- Portfolio assessment
- Rubric
- Running record
- Summative assessment

Here's an example of a question on assessments.

> A student writes a story. Two classmates read the story and make notes on the structure and word usage. Each lists positive aspects of the story, as well as changes the student could make to improve the writing. This process describes what kind of assessment?
>
> ○ Observation
>
> ○ Portfolio assessment
>
> ○ Anecdotal record
>
> ○ Peer review

Did you get the answer? You should have chosen (D). In a peer review, students review each other's work.

What You Need to Know: Speaking and Listening

Finally, for the Speaking and Listening questions, you should be familiar with the following oral communication modes and techniques for presentations.

Oral Communication Modes

- Debate
- Discussion
  - ○ One-on-one
  - ○ Small group
  - ○ Think-pair-share
  - ○ Whole class
- Socratic seminar
- Speech

Presentation Techniques

- Articulation
- Body language
- Clearly written prose
- Concision
- Eye contact
- Imagery
- Organization
- Pauses
- Speed
- Tone
- Visual aids
- Volume

Take a look at the following example question on speech delivery.

> A student is delivering a speech. Those at the back of the classroom cannot hear what the student is saying. Which of the following suggestions would best immediately address the speaker's problem?
>
> Choose **all** that apply.
>
> ☐ Raising vocal volume
>
> ☐ Enunciating clearly
>
> ☐ Using visual aids
>
> ☐ Using imagery
>
> ☐ Quickening speed
>
> ☐ Reorganizing the speech

You should have checked off *raising vocal volume* and *enunciating clearly*.

We covered a lot of content in this chapter. To test your knowledge, try the drill on the next page. Answers and explanations are provided at the end of the chapter.

ENGLISH LANGUAGE ARTS DRILL

Answers and explanations can be found at the end of the chapter.

With which literary school or movement is Ralph Waldo Emerson associated?

○ American Colonialism

○ British Romanticism

○ Transcendentalism

○ Bloomsbury Group

Which of the following is a compound-complex sentence?

○ In the morning, she rose quickly and ate breakfast.

○ The dog barked joyfully when he saw his family.

○ He won the contest, and everyone congratulated him because he had worked so hard.

○ We will drive to meet our friends, and then we will go to the fair.

Of the following, which is NOT an organizational structure for the body content of a nonfiction work?

○ Spatial sequence

○ Chronological order

○ Cause and effect

○ Introduction and conclusion

The following excerpt from a Samuel Coleridge poem is an example of which form of poetry?

Sir, I admit your general rule,
That every poet is a fool,
But you yourself may serve to show it,
That every fool is not a poet.

○ Epigram

○ Limerick

○ Elegy

○ Ballad

Match the following rhetorical appeals to the correct examples.

Pathos _____

Logos _____

Ethos _____

I. "Dr. Jones said most people who smoke will get cancer."

II. "You owe your family for what they have given you."

III. "This graph shows that college graduates earn more."

Identify the work from the following description.

"In this novel, told from the perspective of a child, a lawyer defends an innocent man against racism and injustice. Throughout the course of the book, the child receives a moral education."

○ Charles Dickens's *Great Expectations*

○ Ayn Rand's *Anthem*

○ John Steinbeck's *Of Mice and Men*

○ Harper Lee's *To Kill a Mockingbird*

Which part of the action describes the completion of a story?

- ○ Rising action
- ○ Climax
- ○ Denouement
- ○ Exposition

Which of the following statements include common knowledge that does NOT need documentation in a research paper?

Select **all** that apply.

- ☐ Herbert Hoover served as president of the United States from 1929 to 1931.
- ☐ On April 1, 2012, the Longview police department apprehended more than 20 college students during a raid.
- ☐ In one study, 42 out of 60 participants chose the red button rather than the blue one.
- ☐ Marlon Brando starred in the movie *The Godfather*.

In which of the following would you find persuasive writing?

Select **all** that apply.

- ☐ A letter to a congressman to ask for a change
- ☐ A cover letter for a job
- ☐ An advertisement for a product
- ☐ A historical textbook

Questions 10–12 are based on the following poem.

A noiseless patient spider,
I mark'd where on a little promontory it stood
  isolated,
Mark'd how to explore the vacant vast surrounding,
It launch'd forth filament, filament, filament, out of
  itself,
Ever unreeling them, ever tirelessly speeding them.

And you O my soul where you stand,
Surrounded, detached, in measureless oceans of space,
Ceaselessly musing, venturing, throwing, seeking the
  spheres to connect them,
Till the bridge you will need be form'd, till the
  ductile anchor hold,
Till the gossamer thread you fling, catch somewhere,
  O my soul.

Identify the writer of this poem.

- ○ Henry David Thoreau
- ○ Walt Whitman
- ○ Sylvia Plath
- ○ Alfred Lord Tennyson

What is NOT a theme of the poem?

- ○ Isolation
- ○ Good versus evil
- ○ Spiritual exploration
- ○ The natural world

Match the lines or references with the figure of speech.

Line or Reference	Figure of Speech
"…it stood, isolated;… to explore the vacant, vast surrounding…ever unreeling them, ever tirelessly speeding them."	Alliteration
The spider	Repetition
"Vacant vast" / "seeking the spheres"	Personification
"It launched forth filament, filament, filament out of itself."	Metaphor

To create a safe classroom environment, how should a teacher respond to a student who provides incorrect information during a class presentation?

○ Quickly tell the student he or she was incorrect, and then call the next speaker.

○ Gently laugh at the student to provide levity, and then explain the correct answer.

○ Note the good and true aspects of the student's speech to show support of the student, and clarify the correct answer.

○ Ignore the error since identifying it would cause embarrassment.

Determine the correct word choice in the following statements.

Topics such as immigration **illicit** a strong response from both sides.	illicit
	elicit
If **fewer** people used electricity, there may be a reduction in global warming.	fewer
	less
Between the three of us, Billy is the best person to fix your computer.	Between
	Among

ENGLISH LANGUAGE ARTS DRILL ANSWERS AND EXPLANATIONS

1. **C** Emerson, along with Henry David Thoreau and Margaret Fuller, was part of the Transcendentalist Movement, so (C) is the correct answer.

2. **C** A compound sentence contains two independent clauses. Choices (C) and (D) both contain two independent clauses. A complex sentence contains at least one subordinate clause. Choices (A), (B), and (C) contain subordinate clauses. A compound-complex sentence combines both, and the only answer choice to meet the requirements for both is (C).

3. **D** The introduction and conclusion are parts of a nonfiction work but not the organizational pattern for the body. Choice (D) is correct.

4. **A** An *epigram*, (A), is a short, witty poem, often satirical, so (A) is the correct answer. A *limerick* is also funny but has five lines in the rhyme scheme AABBA. An *elegy* is a poem for someone who has passed away. A *haiku* is a short poem, often about nature, and traditionally has three lines, with 5-7-5 syllables.

5. **Pathos: II; Logos: III; Ethos: I**

   "You owe your family for what they have given you." Pathos persuades by evoking sentiment.

   "This graph shows that college graduates earn more." Logos persuades through the use of facts and figures.

   "Dr. Jones said that most people who smoke will get cancer." Ethos persuades by showing the information is from a credible source.

6. **D** The paragraph describes the plot and a major theme of *To Kill a Mockingbird*, so (D) is correct.

7. **C** The *denouement*, (C), comes after the *rising action*, (A), and *climax*, (B), and wraps up the rest of the story. The *exposition*, (D), is the information that one receives at the very beginning of the story, such as the setting and history of the characters. Choice (C) is therefore correct.

8. **A, D**

   Choices (A) and (D) are considered both facts and common knowledge and do not need a citation in a research paper. However, information from a police report, (B), should be cited, as well as a specific research study, (C).

9. **A, B, C**

   Choices (A), (B), and (C) are all examples of persuasive writing. A historical textbook may have articles of persuasive writing within it, but the main purpose of a historical textbook is to inform.

10. **B** "A Noiseless, Patient Spider" was written by Walt Whitman, so (B) is the answer.

11. **B** Good versus evil is not an obvious theme of "A Noiseless, Patient Spider," while isolation, spiritual exploration, and the natural world are more obvious themes of the poem. Choice (B) is correct.

12.

Line or Reference	Figure of Speech
"…it stood, isolated;…to explore the vacant, vast surrounding…ever unreeling them, ever tirelessly speeding them."	**Personification:** The spider is depicted as having the same emotions or needs as a human.
The spider	**Metaphor:** The spider's throwing out the line for his dinner is the metaphor or analogy for the soul of humans, reaching for a connection.
"Vacant vast" / "seeking the spheres"	**Alliteration:** Alliteration is the repetition of the initial consonants in two or more neighboring words.
"It launched forth filament, filament, filament out of itself."	**Repetition:** Repetition is repeating a word in order to emphasize its importance within a work.

13. **C** The correct answer is (C). While (A) is not unkind, in a safe classroom, teachers should provide validation for the student if he or she is trying to contribute to the class in a positive way. Laughing at the student, (B), may isolate the student from the rest of the class. Ignoring the wrong answer, (D), may cause others to remember a statement that is incorrect and accept it as truth.

14.

Topics such as immigration **illicit** a strong response from both sides.	illicit
	✓ **elicit**
If **fewer** people used electricity, there may be a reduction in global warming.	✓ **fewer**
	less
Between the three of us, Billy is the best person to fix your computer.	Between
	✓ **Among**

Elicit is a verb that means to call forth or draw something out. *Illicit* is an adjective that means something is unlawful. When talking about reducing countable items, such as dollars, use *fewer dollars.* When talking about reducing part of a whole, use *less,* as in *less money.* Use *between* when talking about two people or groups. Use *among* when talking about three or more people or groups.

Chapter 21
Science

SCIENCE SUBJECT ASSESSMENTS

There are six subject tests that address the core sciences.

- Middle School Science (5440)
- General Science: Content Knowledge (5435)
- Biology: Content Knowledge (5235)
- Chemistry: Content Knowledge (5245)
- Earth and Space Sciences: Content Knowledge (5571)
- Physics: Content Knowledge (5265)

The scores required to pass each exam differ from state to state, so check your state's guidelines.

MIDDLE SCHOOL SCIENCE (5440)

Time: 2.5 hours

Format: 125 selected-response (multiple-choice) questions

Remember to check the ETS website for up-to-date calculator guidelines. Go to www.ets.org/praxis/test_day/policies/calculators/.

Calculators are not required. The test will contain a periodic table, various physical constants, and some conversion factors for SI units.

This test is recommended for a beginning teacher of Middle School Science. It tests concepts, terms, phenomena, methods, applications, data analysis, problem solving in science, as well as the impact of science and technology on the environment and human affairs as would be discussed in an introductory college-level course.

Topics	% of Test
Scientific Inquiry, Methodology, Techniques, and History	12%
Basic Principles of Matter and Energy	12%
Physical Sciences	22%
Life Sciences	24%
Earth and Space Sciences	18%
Science, Technology, and Society	12%

Scientific Inquiry, Methodology, Techniques, and History

- Methods of scientific inquiry and how they are used in basic problem solving
- Processes involved in scientific data collection and manipulation
- Interpreting and drawing conclusions from data presented in tables, graphs, and charts
- Procedures for safe and correct preparation, storage, use, and disposal of lab materials
- Safety and emergency procedures in the laboratory
- Using standard equipment in the laboratory
- Historical developments of science and the contribution of major historical figures

For official preparation materials associated with the specific test you are taking, go to www.ets.org/praxis/prepare/materials.

Basic Principles of Matter and Energy

- Structure and properties of matter
- Basic relationships between energy and matter
- Basic structure of the atom

Physical Sciences

- Physics
  - Mechanics
  - Electricity and magnetism
  - Basic waves and optics
- Chemistry
  - Using the periodic table to predict the physical and chemical properties of elements
  - Types of chemical bonding and the composition of simple chemical compounds
  - States of matter and phase changes between them
  - Balancing and using simple chemical equations
  - Basic concepts in acid-base chemistry
  - Solutions and solubility
  - Factors affecting the dissolving process and solubility of substances

Life Sciences

- Basic structure and function of cells and their organelles
- Basic cell reproduction
- Basic biochemistry of life
- Basic genetics
- The theory and key mechanisms of evolution

- Elements of the hierarchical classification scheme and the characteristics of the major groups of organisms
- Major structure and functions of plant organs and systems
- Basic anatomy and physiology of animals, including structure and function of human body systems and the major differences between humans and other animals
- Key aspects of ecology

Earth and Space Sciences

- Physical geology
- Historical geology
- Structure and processes of Earth's oceans and other bodies of water
- Basic meteorology and major factors that affect climate and seasons
- Astronomy

You are expected to have basic familiarity with subjects like physical geology, historical geology, and astronomy.

Science, Technology, and Society

- Impact of science and technology on the environment and society
- Major issues associated with energy production and the management of natural resources
- Applications of science and technology in daily life (basic familiarity)
- Impact of science on public-health issues (basic familiarity)

Middle School Science Practice Questions

A water-based solution is labeled as having a pH of 10. This is because it likely contains a large number of:

○ OH^- ions

○ H^+ ions

○ NaCl molecules

○ H_2O molecules

Here's How to Crack It

This question addresses pH, one of the key concepts of chemistry. It requires the combined knowledge of the definition of the pH scale as well as an understanding of the chemical notation of hydroxide (OH^-) and hydrogen (H^+) ions as well as sodium chloride (NaCl) and water (H_2O).

The pH scale (0–14) is measured in hydrogen ions, with the lower pHs having higher amounts of hydrogen ions. By knowing this, (C) and (D) can be eliminated. Choice (B) is a tempting choice because pH is measured in hydrogen ions; however, a pH of 10 is a high pH, which represents low numbers of hydrogen ions. A basic solution would likely have high numbers of hydroxide ions because hydroxide is a strong base and would have reduced the number of hydrogen ions in the solution, thus raising the pH. Note that (D) may also be a tempting choice because a water-based solution would have lots of water molecules, but the question is asking about the cause of a pH of 10.

Which of the following best describes a solar eclipse?

○ Earth between a new moon and the sun

○ The sun between Earth and a full moon

○ The new moon between Earth and the sun

○ The full moon between the sun and Earth

Here's How to Crack It

This question addresses a basic tenet of astronomy, the positioning of the earth, the moon, and the sun. A solar eclipse is an event that causes a shadow to pass across the sun as viewed from Earth due to the moon passing in between them. Choices (C) and (D) both list the moon in between Earth and the sun. However, (C) correctly lists the new moon phase, which occurs when the moon is backlit because it is on the side of Earth that is facing the sun, so it is the correct answer.

Now try your hand at the following drill. Answers and explanations can be found at the end of the chapter.

MIDDLE SCHOOL SCIENCE DRILL

Answers and explanations can be found at the end of the chapter.

Three dishes of bacteria are grown in three different incubators, each with a different temperature: 25°C, 32°C, and 37°C. Every day for one week the number of colonies of bacteria is counted in each dish, and after one week the totals are 12, 59, and 72 respectively. Which of the following is the independent variable in this experiment?

○ The types of bacteria

○ The temperatures

○ The colony numbers

○ The length of the experiment

Which of the following is the trophic level with the largest amount of biomass?

○ Producers

○ Primary consumers

○ Secondary consumers

○ Decomposers

In the graph below, which distance represents half the amplitude?

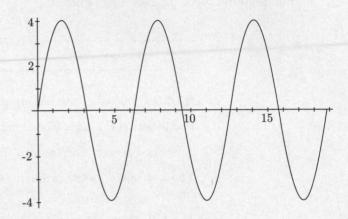

○ 2

○ 4

○ 7

○ 8

Which coefficient on NaOH would properly balance this chemical equation?

$$NaOH + H_2SO_4 \rightarrow Na_2SO_4 + 2H_2O$$

○ 2

○ 3

○ 4

○ None required

Cellular respiration occurs to produce ATP. Which of the following is a reactant in cellular respiration?

○ Water

○ ATP

○ Glucose

○ Sunlight

GENERAL SCIENCE: CONTENT KNOWLEDGE (5435)

Time: 2.5 hours

Format: 135 selected-response questions

This test is recommended for a beginning teacher of secondary science. It uses content knowledge from across the scientific disciplines to test concepts, terms, phenomena, methods, applications, data analysis, and problem solving in science and the impact of science and technology on the environment and human affairs as would be discussed in an introductory college-level course.

Topics	% of Test
Scientific Methodology, Techniques, and History	11%
Physical Science	38%
Life Science	20%
Earth and Space Science	20%
Science, Technology, and Society	11%

Scientific Methodology, Techniques, and History
- Methods of scientific inquiry and design
- Processes involved in scientific data collection and manipulation
- Interpreting and drawing conclusions from data presented in tables, graphs, maps, and charts
- Procedures for correct preparation, storage, use, and disposal of laboratory materials
- Using standard equipment in the laboratory and the field
- Safety and emergency procedures in the laboratory
- Major historical developments of science

Physical Science
- Basic Principles
  - Structure of matter
  - Basic structure of the atom
  - Basic characteristics of radioactive materials
  - Basic concepts and relationships involving energy and matter
- Chemistry
  - Periodicity and states of matter
  - Chemical nomenclature, composition, and bonding
  - Chemical reactions

- Acid-base chemistry
- Solutions and solubility
- Physics
  - Mechanics
  - Electricity and magnetism
  - Optics and waves

Life Science
- Basic structure and function of cells and their organelles
- Key aspects of cell reproduction and division
- Basic biochemistry of life
- Basic genetics
- Theory and key mechanisms of evolution
- Hierarchical classification scheme
- Major structure of plants and their functions
- Basic anatomy and physiology of animals, including the human body
- Key aspects of ecology

Earth and Space Science
- Physical geology
- Historical geology
- Earth's bodies of water
- Meteorology and climate
- Astronomy

Science, Technology, and Society
- Impact of science and technology on the environment and society
- Major issues associated with energy production and the management of natural resources
- Applications of science and technology in daily life
- Impact of science on public health issues

General Science Practice Questions

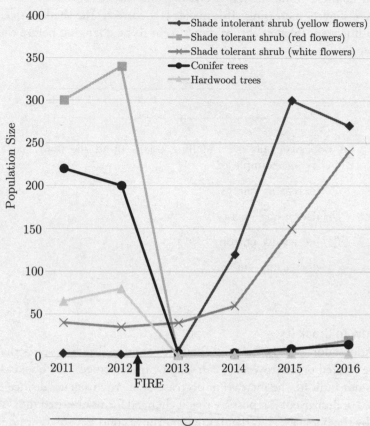

Populations of Species Over Time

Shade intolerant shrub (yellow flowers)
Shade tolerant shrub (red flowers)
Shade tolerant shrub (white flowers)
Conifer trees
Hardwood trees

Population Size

400
350
300
250
200
150
100
50
0

2011 2012 2013 2014 2015 2016

FIRE

If the fire never occurred, which prediction about the population in 2016 is the most supported by the data?

○ The white-flowered, shade-tolerant shrubs would disappear from the region.

○ The number of shade-intolerant shrubs would increase, and the conifers would disappear.

○ Conifers would claim the territory of all colors of the shade-tolerant shrubs.

○ The red-flowered, shade-tolerant shrubs would increase in number, and conifers would decrease.

Here's How to Crack It

This is a question that requires the use of the data trends. The trends occurring before the fire should be assumed to continue since we have no other information to go on. The conifers' numbers were decreasing and the red-flowered, shade-tolerant shrubs were slightly increasing. This makes (D) correct. The shade-intolerant and the white-flowered, tolerant shrubs didn't seem to be changing before the fire, so (A), (B), and (C) are incorrect.

A bookcase falls over, spilling books upon the floor. This is an example of

○ increasing energy

○ decreasing energy

○ increasing entropy

○ decreasing entropy

Here's How to Crack It

This question addresses the Laws of Thermodynamics. The first states that energy cannot be created or destroyed but can only be transformed. The bookcase falling over does not indicate the increase or decrease of energy in general since energy is not created or destroyed. It is possible that it changed forms or exited the system represented by the bookcase, but that is unclear. The Second Law of Thermodynamics states that things are constantly moving toward a state of increasing entropy or disorder. The bookcase falling over would represent increasing disorder and increasing entropy. Choice (C) is correct.

Now it's drill time! Answers and explanations can be found at the end of the chapter.

GENERAL SCIENCE DRILL

Answers and explanations can be found at the end of the chapter.

A sealed flask filled with gas at room temperature is connected to a syringe with a plunger that can move in accordance with the volume of the gas. As the flask is placed into a beaker of ice water, what happens?

○ The plunger indicates a larger volume.

○ The plunger indicates a smaller volume.

○ The plunger begins to oscillate positions.

○ The plunger remains in the same position.

Which of the following techniques directly assists couples with having a child?

○ Gel electrophoresis

○ Polymerase chain reaction

○ Chemotherapy

○ In vitro fertilization

In order for satellites to perpetually orbit Earth, the tangential force of travel away from Earth must be

○ greater than the force of Earth's gravity

○ parallel to Earth's gravitational force

○ approximately equal to the force of Earth's gravity

○ opposite of Earth's gravitational force

A population of peppered moths exists in two colors, black and white. In 1,000 years, it is discovered that the alleles remain at the same frequencies. What best explains this phenomenon?

○ There is no selective pressure acting on moth color.

○ Neither allele is a recessive trait.

○ The peppered moth is a new species.

○ The moths are colorblind and cannot tell what color they are.

Which layer of the atmosphere has the hottest temperature?

○ Troposphere

○ Stratosphere

○ Mesosphere

○ Thermosphere

Remember to check the ETS website for up-to-date calculator guidelines. Go to www.ets.org/ praxis/test_day/policies/ calculators/.

BIOLOGY: CONTENT KNOWLEDGE (5235)

Time: 2.5 hours

Format: 150 selected-response questions

This test is recommended for a beginning teacher of secondary-school biology. It tests concepts, terms, phenomena, methods, applications, data analysis, and problem solving in biology and the impact of science and technology on the environment and human affairs as would be discussed in an introductory college-level course.

Topics	% of Test
History and Nature of Science	14%
Molecular and Cellular Biology	20%
Genetics and Evolution	20%
Diversity and Life and Organismal Biology	20%
Ecology: Organisms and Environments	16%
Science, Technology, and Social Perspectives	10%

History and Nature of Science
- Processes involved in scientific inquiry
- How science is related to other disciplines
- Differences among facts, hypotheses, theories, and laws
- How scientific ideas change over time; contributions made by major historical figures
- Appropriate use of scientific measurement and notation systems
- Reading and interpreting data represented in tables, graphs, and charts
- Constructing and using scientific models to explain complex phenomena
- Procedures involved in the safe preparation, storage, use, and disposal of laboratory and field materials
- Appropriate and safe use and care of laboratory equipment
- Safety and emergency procedures for science classrooms and laboratories

Molecular and Cellular Biology

- Chemical structures and properties of biologically important molecules
- Dependence of biological processes on chemical properties
- Structure and function of enzymes and factors influencing their activity
- Biochemical pathways and energy flow within an organism
- Major differences between prokaryotes and eukaryotes
- Structure and function of cells and organelles
- How cells maintain their internal environment and respond to external signals
- Cellular division, the cell cycle, and how they are regulated
- Structure and function of nucleic acids
- Processes involved in protein synthesis
- Regulation of gene expression
- Differentiation and specialization of cells
- Nature of mutations
- Use of basic laboratory techniques to study biological processes
- Use and applications of DNA technologies and genetic engineering

Genetics and Evolution

- Mendel's laws and predicting the probable outcome of given genetic crosses
- Non-Mendelian inheritance
- Chromosomal and genetic changes that lead to common human genetic disorders
- Sources of genetic variation
- How mutations, gene flow, genetic drift, and nonrandom mating affect the gene pool of a population
- Principles and applications of Hardy-Weinberg Equilibrium
- Mechanisms of evolution
- Evidence that supports evolution
- Genetic basis of speciation
- Models of evolutionary rates
- Scientific explanations for the origin of life on Earth
- Factors that lead to extinction of species

Diversity of Life and Organismal Biology

- Characteristics of living versus nonliving things
- Historical and current biological classification systems of organisms
- Defining characteristics of viruses, bacteria, protists, fungi, plants, and animals
- Characteristics of the major animal phyla

- Organizational hierarchy of multicellular organisms
- Anatomy and physiology of major organ systems in animals
- Maintenance of homeostasis in organisms
- Reproduction, development, and growth in animals
- Characteristics of major plant divisions
- Structure and function of major plant tissues and organs
- Plant life cycles and reproductive strategies
- How plants obtain and transport water and inorganic nutrients
- How plants transport and store products of photosynthesis

Ecology: Organisms and Environments

- Hierarchical structure of the biosphere
- How biotic and abiotic components of an ecosystem influence population size
- Models of population growth
- Relationship between reproductive strategies and mortality rates
- Relationships within and between species
- Changes that occur during ecological succession
- Types and characteristics of biomes
- Energy flow in the environment
- Biogeochemical cycles
- Effects of natural disturbances on ecosystems
- How humans affect ecological systems and biodiversity
- Connections among ecosystems on a local and global scale

Science, Technology, and Social Perspectives

- Impact of science and technology on the environment
- Impact of human activity and natural phenomena on society
- Societal impacts associated with the management of natural resources
- Ethical and societal issues arising from the use of science and technology

Biology Practice Questions

Which of the following is an example of a frameshift mutation for this original sequence?

    AUGCTTTGACCCGAT

○ AUGAUGCTTTGACCCGAT

○ AUGCTTTGAGAT

○ AUGTTTTGACCCGAT

○ TTTGACCCGAT

Here's How to Crack It

A frameshift mutation is a mutation that disrupts the reading frame, which refers to the groups of three nucleotides that will be translated into amino acids. Any insertions and deletions that are not in multiples of three will disrupt the reading frame. Choice (A) adds 3 nucleotides, (B) removes 3 nucleotides, and (D) removes 3 nucleotides. Choice (C) adds a single nucleotide and disrupts the reading frame. The correct answer is (C).

A red blood cell is placed into a solution. Shortly after, the red blood cell is observed swelling and eventually bursting. What type of solution was it placed into?

○ Hypertonic

○ Hypotonic

○ Isotonic

○ Equitonic

Here's How to Crack It

This question puts together your knowledge of osmosis, key terms, and cell membrane permeability. If the cell bursts, it is from an influx of water. This would occur if the inside of the cell were more concentrated than the solution. This would make the solution hypotonic (less concentrated with solute) compared to the cell's interior. Choice (A) would cause the cell to lose water. Choice (C) would not cause noticeable water movement. Choice (D) is not a type of tonicity. Choice (B) is correct.

You guessed it—it's time for a drill. Try the following questions on your own. You can find answers and explanations at the end of the chapter.

BIOLOGY DRILL

Answers and explanations can be found at the end of the chapter.

Which of the following did NOT likely contribute to past mass extinction events on Earth?

○ Insufficient genetic diversity

○ Extreme climate change

○ Meteorite impact

○ Excessive predation

A scientist studies the storage and distribution of oxygen in humans and Weddell seals to examine the physiological adaptations that permit seals to descend to great depths and stay submerged for extended periods. The figure below depicts the oxygen storage in both organisms.

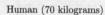

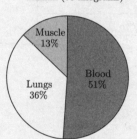

Human (70 kilograms)

Total oxygen store: 1.95 liters

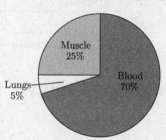

Weddell seal (450 kilograms)

Total oxygen store: 25.9 liters

What conclusion could the scientist make about the oxygen storage per kilogram of body weight?

○ The Weddell seal stores twelve times as much oxygen per kilogram of body weight.

○ The human stores seven times more oxygen per kilogram of body weight.

○ The Weddell seal stores about twice as much oxygen per kilogram of body weight.

○ The human and the Weddell seal store the same amount of oxygen per kilogram of body weight.

Which of the following describes the homeostatic state during high levels of insulin production?

○ Glycolysis activity is greatly reduced.

○ Body temperature is elevated above normal.

○ Glucose is actively being stored as glycogen.

○ There are low levels of citric acid production.

A population of fish within a small pond is monitored over many years, but never seems to go above a certain number. This number represents the pond's

○ total biomass

○ carrying capacity

○ highest trophic level

○ genetic equilibrium

A diploid organism with the genotype AaBbCCDd was identified. Assuming all genes are unlinked, how many genetically distinct gametes can be produced?

○ 4

○ 8

○ 16

○ 32

CHEMISTRY: CONTENT KNOWLEDGE (5245)

Time: 2.5 hours

Format: 125 selected-response questions

This test is recommended for a beginning teacher of secondary-school chemistry. It tests concepts, terms, phenomena, methods, applications, data analysis, and problem solving in chemistry and the impact of science and technology on the environment and human affairs as would be discussed in an introductory college-level course.

Topics	% of Test
Basic Principles of Matter and Energy; Thermodynamics	14%
Atomic and Nuclear Structure	12%
Nomenclature; Chemical Composition; Bonding and Structure	15%
Chemical Reactions; Periodicity	20%
Solutions and Solubility; Acid-Base Chemistry	15%
Scientific Inquiry and Social Perspectives of Science	12%
Scientific Procedures and Techniques	12%

Basic Principles of Matter and Energy; Thermodynamics

- Matter and energy
  - Organization of matter
  - Particulate structure of matter
  - Differences between chemical and physical properties and chemical and physical changes
  - Conservation of energy and the conservation of matter in chemical and physical changes
  - Different forms of energy
- Thermodynamics in chemistry
  - Temperature, thermal energy, and heat capacity, including temperature scales, units of energy, and calculations involving these concepts
  - Concepts and calculations involving phase transitions between the various states of matter
  - Kinetic molecular theory and ideal gas laws
  - Energetics of chemical reactions
  - How the laws of thermodynamics relate to chemical reactions and phase changes

Atomic and Nuclear Structure

- Current model of atomic structure
- Electron configuration of the elements based on the periodic table
- Radioactivity
- How the electronic absorption and emission spectra of elements are related to electron energy levels

Nomenclature; Chemical Composition; Bonding and Structure

- Nomenclature and chemical composition
  - Systematic names and chemical formulas of simple inorganic compounds
  - Names of common organic compounds based on their functional groups
  - Mole concept and how it applies to chemical composition
- Bonding and structure
  - Common properties of bonds
  - Bond types
  - Structural formulas and molecular geometry (shape)
  - Identifying polar and nonpolar molecules
  - Intermolecular interactions
  - How bonding and structure correlate with physical properties

Chemical Reactions; Periodicity

- Periodicity
  - Basis of the periodic table and general layout
  - Periodic trends in physical and chemical properties of the elements
- Chemical reactions and basic principles
  - Balancing chemical equations
  - Stoichiometric calculations
  - Identifying, writing, and predicting products of simple reaction types
  - Chemical kinetics
  - Chemical reaction equilibrium
  - Oxidation-reduction reactions and how to determine oxidation states
- Biochemistry and organic chemistry
  - Important biochemical compounds
  - Common organic compounds (i.e., identify functional groups)

Solutions and Solubility; Acid-Base Chemistry

- Solutions and solubility
  - Solution terminology and calculations
  - Factors affecting solubility and dissolution rates
  - Solution phenomena based on colligative properties
  - Common applications of equilibrium in ionic solutions
- Acid-base chemistry
  - Defining and identifying acids and bases and their properties
  - The pH scale and calculations involving pH and pOH
  - Concepts and calculations involving acid-base titrations
  - Equilibrium relationships in acid-base chemistry

Scientific Inquiry and Social Perspectives of Science

- History and nature of scientific inquiry
  - Processes involved in scientific inquiry
  - Experimental design
  - Nature of scientific knowledge
  - Major historical developments in chemistry and the contributions of major historical figures
- Science, technology, society, and the environment
  - Impact of chemistry and technology on society and the environment
  - Applications of chemistry in daily life
  - Advantages and disadvantages associated with various types of energy production

Scientific Procedures and Techniques

- Collecting, evaluating, manipulating, interpreting, and reporting data
- Units of measurement, notation systems, conversion, and mathematics used in chemistry
- Basic error analysis
- Appropriate preparation, use storage, and disposal of materials in the laboratory
- Appropriate use, maintenance, and calibration of laboratory equipment
- Safety procedures and precautions for the high school chemistry laboratory

Chemistry Practice

Which element has the electron configuration $1s^2\ 2s^2\ 2p^6\ 3s^2\ 3p^3$?

○ Cesium

○ Nitrogen

○ Silicon

○ Phosphorous

Here's How to Crack It

The superscript numbers after the letters *s* and *p* represent the number of electrons in those orbitals. By counting the total number, we see the element has 15 electrons. This would be phosphorus, number 15 on the periodic table.

At a constant temperature, a gas volume is found to be tripled after a change in pressure is applied. If the original pressure was 300 torr, what did the pressure get changed to?

○ 100 torr

○ 200 torr

○ 600 torr

○ 900 torr

Here's How to Crack It

This question requires knowledge of Boyle's law, which states that $V = \dfrac{1}{P}$ or that $P_1 V_1 = P_2 V_2$. Therefore, if the volume were tripled, the pressure would be $\dfrac{1}{3}$ of the original pressure. Choice (A) is correct. Even without knowing the specific law, this could be narrowed to (A) or (B) by the knowledge that it must have been less pressure applied since the gas volume increased.

CHEMISTRY DRILL

Answers and explanations can be found at the end of the chapter.

What is the heat required (in joules) to raise the temperature of 10 g of H_2O by 100°C?

○ 1,000 J

○ 4,180 J

○ 2,970 J

○ 41,800 J

According to Le Châtelier's principle, which of the following would shift the equilibrium to the right?

$$CH_4 + F_2 \rightleftharpoons CF_4 + HF \qquad \Delta H = +38kJ/mol$$

○ Addition of CF_4

○ Removal of F_2

○ Adding a catalyst to the system

○ Increasing the temperature

Which of the following has the shortest bond length?

○ A bond created by sharing 1 electron

○ A bond created by sharing 2 electrons

○ A bond created by sharing 4 electrons

○ A bond created by sharing 6 electrons

How many moles of carbon are in 100 g ?

○ 8.33 moles

○ 12.0 moles

○ 16.7 moles

○ 100 moles

Which of the following represents the most precise data set if the true measurement was known to be 117 mm ?

○ 116, 120, 112, 116, 123

○ 117, 116, 118, 115, 116

○ 120, 121 121, 121, 121

○ 115, 119, 115, 123, 108

EARTH AND SPACE SCIENCE: CONTENT KNOWLEDGE (5571)

Time: 2.5 hours

Format: 125 selected-response questions

This test is recommended for a beginning teacher of secondary-school Earth and Space Science. It tests concepts, terms, phenomena, methods, applications, data analysis, problem solving in Earth and Space Science, and the impact of science and technology on the environment and human affairs as would be discussed in an introductory college-level course.

Topics	% of Test
Basic Scientific Principles and Processes	12%
Tectonics and Internal Earth Processes	17%
Earth Materials and Surface Processes	23%
History of the Earth and its Life-Forms	14%
Earth's Atmosphere and Hydrosphere	19%
Astronomy	15%

Basic Scientific Principles and Processes
- Science methodology, techniques, and history
- Basic principles of matter and energy
- Science, technology, and society

Tectonics and Internal Earth Processes
- Theory of plate tectonics and its supporting evidence
- Deformation of Earth's crust and resulting features
- Characteristics of earthquakes and how they provide information about Earth's interior
- Layered structure of Earth and related processes
- Volcanic characteristics and processes

Earth Materials and Surface Processes
- Identification of minerals
- Cycling of Earth materials
- Characteristics and formation of igneous, sedimentary, and metamorphic rocks
- Earth's surface changes over time

History of the Earth and Its Life-Forms
- How rocks are used to determine geologic time and provide a record of Earth's history
- Fossil records as evidence of the origin and development of life
- Theories of Earth's formation and development of its systems

Earth's Atmosphere and Hydrosphere
- Unusual properties of water and its effect on Earth systems
- Water cycle and the energy transfers involved
- Basic structure and composition of the atmosphere
- Basic physical principles and processes involved in meteorology
- Development and movement of weather systems
- Factors and processes that influence climate and lead to climate zones
- Effects of natural phenomena on climate change
- Characteristics and processes of surface water and groundwater
- Characteristics of glaciers and polar ice and how they move and change over time
- Physical and chemical characteristics and processes of the oceans
- Interrelationships between the oceans and the solid earth
- Interrelationships between the hydrosphere and the biosphere/atmosphere

Astronomy
- Earth's motions and their characteristics and consequences
- Relationships within the Earth-Moon-Sun system
- Characteristics of the components of our solar system and how they formed
- Characteristics of stars and the processes that occur within them
- Characteristics of the Milky Way and other galaxies
- Theories and observations that relate to the origin and development of the universe

Earth and Space Science Practice

Which of the following is NOT a factor in the process of relative dating?

○ The principle of radioactive decay

○ The principle of original horizontality

○ The principle of superpositioning

○ The principle of cross-cutting relationships

Here's How to Crack It

This question requires knowledge of relative dating and each of the principles above. Relative dating is the process of determining the approximate age of something by assessing if it is older or younger than something else, but it does not specifically calculate a numerical age. Another type of dating, absolute (numerical) dating, uses the process of radioactive decay to calculate a precise age. The principle of radioactive decay, (A), is correct.

Which of the following properties of water allows for aquatic life to survive?

○ Very high specific heat capacity of water

○ High density of water molecules after freezing occurs

○ Intramolecular hydrogen bonding between hydrogen and oxygen

○ Hydrophobic interactions that prevent NaCl ionization

Here's How to Crack It

This question requires knowledge of the special properties of water. Several properties of water contribute to the survival of aquatic life, but the only one correctly listed here is the high specific heat capacity, which means that water resists temperature changes. This keeps bodies of water relatively stable in temperature. Water molecules are actually less densely packed in ice than they are in liquid water, so (B) is incorrect. Choice (C) is incorrect because the hydrogen bonding of oxygen and water occurs intermolecularly. (Intramolecular bonding is covalent bonds.) Choice (D) is incorrect because the oceans are full of ionized NaCl, and water is notoriously hydrophilic (water-loving) not hydrophobic (water-fearing). Choice (A) is correct.

———————○———————

Now try the drill questions on your own. Remember, answers and explanations can be found at the end of the chapter.

EARTH AND SPACE SCIENCE DRILL

Answers and explanations can be found at the end of the chapter.

What are the two main metals that make up the outer and inner core of the Earth?

○ Nickel and iron

○ Aluminum and nickel

○ Carbon and iron

○ Aluminum and carbon

Which of the following is NOT a type of volcanic cone shape?

○ Cinder

○ Composite

○ Icelandic

○ Shield

Which direct observational evidence provides the strongest evidence that Earth rotates?

○ The seasons repeat in a cycle.

○ There is an apparent shift of nearby stars as Earth moves from one side of its orbit to the other.

○ The solar diameter varies throughout the year.

○ The length of the daylight period varies throughout the year.

Soil composed of which particle size usually has the smallest capillarity?

○ Coarse sand

○ Clay

○ Silt

○ Fine sand

Weather-station measurements indicate that the dew point and air temperature are getting farther apart, and that air pressure is rising. Which type of weather is most likely arriving at the station?

○ A rainstorm

○ A warm front

○ Cool, dry air

○ Tropical air

PHYSICS: CONTENT KNOWLEDGE (5265)

Time: 2.5 hours

Format: 125 selected-response questions

This test is recommended for a beginning teacher of secondary-school physics. It tests concepts, terms, phenomena, methods, applications, data analysis, and problem solving in physics, as well as the impact of science and technology on the environment and human affairs as would be discussed in an introductory college-level course.

Topics	% of Test
Mechanics	32%
Electricity and Magnetism	19%
Optics and Waves	13%
Heat, Energy, and Thermodynamics	12%
Modern Physics, and Atomic and Nuclear Structure	12%
Scientific Inquiry, Processes, and Social Perspectives	12%

Mechanics
- Vectors and scalars
- Kinematics
- Dynamics and fluid mechanics

Electricity and Magnetism
- Electrostatics
- Electrical properties of conductors, insulators, and semiconductors
- Electrical current, resistance, potential difference, energy, power, and the relationships between them
- Capacitance and inductance
- Differences between alternating and direct current
- How to analyze simple series, parallel, and combination circuits
- How sources generate electric potential
- Magnetic fields, magnetic forces, and properties of magnetic materials
- How a changing electric field produces a magnetic field and how a changing magnetic field produces an electric field

Optics and Waves

- Types of waves and their characteristics
- Wave phenomena such as reflection, refraction, interference, and diffraction
- Fundamentals of the Doppler effect
- Characteristics of sound
- Electromagnetic waves and the electromagnetic spectrum
- Geometric optics

Heat, Energy, and Thermodynamics

- Temperature, temperature scales, and heat capacity
- Mechanisms of heat transfer
- Different forms of energy and transformations between them
- Energy involved in phase transitions between the various states of matter
- Kinetic molecular theory and the ideal gas laws
- Laws of thermodynamics

Modern Physics, and Atomics and Nuclear Structure

- Organization, structure, and states of matter
- Nature of atomic and subatomic structure including various models of the atom
- Relationship of atomic spectra to electron energy levels
- Characteristics, processes, and effects of radioactivity
- Topics in modern physics

Scientific Inquiry, Processes, and Social Perspectives

- History and nature of scientific inquiry
- Scientific procedures and techniques
- Science, technology, and society

Physics Practice

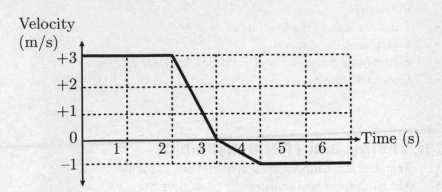

What is the acceleration from 2 to 3 s?

○ –3 m/s²

○ –2 m/s²

○ 2 m/s²

○ 3 m/s²

Here's How to Crack It

Since acceleration is the change in velocity over time, we can find the slope on the

velocity time graph which is $\dfrac{y_2 - y_1}{x_2 - x_1}$ or $\dfrac{0 - 3}{3 - 2}$ = –3 m/s².

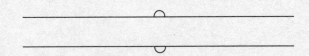

A particle of charge q_1 = +6.0 μC is located on the
x-axis at the point x = 6.8 cm. A second particle of
charge q_2 = –5.0 μC is placed on the x-axis at
x = –3.9 cm. What is the absolute electric potential
at the origin $(x = 0)$?

○ –3.6 × 10⁷

○ –3.6 × 10⁵

○ 2.2 × 10⁻²

○ 2.2 × 10⁻⁴

Here's How to Crack It

The equation for electric potential for a point charge is $V = kq/r$. So $V_1 = kq_1/r_1$ and $V_2 = kq_2/r_2$. Then the absolute electric potential is $V = V_1 + V_2$. $V_1 = 8.99 \times 10^9 \cdot 6.0 \times 10^{-6}/(6.8 \times 10^{-2})$ and $V_2 = 8.99 \times 10^9 \cdot (-5.0 \times 10^{-6})/(3.9 \times 10^{-2})$. Therefore, $V_1 + V_2 = -3.6 \times 10^5$.

Now try the drill on the next page. You can check your answers using the explanations at the end of the chapter.

PHYSICS DRILL

Answers and explanations can be found at the end of the chapter.

An object is dropped from 400 m. What will be its speed when it has traveled half the distance to the ground?

- ○   9.8 m/s
- ○   62.6 m/s
- ○ 1,960 m/s
- ○ 3,920 m/s

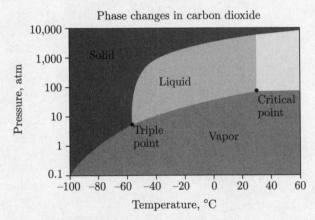

Phase changes in carbon dioxide

As you decrease the pressure from 1,500 atm to 100 atm at –50 °C, what change will occur?

- ○ Vapor to liquid
- ○ Solid to liquid
- ○ Liquid to solid
- ○ Plasma to solid

A small wooden boat floating in a pool of water (density 1 g/cm³) displaces a volume of 500 cm³. What is the buoyant force?

- ○ 0.2 N
- ○ 0.49 N
- ○ 2 N
- ○ 4.9 N

When the length of a wire decreases and the diameter decreases, what is the impact on resistance?

- ○ The resistance of the wire will always increase.
- ○ The resistance of the wire will always decrease.
- ○ Resistance is independent of the wire qualities.
- ○ More information is required to make a conclusion.

Two hydrogen isotopes, hydrogen-3 and hydrogen-2, react to form an atom of helium and a free neutron. This process can be observed occurring in which of the following scenarios?

- ○ Nuclear fusion in the sun
- ○ Radioactive decay in all life forms
- ○ Nuclear fission in a power plant reactor
- ○ In the combustion furnace of a hot air balloon

SCIENCE DRILL ANSWERS AND EXPLANATIONS

Middle School Science Drill

1. **B** The independent variable is the one that is set by the scientist. It is the one thing that differs in each experimental group.

2. **A** The largest biomass is the producers (plants). They are the foundation of the food chain and must have the largest biomass to support the levels above.

3. **A** The amplitude is the distance from the *x*-axis to the peak (or the valley). So, the amplitude is 4. Half the amplitude is 2.

4. **A** If a 2 was added to NaOH, this would balance the atoms on each side of the equation. There would be 2 Na, 6 O, 4 H, and 1 S on each side.

5. **C** Cellular respiration typically starts with glycolysis, and glucose is the hallmark initial reactant in glycolysis.

General Science Drill

1. **B** As the temperature of a gas decreases, the volume of that gas would decrease. This would cause the plunger to indicate a smaller volume of gas.

2. **D** In vitro fertilization is the process of combining eggs and sperm outside the body. The embryo can then be inserted into a uterus to grow and develop.

3. **C** There are two forces that act on orbiting objects, like satellites. The first is the force of the object's velocity sending it on a linear tangent away from Earth. The second is the force of gravity pulling it toward Earth. When these are approximately equal, a satellite will orbit as it perpetually flies out toward space at the same rate it falls back to Earth.

4. **A** After 1,000 years, if the alleles are the same, they must not have been selected for or against. Being recessive would not affect frequency of alleles, only the observed phenotypes, and natural selection affects both recessive and dominant alleles. If the moths were colorblind, this would impact sexual selection practices, but many other selective pressures could have existed on them. If the allele frequencies are unchanged, it seems that neither has been naturally selected.

5. **D** The thermosphere is the hottest layer of the atmosphere.

Biology Drill

1. **D** It is theorized that a meteorite impact or volcanic eruption led to extreme climate changes that caused mass extinction on Earth. If the living things had more genetic diversity, then perhaps more species would have survived, as some of them might have had traits that allowed them to survive the extreme events. It is unlikely that excessive predation caused mass extinction, since each predator eats only certain things, and extinction occurred up and down the food chain.

2. **C** The human stores 1.95 L of oxygen and weighs 70 kg. This is 0.028 L/kg. The seal stores 25.9 L and weighs 450 kg. This is 0.058 L/kg. The seal stores about twice as much per kg.

3. **C** High levels of insulin occur when there is high blood glucose. High glucose would indicate that glycolysis is probably running (since it starts with glucose). Body temperature is not directly related to blood glucose. Glucose being stored as glycogen would likely occur when glucose levels are high. Low levels of citrate indicate that the citric acid cycle is not running well. This indicates that energy stores are low, and this would not occur when there is high blood glucose.

4. **B** The stable number of fish within the pond is an indicator of the pond's carrying capacity, or maximal level that can be supported. This would not represent the total biomass because the pond likely has organisms other than fish living in it. This doesn't tell you about trophic level because you don't know what else lives in the pond. It doesn't tell you anything about the genetic equilibrium because you don't know the genetic variation or alleles present.

5. **B** The gametes could have A or a AND either B or b AND either D or d. All gametes will have C. This means there are 8 possible gametes: $(2)(2)(2) = 8$.

Chemistry Drill

1. **B** The equation for this is $q = mc\Delta T$, where q is the heat energy, m is mass, c is specific heat, and ΔT is change in temperature.

    $q = (10 \text{ g}) \times (4.18 \text{ J/g·°C})[(100 \text{ °C} - 0\text{°C})]$

    $q = (10 \text{ g}) \times (4.18 \text{ J/g·°C}) \times (100\text{°C})$

    $q = 4,180 \text{ J}$

2. **D** Le Châtelier's principle states that the equilibrium will shift depending on the conditions present. Adding more CF_4 (product) would shift it to the left. Removing F_2 (reactant) would shift it to the left. A catalyst does not affect equilibrium. Increasing the temperature would shift it to the right because the reaction is endothermic ($\Delta H > 0$), so heat is required, and thus heat is like a reactant. Adding more reactant would shift the equilibrium to the right.

3. **D** Bond length is shorter the tighter two atoms are attached. With no other information about elements involved, the tightest connection would be with a bond sharing 6 electrons (a triple bond).

4. **A** To determine the number of moles, you must get the molar mass from the periodic table. For carbon, it is 12.0 g. This is the number of grams in 1 mole of carbon. If you set up a proportion, then 12.0 g/1 mole = 100 g/x. Therefore, x = 8.33 moles.

5. **C** Precision refers to how closely the data groups together. This is often compared with accuracy, which is how close the data points represent the true value. Although the true value is 117, the more precise set is the one that is most closely grouped.

Earth Science Drill

1. **A** The core consists mostly of iron, with lesser amounts of nickel and silicon that are combined with a small amount of other elements, most likely sulphur or oxygen.

2. **C** Cinder, composite (also known as a stratovolcano), and shield are all types of volcanic cone shapes. Icelandic is one of six types of volcanic eruptions.

3. **B** Earth rotates on its axis. This axis extends through the poles. Stars will appear to shift during the night. We know that this is caused by Earth rotating, and not by the stars moving.

4. **A** Capillarity refers to the ability of a soil to suck up and hold onto water. When the soil has a large particle size, it is unable to retain the water because the spaces between the particles are large and the water flows out. Thus, large particles have the least capillarity. Soils with smaller spaces between their tiny particles can hold the water (high capillarity) better because the tiny spaces help the water to stick inside. Of the answer choices, coarse sand has the largest particle size followed by fine sand, silt, and then clay.

5. **C** When the dew point temperature and air temperature are equal, the air is said to be saturated. When there is a large difference between the two temperatures, the air contains very low relative humidity. Therefore, (C) is the best answer.

Physics Drill

1. **B** For a free falling object, $V_f^2 = V_i^2 + 2(a)(d)$, where V_f^2 is the final velocity, V_i^2 is the initial velocity, a is acceleration, and d is distance.

$$V_f^2 = 0^2 + 2(-9.8 \text{ m/s}^2)(200)$$

$$V_f^2 = 3920 \text{ m/s}$$

$$V_f = 62.6 \text{ m/s}$$

2. **B**   At −50 °C and 1,500 atm, the phase is solid. When the pressure is reduced, it is now in the liquid phase.

3. **D**   According to the Archimedes principle, the buoyant force pushing upward on an object is equal the weight of the water that is displaced by the object. Therefore, with a displaced volume of 500 cm³, the mass of the water displaced is 500 g. The weight is determined by (*mass*)(*acceleration by gravity*) = (0.5 kg) × (9.8 m/s²) = 4.9 N.

4. **D**   When the length decreases, the resistance decreases. When the diameter decreases, the resistance generally increases. Therefore, more information is required about the length and diameter changes.

5. **A**   If two atoms combine to make a larger atom this is nuclear fusion, which is a process that occurs in the sun. Scientists have thus been unable to harness this type of a reaction to power things on Earth.

Part V
Principles of Learning and Teaching (PLT) Tests

Chapter 22
Overview of the
PLT Tests

PRINCIPLES OF LEARNING AND TEACHING

There are actually four separate Principles of Learning and Teaching (PLT) tests, each for a specific age range:

- Principles of Learning and Teaching: Early Childhood
- Principles of Learning and Teaching: Grades K–6
- Principles of Learning and Teaching: Grades 5–9
- Principles of Learning and Teaching: Grades 7–12

Each test follows the same format, and tests the same topics, but tailors the content to emphasize each test's specific age range. This chapter focuses on the tests for K–6, 5–9, and 7–12, but you can find more information and preparation materials for the Early Childhood exam on the official test page: www.ets.org/praxis/prepare/materials/5621.

WHAT'S ON THE TEST?

The PLT tests measure a range of professional knowledge related to the art and science of teaching. The content covered on the tests is roughly the same as the content you'd see in undergraduate courses in educational psychology and related fields. ETS breaks the content down into five areas:

1. Students as Learners
2. Instructional Process
3. Assessment
4. Professional Development, Leadership, and Community
5. Analysis of Instructional Scenarios (Case Histories)

The chapters in this section focus on these five areas.

What Does the Test Look Like?

The PLT tests are computer-delivered, two-hour-long exams consisting of 70 multiple-choice questions and 4 short-answer (constructed-response) questions based on two case histories. This format is the same for each grade level. The multiple-choice and short-answer sections are NOT timed separately. However, it is expected that you will spend about 70 minutes on the multiple-choice questions and about 50 minutes on the short-answer questions.

Multiple-Choice Questions

There are only four answer choices per question, and there's no penalty for a wrong answer, so you should answer all of these questions—even if you're guessing blindly. A typical multiple-choice question looks like this:

> Teacher Melissa Kolbert allows her students to place their desks anywhere in the room while they do seat work. She programmed a computer to play a brief melody 5 minutes before the end of the class period. When the students hear the melody, they know to finish what they are doing and to put all desks back in rows. Why did Melissa do this?
>
> ○ To use technology in the classroom
>
> ○ To achieve a smooth transition
>
> ○ To get students to be seated at the end of class
>
> ○ To reinforce the idea of student-selected seating assignments

How to Approach Multiple-Choice Questions on the PLT Test

Process of Elimination (POE) is a crucial tool in answering these questions effectively. To help prepare you to eliminate wrong answers on the PLT, you should ask yourself the following questions:

- What's the scenario?
- What do I know about that?
- What would a good teacher do?
- How would I answer the question?
- What's the best answer choice?

Let's try this approach on the question we just read:

> Teacher Melissa Kolbert allows her students to place their desks anywhere in the room while they do seat work. She programmed a computer to play a brief melody 5 minutes before the end of the class period. When the students hear the melody, they know to finish what they are doing and to put all desks back in rows. Why did Melissa do this?

Common sense and good judgment will help you tremendously on the PLT exams. If you think an educational practice is unwise, unfair, or inappropriate, ETS probably does too.

Ask yourself the questions:

What's the scenario? The teacher seems to be making sure that her students have a clear signal and adequate time to get the classroom back in order before the end of class.

What do I know about that? This seems to have something to do with good classroom management. Melissa has her class trained—she doesn't need to yell every day that class is about to end. Giving her students the freedom to sit where they want gives them some control over their learning environment, and they know when they have to give that control back.

What would a good teacher do? A good teacher would do pretty much exactly what Melissa's doing.

How would I answer the question? Answer the question in your own words. Why did Melissa do this? Because she wants a well-managed classroom; because she wants the desks back in their proper places; because she wants to make sure that her students don't just rush off; and because she wants to make sure that the students have enough time to come to a logical stopping point in their work. All of these could be the answer—the right answer should say something like that.

What's the best answer choice? Now, evaluate each answer choice and use POE.

- ○ To use technology in the classroom
- ○ To achieve a smooth transition
- ○ To get students to be seated at the end of class
- ○ To reinforce the idea of student-selected seating assignments

Eliminate (A), as it has nothing to do with classroom management. A smooth transition, (B), means that students will have time to stop their work at a logical place and put their seats back in the proper spots; they won't just rush off, which means Melissa will have a well-managed classroom. Keep (B). Choice (C) is a possibility, so keep it for now. The last choice is not correct; although it mentions student-selected seating assignments, the song she has programmed to play would not reinforce that idea for students. Cross out (D).

You're now left with (B) and (C). While (C) could be a goal, (B) does a better job describing what the melody already accomplishes, so (B) is the correct answer.

Asking yourself these five questions for each multiple-choice question will help you decide what aspect of the PLT content ETS is trying to test.

Short-Answer Questions

The short-answer questions on the PLT are entirely different. You'll see these questions in pairs, with each pair of questions attached to a **case history**—a detailed hypothetical classroom scenario. The scenario is described, sometimes with supporting documentation, such as samples of student work or a transcription of a conversation between a teacher and a student, and then you're asked the questions. Each question typically asks you to identify two ways in which some aspect of the scenario either adheres to or contradicts accepted educational practice, and then to back up your answers using your knowledge of educational theory.

We'll talk about how to approach the case histories in Chapter 27. But first let's take a look at the content you'll need to be familiar with on the PLT.

Chapter 23
Students as Learners

STUDENTS AS LEARNERS

This area is broken up into three subcategories:

1. Student Development and the Learning Process
2. Students as Diverse Learners
3. Student Motivation and the Learning Environment

STUDENT DEVELOPMENT AND THE LEARNING PROCESS

You'll need to know the basic developmental theories and theorists in cognitive, social, and moral development. Here's a brief overview of the big ones:

COGNITIVE DEVELOPMENT

Piaget's Theory

Jean Piaget was a Swiss psychologist whose theory of cognitive development is often alluded to in Praxis questions. You should be familiar with the basics of this theory and some common examples used to illustrate its principles.

Piaget believed that learning happens as people adapt to their environments. He suggested that cognitive development proceeds as follows: when faced with a situation, you first try to use or apply what you already know, and if that doesn't work, you figure out something else based on what's new or different about that situation. The first idea, using your existing framework or *schema*, he called **assimilation**; the second, developing new frameworks, he called **adaptation**. He believed that we are constantly refining our frameworks.

Based on his observations, Piaget theorized that this ongoing process of assimilation and adaptation leads all children to pass through identical stages of cognitive development, but not necessarily at identical times. He identified four stages:

- Sensorimotor (approximate age 0–2 years)
- Preoperational (approximate age 2–7 years)
- Concrete operational (approximate age 7–11 years)
- Formal operational (approximate age 11 years old to adulthood)

Let's review them in order:

1. Sensorimotor Stage

Because most children pass through this stage by the time they reach the age of formal instruction, it is unlikely that you will see questions dealing with it. You should know, however, that things that babies do and the types of games that parents typically play with babies are all relevant to this stage. For instance, one of the characteristics of the sensorimotor stage is understanding **object permanence**— the concept that things continue to exist even though you can't see them. Some educational psychologists and social anthropologists agree that the game of peek-a-boo is practically universal in human culture specifically because it reinforces the concept of object permanence. Another hallmark of the sensorimotor stage is the early development of **goal-oriented behavior**. For example, a very young child who is able to roll over at will, but not yet able to crawl, may consciously roll over multiple times to reach a bottle or favorite toy.

2. Preoperational Stage

At this stage children are developing language skills quickly. They also begin to use symbols to represent objects. Children in this stage will be able to think through simple problems, but only in one direction (i.e., they won't be able to reverse the steps mentally). They also will have difficulty dealing with more than one aspect of a problem at a time. Children in this stage may have difficulty seeing things from another person's point of view. This idea is called **egocentrism**. Although this sounds like a negative quality, it's best understood as the child's assumption that everyone else sees things the same way the child does. For example, a child may assume that everyone likes orange juice simply because she likes orange juice.

3. Concrete Operational Stage

Children in this stage develop the ability to perform a mental operation and then reverse their thinking back to the starting point, a concept called **reversibility**. They demonstrate the concepts of **transitivity** (they can classify objects according to a specific characteristic, even if the object has many different characteristics) and **seriation** (they can put objects in order according to a given criterion such as height or volume). One important concept is that of **conservation**—the idea that the amount of a substance doesn't change just because it's arranged differently. For example, conservation of mass might be demonstrated by taking a large ball of clay and creating several smaller balls of clay out of it. A child in the concrete operational stage will understand that the total amount of clay hasn't changed; a child in the preoperational stage might think that there is more clay (because there are more balls). Children at this age also understand the concept of class inclusion—they can think about a whole group of objects while also thinking about the subgroups of those objects. For example, while thinking about the whole class, a child could also think about how many girls or boys are in the class. At this stage, children can solve concrete, hands-on problems logically.

4. Formal Operational Stage

Not all students will reach the formal operational stage. In fact, some theorists estimate that only about 35 percent of the adult population ever achieves this stage. This stage is characterized by the ability to solve abstract problems involving many independent elements. The thought process necessary to frame and solve such problems is called **hypothetical-deductive reasoning.**

Dewey's Theory

John Dewey was an American philosopher and educator who revolutionized pedagogical theory in the late 19th and early 20th centuries. He adhered to the philosophy of **pragmatism**, which holds that the practicability and usefulness of ideas determine their merit. Accordingly, he believed that educational activities need to be meaningful; curricula should have practical value and be relevant to students' lives. Moreover, Dewey argued that instructional tasks must truly engage the student and enlarge his or her experience; he rejected the rote learning methods that were prevalent at the time in favor of a "hands-on" approach. Dewey's firm belief in democratic principles also led him to reject the rigid hierarchical structure and authoritarianism that characterized the classroom in his day. Remember Dewey's main ideas:

- Learning experiences should be practical and meaningful for the student.
- There should be a "hands-on" approach to learning; students should be able to interact with the learning environment and participate in the learning process.
- Democratic principles should apply in the classroom.

For a comprehensive list of topics covered on the PLT tests, check out the official ETS Study Companion on the Praxis website. Go to www.ets.org/praxis/prepare/materials/ and select your test from the dropdown menu.

Vygotsky's Theories

Lev Vygotsky was a Russian educational psychologist in the early 20th century whose theories you should be familiar with. Here are four of his major ideas that you might see questions about:

- the importance of culture
- the role of private speech
- the zone of proximal development
- scaffolding

Culture

Vygotsky believed that environmental and cultural factors have an enormous influence on what children learn. Piaget argued that children are constantly developing methods of adapting to the world around them; Vygotsky argued that environment and culture dictate what methods the children will find useful, and what their priorities will be.

Private Speech

To Vygotsky, language use is a critical factor in cognitive development. Young children frequently talk to themselves as they play or solve problems. This is called **private speech**. While Piaget would cite private speech as evidence of egocentrism in the preoperational stage, Vygotsky believed that private speech allows children to use language to help break down a problem and solve it—in effect, the children talk themselves through it. He believed that a fundamental stage in development comes when children begin to carry on this speech internally, without speaking the words aloud. Children who routinely use private speech learn complex tasks more effectively.

Zone of Proximal Development

At any given stage, there are problems that a child can solve by herself, and there are other problems that a child couldn't solve even with prodding at each successive step. In between, however, are problems that a child could solve with the guidance of someone who already knows how. That range of problems is what Vygotsky referred to as the **zone of proximal development**. He believed that real learning takes place by solving problems in that zone.

Scaffolding

Scaffolding is another idea fundamental to Vygotsky's notion of social learning. It is about providing children with help from more competent peers and adults. Children are given a lot of support in the early stages of learning and problem solving. Then, as the child is able he/she takes on more responsibility and the supporter diminishes the support. Supportive techniques include clues, reminders, encouragement, breaking the problem into steps, providing examples, or anything that helps a student develop learning independence.

CONSTRUCTIVISM

Piaget's and Vygotsky's theories (among others) led to an educational philosophy called **constructivism**, the idea that learning is a constant assimilation of new knowledge and experiences into each student's unique way of viewing the world. Because each student's viewpoint will necessarily be different from everyone else's, a strict constructivist would be in favor of guided hands-on learning rather than traditional lecture-based teaching, because hands-on learning would be more likely to be related to a student's own experience.

Bruner's Theories

Jerome Bruner was a highly influential psychologist and educator whose constructivist theories helped shaped 20th-century American pedagogy. He is often associated with the notion of a **spiral curriculum,** in which the same subjects are taught to students year after year with increasing degrees of complexity. This method allows students to construct new ideas based upon their experience and existing knowledge. Bruner believed that virtually any subject could be taught to any child, regardless of developmental stages, if the material were presented properly.

Bloom's Taxonomy

- Knowledge
- Comprehension
- Application
- Analysis
- Synthesis
- Evaluation

Students develop thinking skills in roughly the order above. In the early grades, students are limited to facts and other rote knowledge. As they develop, they are capable of processing information at levels of greater and greater complexity. In general, teachers should try to develop higher-order thinking skills (those at the end of the list). Let's take a look at the types of questions that would stimulate these types of thinking. Imagine that a teacher was doing a lesson on the colonization of the United States.

Bloom Taxonomy Level	Description	Question Example
Knowledge	Recalling factual information	What were the names of the New England colonies?
Comprehension	Using factual information to answer a specific question	What crops were common to the New England colonies and the Southern colonies? What were the major religious differences between people in the New England colonies and the Middle colonies?
Application	Taking an abstract concept together with specific facts to answer a question	In which area of the colonies would a Freethinker have been most likely to find like-minded people?

Analysis	Breaking down a question into concepts and ideas in order to answer a question	What characteristics of the New England colonists made them the most likely to rebel against British rule?
Synthesis	Connecting concepts and ideas to create a new product or idea	What steps could the King have taken to appease the New England colonists that might have prevented the American Revolution?
Evaluation	Making considered judgments by breaking down and reconnecting ideas, concepts, and facts and comparing the judgments to standards	In which area of the colonies did the colonists have the best natural resources from an economic standpoint?

So, in planning a U.S. History unit, teachers should build a base of facts and concepts and then develop lessons that encourage students to ask and answer increasingly complicated sorts of questions based on those facts and concepts.

Cognitive, Affective, and Psychomotor Domains

Bloom's taxonomy deals with skills in the **cognitive domain.** The other two widely recognized areas are the affective and psychomotor domains.

The **affective domain** includes class participation, including listening as well as speaking, defending positions, and recognizing the opinions of others.

The **psychomotor domain** includes abilities related to physical prowess ranging from reflexes through basic motions such as catching and throwing a ball, to skilled motions such as playing tennis, or playing the piano. It also includes the ability to communicate through motion, as in dancing or miming.

SOCIAL DEVELOPMENT

Erikson's Eight Stages of Psychosocial Development

You should be familiar with Erikson's Stages of Psychosocial Development. Erikson, a German-born American psychologist, identified eight stages of personal and social development, each of which takes the form of a resolution of an identity crisis. Here they are in chronological order:

1. Trust vs. Mistrust (Birth to 18 Months)

If a child is well cared for during this time, he/she will become naturally trusting and optimistic. The goal is for infants to develop basic trust in their families and the world. Again, due to the age range involved, you will probably not see questions dealing with this stage.

2. Autonomy vs. Doubt (18 Months to 3 Years)

A child learns the mechanical basics of controlling his world—including walking, grasping, and toilet training. The "terrible twos" fall into this stage, with common traits including stubbornness and willful behavior as the child pushes the limits of control and develops autonomy. Children want to become independent and still rely on their support system. Ideally, parents need to be supportive of the child's needs so that the child comes out of this stage proud of his abilities rather than ashamed.

3. Initiative vs. Guilt (3 to 6 Years)

After becoming autonomous, children start wanting to do things. They have ideas and plans and carry out activities. Some activities aren't allowed, and it's important for children to feel that their activities are important and valued by adults. If this feeling isn't there, children believe that what they do is wrong, and guilt develops, which restricts growth.

4. Industry vs. Inferiority (6 to 12 Years)

In these elementary-school years, children are expected to learn and produce. Parental influence decreases. Teachers and peers become more important. Success creates high self-esteem, while failure lowers self-image. Just the perception of failure can cause children to feel inferior, even if the failure is not real. If children can meet their own expectations, as well as those of parents and teachers, they learn to be industrious. If they do not, they risk feeling inferior.

5. Identity vs. Role Confusion (12 to 18 Years)

This is when adolescents answer the question, "Who am I?" It's quite common for teenagers to rebel, some very strongly. Erikson believed that the social structure of the United States was a healthy one for teenagers. They are offered the opportunity and leeway to try out different personalities and roles, and decide which ones suit them best. Acceptance by peer groups is of extreme importance.

Because the last three stages, described below, are stages that adults go through, it is unlikely that you will see any questions about them on the exam. They're listed here only for the purpose of completing the list.

6. Intimacy vs. Isolation (Young Adulthood)

Being able to form mutually beneficial intimate relationships is the defining characteristic of this stage.

7. Generativity vs. Stagnation (Middle Adulthood)

Adults need to be productive in helping and guiding future generations, through contributions in both procreation and profession. Adults who aren't successful in finding ways to contribute may feel disconnected or uninvolved in society or their community.

8. Integrity vs. Despair (Late Adulthood)

Finally, adults need to feel complete and comfortable with themselves and the choices they've made in their lives. They need to accept their eventual deaths.

PLAY AS A FORM OF SOCIAL DEVELOPMENT

Play is an important way in which children learn to socialize. Because most children will have reached the final stage of cooperative play by age 7, this is a developmental idea that is most likely to show up on the Early Childhood PLT. However, it's possible that some wrong answer choices on other exams will make reference to these ideas, so it's a good idea to review these no matter which test type you're preparing for.

Mildred Parten's Stages of Play Development

Mildred Parten, a child psychologist in the 1930s, was one of the first people to study children at play. Here are her stages of play development, which are linked to different levels of social interaction.

1. Solitary Play

Here, children play by themselves. While children may continue to do this throughout their childhoods, in the context of social interaction, this is usually observed in children less than two years of age.

2. Onlooker Play

At around two years old, children will watch others play without doing anything themselves or making any effort to join in. This is closely followed in the same time frame by parallel play.

3. Parallel Play

This is play in which children do the same thing that other children are doing. There is no interaction between the children.

4. Associative Play

Normally, by age four or five, children engage in associative play. Associative play is similar to parallel play, but there is increased interaction. Children will share, take turns, and be interested in what others are doing.

5. Cooperative Play

Finally, usually by age five to seven, children will play together in one activity.

MORAL DEVELOPMENT

Lawrence Kohlberg was a developmental psychologist at Harvard University in the late 20th century who did extensive research in the field of moral education. You should be familiar with Kohlberg's stage theory of moral reasoning. He split moral development into three levels, each of which contains two stages.

Level 1: Preconventional Moral Reasoning (Elementary School)

Rules are created by others.

Stage 1: Punishment and Obedience Orientation

Young children obey rules simply because there are rules, and they understand that they risk punishment by breaking them. Whether an action is good or bad is understood in terms of its immediate consequences.

Stage 2: Instrumental Relativist Orientation

Children internalize the system from Stage 1 and realize that following the rules is generally in their best interests. An action is right or good if it gets you what you want. A simple view of "fair's fair" develops, so that, for example, favors are done with the expectation of something in return.

Level 2: Conventional Moral Reasoning (Junior High–High School)

Kohlberg called this level conventional because most of society remains at this level. Judgment is based on tradition and others' expectations and less on consequences. Individuals adopt rules and sometimes will put others' needs before their own.

Stage 3: Good Boy–Good Girl Orientation

An action is right or good if it helps, pleases, or is approved by others.

Stage 4: "Law and Order" Orientation

An action is right or good if it's expected out of a sense of duty or because it supports the morals or laws of the community or country. This reflects the common sentiment: "It's right because it's the law."

Level 3: Post-Conventional Moral Reasoning

People determine their own values and ethics.

Stage 5: Social Contract Orientation

An action is right or good if it meets an agreed-upon system of rules and rights (such as the United States Constitution). Unlike Stage 4, this phase recognizes that rules can be changed for the betterment of society.

Stage 6: Universal Ethical Principle Orientation

Good and right are relative, not absolute, and require abstract thinking in terms of justice, equality, and human dignity. One's conscience determines right from wrong.

Level 3 is unlikely to be tested because Kohlberg believed that it's not fully attained until adulthood, if it's ever attained at all. It's included here for completeness.

In his later years, Kohlberg decided that Stages 5 and 6 were actually the same.

STUDENTS AS DIVERSE LEARNERS

Not all students learn the same way, and students will have strengths and weaknesses in a variety of areas. The major ideas you should be familiar with are multiple intelligences, different learning styles, gender-based and culture-based differences, and exceptional students.

Multiple Intelligences

What is intelligence? This question may never be fully answered. Nonetheless, you should be familiar with Howard Gardner's work because it might show up on the Praxis. Howard Gardner is a developmental psychologist at Harvard University who, in the mid-1980s, categorized the following eight types of intelligence:

1. Logical-Mathematical Intelligence

This type of intelligence relates to the ability to detect patterns, think logically, and make deductions. Scientists and mathematicians tend to be logical-mathematical thinkers.

2. Linguistic Intelligence

People who have linguistic intelligence are particularly sensitive not only to words themselves, but also to the relationship between the meanings and sounds of words and the ideas and concepts that words represent. Poets and journalists tend to possess linguistic intelligence.

3. Musical Intelligence

Musical intelligence is defined as the ability to recognize and reproduce rhythm, pitch, and timbre—the three fundamental elements of music. Obviously, composers and musicians possess musical intelligence.

4. Spatial Intelligence

People with spatial intelligence have the ability to create and manipulate mental images. They also perceive spatial relationships in the world accurately and can use both the mental and actual perceptions to solve problems. Both artists and navigators use well-developed spatial intelligence.

5. Naturalist Intelligence

This intelligence relates to being sensitive to natural objects like plants and animals and making fine sensory discriminations. Naturalists, hunters, and botanists excel in this intelligence.

6. Bodily-Kinesthetic Intelligence

Bodily-kinesthetic intelligence is the ability to consciously and skillfully control and coordinate your body's movements and manipulate objects. Athletes and dancers need a strong bodily-kinesthetic intelligence.

7. Interpersonal Intelligence

Interpersonal intelligence is the ability to understand and respond to the emotions and intentions of others. Psychologists and salespeople make good use of interpersonal intelligence.

8. Intrapersonal Intelligence

Intrapersonal intelligence is the ability to understand and respond to your own emotions, intentions, strengths, weaknesses, and intelligences.

Gardner believes that we all possess some degree of these intelligences, and that each of these must be relatively well developed in order for us to function well in society.

Although the intelligences are categorized separately, we rarely use them strictly independently. It is difficult to think of a profession or activity that wouldn't combine some of these intelligences. For instance, a pianist needs not only musical intelligence, but also interpersonal (to be able to relate to an audience) as well as bodily-kinesthetic (to control the actions of her hands on the keyboard).

Different Learning Styles

Not all people learn the same way. Different students will process information differently depending on how it's presented. Many theorists split learning styles into the following three categories:

1. Visual Learning

Visual learners learn by seeing. They prefer graphs and charts to summarize information, rather than text or a spoken summary. They prefer maps and diagrams to step-by-step directions. They're more likely to remember faces than names when they meet someone. Traditional lecture-based lessons can be good for visual learners as long as the teacher makes good use of visual aids.

2. Auditory Learning

Auditory learners learn by hearing. They're more likely to remember what was said about a painting they've studied than to be able to describe its appearance. Traditional lecture-based lessons are effective with aural learners.

3. Kinesthetic Learning

Kinesthetic learners learn by doing. They remember things best if they try them out to see for themselves. They're more likely to remember what they were doing when they met someone than what they talked about. Traditional lecture-based lessons are not good for kinesthetic learners. Lessons that involve laboratory work or hands-on experimentation tend to be effective.

Of course, students do not fall neatly into one of these three categories. According to the ETS, good teachers should take into account these different learning styles and plan lessons accordingly.

Gender-Based and Culture-Based Differences

According to ETS, good teachers should recognize that gender and cultural differences could influence student learning. Teachers should examine their own preconceptions and be careful not to reinforce negative stereotypes.

Here are some key facts concerning gender differences:

- Boys are more likely to have adjustment problems in school than girls are.
- Girls tend to outperform boys in the primary grades.
- Boys tend to outperform girls in the secondary grades.
- Some standardized tests are inherently biased against girls.
- Girls tend to do more poorly in math than boys, probably due to societal influences.

If you understand that ETS considers cultural sensitivity very important, you're ahead of the game. Any educational practice that devalues or dismisses cultural differences is probably an example of something NOT to do.

Culture-based differences are too numerous and varied to discuss in detail. Teachers should be aware that societal expectations in a given culture could have an enormous impact upon student learning and behavior. For example, some cultures believe that eye contact from student to teacher is a sign of disrespect, so a teacher would need to be aware that holding such a student to American standards regarding classroom interaction would be inappropriate and possibly traumatic. Similarly, in some cultures, less emphasis is placed on a girl's education than a boy's. A teacher faced with a female student from such a culture would need to understand these gender-based attitudes when interacting with the student's parents.

Exceptional Students

There are some specific requirements for students with specific needs. Because the Praxis is a national exam, individual state requirements won't be tested, but you should be aware of some common terminology:

Individuals with Disabilities Education Act (IDEA)

Passed in its original form in 1975, it now provides special education services to eligible students aged 3 to 21. In 1997, it was reauthorized and modified to allow parents and teachers to be more involved in special education services.

Individual Education Program (IEP)

An IEP outlines the educational goals of a child with special needs. It is created by special education staff, school psychologists, the principal, teachers, the parents, other caregivers, and sometimes the student as well. It will also typically include a mechanism and timeline to show that those goals are being achieved. The IEP must be reviewed annually.

"Least Restrictive Environment"

This phrase means that a child with special needs should have the same opportunities as other students to the fullest extent possible. In other words, students with disabilities should be taught with nondisabled students as much as possible. This is regulated by IDEA.

Mainstreaming/Inclusion

In the 1970s, children with special needs began to be placed in classrooms with children without special needs. That process was called **mainstreaming,** and is now called **inclusion.** It can have social and academic advantages, and it promotes a student's self-esteem and greater understanding and compassion from peers. The drawbacks are that it frequently requires extra help in the classroom and adaptation of the curriculum to meet the needs of the student.

Teachers should also know common strategies for adapting their teaching styles to exceptional children. Important areas include those on the following chart:

Condition	Recommendation
Hearing impaired	• Speak clearly and slowly • Face the student when speaking • Provide adequate visual instruction • Position student in classroom away from other sounds • Learn how to assist those with hearing aids
Visually impaired	• Read out loud • Provide tape-recorded lessons • Ensure appropriate lighting • Move student near front of classroom
Learning impaired	• Provide adequate structure • Provide brief assignments • Provide many auditory experiences and hands-on opportunities
Attention deficit/ hyperactivity disorder (ADHD)	• Reduce distractions • Reduce the length of tasks • Reward on-task behavior • Use progress charts • Allow opportunities to be active • Make sure student understands rules and the assignment
Gifted students	• Provide a variety of challenging learning experiences • Do not isolate from rest of students
Lower socioeconomic status (SES)	• Be aware of the potential for problems at home that could impact a student's performance • Be sensitive to these problems • Do not lower expectations • Provide extra support and motivation

STUDENT MOTIVATION AND
THE LEARNING ENVIRONMENT

Now that we've looked at how children develop and how they learn, let's take a look at how motivation and the classroom environment can have an impact. There are several major theorists you should be familiar with: Edward Lee Thorndike, Ivan Pavlov, Abraham Maslow, B. F. Skinner, and Albert Bandura.

Thorndike's Laws

Edward Lee Thorndike was an early behavioral psychologist whose work led him to three major conclusions:

- **Law of Effect:** An action that produces a positive result is likely to be repeated.
- **Law of Readiness:** Many actions can be performed in sequence to produce a desired effect.
- **Law of Exercise:** Actions that are repeated frequently become stronger.

Pavlov's Conditioned Responses

Ivan Pavlov, a Russian psychologist, proved through experimentation that behavior could be learned according to a system of stimulus and response. His most famous experiment conditioned dogs to salivate at the sound of a bell. He did so by noting that dogs normally salivate at the smell of food, an unconditioned (i.e., innate or reflexive) response to an unconditioned stimulus. The ringing of a bell has no natural meaning for dogs. Such a signal is called a neutral stimulus. He introduced the sound of the bell at feeding time, thereby linking the sound of the bell and the smell of the food in the dogs' minds. Eventually, the dogs salivated at the sound of the bell alone, which was now a conditioned (i.e., learned) response to a conditioned stimulus.

Maslow's Hierarchy of Needs

Abraham Maslow was an educational theorist who believed that children must have certain needs met before they're ready to learn and grow. He organized these needs into a hierarchy, and taught that you couldn't progress to the next level until you'd achieved the previous one. Here's the hierarchy from low to high:

Deficiency Needs
- Physiological needs—food, sleep, clothing, etc.
- Safety needs—freedom from harm or danger
- Belongingness and love needs—acceptance and love from others
- Esteem needs—approval and accomplishment

Deficiency needs are the basic requirements for physical and psychosocial well-being. Desire for these declines once you have them, and you don't think about them unless you lack them.

Growth Needs
- Cognitive needs—knowledge and understanding
- Aesthetic needs—appreciation of beauty and order
- Self-actualization needs—fulfillment of one's potential

Growth needs include the need for knowing, appreciating, and understanding. People try to meet these needs only after their basic needs have been met. Maslow believed that meeting these needs created more desire for them. For example, having adequate shelter and food doesn't make you crave more shelter and food. By contrast, learning and understanding sparks the desire to learn and understand more.

Skinner's Operant Conditioning

B. F. Skinner was a psychologist who believed that you could use a system of positive and negative reinforcements to affect voluntary behavior. He called a positive reinforcement a **reinforcing stimulus,** or **reinforcer**, and the behavior that leads to the positive reinforcement an **operant**. The classic lab scenario is that of a rat pressing a bar in a cage in order to receive food. The pressing of the bar is the operant and the food is the reinforcer. If, after a time, the operant no longer leads to positive reinforcement, the behavior will decrease, and eventually stop. That process is called **extinction**.

A **negative reinforcement** is the removal of an unpleasant stimulus after a certain desired behavior occurs. For instance, a parent wishing to reward a teenager for consistently following a 10 P.M. curfew might extend the curfew until 10:30 P.M.

Don't be confused by the terms "*positive* punishment" and "*negative* reinforcement." Reinforcement is always something we want—punishment never is!

Positive punishment is what we normally think of as being punished for bad behavior. For instance, a teenager that violated curfew rules might be grounded.

Bandura's Concept of Reinforcement

Albert Bandura, a psychologist, theorized that people learn behavior by watching others, trying the behavior themselves, and deciding whether the behavior was beneficial or detrimental. A positive result means that the behavior is *reinforced*, and therefore likely to be repeated. Bandura believed that peer group modeling and images from the media provided very strong suggestions for new behavior patterns.

EXTRINSIC AND INTRINSIC MOTIVATION

One important idea with respect to classroom management is **extrinsic,** or external, motivation (motivation that comes from outside factors) versus **intrinsic,** or internal, motivation (motivation that comes from within). In general, while external motivation can be used, the long-term goal is that students' motivation for learning be intrinsic.

Creating a Positive Learning Environment

Putting all this together means that children will learn best in an environment where they are encouraged to reach their potential, are inwardly motivated to learn, and are exposed to positive behaviors that allow learning to happen. Sounds easy, right?

Here are a few important things to keep in mind:

Consistency

Whatever approach you take to classroom management, you must be consistent. Rules that aren't followed consistently cease to have any weight. There should be consistent, regular procedures for daily activities (such as putting chairs on the top of desks at the end of the day).

Structure

Students need structure and direction. Lessons or tasks should have clear, well-articulated goals. Students should always know what they're supposed to be doing at any given point during the day.

Discipline

Discipline techniques that are too harsh and autocratic (such as Lee Canter's Assertive Discipline) run the risk of suppressing students' internal motivation. Discipline techniques that are too laissez-faire run the risk of not providing enough structure. Striking that balance is challenging, but can be made easier by establishing guidelines immediately. Guidelines should be age-appropriate. First-graders can simply be told that they need to raise their hands and wait for a teacher to call on them before they can start speaking. A sixth-grade teacher might use part of the first day of school having the class as a whole decide what types of behavior should be prohibited, and what consequences should arise from prohibited behavior.

Inappropriate behavior should be dealt with immediately, consistently, and in a manner that does not unwittingly provide positive reinforcement. For instance, a verbal reprimand should occur out of earshot from the rest of the class. A troublemaker who craves attention will continue to act out if the teacher gives him/her attention for each inappropriate behavior. For the student, the teacher's attention is positive reinforcement.

Quizzes Online!
Your Student Tools contain quizzes for each PLT content area so that you can test your knowledge. Register your book to download this bonus study material!

Time on Task

It's easy to lose the forest for the trees, but remember that students are there to learn. Structure and discipline serve to make sure there's as much time as possible available for actual learning.

Transitions

Procedures should be in place for getting students from one task to another in an efficient manner. Suggestions include agreed-upon signals such as flipping the lights on and off or clapping your hands.

TIME TO PRACTICE

Before you move on to the next chapter, check out the quiz for this chapter in your Student Tools. You can download and print a copy of the quiz when you register your book—just follow the instructions on the "Get More (Free) Content" page at the beginning of this book. If you ace the quiz, move on to the next chapter. If you answer several questions incorrectly, be sure to mark them and re-review those topics before test day.

Chapter 24
Instructional
Process

INSTRUCTIONAL PROCESS
This chapter deals with the different ways that teachers can teach material.

CREATIVE THINKING VS. CRITICAL THINKING
A good teacher promotes both critical and creative thinking in her students. The difference between the two might best be described by thinking about the following questions:

- How many different ways can you think of to get from New York to San Francisco?
- What's the best way to get from New York to San Francisco?

Answering the first question involves creative thinking. Answering the second involves critical thinking. Let's compare the two:

Creative Thinking
The first question involves **divergent thinking**—there are many possible answers, and no particular answer is necessarily right or wrong. One technique that a good teacher can use to help with questions such as these is **brainstorming**, in which students are encouraged to come up with as many solutions as possible without stopping to evaluate their merits. Imagine posing the question to a group of active sixth graders. At first, you'd probably get some relatively predictable responses that you'd write down as the students came up with them:

- You could fly; you could drive; you could take a train.

Then, you could start to expect some more "outside the box" ideas:

- You could bike; you could run; you could walk; you could take a boat around the tip of South America and come back up the other side.

And some with less critical thought behind them:

- You could hitchhike. How about a hot air balloon? You could drive to Florida and take the space shuttle. You could wrap yourself up and have yourself FedExed. Could you dig a tunnel?

And after awhile the responses would taper off, and you'd be left with a large list of possibilities on the board.

You should be familiar with two other important ideas regarding creative thinking:

- **Restructuring** is a term that describes the process of thinking about an old problem in a new way. Many educational psychologists believe that time away from the problem is an important element that encourages restructuring—some believe that dreaming is also an important component.
- **Play** encourages creative thinking, and good teachers use well-designed in-class games for this purpose.

Critical Thinking

Let's go back to the results of the brainstorming exercise. There's a large list of possibilities on the board, and you're now ready to ask the second question:

- What's the best way of getting from New York to San Francisco?

This question requires **convergent thinking**—from many possible answers the student is expected to choose and defend the best one. A good teacher will use this opportunity to show how the answer to this question depends on the criteria used. Does "best" mean "cheapest?" If so, then hitchhiking might be a good choice, but you'd have to factor in the cost of food and shelter, because the trip would take longer than it would if you flew. Does "best" mean "quickest?" If so, then flying is probably the best way to go. A good teacher would also seize the opportunity to allow for **transfer**, the application of previously learned skills or facts to new situations. For example, if the class had recently completed a unit on the environment, the teacher could ask, "What if 'best' means 'most environmentally friendly,' but you have to get there within three days?"

Two important aspects of critical thinking are **inductive** and **deductive** reasoning.

Inductive Reasoning

Inductive reasoning occurs when, after viewing several examples, students perceive underlying rules or patterns. For example, students could be given many different parallelograms, and asked what they all have in common. Through measurement and comparison, students might induce that opposite sides of parallelograms are parallel, and that the sum of any two adjacent angles in a parallelogram is 180 degrees.

Deductive Reasoning

Deductive reasoning works in the opposite direction. For example, students might be told that if the sum of any two adjacent angles in a given quadrilateral is 180 degrees, then that quadrilateral is a parallelogram. Then, they'd be given many quadrilaterals, and asked to determine which ones are parallelograms. Both inductive and deductive reasoning are important cognitive skills.

INSTRUCTIONAL STRATEGIES

Different teaching approaches should be taken to stimulate different types of thinking. You should know what options are available to you and which strategies are most likely to accomplish a given educational goal.

Direct Instruction

This is the most common form of teaching, the traditional model in which the teacher stands in front of the room, presents new material, and guides the class toward understanding. You should be familiar with the following concepts:

Hunter's Effective Teaching Model and Mastery Learning

Madeline Hunter, an educational psychologist, expanded on the basic idea of direct instruction and broke the process down into discrete steps:

- Prepare students to learn:
  - Review the previous day's material with a question or two.
  - Get the students' attention with an **anticipatory set**, a question or problem designed to spark students' curiosity and imagination.
  - Outline the lesson's objectives.
- Use input and modeling:
  - Teach well.
  - Organize your presentation.
  - Present the information clearly.
  - Connect new ideas to old ideas.
  - Use examples and analogies.
  - Demonstrate and model new techniques.
- Make sure students understand:
  - Ask both individual and group questions.
- Have students apply new techniques immediately:
  - Work several short examples—guided practice.
  - Monitor student ability—independent practice.

Ausubel's Advance Organizers

David Ausubel's theory expands on some aspects of Hunter's model. **Advance organizers** are the structure (also known as *scaffolding* or *support*) and information that students will need to learn new material effectively. They fall into two categories:

- A *comparative organizer* relates previously mastered material to the material that's about to be presented. For example, a middle-school lesson about sonnet form might begin with a comparative advance organizer that reminds students of a previous lesson on iambic pentameter or simple ABAB rhyme schemes.

- An *expository organizer* is a new idea or concept that needs to be understood before a specific lesson can be understood. For example, a high-school literature class already familiar with rhyme schemes might need an expository advance organizer that discusses the purpose of analyzing poetry and showing that rhyme scheme analysis is just one method of doing so.

Spiral Curriculum

Although this is difficult for a single teacher to implement independently, a **spiral curriculum** revisits topics throughout a student's education, teaching age-appropriate facts and concepts at each stage of the spiral. For instance, a biology curriculum might begin with kindergarteners sorting leaves according to color or shape, whereas a third-grader might learn about the seasonal cycle of leaves, and a sixth grader might learn that leaf shape is an environmental adaptation. Jerome Bruner is the theorist most often associated with this concept.

Demonstrations

Visual learners in particular respond well to demonstrations. Showing is more effective than simply telling. New computer technology allows for imaginative and compelling demonstrations. Good teachers take advantage of all tools at their disposal.

Mnemonics

These provide students with memory devices to help them retain factual information. For instance, "Please Excuse My Dear Aunt Sally" is a common mnemonic for the order of mathematical operations: Parentheses, Exponents, Multiplication, Division, Addition, and Subtraction.

Note-Taking

Students need to be taught how to take notes effectively. One important technique involves giving students a general outline of the major points to be discussed and having them fill in the blanks as the lesson progresses.

Outlining

A clear order of presentation with a well-defined hierarchy of ideas is crucial so that students have an understanding of what the most important parts of a lesson are.

Use of Visual Aids

As with demonstrations, visual aids can make new information stick in students' minds better than it would if it were presented through lecture alone.

Student-Centered Models

In contrast to direct instruction, student-centered models make students, not teachers, the center of attention while new material is being learned. These methods do not lessen the demands on the teacher; in fact, use of student-centered models requires more planning and as much active participation by the teacher as does use of direct instruction. Here are some important student-centered models:

Emergent Curriculum

In this environment, students are given a strong voice in deciding what form the curriculum will take. For instance, students could decide that they were interested in studying leaves. It would then be incumbent upon the teacher to find useful leaf-related activities and experiments that would meet established educational goals. Alternatively, the teacher could present a variety of possible topics, and the students could choose which they wanted to study.

Cooperative Learning

In this model, students are split into mixed-ability groups, assigned very well-defined tasks to accomplish or problems to analyze, and are given individual roles within the group (such as note-taker or illustrator). Students learn from one another and interact in a way that is not possible with direct instruction. One well-known method of organizing cooperative learning in the classroom is called STAD (for Student Teams Achievement Divisions) in which cooperative learning cycles through the following stages:

1. **Teaching,** in which the teacher presents basic material and gives teams a task
2. **Team study,** in which students work on the project
3. **Test,** in which students take individual quizzes
4. **Team recognition,** in which the best-performing teams are rewarded

In another model, called the **think-pair-share method,** students research a topic on their own, discuss their theories and ideas with one other student, and then participate in a classroom discussion.

Discovery Learning

This method is closely aligned with inductive reasoning. Students are given examples and are expected to find patterns and connections with minimal guidance from a teacher during class. Students are encouraged to use *intuitive thinking*, and then make an effort to prove or disprove their intuition given the available information.

Concept Models

Concept models are part of an organizational strategy that helps students to relate new ideas to old ideas. There are three aspects that you should be familiar with:

- **Concept development:** The concept is promoted by the identification of a prototype, or stereotypical example of the concept. For example, if the concept is polygons, a prototype might be a square or a triangle. From the prototype, students generate the definition, in this case, a closed plane figure with a finite number of straight-line sides.
- **Concept attainment:** Students learn to identify examples (pentagons, right triangles) and non-examples (circles, open figures) and sub-define the category according to given criteria (a rectangle is a special polygon having four sides and four equal angles).
- **Concept mapping** or **webbing:** Students draw a pictorial representation of the concepts or ideas about some topic and the links between them. Teachers can look over these maps and discern areas of misunderstanding. There are several different types of methods that currently go by names like "concept mapping," "mental mapping," or "concept webbing."

Inquiry Method

This method is related to discovery learning. A teacher poses a question, and the students have to gather information, formulate, and test hypotheses in order to answer it. Although this method could conceivably be used in teaching almost any discipline, it's particularly well-suited to teaching science and math. For instance, a teacher could pose the question, "Do all triangles have 180 degrees?" Students could then try to find different ways of proving or disproving the statement (e.g., drawing triangles, measuring the angles, and adding them up; comparing the degree measures to a straight line), and eventually conclude that yes, all triangles have 180 degrees.

Metacognition

Teachers can also encourage students to think about their own learning processes and thinking. This is called **metacognition**. For example, a teacher might assign a journal assignment in which students would answer the questions "What did I learn today?" and "How did it relate to things I've learned earlier?"

PLANNING INSTRUCTION

How does a teacher decide what to teach? Ideally, teachers will have long-term and short-term objectives for their students. It's important that these objectives are well-defined because planning instruction and assessment is easier and more meaningful if goals are clearly specified. There are two fundamental approaches to defining objectives. Effective teachers apply both.

Teaching Objectives

Teaching objectives are defined in general terms. To continue with our geometry example from earlier, a cognitive objective might be, "Students will understand the hierarchical relationships among the different types of quadrilaterals." The advantage to a teaching objective is that it's general enough to encompass a wide variety of teaching approaches and techniques. The disadvantage is that it's difficult to measure student understanding of any given concept in all its various forms. Could you write a test that would measure whether students understood all "the hierarchical relationships among the different types of quadrilaterals"?

Learning Objectives

Learning objectives are defined in concrete terms and can be directly observed. Students are expected to exhibit the desired behavior at the end of the lesson(s). For example, "Students will be able to construct a perfect square of a given length using a compass and straightedge." These goals are easy to assess—you could simply watch a student perform the construction—but their specificity makes it difficult to include large-scale concepts. For instance, imagine how long the list of learning objectives would be to describe the body of knowledge and skills covered in the first semester of a geometry class.

The objective type a teacher will use depends on the plan he/she is creating. A daily lesson plan will require learning objectives; a unit or monthly plan will include teaching objectives. Look at the following example.

Type of Lesson	Type of Objective	Example of Objective
Unit Lesson Plan	Teaching Objective	Students will understand the hierarchical relationships among the different types of quadrilaterals.
Daily Lesson Plan	Learning Objective	Students will recite the definition of a quadrilateral. Students will be able to demonstrate the hierarchical distinction between squares and rectangles. Students will be able to prove that every rhombus is a parallelogram.

COMMUNICATION TECHNIQUES

Questions dealing with communication techniques fall into two major categories: (1) culture and gender differences and (2) questioning. Let's explore both of these sectors of communication techniques.

CULTURE AND GENDER DIFFERENCES

You're not expected to know every potentially offensive gesture in every culture, but you should be aware that ETS considers it incorrect to hold all students to North American cultural standards automatically. Awareness of this fact combined with common sense should guide you to the right answer on multiple-choice questions.

As far as gender differences are concerned, you should know that teachers traditionally hold boys and girls to different standards and that this is a practice that ETS condemns. For instance, imagine that a teacher is walking around a classroom, monitoring progress on a particularly difficult math problem. Some studies show that the teacher is simply likely to show girls how to get to the right answer, but will encourage boys to think critically to figure out the problem. When it comes to the test, choose answer choices that treat boys and girls equally in terms of academic expectations.

Some research shows that teachers pay less positive attention to girls than to boys and that they are less likely to encourage assertive behavior in females.

QUESTIONING

Good teachers ask good questions that encourage different kinds of thinking in students. Use Bloom's Taxonomy as a sorting mechanism for different types of questions.

In addition to asking good questions, teachers should also be aware that how questions are asked can have a large impact on student learning. You should be familiar with the following concepts.

Frequency

Frequency simply refers to the number of questions you ask. Socrates notwithstanding, if everything you say is a question, it's difficult for students to learn. On the other hand, nothing is duller than a lecture with no questions. Strike a balance and use questions well to enhance learning.

Equitable Distribution

Call on individual students to ensure that all students are participating. Gear specific questions to specific students, ensuring that a question will be challenging for a given student, but still one the student has a good chance of answering correctly.

Cueing

Cueing is further prompting by the teacher after the initial question is met with silence or an incorrect or partially correct response. For a rote-memory sort of question such as, "What's the capital of Kansas?" a teacher might cue with a reference to a previously learned mnemonic such as, "Remember: 'Everyone in Kansas wears sandals, so…,'" thereby eliciting the student response of "Topeka!" More complicated questions could require more extensive cueing.

Wait-Time

Wait-time is the amount of time a teacher waits for a response after asking a question. Students need time to process the question, think of the answer, and formulate a response. A wait-time of 3 to 5 seconds is shown to have a strong positive impact on student learning.

Further, a good teacher can use questioning as a mechanism to support classroom management techniques. One common technique is called **group alerting**, in which the teacher asks the whole class the question, waits, and then selects one student to answer. Naming the student before the question is asked increases the likelihood that the other students will stop paying attention.

TIME TO PRACTICE

Before you move on to the next chapter, check out the quiz for this chapter in your Student Tools. You can download and print a copy of the quiz when you register your book—just follow the instructions on the "Get More (Free) Content" page at the beginning of this book. If you ace the quiz, move on to the next chapter. If you answer several questions incorrectly, be sure to mark them and re-review those topics before test day.

Chapter 25
Assessment

ASSESSMENT STRATEGIES

Types of Assessments

Just as you would use different teaching strategies to teach different ideas, you should use different assessment strategies to measure student achievement. Here are some terms you should be familiar with.

Norm-Referenced Tests

If you've ever been graded on a curve, then you've experienced a norm-referenced test. This means that your grade depended on how well you did compared to everyone else who took the test.

Criterion-Referenced Tests

Your driver's license test was probably criterion-referenced. Perhaps there were 25 questions, and you needed to answer 20 of them correctly in order to pass. It didn't matter how many people had aced the test or how many people had answered only 10 questions correctly. You needed to prove a certain proficiency in order to pass.

Standardized Tests

The term *standardized* means that test content, conditions, grading, and reporting are equivalent for everyone who takes the test. We tend to think of these tests as purely multiple-choice, but that's not true in all cases. For example, the PLT is a standardized test, but it includes short-answer questions as well.

- Achievement tests—Most standardized tests given are achievement tests, which measure specific knowledge in a specific area.
- Aptitude tests—These tests purport to measure how well a student is likely to do in the future.

Assessments of Prior Knowledge/Pretesting

It's important to take into account the level of knowledge a student has before beginning a lesson or semester. Would it be fair to hold a recent immigrant to the same standards as a native English speaker on an oral grammar test? Probably not. Some curricula are designed so that a specific set of knowledge and skills is necessary before instruction in a new area can occur. Such a set of knowledge and skills is called a **prerequisite competency.**

Structured Observations

These are particularly well-suited to situations in which cooperative learning is taking place. The teacher can observe the interactions within a group and evaluate student performance accordingly. This is an example of an *informal assessment,* meaning that there is no grading rubric or checklist that a teacher follows. An informal assessment is more subjective and situation-specific than a *formal assessment,* such as a standardized test.

Student Responses During a Lesson

This shouldn't necessarily be considered the same as grading on class participation, but a teacher can get a strong sense of student understanding (or lack thereof) based on responses during classroom discussions. This is another example of an informal assessment.

Portfolios

These aren't just used in art class. Portfolios are often used to give students a place to collect their best work over a longer period, such as a unit or even a semester. Teachers can get a sense of the level of student work holistically, without placing undue emphasis on a specific test. Portfolios allow teachers to assess learning growth over a lengthy period.

Essays Written to Prompts

While these take longer to grade and depend upon students possessing sufficient writing skills, essays provide insight into student thought in a way multiple-choice tests cannot.

Journals

Many good teachers use journals not only as tools to promote individual self-expression, but also to gauge understanding.

Peer Assessment

Sometimes it is helpful to have students assess one another, often according to a predetermined set of criteria. This encourages autonomy and responsibility and can help improve students' judgment. In addition, peer assessment frequently requires a more thorough knowledge of the subject matter than would otherwise be needed, which motivates learning and discourages passivity. Such assessments will, of course, typically be less reliable than those of a teacher.

Self-Assessment

Having students assess their own work can also be a valuable tool and, like peer assessment, encourages autonomy and a more active role, while providing teachers with valuable insight. Self-evaluation also helps improve judgment and gives students a better sense of their own subjectivity. As with peer assessment, self-evaluation can, however, be inaccurate and biased, although providing a predetermined set of criteria to guide the student is common practice.

Rubrics

A **rubric** is an assessment that measures and scores a piece of work, action, or behavior. Rubrics explain the expectations, criteria, and characteristics for each degree in a range of quality. Rubrics can be used in any discipline. A rubric's criteria range and degrees should be reviewed with students prior to the assessment process so that students understand the expectations for a particular behavior or assignment.

Characteristics of Assessments

There are some key concepts that you should know with respect to assessments.

Validity

Does the test measure what it's supposed to measure? In addition to ensuring representative content, a well-designed test will correct for factors such as guessing and test anxiety.

Reliability

Barring other factors, would you get about the same score on the test if you were to take it today and then again two weeks from now? If so, the test is said to be reliable.

Raw Score

Your raw score on a given test is the number of points you earned through correct responses, without any statistical adjustments or alterations of any kind.

Scaled Score

Your scaled score on a given test is determined by converting your raw score onto some sort of standardized scale. This is often done when different versions of a test are given to different groups of students (e.g., the SAT), and the various forms may vary slightly in difficulty. Scaled scores are often used for high-stakes exams in the interests of fairness and accuracy of assessment.

True Score

The true score is the score you would get if it measured your knowledge and nothing more. For instance, if you made several lucky guesses, you would get a score higher than your true score; if you didn't sleep at all the night before the test, you would probably get a score lower than your true score. Sometimes the test itself has variations from administration to administration that could impact your score. A well-designed standardized test minimizes those variations.

Confidence Interval

Test writers acknowledge that not all test takers will get their true score each time they take the test. To account for this, they suggest you view any given score within the context of a confidence interval—a range on either side of the score you received. For example, on a given admissions test, scores might range from 200 to 800, with a confidence interval of 30 points at 66%. Let's say you take that test and get a 510. The confidence interval means that the test writers believe there's a 66% chance that your true score is between a 480 and a 540.

Mean

The **mean** is the average of test takers' scores. Add the scores up and divide by the number of test takers.

Median

If you list all scores in mathematical order, the middle score is called the **median**.

Often the median is a better choice than the mean when you want a "representative" score. The mean is affected by extreme scores (both high and low), but the median is always right smack in the middle!

Mode

The **mode** is the score that occurs most frequently.

Standard Deviation

Standard deviation is a statistical idea that tells you how wide the variance of scores is with respect to the mean. Taken together, these last four concepts—mean, median, mode, and standard deviation—can lend some insight into what test results look like as a whole, and how any individual test score compares to the rest of the group. Let's look at two examples.

Here's one group of 20 scores on a test with a maximum score of 100:

Test Scores			
45	59	65	68
69	71	73	73
74	74	79	81
83	84	85	88
92	93	94	100

The average of these scores is 77.5, and the median is 76.5. There are *two* modes here (73 and 74), as both numbers appear twice. In chart form, the distribution of scores looks like this:

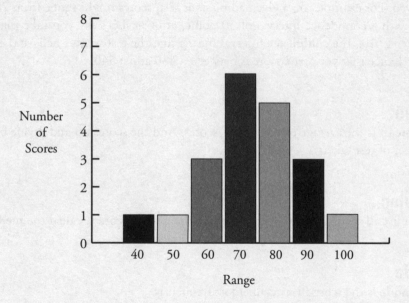

The standard deviation is about 13.2, which means scores are relatively evenly spread out but tend to cluster around the mean. (The curve resembles a normal distribution, or a typical-looking bell curve.)

But what if the scores looked like this?

Test Scores			
52	53	54	56
56	58	59	59
59	59	96	97
98	98	98	99
99	100	100	100

Here, the average is still 77.5, and the median is only slightly different from the last set: 77.5. In fact, according to those numbers, these results are virtually identical. But the mode is 59, and if you see the results in chart form, the differences are even starker:

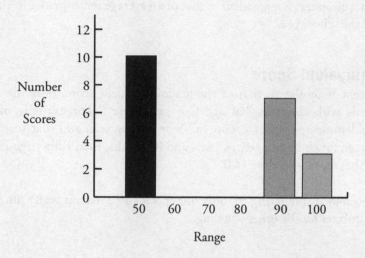

The standard deviation is about 22 points, which means that the scores are not clustered about the mean. But the only way you could tell that without seeing the individual scores (or a graph) would be to know something about the standard deviation.

Finally, there are several ways that you can put an individual score into a larger context.

Percentile Rank

Percentile rank tells you what percentage of the testing population scored worse than you did. For instance, a score in the 72nd percentile means that you received a better score than 72% of the other test takers.

Stanines

The word *stanine* is a contraction of the words "standard nine." Stanines are an artificial scale from 1 to 9 that can be placed on any normal (bell-curved) distribution of scores. The mean is 5, and the standard deviation is 2. For instance, if you had a stanine score of 4, you would be slightly below average. If you had a stanine score of 8, you would be well above average. Stanines are meant to be a broad classification of scores, and are often used instead of a more precise measurement to reduce the chance of attributing too much importance to a particular score.

Grade-Equivalent Score

This is a score expressed in terms of how an average student performs at a certain grade level. For instance, a grade-equivalent score of 10.2 means that your performance on a given test is equivalent to that of an average tenth-grader in the second month of the school year.

Age-Equivalent Score

This concept is similar to that of the grade-equivalent score, only the reference group deals with chronological age (not grade level). For example, if Billy, a 12-year-old student, receives a score of 75 on a given test, and that score was the average score for children aged 14 years and 0 months, then Billy's age-equivalent score for that exam would be 14.0.

While you may be preparing for only one specific PLT test, it won't hurt to complete the quizzes for the other age ranges.

TIME TO PRACTICE

Before you move on to the next chapter, check out the quiz for this chapter in your Student Tools. You can download and print a copy of the quiz when you register your book—just follow the instructions on the "Get More (Free) Content" page at the beginning of this book. If you ace the quiz, move on to the next chapter. If you answer several questions incorrectly, be sure to mark them and re-review those topics before test day.

Chapter 26
Professional Development, Leadership, and Community

TEACHER PROFESSIONALISM

This is a broad topic, but here are some key concepts that may come up on the test.

The Reflective Practitioner

Educators should take advantage of resources available to them in order to become even more effective as teachers. Common resources include the following:

- professional journals and other publications
- professional associations
- professional development activities, such as workshops and conferences
- graduate courses
- independent research
- internships
- other teachers, via learning communities and study groups

The key idea here is for teachers to focus on professional growth, self-evaluation, and improvement. You should be familiar with a variety of reflective practices such as the following:

- reflection journals
- self and peer assessment
- portfolios
- incident analysis
- peer observation

The role of research and debate on teaching practices is also important when it comes to professional development. The test will likely require an understanding of the following:

- how and where to find research on teaching practices
- how to interpret data from research on teaching practices
- how to apply research and data to a variety of educational situations

The Larger Community

Another key concept in the area of professional development is the role of the teacher as a resource and role model for the community in which he or she teaches. This interaction between the teacher and the community is an important aspect of the teacher's job. The community includes the students, students' families, fellow teachers, and other school support personnel like guidance counselors; IEP team members; special education teachers; speech, physical, and occupational therapists; library media specialists; teachers of the gifted and talented; and paraeducators.

According to ETS, there are five basic elements of successful collaboration: (1) develop a plan; (2) identify stakeholders; (3) identify purpose of collaboration; (4) practice and support effective communication; (5) seek support when necessary.

Teachers should know basic strategies for establishing relationships with these community members in order to support the educational process.

Home Environment

A key component of the larger community is students' families, which brings up the issue of home environment. Teachers should be aware of factors outside of school that can influence a student's learning. Changes in family situations ranging from the birth of a sibling to parental divorce can markedly affect a child's performance. Similarly, socioeconomic conditions need to be recognized as an influence. While teachers shouldn't lower their expectations of students with unique situations, teachers should be aware of the potential impact of those situations on a child's performance.

Involving Parents

All studies agree that parental involvement is crucial to a child's success in school. Good teachers take steps to encourage this involvement. On the test, choose answers that describe parents and teachers as equal partners in a child's education as well as display open, two-way communication between parents and teachers. Note that conferences between parents and the teacher should always begin and end on a positive note.

Legal Responsibilities

Another aspect of professional development and leadership is educational legislation and court decisions. For the test, you should be familiar with legal concepts and responsibilities such as

- equal access
- privacy and confidentiality
- First Amendment issues
- intellectual freedom
- mandated reporting of child abuse/neglect
- due process
- liability
- licensing and tenure
- copyright

Common sense should be your guide when answering these kinds of questions on the test. Remember basic guidelines like the confidentiality of student records and mandated reporting of suspected child abuse cases.

Teachers, along with many other professionals who work with children, are "mandated reporters": they have a legal duty to report reasonable suspicions of child abuse or neglect.

The key takeaways here are the following:

1. Teachers should be aware of professional development practices and resources.
2. Teachers should understand the implications of research and debates on teaching practices.
3. Teachers should recognize the role of reflective practice for professional growth and know a variety of activities that support self-reflection and improvement.
4. Teachers should be aware of the larger community (students, families, and colleagues) as well as their role as leaders within that community.
5. Teachers should establish partnerships and collaborative relationships with the community in order to support the educational process.

TIME TO PRACTICE

Before you move on to the next chapter, check out the quiz for this chapter in your Student Tools. You can download and print a copy of the quiz when you register your book—just follow the instructions on the "Get More (Free) Content" page at the beginning of this book. If you ace the quiz, move on to the next chapter. If you answer several questions incorrectly, be sure to mark them and re-review those topics before test day.

Chapter 27
Analysis of
Instructional
Scenarios

CASE HISTORIES AND CONSTRUCTED-RESPONSE QUESTIONS

Following the multiple-choice section of the PLT test, you will be presented with two "case histories" that each deal with a teaching situation with pedagogical implications. Each case history will be associated with several brief "documents" that provide information about the situation (e.g., a homework assignment, a lesson plan, an excerpt from the teacher's journal, and so on). Each case history will have two constructed-response (short-answer) questions attached to it, for a total of 4 constructed-response questions. Your responses to these questions will be scored on a scale of 0–2.

HOW TO APPROACH SHORT-ANSWER QUESTIONS ON THE PLT TEST

These are more complex than multiple-choice questions and will require a more detailed strategy. Here are the steps you should follow:

> **Step 1:** Take Notes and Predict
> **Step 2:** Read the Questions
> **Step 3:** Brainstorm
> **Step 4:** Write the Answer

Let's break each of these down:

Step 1: Take Notes and Predict

The most important thing to know about the case histories is that every piece of information they give you is there for a reason. So as you're reading the case history for the first time, take notes on your scratch paper. You'll be asked to comment on and improve upon the current situation, so pretend that you are evaluating the scenario. If you notice something that seems odd or unusual, write it down. If you notice something particularly positive, write that down, too. You'll soon have a good idea of the situation as a whole, and you'll be well on your way to answering the questions before you even see them. Let's apply this strategy to the following case history:

Scenario:

Mr. Jackson is a first-year teacher at an elementary school in a working-class suburb of a midsize city. He teaches sixth grade, and has a class of 27 students from a variety of ethnic and socioeconomic backgrounds.

1st year—he doesn't have all the answers. Fairly big, and very diverse class.

One student in Mr. Jackson's class, Tim, is grossly overweight. Tim is an average student, performing at about grade level in all academic areas. The other students in Mr. Jackson's class shun Tim, and he has no real friends in the class. Recently, Mr. Jackson has been hearing students verbally abuse Tim in class. Mr. Jackson's response has been to reprimand the verbally abusive student at the time of the incident, but the incidents seem to be escalating in frequency and severity nonetheless.

The Tim situation is a problem. Mr. Jackson isn't doing the right thing by reprimanding the student in front of the rest of the class—he should either do it alone with the student, or with the student and Tim. Disciplining the verbally abusive student in front of the rest of the class calls attention to the student.

A one-time college athlete, Mr. Jackson has no personal experience with being overweight. He notices that Tim brings unhealthy foods to eat at lunchtime.

Does Mr. Jackson know how to relate to Tim's problem?

Mr. Jackson approached Tim to try to discuss these issues with him. Tim said, "I wish you wouldn't even say anything in class. It just makes it worse at recess." Tim's response to the situation has been to become more withdrawn in class.

Tim's embarrassed.

Parent-teacher conferences are in one week. Mr. Jackson knows that both of Tim's parents are obese themselves. Mr. Jackson sympathizes with Tim, but at some level he is surprised that Tim isn't taking steps to correct the problem on his own. Mr. Jackson understands that the current situation is problematic, and realizes that he must take some further action to ensure a positive learning environment for Tim and the rest of his students.

Sounds like Mr. Jackson needs some sensitivity training to help him understand different reasons for obesity. At least he realizes he doesn't have all the answers.

Even before you see the questions, you can anticipate what they're going to be about. This case history has to do with classroom management, student health and social issues, and dealing with parents.

Step 2: Read the Questions
<u>Question 1</u>

Mr. Jackson is correct to be concerned about Tim's current situation.
- Name TWO ways in which the current situation, if left unchanged, could damage Tim's development. Base your response on the principles of teaching and learning and human development.

Mr. Jackson's current method of reprimanding students is not having the effect of stopping the unwanted behavior.

- Suggest TWO alternate strategies that Mr. Jackson might employ to stop the verbal abuse while addressing Tim's concern that punishing other students for teasing him "only makes it worse at recess."
- For each strategy, explain why it would be a preferred strategy to the one Mr. Jackson is using now. Base your response on the principles of learning and teaching and classroom management techniques.

Because you've already thought about the situation, none of these questions should come as a complete surprise. Now think about answering them.

Step 3: Brainstorm
Question 1

Mr. Jackson is correct to be concerned about Tim's current situation.

- Name TWO ways in which the current situation, if left unchanged, could damage Tim's development. Base your response on the principles of teaching and learning and human development.

We already knew Tim wasn't happy. If things don't change, what could happen to him? What do we know? He's overweight, and he's being teased to the point where he has no friends in the class. We're asked to find two ways in which his development could be damaged. How about social development and physical development?

Social

- Peer relationships are important.
- Confronting negativism in a constructive manner is an important social skill.

Physical

- Obesity leads to health risks.

Step 4: Write the Answer
These answers shouldn't be long. Keep two things in mind:

1. Be sure to answer the question directly and give supporting reasons for your statements or suggestions. Cite relevant educational theories where appropriate.
2. Make your answer easy to read by structuring it well. Graders will be reading lots of these answers—they'll appreciate well-organized thoughts.

A high-scoring sample answer might look like this:

The current classroom situation is detrimental to Tim's development in two major areas: social and physical.

First, Tim's current social isolation could lead to emotional problems later in life. Erikson, among other theorists, notes that peer relationships are critical in establishing identity. Having no friends at this age could lead to psychosocial stagnation. In addition, Tim's apparent inability to confront his tormentors suggests that he is incapable of expressing his feelings in a constructive way. This, too, could have negative consequences in terms of interpersonal relationships.

Second, Tim's physical condition needs to be addressed. Childhood obesity rates are rising, as are rates of related medical conditions such as diabetes. The advantages of balanced nutrition and regular exercise are well-documented. Left unchecked, Tim's obesity could lead to serious negative health consequences in later years.

Most of that probably seems obvious to you (although you may have forgotten about the specifics of Erikson's theories), and much is supported by common sense. All you have to do is answer the question by connecting a few meaningful ideas together into several sentences.

ETS would like the above response for many reasons. First, it quickly answers the question with a sentence that also sets up the structure for what is to follow. The paragraphs are well-organized, with words that link ideas together such as "first" and "in addition." Further, the answers are supported by specific references and examples. Notice that the response wasn't particularly long.

You're not looking to get published, and your answers don't need to be worthy of literary prizes. Answer the question, support your responses, and move on.

Let's try the next one:

Question 2

Mr. Jackson's current method of reprimanding students is not having the effect of stopping the unwanted behavior.

- Suggest TWO alternative strategies that Mr. Jackson might employ to stop the verbal abuse while addressing Tim's concern that punishing other students for teasing him "only makes it worse at recess."

- For each strategy, explain why it would be a preferred strategy to the one Mr. Jackson is using now. Base your response on the principles of teaching and learning and classroom management techniques.

Step 3: Brainstorm

We thought about this when we were reading the text. Mr. Jackson could:

- Take the abusive student aside alone.
- Take the abusive student aside with Tim.
- Address the issue with respect to overall classroom expectations, such as rules of behavior.

If he takes the student aside alone, he runs the risk of alienating the student's relationship with Tim even further. Mr. Jackson should include Tim in the discussion.

Why doesn't Mr. Jackson have a code of behavior in place? That's the type of thing that good teachers establish at the beginning of the year to keep situations like this from happening. It's not too late, as long as he doesn't introduce it in direct response to the situation with Tim.

Now, let's put these ideas into a response.

Step 4: Write the Answer

There are two approaches that Mr. Jackson could take that would improve the classroom situation.

First, rather than simply admonishing the attacker in front of the class, he should take the abuser aside with Tim and not only reprimand the attacker for the teasing, but also give Tim an opportunity to express his feelings to his attacker without having the whole class listening in. The advantages of this method are twofold: first, the attacker doesn't get the attention reinforcement in front of the rest of the class, and second, Tim has an opportunity to work on his peer communication skills. Both of these elements are missing from Mr. Jackson's current approach.

Second, in a general forum not directly linked to any particular attack, Mr. Jackson should take an opportunity to set clear, enforceable standards of behavior for the entire class. These standards should include a ban on abusive speech and a penalty for breaking that rule. That way, if the abuser picks on Tim in the future, Mr. Jackson can punish the abuser without linking the punishment to Tim. In contrast to Mr. Jackson's current method, this makes it less likely that Tim would face repercussions "at recess."

Remember that the multiple-choice and short-answer sections are NOT timed separately. Be sure to allocate your time strategically!

PLT PRACTICE: CASE HISTORY, K–6

Answers and explanations can be found at the end of the chapter.

<u>Directions:</u> The case history is followed by two short-answer questions.

<u>Scenario:</u>

Mr. Lewis is a fourth-year teacher in a K–6 elementary school. This is Mr. Lewis's second year teaching third grade. This year, his class is comprised of 23 students—12 girls and 11 boys. At the beginning of the third month of school, Mr. Lewis is about to introduce a new activity called "Reading Journal." He did not try this his first year teaching the third grade, but hopes that this activity will help support the goals and reading curriculum established for third-grade students. The first document is a project plan description of the "Reading Journal," while the second document is a conversation with one of Mr. Lewis's students, Cindy.

Document 1

"Reading Journal" Lesson Plan

<u>Goals:</u>

1. Improve reading comprehension abilities.

2. Improve writing skills and ability to develop critical-thinking skills, as demonstrated in one's writing.

3. Improve speaking and listening abilities.

4. Improve social skills within the class, creating a more positive classroom environment.

<u>Objectives:</u>

1. Students will use the "Reading Journal" to summarize their readings.

2. Students will discuss their readings, and connect the topics to experiences and people in their own lives.

<u>Assignment:</u>

The "Reading Journal"

Each Friday, we will devote one hour of class time to reading. You may choose any book in the class library, in our school library (ask Ms. Sincoff if the book is approved), or any book from home. If you bring a book from home, please bring it to me for approval.

In addition to the class time each Friday, your homework assignment is to read for about two hours per week outside of class.

Each week, you need to make two entries in your journal.

When you start a journal entry, please indicate the book name, author, page numbers you are writing about, and the date of your entry.

Your journal entry should discuss two things:

1. A summary of the pages you have recently completed.

2. Your thoughts on the material. Do you like the book? What is going to happen next? Do you understand the feelings of the characters? Has this ever happened to you?

Assessment:

Every two weeks, each student will turn in the "Reading Journal" to Mr. Lewis.

I will review the journal for the following criteria:

- quality of book summaries
- number of entries during the week
- number of pages read per week

Document 2

Conversation between Mr. Lewis and a student, Cindy

Mr. Lewis	Cindy, I don't have a record of you turning in your Reading Journal from last week. Did you turn that in? I have seen you reading during our Friday sessions.
Cindy	Yes, sir. I read every night.
Mr. Lewis	What have you been reading?
Cindy	Last week I read a book called "Superfudge." This week I'm reading a book called "The Wind and the Willows."
Mr. Lewis	That is an excellent book. It will probably take you a few weeks to complete.
Cindy	I started reading it this Monday, and so far I've read 200 pages.
Mr. Lewis	Wow, that is just fantastic. Do you enjoy the story so far?
Cindy	It is sometimes confusing. I'm not sure I understand all the parts and what is going on.
Mr. Lewis	Well, I hope that you write about it in your journal. That way, I'll know the types of questions that you have.
Cindy	Okay.
Mr. Lewis	I'm very happy to see that you are reading so much. Yet I'm concerned that this level of work is not reflected in your "Reading Journal."
Cindy	Oh, well you said to turn in two a week. That is what I was doing. But I keep reading because I like to read.
Mr. Lewis	Okay, Cindy. Please turn in your journal from last week so I can give you credit for your efforts.
Cindy	Okay.

Directions: Questions 1 and 2 require you to write short answers. You are not expected to cite specific theories or texts in your answer; however, your responses to the questions will be evaluated with respect to professionally accepted principles and practices in teaching and learning. Be sure to answer all parts of the questions.

Question 1

Review Document 1, the "Reading Journal" Lesson Plan.

- Identify ONE strength and ONE weakness of the "Reading Journal" Lesson Plan.
- For each strength or weakness, describe how each item is used in planning instruction. Base your response on the principles of effective instructional planning.

Question 2

In Document 2, Cindy's conversation with Mr. Lewis reveals characteristics about herself as a learner.

- Identify ONE characteristic of Cindy as a learner, and suggest ONE strategy Mr. Lewis might use to support her development.

- For the strategy you suggested, describe how it addresses the characteristics of Cindy as a learner. Base your response on principles of varied instructional strategies for different learners and of human development.

PLT PRACTICE: CASE HISTORY, 5–9

Answers and explanations can be found at the end of the chapter.

Directions: The case history is followed by two short-answer questions.

Scenario:

Ms. Lloyd teaches a sixth-grade mathematics course to 28 students. There are 14 male students and 14 female students. Ms. Lloyd is in her third year teaching this course, and in her fifth year of teaching. She is planning for her self-evaluation. In order to prepare a thorough assessment, Ms. Lloyd begins to gather material that may be helpful for the activity. In the documents below, Ms. Lloyd focuses on a specific class, and three of her students. The class takes place during the month of October, which is the second month of the semester. No formal grades have been given at this time.

Document 1

Profiles of three students

Meg is a challenge. She manages to make comments on almost every topic, but they are rarely correct. She seems so eager to participate, but does not have a good grasp of the material. I've noticed that Meg is frequently the last to leave the school day care. Last week, I was working late on some lesson plans, and the after-school caregiver asked me if I had any additional contact information for Meg since no one had picked her up from school—and it was 7 P.M.! She has also been tardy a number of times—including four times in the last two weeks. I know that Meg lives about 30 minutes from the school, so that could be a factor. But I'd like her to be here on time so we can focus on the more important issues, like building her math skills. With some time and practice, I think she can master the material. She certainly has the right attitude!

Peter is a very quiet student, who is withdrawn from most activities. Yet his performance is just fine. Thus far, he has turned in all the assignments, and would be getting an A– if grades were due this week (they are due in three weeks). Peter seems incredibly shy—he does not like attention from me, nor from other students in the class. He spends most of his breaks or free time playing on his Game Boy, instead of socializing with other students. Previously, I attempted to bring Peter out of his shell by cold-calling on him in class. He responds extremely timidly, which has drawn some laughter from the rest of the class.

Nicole is an excellent student who comes from a very proud family. I taught her older brother two years ago; he was the best student in the class. Nicole is like her brother, but she is beyond even where he was two years ago. I'm afraid that I am boring Nicole with the work that we do. She tends to finish each assignment early and get almost all of the questions correct. She raises her hand to answer a question about as often as Meg, except that Nicole knows the answer! I'd like to find ways to keep Nicole entertained and challenged in the class, but with several struggling students, I'm not sure how to do that. I'm afraid that other students may fall further behind.

Document 2

Self-Analysis

Now that this is my third year of teaching, I'm feeling comfortable with the material, and I can predict the areas that students will struggle in during the year. This year has been somewhat of a challenge, in that the state standards changed, and I know that there is tremendous pressure that this class perform well on the state test, which takes place during the middle of May. As a result, I feel more pressure to keep up the pace—if I don't cover all of the material, the scores of the entire class may suffer. On the other hand, my new pace seems to challenge students more than ever before. I'm not sure if I have a weaker class this year, but more students just "don't get it" than in prior years. The idea of "no one left behind" seems harder than ever.

All of this leaves me with quite a challenge. I'd like to spend more time with students such as Meg, who are struggling with the material. And I don't even have time to think about external issues that are impacting my students—for example, Meg's home life. On the flip side, I'm afraid that students like Nicole are not challenged. Finally, I'm starting to run low on ideas to keep this course innovative and fun. It was so much easier with the English courses I was teaching. Mathematics is more straightforward. I know that many students don't enjoy this class as much as they enjoy other subjects, such as history and English, which provide greater opportunities for creativity.

Document 3

Notes from Class
Tuesday, October 10

Today we reviewed some complicated word problems. I had asked that students prepare questions 1–10 from page 231 in their workbook. About 13 of the 28 students indicated that they completed all ten questions, so I decided to review each of the questions in class. Nicole was the only student to complete all ten questions correctly—including the final question, which only four students in the class got correct. For each question, I asked two students to write their answers on the board. I do this so that I can see how students derive the correct answer, rather than just evaluate if the answer is correct. Meg volunteered to answer question #4, but unfortunately, she did not get it correct. She was one of the students that did not complete the assignment (in fact, she didn't even get to #4, and I wondered why she volunteered). I asked Peter to answer question #6, and he gave the correct answer, but did not want to come up to the board. Thomas was very rude to Peter—I didn't hear exactly what he said, but it was not kind. Peter just sulked in his chair after Thomas leaned over and said something. I told Peter he had to come up to the board, and he quickly wrote his explanation on the board, and then quickly walked back to his desk.

Directions: Questions 1 and 2 require you to write short answers. You are not expected to cite specific theories or texts in your answer; however, your responses to the questions will be evaluated with respect to professionally accepted principles and practices in teaching and learning. Be sure to answer all parts of the questions.

Question 1

Take a look at Document 3 and evaluate Ms. Lloyd's performance for the class on Tuesday, October 10.

- Identify ONE teaching strategy that Ms. Lloyd did well, and ONE teaching strategy Ms. Lloyd could employ to improve her lesson.

- For each strategy identified, explain how it addresses the goals of Ms. Lloyd and the concerns of the class, and how it makes group instruction more effective. Base your response on the principles of effective instructional strategies.

Question 2

Assume that Ms. Lloyd produced a lesson plan before giving the lecture and review on word problems. Assume that no modifications are made for any of her students.

- Suggest TWO modifications, one for Meg and one for Nicole, which Ms. Lloyd could have made that could offer the students a better learning environment.

- For each modification, explain how it will provide for a better learning situation for Nicole and Meg. Base your response on principles of varied instruction for diverse learners.

PLT PRACTICE: CASE HISTORY, 7–12

Answers and explanations can be found at the end of the chapter.

<u>Directions:</u> The case history is followed by two short-answer questions.

<u>Scenario:</u>

Mr. Erving teaches a seventh-grade history class comprised of 26 students. For 12 students, English is the second language; these students represent four different language groups with a wide range of English fluency. Two students are placed in the class on the "least-restrictive environment" provision. Three students have been identified as qualifying for the "gifted and talented" program. One student is repeating the class after having failed it the previous year.

Below is information about Mr. Erving's goals for the year, and specific information about his plans for the week of October 15.

<u>Long-term goals for the class:</u>

1. Students will develop reading and writing skills within the history curriculum.

2. Students will work cooperatively and supportively.

3. Students will develop speaking and listening skills.

4. Students will participate in both formal presentations and informal discussions.

<u>Activities for the week of October 15:</u>

1. Students will begin the class by presenting a history of where they grew up and their native culture. Students will work in pairs. Each student will describe where he or she came from; if they were born in the United States, they will identify the ethnic origin of his or her ancestors. He or she will then present a few facts about that country/region. (1 session)

2. Students will then make a formal presentation on their family background. (1 session)

3. Students will then study the region of their family background in greater detail, using the history text and the Internet. (2 sessions)

4. Students will present "fun facts" about their country of origin. (1 session)

<u>Assessment:</u>

1. Students will be graded on their family-background presentation.

2. Students will be graded on their country-of-origin presentation.

Mr. Erving's impression of three students during the week of October 15

Sarah struggled with the assignment. She is one of the two students in the class under the "least-restrictive curriculum" provision. Sarah seems to have a limited attention span. This was evident during her group work with Cesar, and I could tell that Cesar was frustrated with his partner.

Karen speaks Spanish fluently, and is working hard to improve her English. She performed well during the research portion of the week, but struggled when she was paired with another student. Despite her enthusiasm, it was evident that she did not understand everything that Carrie was telling her during their meeting.

Scott is a gifted student. He spent most of Thursday working on another subject during the class time. When I confronted Scott about this, he indicated that he had completed his research, and was ready to present on Friday. Sure enough, his presentation was one of the best in the class, but I actually believe that Scott could have performed better.

Directions: Questions 1 and 2 require you to write short answers. You are not expected to cite specific theories or texts in your answer; however, your responses to the questions will be evaluated with respect to professionally accepted principles and practices in teaching and learning. Be sure to answer all parts of the questions.

Question 1

Mr. Erving identifies two items for assessment for this week's lesson plan in history.

- Identify TWO additional formal or informal assessment techniques Mr. Erving could use to provide his students with opportunities to demonstrate their learning.

- For each technique suggested, describe how each item is used to assess student learning. Base your response on the principles of informal and formal assessment.

Question 2

In Mr. Erving's notes, he identified several facts about Karen that reveal characteristics about herself as a learner.

- Identify ONE characteristic of Karen as a learner, and suggest ONE strategy Mr. Erving might use to support her development.

- For the strategy you suggested, describe how it addresses the characteristics of Karen as a learner. Base your response on principles of varied instructional strategies for different learners and of human development.

PLT PRACTICE: CASE HISTORY ANSWERS AND EXPLANATIONS

Case History, K–6

1. **Sample Response that Receives a Score of 2:**

    Mr. Lewis' plan has both strengths and weaknesses. One strength is that he has students participate in a writing activity that is connected to a reading activity. By linking the two activities together, Mr. Lewis will help students at this age make connections, and therefore, communicate well. Students will have a better opportunity to learn and demonstrate their learning.

    One way that the plan could be improved is that Mr. Lewis can provide examples of what is expected in the "Reading Journal." Under #2, Mr. Lewis asks students for "your thoughts on the material." He then gives three or four sample questions to answer. However, for students in the third grade, this may be too limiting. Students may answer only these specific questions. That is clearly not Mr. Lewis's goal, for his true goal is to get students to reflect on their thoughts and write their personal feelings. Instead of a specific list, Mr. Lewis should encourage students to write what comes to mind. Or, he could add that students can write about anything that comes to mind.

    Sample Response that Receives a Score of 1:

    The strength of Mr. Lewis' project plan is that it has an assessment section. A necessary part of any project plan is to have an assessment section so that students understand how they will be evaluated. Further, it provides a valuable checkpoint for teachers, so that they can ensure the goals and activities are properly measured with an assessment plan. However, the plan could be improved by listing the average weighting for each of the three categories.

2. **Sample Response that Receives a Score of 2:**

    It is clear that Cindy enjoys reading, but does not hold the same passion for writing. The challenge for Mr. Lewis is to make writing more creative and enjoyable for Cindy, based on her enjoyment of reading. While an alternate response mode is likely unnecessary, Mr. Lewis could ask Cindy to mimic her favorite books by asking her to write her own story in the "Reading Journal." She could take one of the characters in the book, and write about what happens to him or her after the conclusion of the book. This would help to draw direct connections between her reading and her writing. Cindy has displayed much talent as a reader; the challenge now is to bring those same skills to her writing.

Sample Response that Receives a Score of 1:

Cindy is a very strong reader. The fact that she has read almost two novels in two weeks is a tribute to her time spent reading. In fact, those books are a few hundred pages each! Because Cindy enjoys reading, Mr. Lewis does not need to worry about her reading skills. I'm sure they are just fine, unless she glosses over the material too much. But it is clear that she does not have the same passion, and possibly the same skills for writing. She has not turned in her journal, which means that she likely did not complete the writing assignments, in favor of reading more material in her books.

Case History, 5–9

1.   **Sample Response that Receives a Score of 2:**

Ms. Lloyd needs to be creative and find strategies that will challenge and excite students, even with a topic such as math. Math is often described as not being a very creative topic. One way she did this was to engage the students by having them come up to the board to show their work. This creates more incentive for students to complete their work, as positive peer pressure at this stage can be very helpful from a learning perspective. Ms. Lloyd could make sessions more effective by assigning questions to students based upon their skill level. This will keep students appropriately challenged by material they have learned. One strategy that Ms. Lloyd may need to employ is to assess a student's performance based on the completion of homework assignments. Students may not be conditioned to complete their homework, especially if they learn that there are no adverse consequences for completing the material.

Sample Response that Receives a Score of 1:

Ms. Lloyd did a good job in having an interactive exercise. However, she should improve in the way in which she gives different assignments for different students. Clearly, Nicole needs different things to work on. By assigning the same work universally, those at the top of the class will be bored, while those who struggle will not get the attention they need. Ms. Lloyd should plan to maximize her students' scores on the upcoming standardized test. One way to do this is to make sure that advanced students are given the proper material to excel.

2.   **Sample Response that Receives a Score of 2:**

Nicole, who is a bright, independent learner, needs the opportunity for enrichment, which will hopefully keep her more engaged and challenged with the class. We know that Nicole often volunteers to give the answer. If she is not called on, she may be frustrated. However, if she is called on too often, other students may feel disengaged or intimidated by not having the correct answer. Thus, the challenge is to keep Nicole focused in a way that will be positive for both her and the entire class. Ms. Lloyd could offer Nicole a more sophisticated mathematics text, material that focuses specifically on advanced word problems, or the opportunity to create word problems for the class to complete. Nicole could be asked to complete these activities, and then possibly present this information to the rest of the class. That would challenge Nicole to think about the material in a more complex way, and find ways to communicate more effectively.

For Meg, Ms. Lloyd might have a meeting with her and her parents to discuss her performance in math—what is going well, and what is challenging. This would also help to involve the parents in the discussion, and potentially to address the external issues such as Meg's attendance, and the fact that her parents often do not pick her up from school on time. As a result of this meeting, Ms. Lloyd should develop specific assignments for Meg. From the passage, we know that Meg likes to volunteer and be involved in the classroom discussion. Thus, Ms. Lloyd could involve Meg, but frame the way in which she asks Meg questions differently. For example, Ms. Lloyd could ask Meg to explain the steps of the process to solve a math problem, instead of simply asking the answer. This would keep Meg engaged, and help both Meg and Ms. Lloyd identify possible challenges that Meg has with the material. The specific homework given to Meg should involve doing more work in setting up the problem correctly.

Sample Response that Receives a Score of 1:

Nicole needs to be given more detailed and challenging assignments. Ms. Lloyd should take a look at the Mathematics curriculum tested on the state standardized test, and find out what they teach regarding word problems.

Case History, 7–12

1.   **Sample Response that Receives a Score of 2:**

Mr. Erving currently has two formal assessment measures—the students' performance on each of the two assigned presentations. However, Mr. Erving can take measures to ensure that his overall assessment is more than these two speaking opportunities. In order to be properly aligned with the class long-term goals, Mr. Erving needs to include other measures. First, he could give a team grade for group participation. One of Mr. Erving's goals is for students to work cooperatively and supportively. To reinforce this, students should receive feedback on their teamwork during the interview sessions. A second formal assessment would be to provide more details about how the presentations will be scored. Identifying a rubric would be helpful for Mr. Erving so that he can be objective during the presentations. For students, they need to understand the types of things that Mr. Erving will want to see in the presentations—will they be judged on length, quality of research, quality of speaking, or organization of material? Knowing this information will help students focus properly.

Sample Response that Receives a Score of 1:

The assessment section is currently vague. Sure, the teacher will evaluate the two presentations, but it is not clear how or what criteria will be used to give a score. There is a danger that students will feel that the scoring could be extremely subjective unless Mr. Erving provides more details about the scoring criteria. So by revising these two things (scoring for the first presentation and the scoring for the second), Mr. Erving will have done two additional things to improve the quality of his assessment program for this lesson plan.

2.　　　**Sample Response that Receives a Score of 2:**

As an ELL student, Karen has several challenges in order to succeed in this history class. Of paramount importance is the need for Karen to improve her English skills. It appears that she has the right attitude, as noted by Mr. Erving. Yet her language skills are taking away from her ability to achieve the classroom goals, such as developing listening skills, and possibly even working cooperatively. Therefore, Mr. Erving should immediately test Karen on her written and oral abilities in both languages. Once Mr. Erving understands Karen's skills, he can then develop a specific plan to get her back up to speed with the rest of the class.

Sample Response that Receives a Score of 1:

The quality of Karen as a learner is that she is an ELL student. This means that English is her second language, and that she may not know English as well as the native English speakers. Mr. Erving can take additional steps for all of his ELL students to make sure they understand the activities and assignments for the class. He may need to slow down or present information differently so that students like Karen can feel a part of the group.

Chapter 28
PLT: K–6 Drill

PLT: K–6 Drill

Multiple-Choice Questions

For each question, select the best answer. Answers and explanations can be found at the end of the chapter.

In a third-grade class, teams of three have been assigned to solve a series of multiplication problems. This task is an example of what type of learning?

○ Inquiry learning

○ Lecture learning

○ Demonstrated learning

○ Cooperative learning

Which of the following is NOT one of the eight types of intelligence identified by Howard Gardner?

○ Linguistic

○ Musical

○ Spatial

○ Exploratory

Ms. Day's second-grade class is finishing a lesson in mathematics. She then announces, "In five minutes, we will complete work on this subtraction question and begin our discussion of history." This statement is an example of

○ cueing

○ authoritative leadership

○ context clues

○ whole language

Brady, a first-grade student, announces that his favorite TV show is "Reference Boy." He becomes upset when another student, Timmy, mentions that he does not like that show. This behavior is an example of what cognitive development theory?

○ Piaget's preoperational stage

○ Freud's oral stage of personality development

○ Erikson's stage of identity vs. identity

○ Thorndike's law of effect

Mr. Daniels is a first-grade teacher. Which of the following characteristics of his classroom will likely be the most challenging in establishing effective classroom management?

○ All desks are set up so that Mr. Daniels can see the faces of all students in the room.

○ Library books, which are used for group reading assignments, are organized in the back left corner of the room.

○ Classroom rules are posted on the blackboard at the front of the class.

○ Two children with special needs are located at the front of the class.

Which of the following statements is a well-formed learning objective?

○ I will teach students how to subtract two numbers.

○ While in your reading group, pronounce the new vocabulary words on page 12. Help the class pronounce any difficult words.

○ Identify where California is located on a map of the United States.

○ Bring in a guest speaker to talk about the activities of a fireman.

Ms. Bernal is writing a spelling test for her second-grade class. This test will likely have which of the following characteristics?

○ High validity

○ No error of measurement

○ Perfect reliability

○ Low validity

Mr. Elam is in his first year as a fourth-grade teacher. One of his students, Nancy, is struggling with math. Which of the following is likely the most effective step Mr. Elam can take to develop an effective learning plan for Nancy?

○ Ask Nancy about her parents, in order to better understand her socioeconomic status

○ Assign additional math questions for Nancy—practice makes perfect

○ Discuss Nancy's performance with her third-grade teacher, who still teaches at the school

○ Tell Nancy that girls traditionally don't do well in math, and encourage her to do her best

A teacher is using a phonics approach for her first-grade classroom. Which of the following will the teacher most likely witness in the students' performance?

○ Students will know how to associate letters and groups of letters with sounds.

○ Students will have a larger vocabulary than those using a whole-language approach.

○ Students can pronounce words but will likely not know their meaning.

○ Students can decode words from their context.

Which of the following is NOT an effective strategy for teaching a student with ADHD?

○ Provide a quiet environment for testing

○ Ensure that each activity is at least one hour long

○ Create a progress plan for the student

○ Use positive reinforcements when activities are completed

In order to determine how well the students in Mr. Brooks's third-grade class perform in math compared with other students in the state, he should have his students take what type of test?

○ A criterion-referenced test

○ A low validity measure

○ An authentic assessment

○ A norm-referenced test

A student in fourth grade is most likely to be in which of Erikson's stages of psychosocial development?

○ Trust vs. mistrust

○ Initiative vs. guilt

○ Autonomy vs. doubt

○ Industry vs. inferiority

A proper Individualized Education Plan (IEP) includes all of the following EXCEPT

○ what should be taught and how

○ how much time the student will spend with children who do not have disabilities

○ annual goals and short-term objectives for the student

○ an agreement signed by parents and teachers that the IEP will not change for the school year

Steven, a second-grader, completes a standardized reading test. His grade-equivalent score is a 4.3, and his national percentile rank is 93. Which of the following is true about Steven's national percentile score?

○ Steven did as well as 4.3% of the second-graders who completed the test.

○ Steven scored higher than 93% of students who have completed three months in their fourth year of school.

○ Steven scored higher than 93% of students who completed the test.

○ The national percentile shows that Steven has not learned concepts taught in the second half of fourth grade.

Physical education activities are one way to develop which of the following types of learning?

○ Cognitive domain

○ Affective domain

○ Psychomotor domain

○ All of the above

According to Skinner's theories on behavioral development, the practice of giving a student a low grade for poor performance on a test is an example of

○ positive reinforcement

○ negative reinforcement

○ extinction

○ positive punishment

Ms. Brennan's fourth-grade class is studying the process by which cereal is made. The class is currently answering the following question: "What companies should a cereal manufacturer interact with in order to package the cereal?" This task best models what level in Bloom's Taxonomy of Objectives?

○ Knowledge

○ Comprehension

○ Application

○ Evaluation

Mr. Bailey started teaching his third-grade class in the following manner. First, he reviewed the prior day's material. Second, he presented new information for the next lesson. What could Mr. Bailey have done to create a more effective lesson?

○ Introduce a statement or question related to the next lesson to get students curious about the future material

○ Call on a quiet student and ask him or her to explain the next lesson

○ Give a pop quiz to the students

○ Have some students read ahead of time and prepare a quiz for other students in the class

Several tools are recommended when modifying instruction for students who have learning disabilities. Which of the following is NOT a recommended instructional method?

○ Structured, brief assignments

○ Manipulative experiences

○ Cooperative learning

○ Increasingly longer lessons with less public praise

Jamie, a third-grade student, is attempting to learn how to multiply two numbers. Her teacher recommends that she do 100 problems per day until she is comfortable with the process. Which theory does her teacher employ to help Jamie?

○ Thorndike's law of exercise

○ Thorndike's law of effect

○ Skinner's extinction

○ Piaget's sensorimotor theory

Which of the following statements about creating an environment for student learning is NOT true?

○ Objectives should be aligned with the overall goals of the school district.

○ Objectives should be accepted by appropriate national, regional, or state organizations.

○ Objectives should be aligned with students' own achievement goals.

○ Objectives should not be modified for specific student populations; it is important that goals are not compromised.

Tanya is a second-grade student who recently completed a standardized test. She received a score of 100 out of 200, which resulted in an equivalent stanine score of 3. Which of the following statements about Tanya's performance must be true?

○ Tanya scored one grade equivalent above her current grade level.

○ Tanya scored in the 50th percentile.

○ The error of measurement on the test is within 20 percent.

○ Tanya scored below average compared to other students in her class.

Students in a sixth-grade class are trying to solve a problem—how to develop a recycling program for their school. They have invited the local commissioner of sanitation and recycling to speak with the class. The students are at which of the following steps in the problem-solving process?

○ Develop assessment tools to measure the effectiveness of their solutions

○ Brainstorm possible solutions to the task

○ Gather data and information about the problem

○ Develop an implementation plan for the problem

Which of the following instructional strategies is most commonly observed in first-grade classes?

○ The teacher carefully maps out the day's activities, which include numerous structured lessons.

○ The teacher focuses on whole-group discussions and uses various questioning, explaining, and probing techniques.

○ The teacher focuses on two or three long lessons per day, which relate to a common integrated theme.

○ The teacher introduces a topic, and allows students to develop their own plans to address the topic.

Short-Answer Questions

Each case history is followed by two short-answer questions. Read through the case history documents carefully and answer the questions that follow. Be sure to answer all parts of the questions.

Case History 1

<u>Scenario:</u>

Ms. Farrell is about to hold a parent-teacher conference to discuss the results of a series of achievement tests. Ms. Farrell is in her twelfth year teaching third grade at Nessland Elementary School, one of several schools in the South District. This year, her class is composed of 23 students—11 boys and 12 girls. Before her conference, Ms. Farrell is reviewing the documents below in order to prepare her comments about the class's performance.

Document 1

Summary of Results for Third-Grade Classes in South District

	Reading Grade Equivalent	Math Grade Equivalent	Social Studies Grade Equivalent	Writing Grade Equivalent
Nessland Elementary	3.6	4.5	4.1	3.1
All Schools in South District	3.5	4.0	4.1	3.7

	Reading Grade Equivalent	Math Grade Equivalent	Social Studies Grade Equivalent	Writing Grade Equivalent
Nessland Elementary	61%	93%	85%	44%
All Schools in South District	57%	86%	85%	52%

Document 2

Summary of Results for Student Joy Lewis

	Reading Grade Equivalent	Math Grade Equivalent	Social Studies Grade Equivalent	Writing Grade Equivalent
Nessland Elementary	29	34	31%	N/A
All Schools in South District	48%	88%	81%	52%
Grade Equivalent	3.3	4.2	4.0	3.7

Directions: Questions 1 and 2 require you to write short answers. You are not expected to cite specific theories or texts in your answer; however, your responses to the questions will be evaluated with respect to professionally accepted principles and practices in teaching and learning. Be sure to answer all parts of the questions.

Question 1

Ms. Farrell is pleased with the job she has done for the year, as her class is performing above grade level in all areas but one. She is also pleased to see that her class often performs better than those from other schools within the district. Yet she feels that more information may be necessary for her to assess her students' progress effectively.

- Identify TWO reports or inputs that Ms. Farrell could use to get a more complete view of the class's performance.

- For each input identified, describe how that assessment information can be used to guide Ms. Farrell's teaching.

Question 2

Joy's parents are not familiar with the results of standardized tests and want some feedback on her performance.

- Interpret Joy's performance on the standardized test.

- Provide TWO recommendations for what Joy should improve on during the last half of third grade.

Case History 2

Scenario:

Ms. Gemmer is a fourth-grade teacher at Abel Elementary School, where she has taught for the past two years. Below is a conversation she recently had with a student in her class:

Tuesday, 10:45 A.M.

Conclusion of Recess

Tiffany (*smiling*)	Ms. Gemmer, the boys are really funny.
Ms. Gemmer	Oh really? What are they up to now?
Tiffany	They just sang a song about Billy.
Ms. Gemmer	About your classmate Billy? What did they sing?
Tiffany	It's pretty funny. It goes, "Billy, Billy, really stinky. You wear clothes from 1950. You take a bath once a year, cause you stink more than dirty underwear!!"
Ms. Gemmer	Which boys are singing this?
Tiffany	Oh, I don't want to get anyone in trouble. It's just funny.
Ms. Gemmer	Please tell me who was singing, so I can deal with them. Otherwise, I may just punish you too.
Tiffany	Scott and Rick.
Ms. Gemmer	Anyone else?
Tiffany	No. But if you tell them I told you, then they'll get mad at me.
Ms. Gemmer	Don't worry about that. Thank you, Tiffany.

Upon returning from class, Billy did not look happy. In fact, it appeared that he had been crying. Ms. Gemmer noticed that while Billy did not in fact smell, that his clothes were somewhat disheveled, and had numerous stains across the shirt. These were not the result of any recess play; in general, Ms. Gemmer knew that Billy wore many "dirty" clothes. As a majority of her class was affluent, she was concerned that Billy's attire was not a function of finances but of someone not properly caring for Billy.

The following conversation took place immediately after recess:

Ms. Gemmer   Before we move on to our computer assignment, I heard a song I really did not like during recess. Does anyone want to raise their hand and admit that they were singing this song?

No hands are raised; many students are laughing at Rick and Scott, who are no longer making eye contact with Ms. Gemmer.

Mark   I know who did it!

Ms. Gemmer   Thank you Mark, but I want the culprits to identify themselves.

No hands are raised.

Ms. Gemmer   Okay. Fine. I'll deal with this during the lunch period, and those of you who did this, but did not admit it now, will now get twice the punishment.

Ms. Gemmer introduced the computer lesson. Part of this lesson involved students working quietly in groups of three. Ms. Gemmer walked around to each group to monitor their progress. As she reached the group Scott was in, she whispered to Scott, "Please see me at lunch regarding the recess incident." Scott was unhappy, and no longer participated in the assignment. She then walked up to Rick and whispered the same thing. Rick immediately began to cry. When she walked pass Billy's group, she asked Billy how we was doing, leading to this exchange:

Ms. Gemmer   Billy, are you doing okay?

Billy   Yes, Ms. Gemmer.

Ms. Gemmer   Don't worry, I'll take care of the recess problem.

Billy   I don't want to talk about it.

Ms. Gemmer   Then I'll talk about it for you.

Billy   I wish you'd just leave this alone.

Ms. Gemmer   I'm sorry, Billy. But I need to teach people what is right and what is wrong. And that song is not nice.

Ms. Gemmer continued teaching until lunch, when she met privately with Rick and Scott.

Directions: Questions 3 and 4 require you to write short answers. You are not expected to cite specific theories or texts in your answer; however, your responses to the questions will be evaluated with respect to professionally accepted principles and practices in teaching and learning. Be sure to answer all parts of the questions.

Question 3

Ms. Gemmer struggled on how much of this incident she should make public to the entire class versus how much she should deal with it in private.

- Identify one thing Ms. Gemmer did well during this situation.
- Identify two things Ms. Gemmer could do better regarding her handling of this matter. Focus your answers based on your knowledge of managing a positive instructional environment.

Question 4

Ms. Gemmer thinks that Billy's attire may in fact be a sign of problems for Billy.

- Identify TWO things Ms. Gemmer can do to address this issue with Billy and/or his parents.
- Base your response on the principles of teaching and learning and human development.

PLT: K–6 DRILL ANSWERS AND EXPLANATIONS

Multiple-Choice Questions

1. **D** Cooperative learning involves students working together in groups to learn a concept or to complete a task.

2. **D** In addition to the first three answer choices, Gardner's list includes logical-mathematical, bodily-kinesthetic, naturalist, interpersonal, and intrapersonal intelligence.

3. **A** Cueing defines words or other signals that alert students to a coming transition. Ms. Day's announcement prepares students for the transition from math to history.

4. **A** Piaget's theory has four developmental stages. In the second stage, the preoperational stage, students' thinking is egocentric; some students have difficulty understanding the opinions of others.

5. **B** An effective strategy for classroom management is to have books and supplies available at several locations. Arranging the room so that students do not have to stand in line is a key component of classroom management.

6. **C** An objective should describe the actions that students are expected to do once instruction is complete. It should not describe what the teacher will do during the lesson. Choices (A) and (D) describe teacher actions, as does the second half of (B). Therefore, (C) is correct.

7. **A** A test has high validity if it measures how well the students learned the material covered in a particular lesson or curriculum. Because Ms. Bernal is writing a spelling test, it very likely will have high validity—that is, the test will be based on the recent vocabulary her class has studied. Choice (B) is impossible—every test contains some error of measurement. While the spelling test may be reliable, it is a tough argument to say it has perfect reliability. Choice (D) is not valid, as a spelling test is not a predictor for any type of future work.

8. **C** Before Mr. Elam can determine a set of objectives for Nancy, he must determine her prerequisite competencies. The other choices are not aligned with effective techniques to develop Nancy's math skills.

9. **A** This is the standard definition of a phonics approach to reading.

10. **B** Students with ADHD learn most effectively by doing tasks that are small and manageable. Consistently lengthy activities may prove to be challenging for them.

11. **D** Norm-referenced tests are designed to compare students or groups.

12. **D** This fourth stage of Erikson's framework is most common for students in elementary school, between ages 6 and 12.

13. **D** A key component of an effective IEP is that teachers and parents can change the plan at any time, on an as-needed basis. Parents and teachers should meet if either believes that the needs of the student are changing.

14. **C** Choice (B) may be tempting; however, the national percentile rank compares the student's performance to those of all the other students who took the test.

15. **D** While the most obvious type of learning is psychomotor learning (e.g., motor skills), all types of learning can be achieved through physical activities.

16. **D** A negative reinforcement is used to escape an unpleasant situation. For example, students who get an A on the test will not have to do homework for a week. Punishment discourages bad behavior, and we want to discourage students from doing poorly on tests. Positive punishment creates an undesirable situation as a result of a certain behavior. The student does poorly on the test; the student receives a low score.

17. **D** The evaluation stage is defined by making considerable judgments by breaking down and reconnecting ideas.

18. **A** Hunter refers to this as the anticipatory set, which is something said or done to prepare students to focus on the next lesson.

19. **D** Notice that (A) and (D) are contradictory, so one of them is probably correct. Students who have learning disabilities should be given structured, brief assignments.

20. **A** Thorndike states in his Law of Exercise that repeating the response, as in practicing, can strengthen a conditioned response or process.

21. **D** Objectives should be modified to meet the needs of a particular class. The class may be academically diverse, culturally diverse, or linguistically diverse.

22. **D** The word *stanine* is a contraction of the words "standard nine." Stanines are an artificial scale from 1 to 9 that can be placed on any normal (bell-curved) distribution of scores. The mean is 5, and the standard deviation is 2. A stanine score of 3 is below average. Stanines are meant to be a broad classification of scores, and are often used instead of a more precise measurement to reduce the chance of attributing too much importance to a particular score.

23. **C** In the problem-solving process, the students have invited a speaker to offer more information on setting up a program. Therefore, they are in the process of gathering data.

24. **A** Elementary-school students learn best with more structure, shorter lessons, less explanation, more public praise, and experience with manipulatives and pictures. Choices (B), (C), and (D) are more common for middle-school and junior-high students.

Short-Answer Questions

Question 1
Sample Response That Receives a Score of 2:

Document 1 is helpful in that it shows how Ms. Farrell's class performs overall. However, the figures are summations of individual performance. It would be most helpful to have the individual score reports for each student. This will allow her to identify those who need specific help or to identify those that are excelling in a subject. Each group requires a specific learning plan in order to properly develop and challenge the student.

Secondly, Ms. Farrell should seek additional testing information beyond that of one standardized test. From these results, she should create criterion-referenced tests based on her school district curricula. This will help Ms. Farrell specifically identify any concepts or lessons that are difficult for students in her class.

Sample Response That Receives a Score of 1:

Ms. Farrell should speak with the other teachers in South District about how they teach writing. Her class did not perform up to the grade-level equivalent, so she could learn additional techniques from the teachers that were more successful.

An additional piece of information to evaluate is the types of questions that students missed. If many students missed the same questions, then that could provide Ms. Farrell with future lesson plans. She'll need to review those concepts so that students understand them for the future.

Question 2
Sample Response That Receives a Score of 2:

Overall, Joy performed well on her standardized test. The grade-equivalent score shows how a student compares to the achievement of all other students at the same grade level. For example, her 4.2 in math indicates that her performance is the average of those in the second month of the fourth grade. Clearly, she is above average with her peer group (3.4 grade equivalent in that category). Across the state, she is performing around the average in Reading and Writing and above average in Math and Social Studies. Compared to her classmates, she performed above average in Writing, around the average in Math and Social Studies, and somewhat below average in Reading. The teacher should let Joy's parents know that Joy is performing well in school, at least as evidenced by this standardized test. Her parents should continue to motivate and encourage her. The teacher should also recommend that the parents spend extra time with Joy on her reading. Finally, this class seems to do very well in mathematics, so the teacher should review math material with Joy so that she will not fall behind a fast-moving class.

Sample Response That Receives a Score of 1:

Joy performed above average in Reading and Writing and above average in Math and Social Studies. This is evidenced by the grade-equivalent scores above 4 for the latter two subjects.

I would tell Joy's parents to review Reading with her. She performed under the class average and under her grade equivalent score. Further, I would recommend that her parents help her in Writing, because that appears to be a subject where her class is not strong. If the subject matter is not strong in the classroom, parents may want to supplement at home.

Question 3
Sample Response That Receives a Score of 2:

Ms. Gemmer only mentioned that there was an incident; she did not mention Billy by name. This saved Billy further embarrassment by having the song at recess discussed again, but this time to the entire class. Further, Ms. Gemmer did not make this incident a public episode for the class when she quietly asked Scott and Rick to meet her after class to discuss the situation. However, this may have been fortunate for Ms. Gemmer, as earlier actions appeared to be designed to having students publicly identify themselves. Even though I disagree with her request for students to raise their hands, I think she made the problem worse by moving on when no one admitted their guilt. This provides a negative reinforcement to students, basically saying that if you don't answer a tough question, Ms. Gemmer will move on to another topic. Therefore, I would recommend that Ms. Gemmer does not bring up these situations to the entire class unless she is determined to resolve them at that time. Secondly, I would recommend that she not threaten Tiffany with punishment. Tiffany provided valuable input to Ms. Gemmer. Her unnecessary comment to Tiffany could potentially create distrust or uneasiness, and she may find it more challenging for Tiffany to open up in the future.

Sample Response That Receives a Score of 1:

Ms. Gemmer did a horrible job handling this situation. First, she was not friendly to the student that helped her out the most. Second, she didn't punish the kids who made the song. Third, she didn't make the students apologize in front of the entire class to Billy.

I like that she asked Billy if he was okay, which shows that she cares as a teacher. Students who feel appreciated are more likely to do well in school, and likely to develop positive self-esteem, which is critical for students during their elementary school years.

Question 4
Sample Response That Receives a Score of 2:

First, Ms. Gemmer should get more information about Billy's background. She should speak to his teachers from last year, to see if they encountered similar issues with Billy wearing dirty, stained, and torn clothes. If this is a new issue, she can focus on recent changes in Billy's home life. Otherwise, if this behavior has been consistent for a few years, she can use that information when speaking with Billy's parents.

The second thing Ms. Gemmer should do is speak to Billy's parents about his attire. This could be a sensitive topic due to potential financial issues. It is important that Ms. Gemmer describe the problem only in its educational and social context. Specifically, that dirty clothes could cause Billy to become easily distracted or uncomfortable, making it more difficult to pay attention to a lesson. Secondly, these clothes can become a source of teasing, at an age when the need to be accepted by a peer group is quite high. If Billy's parents feel that Ms. Gemmer is describing the issue without any preconceived judgments, they will likely be open to discussing the issue and taking any suggestions made by Ms. Gemmer.

Sample Response That Receives a Score of 1:

Ms. Gemmer knows that constant teasing could have an adverse impact on Billy's development. He could have decreased self-confidence and ability to relate to his peers. Therefore, she should ask him how he ends up so dirty throughout the day. She should ask if he plays too hard during recess, and ends up dirty. She doesn't want to imply immediately that he comes to school disheveled, even if that is the case.

Chapter 29
PLT: 5–9 Drill

PLT: 5–9 Drill

Multiple-Choice Questions

For each question, select the best answer. Answers and explanations can be found at the end of the chapter.

Matthew is having trouble in his eighth-grade algebra class. Mr. Peters, a first-year teacher at the school, believes that Matthew's troubles are due to a lack of effort, not due to confusion about the material. Which of the following statements, if true, would weaken Mr. Peters' assessment?

- ○ Matthew has scored below average in six of the seven tests this year.

- ○ Matthew received a grade-level-equivalent score of 6.2 in the norm-referenced test last year.

- ○ Matthew has not always turned in his homework on time.

- ○ Matthew is doing much better in English than math.

Which of the following statements would behaviorist Skinner argue against?

- ○ Reward systems help lead to desired responses.

- ○ Punishment or extinction is necessary for undesired responses.

- ○ Teachers must teach first things first.

- ○ Students advance at essentially the same rate.

Which of the following is NOT a level of cognitive learning according to Bloom's taxonomy?

- ○ Memorization

- ○ Physical ability

- ○ Understanding

- ○ Application

Ms. Benes is concerned that she will not have enough time this semester to teach all of the state-required curricula for history. Which of the following actions can Ms. Benes take to maximize her learning time with her class?

- ○ Remove some of the early lessons in the curriculum—students likely already know this review material.

- ○ Assign additional homework to move the class at a faster pace.

- ○ Develop strategies to minimize distributing and collecting materials.

- ○ Ask students to identify which sections of the curricula they do not want to study.

Mr. Sullivan is requiring that his sixth-grade class prepare oral book reports as a way to evaluate his students' performance in reading. Which of the following best supports Mr. Sullivan's rationale that an oral book report will motivate the students to read?

- ○ It requires that students read the book, or face the embarrassment of a poor oral report.

- ○ Students gain experience with presentation skills.

- ○ Students are less likely to cheat preparing an oral report than preparing a writing sample.

- ○ Students enjoy public speaking more than reading.

Steven is a strong visual learner in the seventh grade. Accordingly, which of the following activities would be most helpful for Steven's teacher to use in a lesson about immigration patterns in the 1900s?

○ Taking frequent breaks while reading a chapter

○ Discussing the concepts in a group format in class

○ Displaying a diagram that charts movements of certain groups across different continents

○ Presenting a mathematical representation of immigrants across various segments

Concept maps are helpful for all of the following activities EXCEPT

○ outlining term papers and presentations

○ taking notes during a lecture

○ brainstorming with a group

○ evaluating writing assignments

Mr. Windle plans to teach his seventh-grade class a unit on corporate ethics. His first step was to assign a reading chapter from the business textbook. Next, he assigned three questions for the class to answer. Before answering the questions, students were able to meet with one other student to discuss the answers. Then a group discussion would occur during which students would be evaluated based on their participation and quality of responses.

The cooperative learning strategy employed by Mr. Windle is best known as

○ jigsaw

○ think-pair-share

○ STAD

○ demonstration

Mr. Martin is teaching his class a unit on nutrition, and wishes to employ a constructivist approach. Which of the following assignments employs this approach?

○ Students read an undergraduate-level text on nutrition and its impact on the body.

○ Students have a two-part assignment: first, they write a paper on their current nutrition habits. Next, after a lecture about proper nutrition, they amend their papers by indicating what they can improve in their own lives.

○ Students are given a vocabulary list of all important nutrition words. They work within a group of four for one week, before the group is given a spelling test.

○ Students are shown two videos on nutrition, and are then asked to give oral reports about what they have learned.

One curriculum goal within the sixth-grade mathematics course is to learn strategies of calculator computation. Which of the following objectives for students best reflects that goal?

○ Students will use calculators for all mathematical tasks.

○ Students will be quizzed daily on basic mathematic formulas.

○ Students will understand the order of operations.

○ Students will determine whether or not a calculator is needed to solve a problem.

Ms. Smith's class is studying American history. They are asked the following three questions:

- What year did the Revolutionary War begin?
- Who were the Redcoats?
- When was George Washington named president?

These questions reflect which type of learning, according to Bloom's Taxonomy?

○ Knowledge

○ Application

○ Analysis

○ Evaluation

Which of the following is NOT one of four stages of cognitive development, as proposed by Jean Piaget?

○ Proximal

○ Sensorimotor

○ Concrete Operations

○ Preoperational

Which of the following is NOT an effective strategy in teaching a student with ADHD?

○ Seat the student near the teacher's desk, but include him or her as part of the regular class seating.

○ Assign only one task at a time.

○ When providing daily announcements to the class, ask whether the student took his or her medication.

○ Have preestablished consequences for misbehavior.

Mr. Banham:	Who can tell me the cube root of 64? Christine?
Christine:	It is 4.
Mr. Banham:	Correct. Great job. Christine gains 10 points toward her day of no homework.

The above exchange is best supported by what theory and theorist?

○ Skinner and negative reinforcement

○ Maslow and intrinsic motivation

○ Bandura and causal relationships

○ Vygotsky and hierarchy of needs

Mr. Farello wants his seventh-grade science class to understand how temperatures vary across the United States. What is one technique Mr. Farello can use as an inductive thinking approach to the problem?

○ Ask students to brainstorm about different types of weather

○ Provide students with a chart that shows different temperatures in different regions

○ Give an overview lecture on how temperature is measured

○ Ask students to write their own theories, and then have the class try to disprove them

Ms. Jones likes to conclude her mathematics class with a "lightning round," during which students will shout out the answer to her questions as quickly as possible. This practice is contrary to the benefits associated with what concept?

○ Wait-time

○ Concept attainment

○ Social reasoning

○ Memorization and recall

Which of the following is NOT part of Madeline Hunter's "seven step lesson plan"?

○ Objectives

○ Anticipatory set

○ Guided practice

○ Invention

Which of the following events is most aligned with the theories of emergent curriculum?

○ Students decide what grades they should receive.

○ Students help to determine what is taught based upon their interests and desires.

○ Parents and teachers align to determine the best course of action for students.

○ Teachers will not deviate from state-designed curricula.

On the sixth-grade social studies test at Butterick Middle School, the results were as follows:

Mean:	74.5
Median:	76.0
Mode:	81.0

Which of the following statements is true?

○ Students at Butterick scored below the national average for sixth-grade classes.

○ More students received a score of 76 than any other score.

○ The average score for the class was 81.

○ An equal number of students scored above and below 76.

In a continual effort to improve, Ms. Dooner seeks out different ways to refine her teaching style. Which of the following demonstrates her role as a reflective practitioner?

○ Brainstorming with other colleagues

○ Reading professional literature on the latest research

○ Joining a professional association

○ All of the above

Upon the completion of each test, Ms. Alldredge asks her class to fill out a one-page questionnaire, entitled "Next Time..." The form asks students to think about what they could do next time to learn more effectively. Students receive this form regardless of how they perform on the test. Through this effort, Ms. Alldredge is developing which of the following skills?

○ Reinforcement

○ Metacognition

○ Scanning

○ Conceptual differentiation

Two weeks into the school year, Ms. Brown is worried about a group of eight students, who seem to be falling behind. Of additional concern, she realizes that all eight students are ELL students. In order to address their needs as learners, what could Ms. Brown do to address the situation best?

○ Begin tutorial sessions with the eight students to review the basic material already covered

○ Create a different set of expectations for these students, as they will have more difficulty than will students whose native language is English

○ Test all eight students on proficiencies in their first language and English, in order to understand their current performance levels

○ Move the students into their own group to provide more support and allow other students to move at a different pace

In Ms. Nevin's fifth-grade class, the students are given two hours to play in the treasure chest, which contains many common household items. The goal during the play time is to create a representation of an animal out of these items. This type of play is considered

○ constructive play

○ parallel play

○ inductive play

○ causal play

Paul received the results of his eighth-grade computer test. He was told he received a stanine score of 5, and a percentile rank of 61. Which of the following statements is true?

○ He missed six questions, for a total of 61 percent correct.

○ He received an average score, scoring above 61 percent of students who completed the test.

○ His average performance was the equivalent of a sixth-grade student, and he answered 61 percent of the questions correctly.

○ His performance is the equivalent of an eighth-grade student in the sixth month.

Short-Answer Questions

Each case history is followed by two short-answer questions. Read through the case history documents carefully and answer the questions that follow. Be sure to answer all parts of the questions.

Case History 1

Scenario:

Ms. Johnson teaches a seventh-grade English class of 24 students. Fourteen of the students are male, and 10 are female. For nine of the students, English is the second language. These nine students represent three different language groups. The English fluency skill of the nine students varies widely. In addition to these students, Ms. Johnson teaches two more students who have been placed in the class on the "least-restrictive environment" provision. Three other students have been identified as strong performers, and have qualified under the "gifted and talented" program. Finally, one student is repeating the class, after receiving several failing grades the previous year.

Ms. Johnson has determined the following goals for the class.

Goals:

1. Develop skills working cooperatively.

2. Improve reading, writing, and critical thinking skills within the English curriculum.

3. Develop speaking and listening skills, in both group discussions and formal oral reports.

4. Learn to appreciate the diverse works of literature present in our world.

Last week, Ms. Johnson wanted to focus on the third goal. She came up with the following activities:

- Students will meet in pairs to introduce themselves. Then each student will introduce the other to the class.

- Afterwards, each student will be asked to find something they have in common with another student. Another interview will take place, during which they will need to identify another thing the two students share in common.

The exercise did not go as well as Ms. Johnson had hoped. Here are her notes summarizing the exercise:

Today was not ideal. The interview exercise seemed like a good idea, but it turned out to be more difficult than I had imagined. Most students simply gravitated to the friends they already knew in the class. As I walked around, I found many pairs discussing random topics, instead of getting to know each other. Some students, like Stephanie, lost focus during the exercise. She couldn't remember anything about her partner, Stephen, when she was asked to present to the group. Other pairs weren't sure what to do. Seo-yun and Ha-yoon, neither of whom speaks fluent English, conducted their interviews in Korean, despite my request to carry out the exercise only in English. Other students thought the exercise went too long—it did take up two class periods.

Today Ms. Johnson is preparing grades for the first progress report. As she reviews the performance of her students, she talks over the grades with her principal. She notes:

I don't feel like I'm really helping anyone. It is such a diverse class. My strong students are probably bored; I spend too much time making sure our IEP students have their needs met; and I'm really frustrated with the poor English skills of some of our students. I just don't know how other teachers let them slip through the cracks, but it's up to me to fix this. At times I feel like I need five separate lesson plans to work effectively with these 24 students. I know that one size never fits all, but right now, one size seems to fit no one!

Question 1

Ms. Johnson set up four objectives for her class to achieve this year.

- Select TWO of the four objectives, and for each objective, identify one strategy Ms. Johnson might employ to meet her goal, given the current makeup of the class.

- For each of your strategies, explain how the strategy will help Ms. Johnson meet her objectives. Base your response on principles of planning instruction and/or language development and acquisition.

Question 2

Ms. Johnson noted that the "interview" exercise did not go as well as she had hoped.

- Identify TWO things Ms. Johnson could have done to make the exercise more effective.

- For each item identified, explain how that action would have made the exercise more useful to the class. Base your response on the principles of effective instructional planning.

Case History 2

Scenario:

Tammy is an eleven-year-old fifth-grade student who lives with her father about an hour from the school district. She attends the school because her permanent address is listed as her mother's address, which is located within the school district. Tammy often arrives at school late. Tammy often appears to be fatigued at school, and on several occasions has fallen asleep at her desk. Despite very strong achievement scores, Tammy is not performing well in school, as her assignments are often incomplete. Ms. Ramos, Tammy's teacher, has asked another teacher to view the class, in hopes that she can provide some additional recommendations on how to improve Tammy's performance. Before Ms. Jimenez views the class, Ms. Ramos sends her this note:

Ms. Jimenez, thank you for agreeing to visit my class. I hope that you can help me find some solutions in dealing with Tammy. She has been an excellent student, but her performance has dropped recently, and it is very frustrating. I'm concerned that something may be troubling at home. She looks exhausted when she arrives at school, and is so tired that she simply doesn't concentrate as much as she should. Other students have started to notice, and she is now being teased as "Tired Tammy." I look forward to your comments. Thanks, Ms. Ramos.

Classroom Observation

On the day of Ms. Jimenez's visit, Ms. Ramos begins the class with a discussion of how businesses deal with money. Tammy is not present yet. Ms. Ramos reviews the definitions of income, expenses, and profit, concepts covered during the previous lecture. A few minutes into class, Tammy walks in, and hands Ms. Ramos a tardy slip. A few students giggle at Tammy, who arrives late for the third consecutive class period. Ms. Ramos quiets the class down, and continues to review key definitions.

Next, Ms. Ramos announces that there will be an activity: "Today, we are going to all run a small business by playing a game in your table groups. There are five different roles that you will need to play. Person 1 will be the banker, who holds the money. Person 2 will be the business owner, who pays the bills to the bank. Person 3 will be the accountant, who collects the money from the customer, and tracks the income and the expenses. Person 4 will be the customer, who gives money to the business owner for the product. Person 5 will be the supplier, who will supply the product to the business owner. Use the game pieces and boards that I'm currently distributing to start the game. Please do this for twenty-five minutes, and we will see which group made the most money."

As Ms. Ramos passed around the materials, Tammy's table group starts to discuss the roles that each person will play. There is lots of confusion. "What does Person 2 do again?" asks Tammy. Another student angrily snaps back, "Pay attention, dork." This quiets Tammy, who chooses not to volunteer for a position, but instead waits until the other four students have chosen roles. She is told that she is the banker.

The game progresses, and Ms. Ramos stops by to see how Tammy's group is performing. Cesar drew a card, which said, "Pay business expenses for electricity for $100." When Cesar handed Tammy a $100 bill, she looked confused. Ms. Ramos replied, "Tammy, if you were paying attention, you would know that Cesar just paid an expense. Focus on the game, please." Tammy took the money from Cesar, and looked upset as Ms. Ramos walked away. Tammy looked away from the game board, and stared out the window, fighting back tears.

When the activity ended, each group was told by Ms. Ramos to find the amount of profit or loss made by their group. When Carrie, one of Tammy's group members, went to get a calculator, Tammy stopped her and said, "We made a profit of $300. I already added it up." Carrie said thank you, and wrote the figure down. After each group shared their results, each student turned in the summary papers to Ms. Ramos. Ms. Ramos noticed that Tammy had not completely filled out the form. Instead, she had put her head down and rested while the other team members were finishing their roles. Ms. Ramos asked her why she did not complete all aspects of the assignment. Tammy shrugged her shoulders and walked back to her seat.

Post-Observation Notes

Ms. Jimenez writes, "I can understand your confusion about Tammy. There were times when she grasped concepts much faster than other students. At other times, however, she appeared uninterested, and shied away from both participating and dealing with other students. A few students teased her, which may be a reason for concern, but I think there may be something else. She doesn't seem to be your happy-go-lucky fifth-grader, and clearly looks to be a student that is not getting proper amounts of rest."

Directions: Questions 3 and 4 require you to write short answers. You are not expected to cite specific theories or texts in your answer; however, your responses to the questions will be evaluated with respect to professionally accepted principles and practices in teaching and learning. Be sure to answer all parts of the questions.

Question 3

Ms. Ramos believes that Tammy's home environment could be a reason for the challenges Tammy faces at school.

- Identify TWO specific actions Ms. Ramos can take to connect Tammy's home environment with her school performance.

- Explain how each action could benefit Tammy's learning. Base your response on the principles of fostering strong school-parent relationships.

Question 4

It is mentioned that many students were confused before starting the small business game.

- Suggest TWO actions Ms. Ramos could have made in the planning and/or implementation of the group work that would have made the activity more successful.

- For each action, explain how the change could make the activity more successful. Base your response on the principles of planning instruction.

PLT: 5–9 DRILL ANSWERS AND EXPLANATIONS

Multiple-Choice Questions

1. **B** This score indicates that Matthew is not performing up to a standard consistent with his grade level. His troubles in algebra may not be due strictly to a lack of effort; prior score results show that he did not understand the basic material. Many students have trouble learning because they have not mastered the basic skills necessary for understanding a more complex concept.

2. **D** Many behaviorists, including Skinner, caution that student development, especially in elementary and middle school years, progresses at different rates. Moving students along at the same rate holds some back, and pushes others too quickly.

3. **B** The three levels of cognitive learning are commonly defined as memorization, understanding, and application.

4. **C** Teachers need to maximize their allotted time for learning. Many transitional activities, such as distributing materials, can remove valuable minutes from the day that could otherwise be used for learning. Choices (A), (B), and (D) would give Ms. Benes more time, but at a cost to the students' education.

5. **A** Most students will read the book to prevent embarrassment. Choices (B) and (C) deal with issues outside of motivation. Choice (D) does not provide a reason as to why students would want to read the book.

6. **C** A diagram will be helpful for Steven, who learns best with visual displays. While (D) could be considered, (C) is a more complete answer.

7. **D** Concept maps represent information visually. Concept maps are not the same as scoring rubrics, which can be helpful in evaluating writing assignments.

8. **B** In a think-pair-share strategy, a concept is introduced, a student gets to review the material with another student, and the material is then discussed with a larger group.

9. **B** The constructivist approach is based on the premise that learning is the result of mental construction: students learn by fitting new information together with what they already know.

10. **D** Choice (A) is misleading. The goal of the course is to learn strategies for calculator computation. In order to employ any strategies, students must know when it is appropriate to use a calculator. Choice (A) is not a reflection of this goal. Choose (D).

11. **A** Knowledge is the first order of learning in Bloom's taxonomy. The three questions that Ms. Smith asked require remembering, recalling information, and memorizing, which are all aspects of knowledge learning.

12. **A** The four stages of Piaget's theory on cognitive development are sensorimotor, preoperational, concrete operations, and formal operations.

13. **C** While a reminder may be helpful, teachers should avoid publicly reinforcing that the student with ADHD is in any way different or in need of special help. This could lead to ridicule and criticism of the student.

14. **A** Skinner believed that behavior which is reinforced will reoccur, and that negative reinforcement is particularly effective.

15. **B** An inductive approach to learning makes generalizations and theories based on a specific set of information. Once students are provided the data, they can then make theories about temperature changes. Choices (A) and (D) suggest an opposite approach.

16. **A** Research on wait-time, the time between a teacher's question and a student's response, indicates that the longer the wait-time, the higher the quality of response and the greater the level of participation. While the practice in Ms. Jones' class is likely entertaining, wait-time research suggests that students are not given enough time to provide optimal responses.

17. **D** The popular "seven step lesson plan" from Madeline Hunter could have up to nine elements: objectives, standards, anticipatory set, teaching (input, modeling, and check for understanding), guided practice, closure, and independent practice. Not all lesson plans will involve all nine steps.

18. **B** Emergent curriculum describes the kind of curriculum that develops from the interaction of all classroom participants, including the students.

19. **D** The median is defined as the middle value in a series of numbers. Therefore, an equal number of students scored above and below 76.

20. **D** On the test, you may be asked questions about how teachers can improve. The test writers love to promote the concept of the teacher as a reflective practitioner.

21. **B** Metacognition is the process of thinking about thinking. By having students reflect on their own learning behaviors, they will be able to determine strategies that enable them to learn more effectively in the future.

22. **C** Before Ms. Brown can devise effective learning strategies, she needs an accurate assessment of her students' current performances and skill sets. Choices (B) and (D) are absolutely wrong. Lowering expectations is not a long-term effective teaching method.

23. **A** Constructive play is a tool to help stimulate the imagination and creativity of children, and has been found to have a positive impact on the learning and development of children.

24. **B** A stanine, or standard nine score, is designed to represent scores on a 9-point scale. Generally, scores of 4, 5, or 6 are average. A percentile rank of 61 is used to compare Paul's performance with that of other students. He scored higher than 61 percent of the students who took the test.

Short-Answer Questions

Question 1
Sample Response That Receives a Score of 2:

One goal is to develop speaking and listening skills. To develop these skills, Ms. Johnson can include activities such as having students report aloud about the books they've read, while other students note what is important about each, and ask questions about the books. Students can then be placed into groups and choose a book that was important to them. The group would select one or two for presentations to the class. This strategy will develop speaking and listening skills, while possibly generating more interest in books that other students would be interested in reading.

Another goal is to improve reading, writing, and critical thinking skills. Ms. Johnson could have each student maintain a folder of literature entries for several weeks. Then, the student would select two for review and analysis. The student would then rewrite two entries, adding information on why the entries are important to them, and turn them in to Ms. Johnson for evaluation. This adds purpose to the assignment of maintaining a journal.

Sample Response That Receives a Score of 1:

The second goal listed by Ms. Johnson is to improve reading, writing, and critical thinking skills. One way this can be done is to ask students to find situations of conflict within the books they've read. Students will need to explain why the conflict arose, what the different opinions were from the characters, and what the resolution was. This could be used to start a discussion on the different types of conflict that people go through every day. Ms. Johnson would be helping the class with life lessons in addition to helping them with English. It would also help the class work cooperatively.

Question 2
Sample Response That Receives a Score of 2:

With a number of ELL students in her class, Ms. Johnson may need to give more detailed directions on her expectations for conducting an interview. Before students break off into pairs, she could present a model of an interview and an introduction. One way to do this would be to show a video of a pair of students completing the task. Another way would be to ask a student (either a gifted student or the student who did the exercise last year) to interview and introduce Ms. Johnson. This would provide a framework and visual understanding so that the ELL students can be successful in the task.

A second recommendation would be to assign students to specific pairs. Part of the goal of the exercise is to meet new students. By determining the pairs in advance, Ms. Johnson can ensure that students have an opportunity to meet new people. The interview will be more effective if you are unfamiliar with a person.

Sample Response That Receives a Score of 1:

It did not appear that Ms. Johnson put a time limit on how long the interview should take. Students will be more effective if they understand the amount of time allotted to the exercise. Otherwise, some students may finish too early, while others will take so long they may not complete the task in time. More structure is necessary from Ms. Johnson.

Secondly, she has not presented any evaluation criteria. Evaluation criteria will help students understand how their performance will be measured.

Question 3
Sample Response That Receives a Score of 2:

First, Ms. Ramos can collect as much information as possible about Tammy to use in a meeting with Tammy's father. Collecting information in advance will help establish a positive relationship with the father, and help identify Tammy's strengths and needs. Observation information could include the number of times Tammy is tardy; the number of times Tammy has arrived at school unkempt; and specific examples of times when Tammy has failed to work to her grade level. This observation information could be augmented by recording Tammy's strengths, and by researching information about how students of Tammy's age deal with parents who are separated or divorced.

Second, Ms. Ramos should organize a parent conference to address her concerns about Tammy. By showing a sincere interest in Tammy's future success, Ms. Ramos can work to establish a positive relationship with Tammy's father.

Sample Response That Receives a Score of 1:

First, Ms. Ramos needs to call a meeting with Tammy's father, and if possible, her mother. This will help connect the home environment with the school performance. They can discuss Tammy's performance and hopefully identify why her performance has changed, and why she isn't living up to her potential as shown on the standardized tests. Ms. Ramos may also want to bring the observation notes from Ms. Jimenez. In this way, a neutral third party can provide information, so that hopefully the parents and Ms. Ramos can work together to help Tammy improve.

Question 4
Sample Response That Receives a Score of 2:

Ms. Ramos quickly defined the roles of the five individuals in each group. However, there was nothing present so that students could retain that information. Therefore, Ms. Ramos could display posters that illustrate what students are to do; a poster for each of the five roles would help students remember the different roles, and what each role needs to do.

Secondly, Ms. Ramos allowed the class to become a bit chaotic when she passed out the material. For such a large activity, she could have used volunteers, or even the observation teacher Ms. Jimenez to help pass out material in advance. In this fashion, transition time is reduced, and students would be able to use the visual clues of the game board to understand the rules explained by Ms. Ramos better.

Sample Response That Receives a Score of 1:

Ms. Ramos should teach or review group work behavior and expectations before the work begins. This would help students to participate appropriately in each activity. Further, she should give warnings on how much time is remaining, so that students know when they are about to finish the activity. This helps them pace themselves appropriately.

Chapter 30
PLT: 7–12 Drill

PLT: 7–12 Drill

Multiple-Choice Questions

For each question, select the best answer. Answers and explanations can be found at the end of the chapter.

On a tenth-grade mathematics test, Kathy received a grade-equivalent score of 12.4 and a percentile rank of 91 percent. Which of the following statements is true?

○ Kathy missed only 9 percent of the questions on the test.

○ Kathy performed as well on the test as the average twelfth-grade student in the fourth month of instruction.

○ Kathy can successfully complete 91 percent of the curriculum of a typical twelfth grader in the fourth month of instruction.

○ Kathy's ranked 91st of all students that have completed the test nationwide.

Archimedes was asked to find a method for determining whether a crown was pure gold, or if it was alloyed with silver. Thinking over how to solve the problem, he stepped into a bath, and realized that a pure gold crown would displace less water than an alloyed crown. "Eureka!" he shouted.

The learning process of Archimedes is best described as

○ accidental learning

○ discovery learning

○ emergent learning

○ cluster learning

A teacher would like to get information on how well her class understood her lecture on the Constitution. Which of the following tests would give the best information?

○ Criterion-referenced test

○ Norm-referenced test

○ Portfolio assessment

○ Standardized test

Lindsey is struggling in her tenth-grade class. Her records show that she has performed above-average in the ninth grade, and her teacher reports that she has a good attitude and desire to succeed. However, Lindsey's performance on most tests is poor.

Which of the following could Lindsey's teacher do to encourage Lindsey?

○ Involve Lindsey's parents, and send them notices whenever Lindsey does poorly on an assignment.

○ Match up Lindsey with a student who performs well, and hope that the other student can motivate Lindsey.

○ Match up Lindsey with another student who is struggling, so they can work at their own pace.

○ Divide Lindsey's work into small pieces, and provide feedback with each part of an assignment.

With which one of the following statements about effective instruction would Howard Gardner most likely agree?

- ○ Teachers must find eight different ways to teach every type of learning material to correspond with the eight different types of intelligence.

- ○ Students must learn different types of intelligence at different times; these intelligences must build on one another.

- ○ Intelligence and morality must be separated, and the two should not work together.

- ○ Educators need to develop new approaches to better meet the needs of the range of learners in their classrooms.

Which of the following is an example of a spiral curriculum, as popularized by Jerome Bruner?

- ○ Students are given a difficult problem; the tools to address the problem are presented, and then a quiz is given to test comprehension.

- ○ Students are given aid from teachers each step of the way, so that they can grasp the material.

- ○ Students are given a new lecture; before the work is completed, the basics are reviewed, and then are built upon to further the learning process.

- ○ Students move at their own pace, based on successful performance on criterion-referenced tests.

Which of the following statements is a well-formed learning objective?

- ○ I will teach students how to solve trigonometric functions.

- ○ While in your reading group, try to identify the use of foreshadowing. Provide examples to the class on foreshadowing.

- ○ Identify the natural resources present in the United States that are not present in Asia.

- ○ Bring in a guest speaker to talk about the trade deficit.

Which of the following is an example of punishment in Skinner's theory of operant conditioning?

- ○ Detention

- ○ A "no homework day"

- ○ Silence in the classroom

- ○ A test

George, a ninth-grade student, comes to school on a Monday morning with severe bruising on his face and arms. When his teacher, Ms. Jefferson, asks him what happened, George says that his father beat him. The best course of action for Ms. Jones to take would be to

- ○ get George's father's side of the story as soon as possible so that she can determine who is telling the truth

- ○ immediately report George's statements to the school principal and follow his or her instructions as to whether or not to call the police

- ○ report the conversation to the local Child Protective Services office or to local law enforcement

- ○ document the conversation with George and continue to monitor the situation closely, watching for any signs of abuse

Vygotsky's ideas about the "zone of proximal development" are best articulated by which of the following learning techniques?

○ Students should work at their own pace independently in order to advance in concepts when they are ready.

○ Students should review basic concepts first and then receive new material with teacher assistance, thus building on previously learned concepts.

○ A challenging concept is taught and expected to be learned, even if the basic building blocks of that concept were not previously covered.

○ Seeking help from an instructor is not encouraged, as it may stifle development.

Students who do not have basic needs met will not be able to achieve the advanced levels of learning, such as the fulfillment of one's potential.

This statement is best supported by the works of what theorist?

○ Abraham Maslow

○ Howard Gardner

○ John Dewey

○ Jerome Bruner

Mr. Abato is designing a lesson plan for his twelfth-grade science class. In preparing a lesson on genetics and cell division, he plans to present a short lecture on the basics of genetics, and then show a video explaining how cells divide. What other activity could he employ which would focus on the students that are kinesthetic learners?

○ Provide step-by-step instructions on how a cell divides

○ Reinforce the lecture with a laboratory session, wherein students will recreate the cell division process

○ Bring in an expert on genetics as a guest-speaker for the class

○ Assign a reading assignment in advance of the lecture

In Ms. Lepson's eleventh-grade computer class, teams of three have been assigned to solve a programming problem. The team will receive one overall grade for their performance on the assignment. This structure is an example of what type of learning?

○ Cooperative learning

○ Demonstrated learning

○ Exploratory learning

○ Parallel learning

Ms. Chamberlin would like to increase the level of participation by students during class discussions. Which of the following techniques is most likely to improve the level of participation and the thoughtfulness of students' responses?

○ Implement a reward system for answering questions, such as a day with no homework

○ Post a ranking of students, ordered by the number of times they answer a question

○ Ask more leading questions, with clues to the correct answer

○ Increase the wait-time between the conclusion of her questions and calling on a student to give an answer

Which of the following ideas best incorporates the concept of scaffolding?

○ Students will role-play important events being studied.

○ For a novel currently being studied, new vocabulary can be supported by linking words on a webpage to a separate page with definitions.

○ Take students on a field trip to a relevant site, and have them take pictures of items that relate to the subject being studied.

○ Ask students to create their own test, based on the subject material currently being studied.

Ms. Bryant's eleventh-grade class took the SAT, a standardized test used for admission to many colleges and universities. Her class performance is summarized below:

Mean: 1240

Median: 1000

Mode: 980

Which of the following statements is true about the performance of Ms. Bryant's class?

○ The performance of some individuals was extremely high, raising the overall average.

○ An equal number of students scored above and below 980.

○ The mean score was below the norm for eleventh-grade students.

○ More students scored 1240 than any other score.

Today Noelle attended her twelfth-grade science class. There was a discussion on genetics. The class attempted two problems as a group. For homework, Noelle will be required to review her notes on the lecture, and to be ready to try three more group problems tomorrow.

What stage of the lesson plan is Noelle's class currently performing?

○ Anticipatory set

○ Closure

○ Independent practice

○ Guided practice

Steven is having problems in his high school classes. The school counselor believes that Steven is having problems at home. His parents have divorced, and there may be abuse within the family. The counselor believes that his home situation must be addressed before his academic issues can be solved.

What theory best supports the counselor's beliefs?

○ Skinner's theory of negative reinforcement

○ Maslow's hierarchy of needs

○ Bandura's extinction theory

○ Freud's theory of id, ego, and superego

Ms. Lloyd has a new student in her class, Cynthia, who was diagnosed with ADHD. Cynthia will be the only student in the class with ADHD. What can Ms. Lloyd do to provide a positive learning environment for Cynthia?

○ Introduce Cynthia to the class, and announce that she has ADHD, so that other students can help keep her on track

○ Seat Cynthia in the back of the class, away from the teacher and most other students

○ Create a consistent class schedule, with predetermined transitions

○ Keep the same set of rules for Cynthia as for all other students

The formal operational stage of Jean Piaget's stages of cognitive development is most closely associated with which age group?

○ Infants

○ Toddlers

○ Elementary-school students

○ Adolescents

Mr. Snow is teaching a tenth-grade literature class. The class has completed a novel, and is required to write an essay answering the following questions:

- What criteria would you use to assess the strength of the main character?

- Do you agree with the outcome of the novel?

- What is the most important message from the novel?

These questions measure what type of learning, according to Bloom's Taxonomy?

○ Knowledge

○ Comprehension

○ Synthesis

○ Evaluation

Mr. Prior believes that the best way to teach his ninth-grade English class is to employ a constructivist approach. He could do this by using which of the following strategies?

○ Students will read material at a level significantly more challenging than the student's reading level today.

○ Students will analyze passages to understand the syntax, structure, and vocabulary of each sentence. Then students should diagram the sentences.

○ Students will read a new passage. In writing a summary of the passage, they will be asked to associate the passage with prior readings and with events from their own lives.

○ Students will read the passage, pair up with another student, and then present a summary of the passage to the larger class.

In Mr. Heller's eleventh-grade business class, the students are currently studying fiscal policy. In order to convey the material, he has broken up the class into groups of six. Then, after a series of lectures, he allows the teams to meet for two group sessions to review the material. Next, a test is given, and the cumulative score of all six members is used to determine a grade. Each team member receives the same overall letter grade.

Mr. Heller is using what cooperative learning technique?

○ Jigsaw method

○ Think-pair-share

○ Student Teams-Achievement Divisions (STAD)

○ Portfolio

Keith, normally a very strong student, is struggling with an assignment in his twelfth-grade history class. The assignment is to analyze the inaugural address of President John F. Kennedy, and write a paper discussing the speech's impact. Thus far, the class has been told to read the address contained in their history book. Keith has told his teacher that he is having difficulty understanding the meaning of the speech. What is the most plausible reason Keith is struggling with the assignment?

○ Keith is not interested in history.

○ Keith does not recognize the reward system in place for completing the assignment.

○ Keith may be a strong auditory learner; hearing the speech may help him with the assignment.

○ Keith may have difficulty reading.

Short-Answer Questions

Each case history is followed by two short-answer questions. Read through the case history documents carefully and answer the questions that follow. Be sure to answer all parts of the questions.

Case History 1

Scenario:

Mr. Watson is teaching an elective economics class of 21 twelfth-grade students, made up of 11 males and 10 females. Students must have completed three years of high school mathematics in order to participate in the class. Some of the brightest students at the high school participate in the class, and Mr. Watson is considered one of the most interesting and dynamic instructors. He is beginning his final month of instruction, five weeks before graduation.

Document 1

Project Plan

Consumer Finance Exercise

May 8

Objectives: Students will:

1. Review and use concepts about consumer finance to solve problems.

2. Demonstrate mathematics skills as they relate to personal finances.

3. Use creativity to finance deals in multiple ways.

4. Use higher-order thinking skills to determine whom to approve for credit.

Assignment:

1. Students will work in groups of four; each student will be a member of a credit card consumer finance company.

2. Each group will select ten sample customers from a list I will provide.

3. For each customer, the group will determine whether to approve or deny the applicant based on his or her credit and the specific credit request (amount to finance, desired rate).

4. Each customer should also be matched using the "Loss Rate" handout to compare how customers have performed historically.

5. Each team will present their results to the class as a whole, and will make a presentation with their recommendations.

6. Creativity in restructuring deals is encouraged—each team should strive to finance as many customers as possible.

7. All students on the team must participate.

Activities:

1. Discussion on consumer finance principles—2 sessions

2. Group work—select ten sample customers; determine results—2 sessions

3. Group work—prepare presentations and Excel worksheets—1 session

4. Group presentations—3 sessions

5. Review of work and quiz on consumer finance—1 session

Assessment:

1. Group work: individual and group grade

2. Group presentation: individual and group grade

3. Excel spreadsheet: team grade for quality of decisions

Document 2

Review after Lesson Plan Complete

May 24

Below are notes taken by Mr. Watson after the conclusion of this lesson plan:

I really thought this would be an exciting lesson plan. Students will soon be out in the real world, and I thought they'd enjoy gaining this valuable experience of applying for a credit card. Students need to understand the value of one's credit history, and the role it can play in consumer finance. But the class was pretty out of control during these sessions—they spent more time discussing prom, graduation, and summer than the FICO scores of their "customers." I think my class may just be lazy right now. I'm not sure I can give assignments like this toward the end of the year—students are just too burnt out, and "senioritis" is at an all time high. The threat of a poor grade just doesn't seem to work anymore, as many are preoccupied with where they will attend college, if they choose to at all. Next year, I'll do this lesson during the first semester.

Directions: Questions 1 and 2 require you to write short answers. You are not expected to cite specific theories or texts in your answer; however, your responses to the questions will be evaluated with respect to professionally accepted principles and practices in teaching and learning. Be sure to answer all parts of the questions.

Question 1

Document 1, Mr. Watson's project plan for consumer finance, demonstrates several aspects of effective instructional planning.

- Identify TWO strengths of Mr. Watson's project plan.

- Explain how each strength demonstrates an aspect of effective instructional planning. Base your response on the principles of effective instructional planning.

Question 2

Review Mr. Watson's project plan, described in Document 1.

- Recommend TWO ways in which Mr. Watson could strengthen the assessment section of his project plan in order to provide students with a better opportunity to demonstrate their learning.

- For each recommendation, describe how it would improve Mr. Watson's ability to assess his students' accomplishments on this project. Base your response on the principles of assessment.

Case History 2

Scenario:

Kevin is a tenth-grade student and gifted athlete who plays on the varsity football, basketball, and baseball teams. Only a sophomore, he is considered the best athlete in the school, and certainly the most popular. The local press has named Kevin "a sure thing" to play professional sports one day, and that day may be as soon as two years away.

Mr. Foster is Kevin's tenth-grade English and homeroom teacher. Mr. Foster is very concerned about Kevin's performance in English, and in other subjects as well. Mr. Foster has gathered the following documentation together in preparation for a conference with Kevin's parents.

Document 1

Semester 1 Progress Report

November 15

Course	Grade
Geometry	C–
World History	C–
Physical Education	A–
Religion	C–
English	D
Biology	C
Preliminary GPA	**1.97**

Document 2

Results of Kevin's Diagnostic Test

October 15

Results for Kevin			
	Reading Skills	**Mathematics Skills**	**Writing Skills**
# of Questions	50	50	2
# Correct	13	17	N/A
Percentile	37%	23%	42%
Grade Equivalent	9.1	8.3	9.6
Notre Dame High Median	61%	74%	77%

Document 3

Transcript of Meeting Between Mr. Foster and Kevin's Parents, Brian and Jolene

Brian	We're very concerned with this grade of a D. Kevin received a B+ in English last year. How could he drop so quickly?
Mr. Foster	Kevin's grade is based on the number of assignments he has turned in, and the quality of those assignments. Thus far, he has failed to turn in three assignments, and the overall quality of his work has not been up to standards.
Brian	We've spoken with his football coach, who indicated that you grade harder than any other teacher. Kevin can't be penalized because he is in your class. Why isn't there consistent grading?
Mr. Foster	I'm sorry you feel that way, but my grading is based upon the work of all students. I have no desire to create a grading scale divergent from others. I simply evaluate the quality of work that students do.
Brian	You need to understand that Kevin needs to get at least a C in this class, in order for him to stay academically eligible. Anything below a 2.0, and Kevin can't play. You seem to know that—everyone else has recognized that Kevin is trying and has given him no worse than a C–. And let's be realistic—keeping Kevin eligible is the most important thing for his future.
Mr. Foster	I understand how much Kevin likes to play sports. By focusing on his work, he can remain eligible to play. I will not use his extracurricular involvement as a factor in my grading.
Brian	Well, maybe Kevin needs a new English teacher.
Mr. Foster	I'm sorry you feel that way. You are welcome to discuss this with the principal.
Jolene	Fine, we will. Everyone seems to help Kevin do his best. You seem determined to punish him for not being as strong as your other students.
Mr. Foster	That's not true, and I'm disappointed you feel that way. This conversation is over.

Directions: Questions 3 and 4 require you to write short answers. You are not expected to cite specific theories or texts in your answer; however, your responses to the questions will be evaluated with respect to professionally accepted principles and practices in teaching and learning. Be sure to answer all parts of the questions.

Question 3

In Document 3, it is clear that there is tension between Mr. Foster and Kevin's parents.

- Identify TWO things Mr. Foster could do to have a more meaningful conversation with Kevin's parents.
- For each action identified, discuss how each action will help to focus on Kevin's educational welfare and the development of an effective parent-teacher relationship. Base your response on the principles of fostering school-parent relationships to support student learning.

<u>Question 4</u>

Assume Kevin's parents asked Mr. Foster about the results of the standardized test scores, displayed in Document 2.

- Provide TWO unique descriptions of Kevin's performance on the standardized test.

- For each description, compare Kevin's performance with those of his classmates and those of students statewide.

PLT: 7–12 DRILL ANSWERS AND EXPLANATIONS

Multiple-Choice Questions

1. **B**   A grade-equivalent score shows that a student performed at a level equivalent to the average student of a certain grade. In Kathy's example, she performed as well as the average twelfth-grader in the fourth month of instruction performed on that test.

2. **B**   Discovery learning takes place when the learner draws on his own experience and prior knowledge to gain insight.

3. **A**   A criterion-referenced test is designed to test specific information. These tests are often created by teachers to review specific subject material.

4. **D**   Immediate feedback is key to diagnosing learning deficiencies and properly motivating students. Lindsey will learn best when given continuous positive reinforcement.

5. **D**   Gardner's work on multiple intelligences suggests that students have different abilities and strengths, as well as different ways of learning. While (A) is too extreme (it is neither practical nor effective to try eight different approaches for each topic), the need to develop new approaches is endorsed by Gardner.

6. **C**   The concept of a spiral curriculum is to constantly review and build on past results in order to further the learning process.

7. **C**   An objective should describe the actions that students are expected to do once instruction is complete. It should not describe what the teacher would do during the lesson. Choices (A) and (D) describe teacher actions, as does the second half of (B).

8. **A**   Detention is often seen as punishment.

9. **C**   Teachers are legally required to report any reasonable suspicion of child abuse to the police or child welfare services. George has obvious signs of a beating and implicated his father, so Ms. Jefferson is obligated to report in this instance.

10. **B**   The theory of the zone of proximal development states that students have an ability to grasp new material that is closely aligned with prior material. In order to learn new concepts, assistance from teachers and other students may be necessary.

11. **A**   This question relates to Maslow's theory of the hierarchy of needs. Maslow stated that there is a set hierarchy of needs, and that advanced needs (such as knowledge, understanding, and fulfillment of one's potential) can be met only once deficiency needs (such as shelter, food, and love) are met.

12. **B** A kinesthetic learner does best when he or she has an opportunity to "learn by doing." A laboratory environment provides the opportunity for students to understand cell division by participating and seeing the results themselves. Students who learn in this fashion learn best by being active participants in the learning process.

13. **A** Cooperative learning involves students working together in groups to learn a concept or to complete a task.

14. **D** Research on wait-time shows that the longer a teacher waits before calling on a student, the higher the level of participation, and the better the quality of responses. Choices (A) and (B) may lead to greater participation, but will not necessarily increase the quality of the response.

15. **B** Scaffolding is coaching or modeling to help students understand material until students develop these new skills and display confidence in their ability to handle the material without support. When the student achieves competence, the support is removed. The student continues to develop the skills or knowledge on his or her own. Choice (B) provides an example of scaffolding with new technology tools.

16. **A** You should be able to get to (A) by eliminating the other three answer choices. Choices (B) and (D) use incorrect definitions for median and mode, respectively. We have no information to support (C). When the mean is higher than the median, it means that the strength of the performance of the students above the median outweighs the performance of those scoring below the median. In the example shown, several students must have scored quite high in order to raise the mean 200+ points above the median.

17. **D** In Madeline Hunter's "seven step lesson plan," the class currently exhibits the stage of guided practice. The class is reviewing problems as a group, before attempting problems on their own. Choice (C) relates to the homework assignment.

18. **B** Maslow believed that certain lower-level needs must be met before higher-level needs can be fulfilled. If Steven is having issues with safety, shelter, and avoidance of pain, it will be very difficult for him to learn self-confidence and other traits necessary for strong academic performance.

19. **C** Students with ADHD tend to have difficulty with multiple transitions and frequent distractions. A consistent class schedule will help minimize the distractions. Choice (D) may seem correct; however, there should occasionally be different sets of rules, such as the amount of time allocated to complete a test.

20. **D** This is the final of four stages in Piaget's stages of cognitive development. Not all teenagers or adults will reach this stage, but for those who do, it tends to occur during early adulthood.

21. **D** This higher-order thinking involves developing opinions and making value judgments.

22. **C** The constructivist approach is an approach to teaching and learning based on the premise that learning is the result of mental construction: students learn by fitting new information together with what they already know.

23. **C** This method, popularized by Slavin in 1995, entails giving all members of the group the same grade. This encourages team behavior to ensure that all members comprehend the material.

24. **C** We know that Keith is normally a strong student, which makes (A), (B), and (D) less likely. Choice (C) provides a plausible explanation. Thus far, Keith has only read the speech. If he were to hear it, and he is a strong auditory learner, he may be able to perform better on the assignment.

Short-Answer Questions

Question 1
Sample Response That Receives a Score of 2:

Mr. Watson's project plan is strong because it requires each student to participate in the group activities. This ensures that each student will contribute something to the project. Further, this is reinforced in the assessment section with team grades for both the group work and the group presentation. This will help facilitate participation within the groups, and allows each individual to make a contribution. Secondly, Mr. Watson has linked activities to the assessment section in many ways. The group work discussed in activities 2 and 3 are assessed under Assessment 1, and the group presentation activity 4 is assessed under Assessment 2. With the goals, assignments, activities, and assessments closely linked, Mr. Watson is able to deliver an effective instructional plan.

Sample Response That Receives a Score of 1:

This project plan is strong, and demonstrates aspects of effective planning. A very important feature of Mr. Watson's plan is building on prior knowledge. He tells the students that they are going to use their background in mathematics to learn about consumer finance. By reviewing this information first, he provides the necessary backdrop to then move on to a new concept. By building on prior knowledge, students get a much better opportunity for success. This is definitely one strength of Mr. Watson's project plan.

Question 2
Sample Response That Receives a Score of 2:

First, while many aspects of the project plan are linked, there are a few gaps that Mr. Watson should address. Students are told that they will have an activity during the final session in which they will take a quiz, but that quiz is not part of the assessment section. Does the quiz not count? My guess is that it does, and Mr. Watson should add that quiz as part of his overall assessment strategy. Each activity should be linked to the other parts of the project plan, including the assessment section.

Second, Mr. Watson could add some more details about the assessment section. For instance, he could provide the relative weight of each part of the assessment. This might encourage the students to include information that they might have otherwise left out.

Sample Response That Receives a Score of 1:

Mr. Watson needs to make sure that he links the assignments and activities sections with the assessment section. For example, he tells students that they will be evaluated based on the Excel spreadsheet they put together; however, there is no assignment that states that they will be asked to make an Excel spreadsheet. The same aspect is true with the quiz—it appears in the activities session, but is not part of the formal assessment. If he links these things up, he will have a more effective project plan.

Question 3

Sample Response That Receives a Score of 2:

Mr. Foster should be rewarded for not caving to parental pressure in changing Kevin's grade. However, he could employ strategies to make the conversation more meaningful. Mr. Foster should review Kevin's work with his parents to help them identify the areas where he is struggling. This would help to make Kevin's parents an integrated part of the teacher-parent team. Further, it would allow Mr. Foster and Kevin's parents to have an objective discussion about the issues. By reviewing specific work, Mr. Foster will focus the conversation on Kevin's learning issues, not outside issues like sports eligibility, or the grading of other teachers.

A second strategy Mr. Foster could employ would be not taking the comments from Kevin's parents personally. While he initially showed good active listening techniques, it appears that Mr. Foster grew frustrated by the end of the conversation and quickly cut it short. Mr. Foster should recognize that the comments are not directed specifically to him; even if they were, he needs to remain focused on the issues, which are Kevin's learning challenges. By staying objective, Mr. Foster can create good will with the parents.

Sample Response That Receives a Score of 1:

Mr. Foster should bring the principal with him for this conversation to help back him up. It appears that he is being criticized for doing his job as a teacher. Sometimes, it is necessary to ask for administrative support to help a teacher stand strong on an issue, and this appears to be the case. Further, he should bring in other teachers to discuss Kevin's performance. Just because the English score is a D doesn't mean that he is doing well in other courses. This is clearly shown in his preliminary report in Document 1.

Question 4

Sample Response That Receives a Score of 2:

Kevin scored in the 37th percentile in the Reading section of the test. This means that he scored better than 37 percent of the students who took the test (and conversely, below 63 percent of students who completed the test). He compares unfavorably to the class median percentile of 61, which shows that students at his class level seem to be performing stronger than an average class. Finally, his grade-equivalent score is 9.1, meaning that his performance is below his expected level (10.2), and that his score is the equivalent to the average score of students in the first month of the ninth grade.

Kevin scored in the 23rd percentile in the Math section of the test. This means that he scored better than 23 percent of the students who took the test (and conversely, below 77 percent of students who completed the test). He compares unfavorably to the class median percentile of 74, which shows that students at his class level seem to be performing stronger than an average class. Finally, his grade-equivalent score is 8.3, meaning that his performance is far below his expected level (10.2), and that his score is the equivalent to the average score of students in the third month of the eighth grade.

Sample Response That Receives a Score of 1:

Kevin scored in the 37th percentile in Reading, the 23rd percentile in Math, and the 42nd percentile in Writing. So he performs the best in Writing, but he is below the 50th percentile in all areas. This should be reason for concern, as he is below in all categories, and he is below the class median for all subjects as well. It is interesting to note that he got more questions correct in Mathematics than in English, even though he got a lower percentile.